LOCAL GOVERNMENT
ECONOMICS

Also by Stephen J. Bailey

PUBLIC SECTOR ECONOMICS: Theory, Policy and Practice

Local Government Economics

Principles and Practice

STEPHEN J. BAILEY
Professor of Public Sector Economics
Glasgow Caledonian University

MACMILLAN

First published 1999 by
MACMILLAN PRESS LTD
Houndmills, Basingstoke, Hampshire RG21 6XS
and London
Companies and representatives
throughout the world

ISBN 0–333–66907–X hardcover
ISBN 0–333–66908–8 paperback

A catalogue record for this book is available
from the British Library.

This book is printed on paper suitable for recycling and
made from fully managed and sustained forest sources.

10 9 8 7 6 5 4 3 2 1
08 07 06 05 04 03 02 01 00 99

Printed and bound in Great Britain by
Creative Print & Design (Wales), Ebbw Vale

Contents

List of Figures

List of Tables

Preface

This book is designed for students with a good understanding of public sector economics. It provides progression from the author's earlier book *Public Sector Economics: Theory, Policy and Practice* (Bailey 1995), addressing many of the same themes but at a more advanced level, and specifically within the context of local government. Suitable for both UK and international readerships, it reflects the multidisciplinary nature of local government and is aimed at final year students on economics or multidisciplinary degrees, and at postgraduate taught Masters students.

There is an inherent tradeoff between aiming at a wider or a more specialized readership but the author hopes that this text achieves a reasonable balance in being accessible to non-specialists as well as those specializing in economics. The introductions to Chapters 1 and 15 and the list of contents provide the reader with an immediate indication of the ultimate objective of this book and of the topics covered within it.

Local government economics is taught on an increasingly wide range of courses in many countries. However, there is a marked sparsity of current teaching texts. The existing literature is notable for its concentration on edited works of research and conference papers and its focus on the traditionally narrow field of fiscal federalism.

The last UK teaching texts in this area were published many years ago (Foster *et al*. 1980; King 1984). An edited volume of research papers has been published more recently (King 1992), but this is not a teaching text. Other related UK books are in the area of local government finance and concentrate on administrative or public policy aspects, with little or no consideration of economics.

There is a similar marked absence of recent American teaching texts in this area. Wallace Oates' classic work *Fiscal Federalism* dates back almost three decades (1972). Oates subsequently published two edited volumes (Oates 1977, 1998) and a set of his own published papers (Oates 1991). See also Wildasin (1986).

Other publications in the field include a research volume based on a doctoral thesis (Levaggi 1991), sets of edited papers (Owens and Panella 1991; Pola *et al*. 1996; Ahmad 1997), and a series of research monographs on fiscal federalism published by the Australian National University in the 1970s. There are also a number of other American books dating from that decade. More recently, the International Monetary Fund published an edited text on fiscal federalism (Ter-Minassian 1997).

Fiscal federalism covers a much narrower field than is covered in this book. The area of local government economics has become much broader during the last decade or so, such that fiscal federalism, though still an important component, is no longer the principal focus in many countries. In particular, increasing attention has been paid to the impact of local government spending and taxation on macroeconomic policy, to supply-side initiatives, to use of charges, to privatization, to the purchaser–provider split, to efficiency and to the quality of services. All of these new policy areas are considered in this book.

In summary, this book provides a much-needed, up-to-date treatment of local government economics, broadly defined. While it focuses on local government economics *per se*, it attempts to demonstrate the relevance of the discipline to principles and practice. Specifically, the approach adopted in a number of the chapters is intended to demonstrate how economics can be used to provide theoretical justification for the some of the principles contained within the European Charter of Local Self-Government.

The European Charter is increasingly being adopted throughout the European Union, including those countries which have recently entered the EU or are in the process of doing so. More generally throughout Europe, the breakup of the former Soviet Union and subsequent further disintegration into smaller nation states has led to the rapid creation of local governments and a consequent need for training and education programmes at universities. Such countries often look to Western Europe and North America when examining alternative systems of local government structure, functions and finance. English is almost invariably their second language and is increasingly being used in graduate and postgraduate teaching programmes in European universities. Hence, it is hoped that this book will fulfil the need for a teaching text covering local government economics.

It is hoped that the student, having read this book, will have a detailed understanding of the importance of economics for this crucial component of the public sector and of the welfare state. Put simply, there is a lot of economics in local government, much more than is generally appreciated by non-economists. Therefore any teaching of local government which does not include relevant economic theory can only be regarded as seriously deficient in its coverage of the multidisciplinary basis of local government.

STEPHEN J. BAILEY

Acknowledgement

Chapter 11 was written jointly with Stephen Connolly and is incorporated in this volume with his permission.

S. J. B.

1 Introduction to Local Government Economics

INTRODUCTION

The traditional approach to local government economics is that of fiscal federalism. This is the result of the development of local government economics in federalist countries, particularly the USA and Canada, but also Australia, Germany and so on. The fiscal federalism literature uses efficiency criteria in assigning individual public sector activities and revenue sources to the various levels of government within federal systems. It refers to market failure, tax incidence, public choice, and other theories to determine the level of government most appropriate for delivery of specific public sector outputs.

There is a presumption in favour of decentralization because it facilitates the matching of public sector outputs and local preferences, so promoting allocative efficiency. However, the degree of decentralization is constrained by loss of any economies of scale in service provision, and by the limited scope for decentralization of the distribution and stabilization functions of government. Fiscal federalism prescriptions are further complicated by externalities and interjurisdictional spillovers, as well as by the assignment of major taxes to the national government level.

Although developed as an ex-post rationalization of the USA's federal system of government (which owes its existence more to political history than to economic prescriptions), King (1984) emphasized the general applicability of the prescriptions of fiscal federalism to non-federal countries such as the United Kingdom. Those prescriptions can be used to analyse the design and operation of multi-level government in any country. They therefore feature strongly in this book.

However, this text is not solely restricted to fiscal federalism. Local government economics has become much broader during the 1980s and 1990s. Increasing attention has been paid to the impact of local government spending and taxation on macroeconomic policy, to supply-side initiatives, to use of charges, to privatization, to the purchaser–provider split, to the internal efficiency of local governments and to the quality of services. These new policy areas are considered in this book. Hence, it fits better into the broader political economy mould than into the more narrowly prescriptive fiscal federalist framework.

While providing coverage of European practice in general, the text focuses on the UK for more in-depth examples of the definition of local government, decentralization, fiscal stress, intergovernmental grants, local property taxes, charges, local government reform, competition, and service quality. Although mention is made of specific services or topics to illustrate theoretical and analytical points, it does not provide detailed coverage of particular services such as housing and planning, nor of issues such as transport and the environment.

In providing the introduction to local government economics, this chapter considers the definition of local government and its democratic and economic roles. It also sets down the principle which can be used to determine which particular services should be provided at the local level and signals the diversity of practice to be found in subsequent chapters. Finally, it sets out various models of local government which are necessary for a fuller understanding of the analysis of subsequent chapters.

Ultimately, the objective of this book is to develop a set of economic principles justifying the existence of local government and providing guidance in respect of its functions, size, structure, financing, methods of operation, and freedom from central control of its expenditures. These principles are set down in the final chapter.

DEFINITION OF LOCAL GOVERNMENT

Local governments (the term being used interchangeably with 'local authorities', 'councils' and 'municipalities) are sometimes simply referred to in the economics literature as 'subcentral authorities'. Although accurate, this generic term fails to distil the essence of local government. Local governments can be thought of as democratically-elected bodies whose jurisdiction is of a local (rather than regional or national) scale, backed by powers to levy local taxes by which to exercise genuine discretion over service provision (Cole and Boyne 1995). However, they vary substantially in (both geographic and demographic) size, often share subordination to the centre with other non-local public sector organizations, sometimes include non-elected bodies such as intermunicipal enterprises, may be single-purpose or multi-purpose and may not, in fact, have powers of local taxation. Hence, there is no subset of characteristics by which to define 'pure' local government and distinguish it from regional, state or provincial government or from other subnational public bodies.

The defining characteristics of local government are its position on a continuum of more or less local criteria, rather than there being clearly distinct categorical differences between these various subnational bodies. Difficulties in deriving a clear definition of local government make comparative analysis problematical because it is not always possible to compare like with like. It may even be difficult to construct a precise definition of local government in a single country at a particular point in time. For example, recent reforms to the structure, functions and methods of operation of local government in the

UK have been so radical that 'it is, therefore no longer clear what the term "local government" means in the contemporary British context' (Cole and Boyne 1995, p. 191).

Nevertheless, the general conception of local government is one of a locally-elected democratic statutory organization below the level of the state, province or region, providing public sector services to the populace within the area of its jurisdiction. This conception of local government will suffice for the purposes of the subsequent economic analysis.

Local governments have a *power of general competence* in most European countries, meaning that they have general powers to undertake any activities (unless specifically forbidden or already undertaken by other bodies) which they consider to be in the local public interest. In the UK, however, local governments can only undertake activities which they are statutorily authorized to do by central government. Any activity which is not specifically authorized is likely to be *ultra vires* (a Latin term meaning 'beyond the powers') and so illegal.

This different international practice only partially reflects the distinction between federal and unitary states. In the former, constitutional and legislative power is divided between federal government at the centre and the subnational governments in regions, states or provinces. However, over 80 per cent of the world's nations are unitary states, the national parliament being the single source of constitutional power and legislative authority. In many European unitary states, however, the constitutional status of local government is formalized and protected in a written constitution which guarantees the principle of local self-government. The UK has no such written constitution and local government is therefore constitutionally subordinate to central government, so explaining the constraint of *ultra vires*.

What little discretionary powers UK local government has had seem to be increasingly constrained. Some powers have been taken away from local government and those remaining have become subject to greater central control. Central government calculates what it thinks each local government should spend on individual services and constrains its revenue sources accordingly. This centralizing trend in the UK contrasts sharply with the decentralizing trends in most other European countries, although limited decentralization was planned by the UK government at the time of writing (see Chapter 2).

However, it would be wrong to suggest that there are no differences between UK local governments in terms of their provision of services to their local electorates. There are, in fact, substantial differences within and between metropolitan and rural local governments in the UK. They still have some ability to determine their own political priorities and introduce their own policy initiatives in response to the preferences of their own local citizens. There are also centrally-prescribed differences in the structure and service responsibilities of local governments within the different constituent parts of the UK (that is, England, Northern Ireland, Scotland, and Wales).

Such diversity is not peculiar to the UK, however (see Chapter 2), and does not necessarily negate the generic applicability of the theoretical framework and principles set out in this book and summarized in Chapter 15.

The relationship between central and local government in the UK is determined by legislation, conventions and voluntary co-operation. The ill-defined status of local government combines with changing perceptions of local autonomy, accountability, equity and the need for macroeconomic control, causing the relationship between central and local government to be in a state of continuous change.

> The statutory provisions thus provide only a loose framework within which local authorities are left with a very wide but largely undefined measure of discretion. The limits for central government intervention have thus become a matter for political determination ... reinforced by the provision of financial incentives through the grant scheme. (NAO 1985, pp. 11 and 18)

Past attempts to differentiate between permissive and mandatory functions and to define minimum statutory requirements proved unsuccessful (for example, Cmnd 7643). While UK local authorities provide services for national as well as local purposes, precise standards of services are not normally prescribed. Central–local relations therefore revolve round central government's need to constrain local government's actions.

LOCAL GOVERNMENT'S ROLE IN THE DEMOCRATIC SYSTEM

The conventional argument for local government is that it secures the public interest in facilitating representative democracy, a crucial component of the democratic state in promoting pluralism, participation, and public choice (Young 1988). *Pluralism* refers to the capacity of the system of government to accommodate alternative political views so as to avoid a tendency towards centralized autocracy. Local governments are a means of accommodating pluralistic views within society. *Participation* refers to the role of local government in providing the opportunity for people to take an active part in government, acquiring the habits and skills which underpin the democratic infrastructure. *Public choice* refers to the role of local governments in providing services in accordance with local needs and preferences, rather than according to uniform national standards. Put simply, local needs and preferences should be locally defined.

It is argued that local government provides opportunities for participation by citizens in a number of ways (Council of Europe 1995a).

1. It provides additional opportunities for voting.

2. It confers upon citizens other participatory rights, including pressure group activities.
3. Local government politicians tend to be more fully representative of the population than is central government, particularly in terms of the proportion of women holding political office.
4. It acts as a training school for democracy, particularly in the emerging democratic systems of the central and east European countries.
5. It extends the *instrumental* concept of the individual consumer into a *developmental* concept of citizen in a wider community so that voting is not simply an expression of self-interest.
6. Local government represents subnational communities as territorial collectivities, for example, in the field of local economic development, and so provides a counter to the supposed tendency for the nation state to be captured by producer interests.
7. Local communities are able to resolve their internal conflicts for themselves without recourse to central government, so enhancing the political stability of the nation state.
8. Decentralization is also likely to produce more diverse and innovative policies and ways of dealing with particular issues, piloted first at the locality. Mistakes at local level will be of lesser impact than those resulting from decisions of national government.

These points are either assertions or, at best, their effectiveness is not proven. For example, it is questionable whether local government really does develop the political capacity of society by providing a training ground for the running of the democratic system. It may instead be dominated by the national political party system, local people perhaps having a poor understanding of the local governments in which they live. However, it would not seem unreasonable to take the view that, while there is scope for improving democratic decision-making, local government works sufficiently well to constitute an important mechanism by which people can participate in democratic processes.

Hence, it can be argued that the ultimate justification for local government rests in *political* theory. Political scientists emphasize that local government is not simply a mechanism for the delivery of public sector services. Though acknowledging this crucial point, much of the *economic* theory elaborated in this book necessarily concentrates on the role of local government in promoting efficiency through its service delivery function. The service provision of local government has underpinned the expansion of the postwar welfare state in virtually all Western democracies. The UK government even went so far as to state that 'the main role of local government is to provide services in a way which properly reflects differences in local circumstances and local choice' (Cmnd 9714, p. vii). This statement refers to the economist's realm of allocative efficiency.

THE ECONOMIC ROLES OF LOCAL GOVERNMENT

Economic theory necessarily emphasizes the *instrumental* role of local government in providing public services and seeks to determine the conditions for maximization of economic welfare. This approach is valid as long as the partial nature of economic analysis is recognized – partial in the sense of not incorporating political, sociological and other perspectives and, within economics, partial in that it is not a general equilibrium analysis.

At its broadest level, the creation of stronger local democratic institutions can be seen as a form of national capacity-building and institutional strengthening, a necessary prerequisite of sustainable long-term economic development. In effect, this is a strategic supply-side policy comparable with the development macro model of public expenditure growth associated with Rostow and Musgrave. In such cases decentralization responds to the need, first, to reduce the inherent inefficiencies of a centrally-controlled system, second, to facilitate privatization and, third, to relieve the strained finances of national governments.

More specifically, the four main economic roles of government are the allocative, distributive, regulatory and stabilization roles (Bailey 1995, ch. 2). It is usually argued that stabilization and income distribution are properly the concern of central (national) government while resource allocation is primarily the concern of local governments (Oates 1972; King 1984; Musgrave and Musgrave 1989). Though it is also usually argued that the regulatory function is best undertaken by central government, the division of that function between central and local government necessarily reflects the division of service responsibilities between those tiers of government.

1. The Allocation Function

A perfectly competitive market economy necessarily achieves a Pareto optimal allocation of resources because all product and factor prices reflect their respective marginal costs. This results in equality between the marginal rate of substitution in consumption and the marginal rate of transformation in production for each commodity ($MRS = MRT$). In such circumstances, it is not possible to increase output by reallocating the factors of production, nor is it possible to increase welfare by altering the distribution of commodities between individuals. Put simply, it is not possible to make one person better off without making at least one other person worse off.

Markets fail to achieve allocative efficiency if they are less than perfectly competitive or if not all costs and benefits are reflected in market prices. Monopoly power leads to *market failure*, as does failure to establish property rights. The latter occurs in the cases of public goods, externalities and other cases of high transaction costs (see Chapter 3). Government intervention, at whatever level, can only be justified in such cases if it corrects for market failure. The possibility of *government failure* has to be recognized as a constraint on the justification for intervention.

Market failure at the local (as distinct from the national) level may relate to local *natural monopolies* (such as water and sewerage services), to local *public goods* (for example, local street lighting, local environmental health and trading standards), local *merit goods* (such as housing of adequate standard), or to local *externalities* (for example, relating to unacceptable or beneficial land use in a neighbourhood). These forms of market failure are the usual justifications for government intervenion in the economy.

Natural monopolies do not necessarily require direct provision of services by local governments themselves, regulation being an alternative form of intervention used for water and sewerage services in England and Wales (Bailey 1995, ch. 14). Very few local government services are pure public goods. Services such as education, recreation and personal social services are private goods, since they are both excludable and rival in consumption. They may display significant positive externalities but they are still private goods. The economic concept of merit goods relates to preferences at a point in time and the tendency for consumers to be myopic in the time preference of their market decisions. In other words, they emphasize the immediate future and so neglect the long-term effects of, say, inadequate housing or education. Government intervention is therefore justified in such cases.

However, the concept of merit goods is not robust since it incorporates normative stances (that is, paternalism), for example the judgement by central or local government of whether an individual's valuation of the personal benefits of consumption of a particular service are acceptable. If it is not then the government over-rides consumer sovereignty. Externalities, while a robust economic concept, are difficult to measure in monetary terms both because service output is often difficult to measure and because its monetary value may be derived from imperfect markets.

The following example clarifies the nature of externalities at the local level. A pupil's school education may create benefits not just for that particular pupil but also for others living both within the local government area and outside it. Positive externalities spilling over local government boundaries to benefit those living in other local jurisdictions are often referred to as *spillover benefits*. More generally, *spillover effects* or *spillovers* are terms used to refer to both positive and negative interjurisdictional externalities. In the schooling example, education and training services provided by one local government for its own citizens may benefit other local government areas if its citizens outmigrate, the increased supply of skilled and educated workers creating the conditions for economic growth in those other local governments.

Positive spillovers could be internalized either by extending the boundaries of local authorities or by making central government responsible for supply of services creating spillovers. The former is only practicable where spillover effects are fairly restricted in geographical terms. Alternatively, local governments' provision of such services could be subsidized by central government in order to achieve an economically optimal level of supply without the need for boundary reforms or central controls, both of which may be politically contentious. The latter is the least appropriate arrangement if local preferences are to be reflected in decisions concerning the volume and standard of service.

Intervention at the local government level to deal with negative externalities can be by direct administrative means or by indirect means using market mechanisms. Administrative mechanisms (for example, imposing physical limitations on polluting activities) may be difficult to enforce and so costly to put into effect. Market mechanisms require local taxes to be levied on commodities creating negative externalities. For example, local taxes could be levied on effluent discharges into local rivers and coastlines but, again, it may be difficult and expensive to monitor the volume and toxicity of discharges. Alternatively, local licences to pollute could be auctioned to the highest bidder.

A minimum price could be set for the licence, that price incorporating the monetary value of the negative externality. The revenues so raised could then be used to compensate those groups adversely affected by the negative externality, such that their level of economic welfare is not reduced by that activity – the so-called *Scitovsky compensation test*. This test is a much less restrictive approach than the *Pareto optimum* discussed above. The latter can only demonstrate a welfare improvement where at least one person is made better off and no one else made worse off by an activity. In contrast, the compensation test can demonstrate a net welfare gain (or loss) where there are those whose welfare is reduced by an economic activity as well as those whose welfare is increased.

In practice, it may be difficult to determine the monetary value of the negative externality and such a procedure leaves unresolved the question of whether or not to compensate those who are adversely affected by the negative externality. That political decision is not resolved by the Scitovsky compensation test for an improvement in allocative efficiency, where those who gain from an economic activity creating a negative externality can compensate those adversely affected by it and still be better off. Compensation does not have to occur for there to have been a gain in allocative efficiency and so the normative judgement of whether or not compensation *should* be paid is a political decision. However, central government should intervene on allocative grounds where negative spillover effects occur (see 3 below).

In summary, local governments have a potentially substantial allocative role in responding to cases of market failure at the local level, provided that intervention is not counter-productive in exacerbating market failure. For example, assuming *ceteris paribus*, it would be counter-productive for local governments to pass legislation creating statutory (as distinct from natural) monopolies if the result was reduced competition among, say, providers of public transport.

2. The Distribution Function

It is generally argued that local governments should not undertake redistribution of income (via taxes and subsidies) because of the inefficiencies it would create. A local government adopting programmes with substantial redistributional objectives would have to tax high-income groups in order to pay subsidies to low-income groups. Low-income groups would have an incentive to move into the local government area but high-income groups would have an incentive to move out. Hence, tax rates on the higher-income groups would have to rise in order to compensate for the diminishing per capita tax base. In turn, this would increase the incentive for high-income groups to move out.

Alternatively, if the local government feels that it cannot tax high-income groups beyond a certain ceiling, then the funds available for redistribution to low-income groups will fall in per capita terms as low-income groups move into the area. In either case, the redistributive policy would therefore ultimately fail. This outcome is borne out by the history of poor relief in England (Foster *et al.* 1980). Hence, it has long been argued by Oates (1972) and others that redistributive policies are best undertaken by central government, since it reduces the incentive for migration of income groups from one local government to another.

Since migration is costly, and more costly the larger the local government area (for example, because of the need to commute to one's place of employment), local redistributive programmes would have to be substantial and expected to persist over the long term. Otherwise it would not be worth migrating. Hence, programmes which are mildly redistributive between original incomes and post-tax disposable incomes are feasible at the local level. Moreover, modestly redistributive outcomes may be broadly acceptable to higher-income groups.

First, high-income groups may support redistribution from a sense of altruism, relief of the poor being a public good in this case. However, the 'free-rider' problem may frustrate such altruistic behaviour. Second, high-income groups may support redistribution because they expect to benefit from positive externalities at the local level. For instance, if there is perceived to be a positive relationship between income inequality and crime then redistribution reduces crime in the locality. The existence or not of such a link is a particularly contentious issue, since it may be used to condone, or even justify, crime. Moreover, there may be a general expectation that the relief of poverty is still a central government function and the hypothesized strong positive relationship between income inequality and crime may be contested as to its factual accuracy or, even if established, its moral acceptability.

It will be seen later that local governments in many countries are part-financed by a local income tax. There is therefore redistribution from *original* to *disposable* incomes. There is, of course, further redistribution between disposable income and *final* income, the latter taking account of the redistributive aspects of service provision. The extent of redistribution from original to final income is constrained by payment of equalizing intergovernmental grants, by ceilings on local tax rates, and by statutory entitlements to local government service provision irrespective of income. While merit goods such as subsidized municipal housing can be expected to redistribute final income in favour of the poor, higher take-up rates of services such as post-compulsory school education by the children of high-income groups actually redistributes final income in favour of affluent groups.

Therefore, while redistribution is best undertaken by central government because of the potential for inefficiency to be created by migration, local governments do perform some redistributive functions.

3. The Regulatory Function

In most cases, local governments will be acting as agents for central government in carrying out the regulatory function. Regulatory functions may relate to town and country planning, policing central legislation relating to trading standards, the local environment (for example, pollution) and so on. In the pollution licences example above, allocative inefficiency would be exacerbated if local governments abused their monopoly power to issue licences, raising their prices above those necessary to 'buy out' the monetary value of the negative externality. The potential for monopoly abuse and the existence of spillover effects mean that policy relating to pollution licences is perhaps best determined at central level, local authorities merely acting as agents for central government.

The UK land-use planning system is another interesting example of regulation by local government. National legislation regarding spatial planning vests responsibility for its implementation in local government. Local authorities act as agents of central government in regulating land use so as to avoid or minimize the undesirable aspects of urban development (such as factories with polluting emmissions in the middle of housing areas). Developers of land wishing to build residential, commercial or industrial premises have to seek planning permission from the local government in whose area of jurisdiction the proposed development is to take place. Permission can be refused, subject to the right of appeal, if there would be locally unacceptable consequences arising from the development. Planning consent is issued by means of an administrative regulatory mechanism dealing with market failure at the local level.

The alternative is a market-led system of land development based on the auctioning of planning permissions to the highest bidder (Evans 1988). Negative externalities (such as increased congestion) could be bought out by use of a reserve price in the auction and compensation paid to those people adversely affected by the development. However, auctioning would only be effective if the local development market was competitive, so that collusion between developers could be avoided when bids were being made. Collusion would occur if developers agreed not to put in competitive bids but rather agree to share out available land and structure their bids accordingly. Administrative mechanisms may be preferable to market mechanisms in such cases.

4. The Stabilization Function

It is generally argued that local governments should play no part in stabilization of the economy through macroeconomic policy. They would, of course, be unable to engage in 'beggar my neighbour' balance of payments policies through manipulation of exchange rates, imposing tariffs and quotas on imports, or subsidizing exports. Locally-differential prices and incomes policies would be difficult or constrained because of national public sector pay agreements. Locally-preferential public procurement policies regarding local government purchases of supplies and services (in order to stimulate the local economy) would be contrary to the European Union (EU) public procurement directive which prohibits discrimination in the award of public sector contracts because it is anti-competitive.

Decentralizing monetary policy would be contrary to current centralizing trends in the EU's move towards a single currency. It would contradict arguments for the need to co-ordinate monetary policy at the international level. If local governments competed with each other in terms of expansionary monetary policy in an attempt to stimulate their local economies at the expense of other local governments, the result could be highly inflationary.

Similarly, in terms of fiscal policy, local governments may compete with each other via budget deficits, each seeking to expand aggregate demand in their own local economy at the expense of other areas. However, the open economies of local governments would inevitably mean that the benefits of expansionary fiscal and monetary policies would leak out of the local economy (because of a high marginal propensity to import goods and services from other local government areas), such that multiplier effects would be small (that is, assuming *crowding in*).

In fact, *crowding out* may occur, since local governments increasing deficit-financed spending may simply replace private expenditures in the locality, if local residents buy their local government's bonds. Ultimately, such local governments would have to offer higher interest rates on their bonds in order to attract loanable funds from outside their jurisdiction. Alternatively, the attempt to control interest rates would lead to an expansion in the money supply, with the inflationary consequences already noted and leading to the crowding out of private expenditure by public spending (Bailey 1995, ch. 5).

High local government spending and low local taxes would also induce inward migration which, if unemployment were not to increase, would require even greater budget deficits. This pressure towards ever greater fiscal stimulus would be potentially unstable. It would create allocative inefficiency if the increased labour force led to diminishing marginal returns to labour (assuming capital is fixed).

Hence, demand-side approaches to stabilization policies are at best of limited effectiveness because of small multipliers and, at worst, counter-productive because of crowding out. For these reasons, local economies would be better served by local government supply-side policies relating to local economic development through creating conditions to stimulate the small firm sector.

RESOLVING CENTRAL–LOCAL OVERLAPPING ROLES

In principle, where local autonomy conflicts with central government's stabil-ization and distributive roles, the degree of local discretion may be repres-ented by the choice between the following:

1. *the centralized constraints model*, where central government sets out a set of constraints which local governments are required not to breach but within which they can operate with full autonomy;
2. *the bargaining model*, where local government's autonomy is established within the constitution and with which central government must there-fore negotiate in order to secure its compliance with national policies. The problem with this approach is how to ensure that each and every local government honours the bargain, possibly only mutually agreed at great expense.

In practice, the degree of local discretion may be the outcome of historical evolution of the state rather than an explicit choice between those two models. Indeed, the relationship between central and local governments may be in a more of less continuous state of flux in reflecting changing perceptions of the need for local autonomy, accountability, provision of welfare services and macroeconomic control. This is the case even when an explicit choice has been made between a federal system (as in the USA and Germany) or a unitary system (as in the UK) since it is not necessarily the case that federal systems of government are more decentralized than unitary systems. Each of these can have different degrees of decentralization.

THE PRINCIPLE OF JURISDICTIONAL RESTRICTION

Local (and regional) governments should generally provide services whose benefits are restricted to a single jurisdiction, for example local roads, local public transport, local parks and other leisure and recreation facilities, local (and regional) water and sewerage services. At the other extreme, central government should provide national services such as defence, motorways and the system of justice. In the intermediate case, where there are significant benefits extending beyond administrative boundaries, the situation is less clear cut, for example education and health care.

There may be some sharing of responsibilities between central and local government in such cases, either a formal separation of parts of the education service (say university versus school education, respectively) or a less formal system of influence and guidance from the centre. In the UK, local government provision of services is determined neither by formal constraints alone nor by free local choice but rather by a complex mixture of pressures and influences emanating from national government departments, past practice, pressure group influences, professional attitudes, political influence and statutory provisions.

Ultimately, the division of service responsibilities between central, regional and local governments reflects past practice and historical factors more than the strictures of economic efficiency.

> In fact, strong legal protection of the main features of municipalities (including their boundaries) is arguably more important for the upholding of the principles of local self-government than any marginal improvements in local public services' efficiency and in the levels of citizen participation in local public life. (Martins 1995, p. 457)

Not surprisingly, therefore, there are substantial differences in the array of powers attributed to local governments in different countries and territorial administration systems vary enormously in terms of administrative structures, political cultures and the dynamics of central–local relations. This diversity of practice does not simply reflect the differences between federal, regional and unitary states, since each is compatible with one or two or more tiers within the local government structure.

MODELS OF LOCAL GOVERNMENT

The models of local government correspond broadly to the more general models of government (Bailey 1995, ch. 7). The latter are the:

- *despotic benevolent model* (where the government knows best and its actions take account of market failure in maximizing economic welfare);
- *fiscal exchange model* (where the government provides services solely in accordance with voters' willingness to pay taxes);
- *fiscal transfer model* (where the provision of public sector services is used to pursue social policy objectives); and the

- *leviathan model* of government (where despotic self-serving bureaucrats and politicians maximize their own welfares, rather than those of national and local citizens).

Recognition of these different models of government effectively recognizes the need to take account of the range of 'actors' or 'stakeholders' within governmental institutions and also the power relationships between them (see Chapter 13). This is in sharp contrast with the standard neoclassical approach which simply refers to 'the government' and 'the citizen' in highly standardized and abstract ways, failing to take account of the wide range of people who have a stake in what the government does.

The range of stakeholder representation in the private sector (that is, producers and consumers) reflects commercial market exigencies (that is, economic power). The range of stakeholder representation in the public sector (local politicians, local government bureaucrats, local citizens, the users of local government services and so on) ultimately reflects the distribution of political power. Hence the range of stakeholder representation is ultimately determined by the distribution of power within the organization and the model of government within which it operates. There are three main models of power relationships within local authorities (Wilson and Game 1998):

1. *The formal model*, where power relationships are determined by the legal-institutional framework of decision-making by the council, committees and departments – put simply, councillors (local politicians) make policy and officers (bureaucrats) implement it. This static model fails to reflect fully the complexity, variety and dynamic evolution of decision-making structures within local authorities.
2. *The technocratic model*, where power resides in officers due to their specialized knowledge and abilities in contrast with the stereotype of non-specialist, amateurish, part-time councillors – put simply, officers are the dominant force in local politics due to their monopoly of information and competences. This imbalanced model fails to recognize the existence of high-calibre council leaders and chairs of committees, ignores the existence of policy-making by well organized political party structures, and makes too much of asymmetric information.
3. *The joint-elite model*, where policy-making is dominated by a small core of councillors and senior officers – again a static model, failing to reflect both the dynamism of internal power relationships and the role of junior officers and backbench politicians in proposing policy changes and new intiatives based on their direct operational experience and creative energy.

None of these models is sufficient on its own in describing the reality of the distribution of power within local governments. Elements of all three may be relevant, officer power perhaps being greater where policy-making is weak or constrained by hung councils (that is, where no single political party has control of the council and its decision-making), elite group influence perhaps being greater where there are divisions between and within departments, and the formal model perhaps being most relevant where there are highly motivated, assertive councillors of both the New Urban Left and Radical Right.

Though it may not be possible to develop a robust model of local government because of these differing power relationships, nevertheless it is possible to modify the standard models of government in order to reflect the specific features of local government. In particular, the despotic benevolent government model in its local government form can be referred to as the traditional *command council*, a rational, paternalistic, hierarchical, bureaucratic machine driven by standardization and economies of scale. It provides services *to* users rather than *for* or *with* them. Councillors operate through the committee system, chief officers are 'barons in their own fiefdom'. In this case no separate representation of service users is required as long as the local government is omniscient.

A separate representation of service users certainly is required in the *fiscal exchange model* because local government is simply a service-delivery instrument, providing services in response to citizens' and users' demands and tax payments and/or service charges for them. This is particularly the case if voting mechanisms are incapable of registering service users' and citizens' preferences for different standards or quality of services. Ultimately, therefore, it is the taxpayer and/or service user who defines both service levels and quality in accordance with willingness to pay taxes and/or charges.

Both of these models underpin the analysis of Chapter 12. Where full-cost charges are levied as payment for receipt of services and use of service is voluntary, it is the client or customer (rather than citizen) who defines quality. Where charges do not fully cover service costs, such that subsidies must be financed by taxpayers, both taxpayers and customers will have a say in the definition of quality but the ethos is predominantly consumerist (see Chapter 14).

Councils' identities are perhaps derived more from the services they provide than from the local democratic process. Customer-care charters tend to proliferate within a highly managerial system, the role of politicians being downplayed, possibly leading to a loss of corporate vision and direction. As a consequence, there may be a parallel shift to a company ethos, the enabling of service provision being interpreted in market terms so that market-based provision replaces social provision (but see Chapter 12). A market-based approach is positive rather than normative in that it does not say what government *should* do.

The danger of defining the public realm as the arena in which we exchange taxes for public services is that we reduce politics to service consumption, rather than authoritative decision based on collective commitment. The concepts which we use to understand the public realm are different from those of the market, emphasising need rather than demand, citizenship rather than consumption, and 'voice' rather than 'exit'. The liberal concept of the state [is an] ... impoverished view [which] provides justification for a very thin state concerned with procedural rather than substantive justices. (Walsh 1995, pp. 251–2)

In terms of the *fiscal transfer model* (where both quantity and quality of services, and their distribution, may be an instrument of social policy), stakeholders include particular groups of users, taxpayers and their political representatives who, constituting a political majority, adopt policies which skew the financing, quantity and quality of public services in their favour. In its most socially progressive form, this model is associated with an ethos of community, local authorities being a truly democratic institution (rather than local administrator of services) with a social approach to local issues and entailing accountability to local citizens (as distinct from consumers). The local authority provides leadership in an enabling partnership with the local community (services **with** rather than **for** or **to** local citizens).

The *leviathan model* is as applicable at the local government level as it is at the national level. In the former case, providers are despotic self-serving local bureaucrats who seek to limit stakeholder representation in order, for example, to adopt those definitions of service quality which promote their own interests (see Chapters 13 and 14). Definitions of (and stakeholders' interests in) quality will be construed so as to divert resources (through more spending) in favour of service providers. Local bureaucrats will favour those definitions of service quality which bring forth increased spending, so promoting budget maximization for their programmes with all the improved career benefits and personal aggrandizement which that involves for them. The leviathan model fits within the *public choice* school of economic theory which hypothesizes that public servants themselves seek to maximize their own welfares (see Chapter 5).

CONCLUSIONS

The treatment of local government economics in this book is much broader than the traditional approach which is restricted to fiscal federalism. It goes beyond the assignment of functions and finance to different tiers of government in that it adopts a broader political economy approach. This reflects recent developments in the operations of local government and development of the discipline itself. The multidisciplinary nature of local government studies must be recognized in order to appreciate both the potential contribution of economic theory and its limitations. Its greatest potential contribution to the study of local government lies in its integration with other academic disciplines. Such integration is attempted in this book.

The definition of local government is difficult and the tortuous debate regarding alternative definitions requires recourse to political science. The economic analysis in this book is qualified, but not invalidated, by the democratic role of local government, as distinct from its role as a provider of public sector services. Local government operations have potentially substantial effects on the economic efficiency of the economy. The economic analysis of local government actions is therefore as legitimate as other analyses by political scientists, sociologists and other academic disciplines.

The conventional economic argument is that the main role of local government should be limited to the allocation function, namely dealing with market failure. Attempts to adopt the distribution and stabilization functions are likely to cause inefficiency. The regulatory role may, or may not, be undertaken on behalf of central government.

In practice, however, local government actions may contain elements of all four roles. Hence, there is the distinct possibility that central government and local government roles may overlap. While it may be difficult to resolve that duplication, it will be diminished by the principle of jurisdictional restriction.

Models of local government are a subset of the general models of government and explicitly take account of the distribution of political power within local democratic institutions. Though it is not possible to determine a priori which model is most valid, those models underpin the analysis of later chapters.

2 The Economic Efficiency Case for Decentralized Government

Public responsibilities shall generally be exercised, in preference, by those authorities which are closest to the citizen. Allocation of responsibility to another authority should weigh up the extent and nature of the task and requirements of efficiency and economy.

(European Charter of Local Self-Government: Article 4)

INTRODUCTION

The relationships between size of local governments, the efficient provision of their services and the degree of citizen participation in local public life have been the focus of debate in many developed countries since the early 1950s. The European Charter of Local Self-Government clearly incorporates the principle that local governments should be as small as possible. Formulated by the Council of Europe in 1985, the Charter has since been ratified by almost all member states of the Council of Europe. Within the European Union, the decentralization principle has been adopted under the name of '*subsidiarity*', that government powers should be exercised at the lowest level of government possible.

This chapter sets out the economic theories underpinning the economic rationale for decentralized government and demonstrates the contribution economic theory can make to the debate concerning the optimum size of local government. In so doing, it refers to both allocative and technical efficiency in the production of local government outputs. It also considers the actual degree of decentralization within European countries.

DEFINING DECENTRALIZATION

There are three forms of decentralization and these must be kept conceptually distinct in order to appreciate that which is of relevance to the economic theories to be developed.

1. *Economic* decentralization is concerned with the location of economic decisions, these being decentralized by definition within perfectly competitive markets (that is, consumer sovereignity).

18

2. *Political* decentralization refers to *devolution* of political decision-making to local and regional governments. Subnational governments are vested with powers to levy their own taxes and user-charges to finance provision of a self-determined mix and level of public sector outputs. This is the form of decentralization to which the European Charter of Local Self-Government refers.

3. *Administrative* decentralization refers to the creation of regional offices of central government departments with or without decision-making powers independent of sanction by the centre. The former is administrative *discretion* (that is, the ability to make operational decisions within set policy parameters). The latter is simply administrative *decentralization*.

These three forms of decentralization are not necessarily mutually exclusive (see Chapter 4). The opening quotation clearly implies an interrelationship between economic and political decentralization, the former being more decentralized (to the individual in the market) than the latter (to the individual as part of a collective decision-making organization). Some measures may facilitate more than one form of decentralization. For example, the use of education vouchers can facilitate both economic and administrative decentralization within any given structure of political (de)centralization. The voucher entitles the holder (for example, a parent) to a specified range of educational services (in this case, for a child) which can be chosen from alternative service providers (that is, schools). Hence, there is economic decentralization through increased consumer sovereignty and administrative decentralization from the local government to the individual school level.

THE ALLOCATIVE EFFICIENCY CASE FOR LOCAL GOVERNMENT

Chapter 1 set out the case for the economic role of local government being restricted to the *allocative* role, adjusting for instances of local market failure. However, that analysis did not provide any guidance concerning the appropriate size of local government, either in terms of the number of its citizens, its service responsibilities, or its geographical area. The above quotation from Article 4 of the European Charter of Local Self-Government clearly refers to population size, as does subsidiarity. In principle, the optimal size is that which can most accurately match supply with the demand for public sector outputs. Centralized choices lead to uniformity of provision, failing to take account of local variations in preferences. Hence, local government is preferable to central government in this respect because nationally uniform services create a loss of consumers' surplus, as illustrated in Figure 2.1.

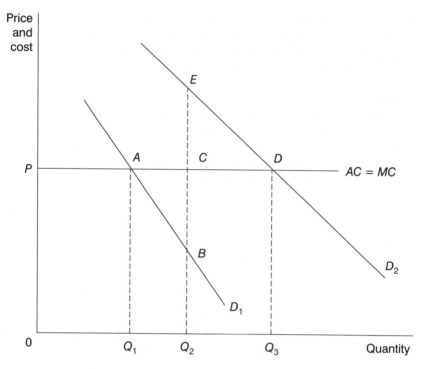

Figure 2.1   *The allocative efficiency case for local government*

Assume constant costs in producing the output such that the cost function is a horizontal straight line (so that average cost, AC, equals marginal cost, MC). Assume also that society is either composed of only two individuals (or, alternatively, of two groups with identical preferences within the group but different preferences between them) represented by demand schedules D_1 and D_2. Assume further that national government would decide to produce output Q_2. However, at price P, group 1 demands Q_1 while group 2 demands Q_3, respectively less than and greater than Q_2. Group 1 is therefore forced to consume more of the output than it wishes, the cost of the additional enforced consumption (Q_1ACQ_2) being greater than willingness to pay (Q_1ABQ_2). Likewise, group 2 is deprived of extra consumption for which it would be willing to pay Q_2EDQ_3, compared with a cost of only Q_2CDQ_3. Hence group 1 incurs a deadweight loss of welfare measured by the area ABC while group 2 experiences a loss of CDE.

The creation of two local governments would therefore lead to a welfare gain through improved allocative efficiency compared with choices at national level. Decentralized public choices are Pareto efficient simply because of the removal of the deadweight loss of consumers' surplus. This result is referred to as *Oates' decentralization theorem* (Oates 1972). The essence of the theorem is that local governments be created such that preferences vary little within localities but vary strongly between them. It relates to *economic decentralization* in that it is concerned with the location of economic decisions and is concerned only with *allocative efficiency*, having no direct effect on any technical or *X-inefficiency* created by self-serving behaviour of bureaucrats and so on (see Chapters 3 and 5). The actual size of allocative inefficiency or welfare loss depends on:

1. *The size of the disparities between central and local choices*: the greater the heterogeneity of preferences the greater the welfare losses because the distance between the two demand schedules increases, and so do the sizes of areas *ABC* and *CDE*.
2. *The slopes of the two demand schedules*: the more inelastic (and hence steeper) they are, the larger are areas *ABC* and *CDE* (D_1 and D_2 each pivoting on *A* and *D* respectively). Hence, deadweight loss varies inversely with the price elasticity of demand. The deadweight loss of consumer's surplus will vary from service to service reflecting the heterogeneity of preferences and price elasticities of demand.
3. *The extent of any economies of scale* in production of the output: assuming *ceteris paribus*, an inverse relation between the rate of output and unit costs increases the optimum size of subcentral government acting as a tradeoff against loss of consumer surplus (see below).

Note that the model assumes conditions of constant costs. However, the presence of economies or diseconomies of scale violates this assumption. The model will be similarly affected by a relaxation of any of the other underlying assumptions which are discussed below. First, however, note that while there have been few attempts to estimate the loss arising from these three factors, Bradford and Oates (1974) suggest that the welfare losses associated with uniform provision of public services can be quite large. Such estimates are of less validity the more this theorem is subject to the following qualifications.

1. *The demand schedules assume a direct market-type relationship between payment and service takeup*, whereas most public sector services are financed by taxation, liability to pay taxes not being conterminous with service use. Hence, the vertical axis in Figure 2.1 is misleading in implying that consumers pay in direct proportion to the output they consume. This will only be the case where (full-cost) user-charges are levied, in such a case begging the question why collective choice is required for such individualistic consumption. Otherwise liability to pay taxes varies in accordance with incomes and/or expenditures, rather than in respect of consumption of local government services.
2. *Alternatively, the system of electoral representation is assumed to reflect fully citizens' willingness to pay tax prices*. This will not be the case where

'first-past-the-post' majority voting systems are adopted. Some preferences will not be reflected in decisions regarding supply. Minorities, for example, may be permanently underrepresented, or even not represented at all. In fact local governments may be prone to exploit their monopoly powers in providing services *to* (rather than *for* or *with*) their largely captive 'market' of service users (see Chapter 1). Until quite recently in some countries, users have rarely been treated as customers with rights to receive information, make choices and obtain redress where appropriate (see Chapter 12). Local governments have tended to emphasize quantity rather than quality of output, relatively little attention being paid to flexibility, choice and other aspects of quality (see Chapter 4).

3. *It assumes a fiscal exchange model of government,* whereby central and local governments simply respond to the demands of citizens, providing outputs in exchange for agreed tax payments. This is a very narrow view of local government as service provider, rather than as an integral and essential part of the system of democracy (see Chapter 1). Such responses would require local governments to consult their electorates' wishes on expenditures and associated tax levels on a regular and frequent basis whereas, in fact, very few do. They rely instead on electoral representation.

4. *The theorem is unrealistic in assuming identical preferences within each group.* Alternatively, compared with a representative (or median) voter, some individuals and groups of voters whose preferences differ from those of the median voter may be politically marginalized such that there may still be a loss of consumers' surplus despite decentralization. This would be the case if 'distributional coalitions' (see Chapter 5) acting as pressure groups exploit power arising from institutional form in order to serve themselves rather than the local community, for example under the fiscal transfer model of government (see Chapter 1).

5. *It applies to individual service outputs* but local governments are usually multifunctional, providing a whole array of services for which citizens vote as a package. Single-issue voting is the exception rather than the norm.

6. *The demand schedules assume that willingness to pay reflects all the costs and benefits of public sector outputs.* In fact, deadweight loss will be offset to the extent that increases in provision of, say, education and police protection generate substantial benefits spilling over local government boundaries. In principle, such spillover effects can be addressed within the omniscient *despotic benevolent model* of government (see Chapter 1) by the payment of allocatively efficient subsidies from central to local government which serve to lower the cost schedule and so encourage allocatively optimal provision of such services. Spillovers will presumably be smaller for refuse collection and other purely localized services than

for, say, education. Hence, reference to spillover effects to justify increasing centralization should not be overplayed.

7. *It ignores the legitimacy of values other than allocative efficiency*, especially equity and social integration. For example, the national interest may legitimately override the local interest where it is a national policy to banish the occurrence of racial or religious discrimination in the provision of local government services.

8. *It strictly only justifies decentralization of choices* rather than of government *per se*. However, although it is concerned with *economic* decentralization of economic decisions, Oates' decentralization theorem clearly relates to *devolution* in that it matches collective services with citizens' willingness to pay local and regional taxes. Devolution is a necessary concomitant of the decentralization of collective economic decisions.

9. *This neoclassical analysis is devoid of institutional form* and its associated distribution of political power (see Chapter 1). Recourse has to be made to disciplines other than economics in order to make recommendations about institutional form and democratic process. Instability in institutional form or democratic process could mean that allocative efficiency may not result.

10. *Bureaucrats may exploit information asymmetries in order to serve their own interests rather than those of local voters, such that decentralization does not eliminate the loss of consumer surplus*. For example, bureaucrats may exaggerate the benefits of services and disguise (understate) their costs in order to maximize their budgets and so improve their own prospects of promotion and status, for example under the *leviathan model* of government. This creates X-inefficiency (see Chapter 3).

11. *It does not necessarily justify the current size of local government in any particular country*. In principle, it justifies the smallest possible scale of local government consistent with not incurring substantially higher costs of provision of public sector outputs due to loss of any economies of scale (see below). At the extreme, there should be as many local government jurisdictions as there are discrete sets of preferences. Given that this would be inefficient in cost terms, some aggregation of locally heterogeneous preferences is inevitable.

12. *The theorem does not require that local or regional governments should themselves provide the service*. Their provision (for example, collection of domestic waste) could be contracted out to private firms (see Chapter 12). If, in fact, consumers' preferences were highly heterogeneous and market provision were possible, then the theorem justifies provision of local public services through the market. Alternatively, such services could be provided by some sort of non-profit community association or club or some form of public-private organization. In the USA, for example, there are 150 000 or so 'residential community associations'

(essentially private clubs) providing specified 'public' services (see Chapter 8). The growth of private policing is an example in the UK (Johnstone 1992).

Points 4, 9, and 10 above relate to government failure, a potentially serious counterbalance to Oates' decentralization theorem. However, despite all these qualifications, Oates' theorem provides a theoretical rationale for local autonomy in decision-making by highlighting the adverse welfare consequences of centralized choices. It therefore provides the public choice justification for decentralization since, by achieving allocative efficiency, it maximizes social welfare.

The size of the welfare losses are presumably reduced the smaller the scale of local government because each local government's population becomes more homogeneous and outputs can more accurately reflect local demands. It seems intuitively plausible that the smaller the population size of a community the greater each individual citizen's impact on local collective decision-making, so supporting the decentralization theorem.

This assumes either that the boundaries of smaller local government are drawn specifically to separate heterogeneous groups or that populations spatially re-sort themselves into homogeneous communities. Both seem plausible, although the first may require periodic adjustment of local government boundaries (see below) and the second assumes Tiebout's 'voting with the feet' (see Chapter 4). Hence, some tradeoff of welfare gain and increased costs associated with smaller size seems inevitable. The optimal size of jurisdictions will be determined by that tradeoff but, in practice, little is known about the relative sizes of gains in allocative efficiency and losses in economies of scale for different services as the size of jurisdictions is reduced.

Political scientists often dismiss the economist's emphasis on balancing the costs and benefits of decentralization, typically arguing that 'the prime requirement for good government is that it be democratic, not that it be efficient' (Commission for Local Democracy 1995a, p. 3). It is notable, therefore, that local decision-making inputs are not allowed by central government in the case of the UK's National Health Service (which is *not* part of UK local government).

TECHNICAL EFFICIENCY AND ECONOMIES OF SCALE

Whereas allocative efficiency is a broad concept relating to the economically optimal allocation of resources throughout the economy (see Chapter 1), technical efficiency relates to the production of outputs at the level of the firm or organization. Technical inefficiency arises when the firm or organization is not operating at minimum cost. This cause of inefficiency is conceptually distinct from the cost effects of any self-serving behaviour by bureaucrats (referred to in point 10 above).

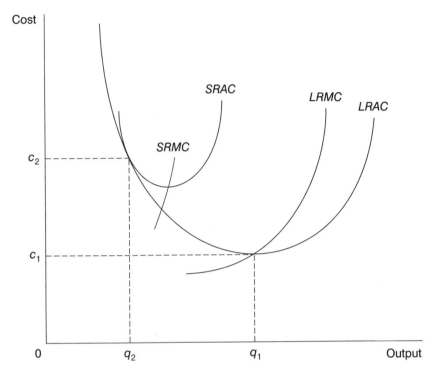

Figure 2.2 *Economies of scale*

Internal economies of scale exist when increasing the productive capacity of a firm causes total production costs to increase proportionately less than output. In other words, long-run marginal cost (*LRMC*) is less than long-run average cost (*LRAC*). Economies of scale arise due to a number of factors. First, indivisibilities in plant or production processes. Second, greater specialization and division of labour as the scale of output increases. Third, fixed levels of overhead administrative or management processes which must be undertaken whatever the scale of output. Fourth, pecuniary economies arising from buying inputs in bulk. The *LRAC* of production falls in such cases (see Figure 2.2).

Calculation of *LRAC* (total cost divided by the number of units produced) assumes that all inputs have been adjusted so as to minimize costs of the given level of output by making the most economical use of factors of production. This is the case in Figure 2.2 if market size limits output to q_2. However, once the plant is built in accordance with optimal capacity q_2, then some factors (usually assumed to be capital) will be fixed in the short run. Hence, any deviations from the optimal level of output (that is, where unit costs are minimized) will lead to short-run average cost (*SRAC*) being greater than *LRAC*, since inputs are no longer being combined in optimal proportions. For example, more or less labour may be applied to the fixed amount of capital, leading to diminishing returns to labour. This is demonstrated in Figure 2.2, *SRAC* lying above *LRAC* at all levels of output other than the optimal level.

The range of output up to q_1 displays economies of scale since *LRAC* is falling (for example, from c_2 to c_1 as the *alternative* scales of output expand from q_2 to q_1). Thereafter, diseconomies of scale result in *LRAC* increasing for successively greater alternative levels of output above q_1 since *LRMC* is greater than *LRAC*. This may be due to a more than proportional increase in the complexity of management processes as the scale of output increases, such that administrative costs per unit of output rise. Such managerial diseconomies cause *LRAC* to increase so that it would not be allocatively efficient to expand production above q_1. Instead, replication of plants with capacity q_1 is the most economical way of meeting demands requiring output in excess of q_1.

THE TRADEOFF BETWEEN DECENTRALIZATION AND ECONOMIES OF SCALE

As already noted, the existence of substantial economies of scale would serve to qualify the allocative efficiency case for small local governments in accordance with Oates' decentralization theorem. Therefore the economically optimal (output) size of local government is where the marginal social cost equals the marginal social benefit. This occurs when any gains from increased size (economies of scale) exactly balance the losses (reduced ability to respond to preferences which vary among citizens). Note, however, that gains may also include the internalization of spillover benefits as size increases (see Chapter 1). This means that optimum size can only be determined in terms of the provision of a single service and that optimum size may differ in respect of different services.

However, the costs and outputs of services, and the benefits obtained from their consumption, are difficult to measure. The benefits of those outputs are difficult to determine, being complicated by the existence, if any, of (largely intangible) externalities and so on. Nonetheless, in principle, there is clearly a tradeoff between the benefits of smaller size in terms of Oates' decentralization theorem and any lost economies of scale. Hence, both *demand-side* and *supply-side* factors must be taken into account when determining the optimal size of local governments in efficiency terms.

The severity of that tradeoff will be greater the more pronounced the U-shape of the *LRAC* schedule in Figure 2.2. A very flat U-shape (with a shallow cost gradient) would mean that the cost consequences of deviating from q_1 would be much less than if the U-shape were very pronounced (a steep cost gradient). Indeed, if the *LRAC* curve was flat-bottomed over a wide range of output (because of constant returns to scale) then there would be no cost consequences arising from reducing the size of local governments until the point of minimum efficient scale (q_1) was reached. More generally, the less pronounced the U-shape, the greater the net improvement in demand-side allocative efficiency arising from decentralization. This demand-side improvement will offset, over a wider range of output possibilities, the increased supply-side economic inefficiency arising from local governments below the minimum efficient scale. Clearly, the determination of the optimal size of local governments requires estimation of the consumption benefits arising from decentralization and of the production cost benefits arising from increasing scale.

However, like Oates' decentralization theorem, the theory of economies of scale is axiomatic, a self-evident truth, given the assumptions relating to the model of production from which it is derived (for example, the assumption of indivisibilities of capital). Economies of scale may not be directly applicable to the operations of local government for the following reasons.

1. *Having been developed in respect of large-scale manufacturing activities, the model requires a highly standardized output of a single good or service.* Some local government outputs are highly standardized, especially technical services such as kilograms of domestic waste collected, litres of water delivered and cubic metres of sewage treated. This is the 'natural monopoly' case discussed in Chapter 1. However, many other local government services are non-standardized by design in meeting the differential needs of service users; for example, child care services or community care facilities for the elderly and disabled. There will be limited potential for substantial economies of scale in the latter cases.
2. *It assumes clearly definable and measurable costs* for the single output in question (see below).
3. *It assumes a clearly definable and measurable output.* However, the outputs of many local government services are intangible in that they do not consist of intermediate consumption goods (for example a car, which provides personal transport services). Instead, consumption and production are often simultaneous (for example, social workers providing advice to clients and teachers instructing pupils). Such outputs are clearly difficult to define and measure.

It may be possible to circumvent these problems in modelling economies of scale by undertaking empirical studies. There are three techniques.

1. 'Engineering Studies'

These proceed by asking managers and professional bodies for their views about optimal scale and the steepness of cost gradients. However, the responses will tend to be biased in favour of maintaining or improving the job opportunities of respondents, especially if structural reorganization depends on those responses. Such methods are often used informally in the run up to reorganization of local government.

2. 'Survivor Tests'

These involve the longitudinal analysis of the size distribution of firms in order to see if certain sizes of plant survive or fail or, alternatively, increase or lose market share. The former variant of this technique is clearly inappropriate, since local governments are rarely allowed to become bankrupt. The latter variant may be useful if local governments actively compete to attract households and businesses to their areas (see Chapter 4 on the Tiebout Hypothesis).

3. Studies of Bivariate Correlations between Population Size and Service Costs of Local Governments

These generally proceed by means of cross-sectional studies in order to see if, at a particular point in time, demographically larger local governments have lower per capita service costs than smaller ones. If so, costs are assumed to be a negative function of population size. The shortcoming of this technique is that it either ignores other factors which influence costs or assumes that they do not vary systematically between demographically large and small local governments (that is, are not colinear with size). In fact, it is generally recognized (and confirmed by research) that the population size of local governments is positively correlated with per capita expenditure needs. For example, the greater the urban scale the more likely local governments are to have high proportions of single-parent families (who have relatively high needs for municipal housing) and to face more need to provide child welfare services (see Chapter 6).

The results of many studies making use of this third technique suggest that the per capita costs of service provision tend to rise with population size (Boyne 1995). However, those studies almost invariably rely on very crude definitions and measures of the key variables in the economies of scale model, namely total output, units of output and unit costs of provision. The main problems are as follows.

1. *It is not possible to derive a composite measure of the output of multifunctional local governments.* Output is measured by kilograms of refuse collected, meals provided and so on. Such divergent forms of output cannot be combined in a composite measure of total local authority output.

Hence, it is not possible to derive a measure of scale. To get round this problem most studies use total population as a proxy for service output and therefore of scale. This is not valid because residents are clearly not the units of output depicted in Figure 2.2. They are recipients of service output rather than the output itself. Nonetheless, some studies assume both that total population is an accurate measure of need to spend and that spending accurately reflects that need. However, total population is not the primary determinant of need to spend since the need generated by a given population total can be expected to vary in accordance with its socioeconomic and demographic structures. It may also be invalid to assume that output is responsive to current need since it may, instead, reflect historical commitments such as debt charges relating to past physical investments.

2. *The measurement of costs is also problematic.* First, it is difficult to assign to individual services the overhead costs of central departments (for example finance) and of running the system of democracy. Second, local government capital costs are influenced by the use of historic or current replacement costs, by the period over which assets are depreciated and whether depreciation is 'straight line' (where the book value of an asset is reduced by equal successive amounts over its assumed lifetime) or 'accelerated'. In any one year, capital accounting costs will be increased by the use of current replacement costs, shorter assumed lifetimes and accelerated depreciation. Third, local government accounting costs are not measures of economic costs, in particular not being based on opportunity costs (a measure of the true economic cost of using an asset for one particular use rather than another).

3. *The measurement of unit costs is therefore also problematic* if neither output nor costs can be accurately measured.

4. *Variations in cost per unit of output may reflect differences in service quality rather than differences in the scale of output.* Either it has to be assumed that quality of output is constant in all local governments or quality has to be directly measured and accounted for in the model. Both are particularly problematic if quantity and quality of output are interdependent. For example, costs rising as a positive function of output may reflect increasing quality rather than diseconomies of scale. This would be the case where increased choice is made available to service users. Alternatively, where costs are a decreasing function of output, this may reflect increasing standardization and so reduced responsiveness to users and therefore poorer quality of output.

5. *Costs may reflect the degree of urbanization.* In that population size is positively correlated with urban scale and that the degree of urbanization is positively correlated with service costs, expenditure may be a positive function of population size. Urbanization may be positively correlated with service costs because of more expensive land and premises, higher

labour costs and provision of regional services to city hinterlands (see Chapter 6). Labour costs may be higher in urban areas as a result of higher rates of unionization of the workforce and so higher rates of pay and/or staffing.

6. *Scale effects may not be related to the population size* of local authorities but, instead, be related to the size of individual schools, crematoria facilities and so on. This is the distinction between firm size and plant size respectively. If larger local governments decentralize provision of their services, the smaller average plant size may lead to diseconomies of scale, not of large 'firms' but of small 'plants'.

7. *Modelling problems affect the results.* First, linear tests of the relationship between costs and population size may cancel out U-shaped cost effects, resulting in insignificant results. Second, since local government expenditures are influenced by a large number of factors, it is necessary to undertake multivariate (rather than bivariate) studies of service costs, all factors in addition to population being separately accounted for in any longitudinal study.

8. *Any scale effects relate to individual services whereas local government provides a multitude of service outputs.* Optimum scale for provision of one service may lead to diseconomies of scale for another. Hence, there cannot be one optimum size for a given local government applicable to all its services. Unless local governments are restricted to provision of single services, optimum scale will therefore be a compromise depending on a ranking of relative priorities for the many services provided by a single local government.

In general, these problems have not been fully addressed in empirical analyses of the relationship between population size and spending per resident. They are therefore not valid tests of the influence of scale on unit costs, since they have not been properly related to the economic theory of economies of scale. 'There is, as yet, no useful evidence on the key questions concerning economies of scale' (Boyne 1995, p. 220).

Although it has been seen that it is difficult to confirm or deny the existence of scale effects, the conventional wisdom has been that technical efficiency is a function of population size. This conventional wisdom has often been used, first, in specifying a minimum or maximum population size for local government and, second, when subdividing services between tiers of subnational government (for example, county and municipality, or local and regional).

(a) Maximum Population Size

This does not simply reflect any diseconomies of scale. It may also be constrained by the general belief that the level of citizen participation in local politics (not just voting) and the quality of local democracy (for example in terms of well-informed citizens and their access to decision-makers) are negative functions of local government size. However, the impact of an individual on a group diminishes very rapidly as size exceeds 50 persons such that there is little difference in the individual's impact on two alternative group sizes of 1000 and 100 000 persons. Ultimately collective decisions are precisely that, the bigger the collective group the more the individual's preferences are subsumed by the collective preference. Local politicians may, however, be more responsive to individual voters in smaller communities simply because they tend to be more accessible the smaller the local government. In fact, research suggests that large local governments are no less accessible to citizen participation than small ones (Smith 1985). They may, in fact, be less oligarchic than small local governments and provide more opportunities for participation (for example through decentralization of administration and of user-group representation) specifically in recognition of the need to be more responsive to the divergent preferences of citizens.

Where maximum population size is not sufficient to reach the point of minimum efficient scale for some outputs, there are two possibilities. First, intermunicipal cooperation may achieve economies of scale. Voluntary creation of federations of small local governments or of intermunicipal enterprises are sometimes used for provision of public utility services such as public transport, energy, water and sanitation and waste removal. For example, 'special districts' are common for water supply and fire protection in the USA, as are 'secondary communes' in the Nordic countries. In bordering on fragmentation, this may make more difficult routine dealings with central government. Also the more 'governments' there are serving a given population the higher the costs of representation. In such cases citizens face greater difficulty in understanding and controlling government, serving to reduce accountability and perhaps increasing allocative inefficiency. Moreover, it may involve some standardization of services despite heterogeneous preferences and so be contrary to Oates' decentralization theorem. Hence, in being at the cost of democratic accountability, intermunicipal enterprises are best suited to technical services rather than those with substantial social or political features. This is in fact common practice (Council of Europe 1995b).

Second, local authorities too small to achieve economies of scale may still be able to capture such cost savings by contracting out their supply to private sector firms large enough to gain economies of scale, for refuse collection and maintenance of local roads for example (see Chapter 4). There is little evidence of this in practice, however, at least in the UK (see Chapter 14).

(b)   Minimum Population Size
This may reflect the need to ensure administrative capacity in terms of financial, technical, human and other resources and to avoid administrative overload for central government in dealing with lots of small local governments. Where minimum size is still so large that it incurs diseconomies of scale for a

particular service output, decentralization of service provision may be the optimum response, for example in the management of municipal housing.

Where minimum population size encompasses diverse groups of residents with discrete preferences, the resulting allocative inefficiencies caused by provision of standardized services can be overcome by decentralization to neighbourhood areas within individual local governments and increased inputs from the neighbourhood's elected representatives and residents (see Chapter 4).

A priori, local voters find it easier to vote out of office local rather than national governments and can vote on a much narrower range of local issues than is possible for national government which, *inter alia*, invariably has responsibility for national defence, foreign policy and macroeconomic policy. This assumes that local elections are contested on local issues rather than being seen as mid-term referenda on the performance of national government.

On the other hand, larger size may improve territorial justice by allowing combination of rich and poor populations, so reducing local disparities in resources and expenditure needs per head. The smaller are local governments the greater the disparities in per capita local taxable resources and expenditure needs and so the greater the need for central government intervention in the form of intergovernmental grants (see Chapter 9). It is a paradox that smaller size has the potential to increase local democracy and yet requires greater central government intervention to address resource inequalities in relation to need.

(c)   Optimum Population Size

A formal model of optimum population size has been developed by King (1996). The model relates to single service functions and is based on a highly restrictive set of assumptions. In particular, it assumes that population (as distinct from output) is the relevant determinant of size, that the objective is to maximize the sum of individual utilities, that all citizens have equal incomes and equal marginal utilities of income, that those incomes and marginal utilities are constant over time, that service production technologies are also constant over time, and that local authority boundaries are infinitely variable. These assumptions ignore the problems of interpersonal comparisons of utility and social welfare functions. They also ignore cultural, ethnic, religious and other factors which influence tastes (that is, not just income).

However, such assumptions are necessary if an economic model of size is to be developed and the model can, nonetheless, provide valuable analytical insights. In particular, King concludes that the optimum size of local authorities is likely to change over time and that, although structural change is costly, size must be periodically redetermined if allocative efficiency is to be maintained. The period between reform of boundaries will reflect the speed at which incomes and service technologies change and also reflect the costs of restructuring, However, a period of less than two decades or so between major reform is unlikely to be justifiable in allocative efficiency terms.

Nevertheless, it must be recognized that a progressive shift in the local governance structure from direct provision of services to enabling their provision (for example by the private sector) may shorten the period between structural reforms and is likely to justify smaller local governments (see Chapter 12). Put simply, optimal size is a dynamic rather than static concept.

THE DEGREE OF POLITICAL DECENTRALIZATION IN PRACTICE

Centralization and decentralization are not a dichotomy but, instead, a continuum. Even written constitutions may be subject to changing interpretations and provisions regarding local self-governance. The degree of political decentralization is usually measured in four main ways:

1. *the range and importance of functions undertaken by local governments* in their own capacity rather than as agents of central government;
2. *the legal basis for local government autonomy*, for example whether it is vested with general competence powers to undertake activities not expressly prohibited or assigned to other levels of government or whether it can only undertake such activities as are explicity authorized by central government (see Chapter 1);
3. *the proportion of public expenditure accounted for by local governments net of necessarily national expenditures* such as defence and, again, assuming that local governments are not simply acting as decentralized administrative units for national government; and
4. *the degree of dependence of local governments on intergovernmental grants* paid to them by central government, local autonomy being less the greater the proportion of local revenues derived from central government and the greater the proportion of that revenue in the form of conditional (categorical) grants for specific services rather than general (unhypothecated) grants for the generality of services (see Chapter 9).

Despite differences in the degree of decentralization amongst different countries, general trends can be discerned from international practice.

1. Concern with Economies of Scale has been Predominant

A concern for improved efficiency of service delivery led to dramatic reductions in the total number of local governments in many European countries between 1950 and 1992 (see Table 2.1). Three countries reduced the number of their local governments by 80 per cent or more over that period and six by

Table 2.1   *Total number of local authorities, 1950 and 1992*

Country	1950	1992	Change Number	%
Austria	3999	2301	−1698	−42
Belgium	2699	589[a]	−2080	−78
Bulgaria	2178[b]	255[a]	−1932	−88
Czech Rep.	11 051	6196[a]	−4855	−44
Denmark	1387	275	−1112	−80
Finland	547	460	−87	−16
France	38 814[c]	36 763[d]	−2051	−5
Germany[e]	24 272	8077	−16 195	−67
Greece	5959	5922	−37	−0.6
Hungary	n.a.	3109	n.a.	n.a.
Iceland	229	197	−32	−14
Italy	7781	8100	+319	+4
Luxembourg	127	118	−9	−7
Malta	n.a.	67	n.a.	n.a.
Netherlands	1015	647	−368	−36
Norway	744	439	−305	−41
Poland	n.a.	2459	n.a.	n.a.
Portugal	303	305	+2	+0.7
Slovakia	n.a.	2467	n.a.	n.a.
Spain	9214	8082	−1132	−12
Sweden	2281	286	−1995	−87
Switzerland	3097	3021	−76	−2
Turkey	n.a.	2378	n.a.	n.a.
United Kingdom	2028	484	−1544	−76

Source: Council of Europe (1995a), reproduced with permission of the Council of Europe.
Notes:
n.a. denotes not available.
a: Data relate to 1991.
b: Data relate to 1949.
c: Data relate to 1945.
d: Data relate to 1990.
e: West Germany only: 1950 data for the ex-Soviet East Germany not available.

60 per cent or more. However, an increasing concern for the locality was evident in the creation of decentralized administrative processes and even the creation of submunicipal authorities.

2. Local Governments Remain Small in Most Countries

The average population per local authority varies widely from less than 2000 in France, Greece, Iceland and Slovakia to over 30 000 in Bulgaria, Portugal,

Table 2.2   *Population size of local authorities, 1990*

Country	Average population per local authority	Percentage of municipalities by size of population				
		Less than 1000	*1001– 5000*	*5001– 10 000*	*10 001– 100 000*	*Over 100 000*
Austria	3340	25.8	65.7	5.6	2.7	0.2
Belgium	16 960	0.2	17.1	29.0	52.3	1.4
Bulgaria	35 000	0	8.2	21.9	63.6	6.3
Czech Rep.[a]	13 730	79.8	15.9	2.1	2.1	0.1
Denmark	18 760	0	7.0	44.0	47.6	1.4
Finland	10 870	4.9	44.6	26.3	22.9	1.3
France	1580	77.1	18.1	2.5	2.2	0.1
Germany[b]	4925	53.6	30.4	7.1	8.4	0.5
Greece	1700	79.4	17.3	1.3	1.9	0.1
Hungary	3340	54.3	37.1	4.2	4.1	0.3
Iceland	1330	83.3	13.2	1.5	1.5	0.5
Italy	7130	23.9	49.0	14.2	12.2	0.7
Luxembourg	3210	51.0	41.0	5.0	3.0	0
Malta	5425	11.0	45.0	28.0	16.0	0
Netherlands	23 200	0.2	11.0	27.6	58.4	2.8
Norway	9000	3.9	52.4	21.4	21.6	0.7
Poland	15 560	0	27.7	47.3	23.3	1.7
Portugal	32 300	0.3	8.2	25.0	59.0	7.5
Slovakia	1850	67.7	27.9	1.8	2.5	0.1
Spain	4930	60.6	25.6	6.4	6.7	0.7
Sweden	30 040	0	3.1	19.2	73.8	3.9
Switzerland	2210	59.5	31.5	5.3	3.5	0.2
Turkey[c]	23 340	0.1		79.3	17.2	3.4
United Kingdom[d]	118 440	n.a.	n.a.	n.a.	n.a.	n.a.

Source: Council of Europe (1995a), reproduced with permission of the Council of Europe.
Notes:
n.a. denotes not available.
a: Data for 1/1/91
b: Data relate to all of Germany.
c: Data for Turkey cannot be split between 1001–5000 and 5001–10 000.
d: All local authorities in the UK have more than 10 000 inhabitants. The average population of local authorities in 1990 was 127 000 in England, 91 620 in Scotland and 75 370 in Wales (Council of Europe 1992). The overall average of 118 440 in 1990 rose to 139 300 in 1995 (Chandler 1996).

Sweden and the United Kingdom, the UK having by far the largest local governments (see Table 2.2). However, the average conceals many small local authorities. More than half the local governments (municipalities) in 10 countries have fewer than 1000 inhabitants and 15 countries have more than half with less than 5000 citizens. At the other extreme, five countries have a majority of municipalities with more than 10 000 population, almost half for

Denmark and all in the UK. Hence, there is considerable variation *within* as well as *between* countries.

3. Considerable Variation in the Average Number of Inhabitants Represented by One Elected Representative

Four countries have less than 300 while five countries have over 1000 (see Table 2.3).

Table 2.3   *Elected representatives, municipalities and population, 1992*

Country	Total no. of elected representatives in municipalities	Average no. of elected representatives per municipality	Average no. of inhabitants represented by one elected representative
Austria	n.a.	n.a.	n.a.
Belgium	12 698	22	783
Bulgaria	n.a.	n.a.	n.a.
Czech Rep.[a]	69 878	12	138
Denmark	4737	17	1084
Finland	12 567	28	394
France[b]	501 591	14	116
Germany[c]	227 474	20	250
Greece	1801	11	5581
Hungary[d]	25 000	8	415
Iceland[d]	1150	6	194
Italy	145 242	18	397
Luxembourg	1088	9	349
Malta	425	6	588
Netherlands	n.a.	n.a.	n.a.
Norway[d]	7670	17	515
Poland	55 544	23	689
Portugal	8760	29	1125
Slovakia	n.a.	n.a.	n.a.
Spain	66 760	8	597
Sweden	12 887	45	667
Switzerland	n.a.	n.a.	n.a.
Turkey	29 351	12	2331
United Kingdom[d]	22 000	42	2605

Source: Council of Europe (1995a), reproduced with permission of the Council of Europe.
Notes:
n.a. denotes not available.
a: Data for 1990
b: Data for 1983
c: Excludes four new Länder for which data is n.a.
d: Estimated data

4. The Public Sector is Becoming Increasingly Complex in Many Countries

There is clearly an enormous diversity of practice among European countries in the size of local governments. This diversity relates not only to differences between different countries but also within individual countries, Table 2.2 shows that many countries have local governments with populations both less than 1000 and more than 100 000. These substantial differences in the sizes of municipalities in different European countries obviously cannot be explained simply by economic factors such as economies of scale or Oates' decentralization theorem. Each country has its own peculiarities and socioeconomic and ideological context.

For example, the UK has become increasingly centralist since 1945, there being no written constitution to guarantee local autonomy. The success of centralized wartime planning 1939–45 and the subsequent growth of the welfare state resulted in increased control by national government over the expenditures, revenues and provision of services by local governments. It is not yet clear whether such centralizing tendencies will be reversed by the UK Labour government's plans to introduce devolution of powers to Scotland and Wales by 1999 (Cm 3658, Cm 3718). Devolution has been justified partly because those two countries elected a majority of Labour members of parliament almost continuously between 1945 and 1997 but had Conservative UK central governments for 34 of those 51 years.

There were attempts to decentralize large parts of the UK public sector during the 1980s and 1990s through the creation of almost 5000 quasi-autonomous non-governmental organizations (quangos), including 'executive agencies' (see Chapter 4). However, in being run by ministerial appointees, they were arguably even less accountable to citizens than the centrally-dominated system they replaced. Nonetheless, they are estimated to spend nearly two-thirds as much money as local government receives from central government (Commission for Local Democracy 1995b).

Other reforms offer the potential for more local accountability. Provision is being made for increased user choice in health and education, but economies of scale seem to be leading to increasing concentration of services offered through competitive tendering – as diverse as leisure, refuse collection and rental housing. While contracted services can be made more responsive to users' preferences, there is little evidence that this has occurred in practice (see Chapter 14).

Elsewhere, separatist and decentralization issues have been prominent, often reflecting cultural and linguistic issues – for example, Catalonia in Spain and Quebec in Canada. Countries in central and eastern Europe have tended to move towards increasing decentralization. Following the collapse of the former Soviet Union, many of the central and eastern European 'economies in transition' created new systems of local government in the early 1990s as part of the decentralization of the former socialist state (Bird *et al.* 1995). As already noted in Chapter 1, decentralization is an aid to political stability. It also facil-itates nation-building and is coincident with privatization, attempts to achieve macroeconomic stability and to maintain a social safety net during radical economic restructuring. Essentially, however, it has been introduced to utilize public resources more efficiently than in the past and to facilitate the transition from a command to a market economy. In this case, the develop-ment (or reintroduction) of local self-government is a prerequisite of demo-cratic institution-building. The relationship between population size, efficiency and citizen participation has therefore been re-emphasized as an issue.

In addition, highly specific institutions are being developed in some Euro-pean Countries and elsewhere, for example the growth of single-function special districts in the USA to provide highways, sewers, hospitals, libraries, fire protection, housing and so on. The USA has also developed metropolitan area governments to take strategic decisions affecting central city governments and their surrounding suburban governments (Oates 1990).

CONCLUSIONS

Neither Oates' decentralization theorem nor the theory of economies of scale have proven particularly useful in providing clear guidance regarding the appropriate size of local governments. Moreover, King's formal model of optimum population size is based on highly restrictive assumptions. The indeterminacy of economic theory is particularly unfortunate in countries such as the UK where local government boundaries have been subject to periodic restructuring.

Failure to determine the extent of any economies or diseconomies of scale is only important, however, if they are so strong, and the services in question so overwhelmingly important, that they alone should determine the size of local governments. Moreover, almost any scale of local government will leave unresolved allocative inefficiences. Allocative inefficiencies may be caused by service charges because market failure has not been properly addressed. They may also be caused by local taxes not being directly related to benefit or to costs of service use, for example because of their partial coverage of voters and service users, and perhaps causing disincentives-to-work effects. Allocative inefficiencies may also result from intergovernmental grant systems, which may stimulate expenditures greater than required for the purposes of allocative efficiency (see Chapter 11).

Being more useful as a conceptual than practical tool, Oates' theorem can-not be used to justify a particular level of decentralization. Even as a concept it is highly qualified. However, it would not be valid to conclude that central-ization is the answer, since that too causes allocative inefficiencies. Moreover, how far should centralization go – to the nation state or to the European Union level?

In practice, the actual size of local governments is determined not by theoretical considerations relating to Oates' decentralization theorem and economies of scale but, instead, by historical, administrative and other factors. In addition, besides paying attention to economic prescriptions, account must also be taken of disciplines other than economics in deciding the optimal degree of decentralization. For example, although the multidisciplinary prescription about optimal size may be suboptimal in economic terms, services with substantial economies of scale could be provided by means of intermunicipal enterprises, owned by a number of local governments which are individually too small to achieve scale economies.

Moreover, decentralization cannot be considered in isolation. It is not the only means of strengthening the 'voice' of citizens in order that service provision more closely reflects their preferences. Other means may offer greater potential for improved allocative efficiency than decentralization on its own account. Ongoing adjustments to the level of decentralization as service technologies change may be prohibitively costly. Alternative ways of strengthening voice are considered in the following chapters.

Finally, although this chapter has been concerned with the economic theories of relevance to the optimal size of local government, the principles considered can also be used to assess the appropriateness of arrangements for local spending and taxation. For example, Oates' decentralization theorem obviously requires local (rather than national) citizens to bear the costs of the services they require to be provided. This therefore has implications for the use of charges (see Chapter 7), for the types of taxation appropriate for local governments (see Chapter 8), for the balance between borrowing and current taxes to finance present day expenditures (see Chapter 5), and for the particular types of intergovernmental grants in use (see Chapter 9).

3 Exit and Voice within Local Government

INTRODUCTION

In Chapter 2 a potential tradeoff was identified between technical efficiency gains from economies of scale and allocative welfare losses as the demographic size of local government varies, smaller size resulting in increased welfare but loss of potential economies of scale for at least some services. Welfare losses due to increasing size occur as a result of two factors.

1. The individual's scope for movement to a neighbouring authority providing the desired mix of service levels and local tax costs is diminished the bigger (and, hence, fewer) are local governments.
2. The individual's preferences are more difficult to articulate (and therefore satisfy) the greater the population catered for.

These factors are refered to as *exit* and *voice* respectively.

Both exit and voice are concerned with the articulation and implementation of choices regarding the provision of goods and services. Exit is linked to choice via competition, which allows choice from among alternative suppliers, Voice is used where competition is absent or inappropriate as a vehicle of choice. It is often supposed that voice is more suitable than exit in expressing preferences for local government services and the reverse for private sector services.

The exit–voice concept is an important analytical framework in the social sciences. It has been used to examine decline in a wide variety of organizations, including corporate enterprises, trades unions, political systems, public services and local government. It is a component of the theory of organizational slack, emphasizing quality issues, and fits within the broader framework of political economy.

This chapter considers the nature of exit and voice, examines the factors which influence the choice between exiting and use of voice, considers whether they are necessarily mutually exclusive options and demonstrates how they affect allocative efficiency. It provides a conceptual framework which will be used in subsequent chapters to analyse the financing and provision of local government services.

40

THE DEVELOPMENT OF THE EXIT–VOICE ANALYTICAL FRAMEWORK

The concepts of exit and voice were crystallized by Hirschman (1970, 1976). *Exit* refers to the ability of consumers to choose among alternative suppliers of a given product and therefore depends on a market mechanism. The service user who is dissatisfied with the quality of service being provided by the current supplier can opt for another instead, therefore exiting the first. *Voice* refers to the expression by consumers of their preferences for quantity and quality of output in an attempt to change, rather than escape from, an unsatisfactory service. Voice is expressed to service managers or political representatives through individual or collective petition. Expression of voice requires administrative mechanisms, ranging from voting systems, through customer surveys to complaints procedures. It is therefore more costly in resource terms than exit. Although voice was not referred to directly in the Oates' decentralization theorem, the welfare gains arising from decentralization are clearly based upon expression of voice (see Chapter 2).

Hirschman argues that the performance of organizations (whether in the public or private sectors) will tend to deteriorate over time because organizations do not constantly strive to maximize their primary goals and objectives. Contrary to the standard assumption of the classical theory of the firm, for example, private sector firms may not maximize profits, instead earning a satisfactory level of profits (Simon 1952, 1959). Defenders of the neoclassical theory of the firm argued that such *satisficing* behaviour exposes firms to the threat of takeover by other companies seeing the possibility of higher profits. That threat serves to limit the extent to which performance deteriorates.

Nonetheless, Cyert and March (1963) developed Simon's *behavioural* approach to the theory of the firm in describing actual decision-making processes within corporations and introducing the concept of *organizational slack*. This inefficiency is internal to the organization, costs being greater than the minimum, and became known as *X-inefficiency* (Leibenstein 1966; see Chapters 2 and 5). It is distinct from allocative inefficiency at the level of the economy, for example unwanted provision of services resulting in excess capacity. Separation of ownership and control of the modern corporation affords management considerable discretion (limited by the threat of takeover in the capital market) to maximize their own utilities rather than those of the shareholders and owners (Williamson 1963, 1974). Rather than maximize profits in order to maximize shareholders' welfares (through higher dividends and capital gains on share holdings), managers may maximize their own utility functions. Those functions are hypothesized to be positively related to the number of subservient staff reporting to them, to their scope for discretionary investment behaviour, and to managerial expenses in excess of those strictly required to continue the firm's operations.

This managerialist/behavioural challenge to the neoclassical theory of the firm can be generalized to public sector organizations (and to voluntary sector organizations) by means of the *principal–agent model*. In the private sector the principal is the owner (that is, shareholders) of the company and the agent the manager(s). In the public sector the principal refers to citizen–voters (or their political representatives), the agent being bureaucrats (see Chapter 5). Both the principal and the agent are assumed only to be concerned with their own utilities, not that of the other. The agent incurs disutility from the effort necessary to provide for the needs of the principal. The principal cannot fully monitor the agent and so must incorporate into the agent's employment contract a set of incentives which will induce the agent to maximize the principal's utility. Appropriate and effective contract incentives combine with the threat of termination of contract to solve the principal–agent problem in the principal's favour. However, neither shareholders nor citizen voters write contracts for managers and bureaucrats. They tend to be written by managers or bureaucrats themselves in the private and public sectors, only minimally overseen by company directors or by elected representatives.

These control problems create the conditions for a deterioration in organizational performance. Hirschman argues that the deterioration typically takes the form of an absolute or relative reduction in quality of output. That deterioration is made evident to the management of the organization either as some customers or members choose the exit option and leave the organization and/or because they voice their dissatisfaction.

In a market context, exit leads to a fall in revenues. This can be shown diagramatically in Figure 3.1, where output demanded and supplied is on the horizontal axis in both of parts (a) and (b). Quality is shown on the vertical axis in part (a) while price is shown in part (b). In part (a), quantity demanded falls from Q_1 to Q_2 when quality of output deteriorates from L_1 to L_2. The resulting fall in revenue is measured in part (b) by the area TQ_1Q_2S, price being assumed to remain constant at P_1 (for example, because it is an administered price). This fall in revenue impacts adversely on the firm's profits and stimulates a corrective response. The more elastic is demand in respect of quality the greater the revenue loss. This can be visualized in Figure 3.1(a) by pivoting the demand curve on point E so as to lessen its slope and therefore increase the revenue loss rectangle in Figure 3.1(b). Clearly, more will exit the greater the quality elasticity of demand.

Voice is expressed by non-exiting customers and may be strengthened by a high-quality elasticity of demand, since the consequences of lack of remedial action are so great in terms of substantial levels of exit and consequent revenue loss. Voice may also be strengthened by the degree of discontent of non-exiting customers.

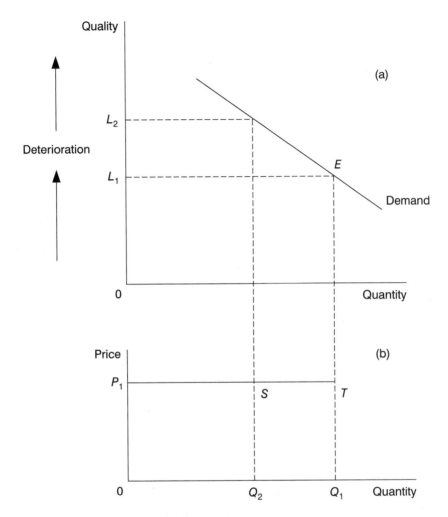

Figure 3.1 The impact of quality deterioration on revenue

Exit is impersonal and indivisible: either one exits or one does not exit. In contrast, voice can be graduated between the extremes of faint grumbling to violent protest. It has none of the anonymity of perfectly competitive market transactions, instead requiring articulation of one's wants and needs. Voice therefore requires representation via negotiation or political action.

Hirschman argued that exit is the realm of economics whereas voice is the realm of politics, there being a 'fundamental schism' between economics and politics (Hirschman 1970, p. 15). However, this is an over-simplification in that economic theory does incorporate voice mechanisms, albeit in a highly restricted way.

EXIT AND VOICE IN ECONOMIC THEORY

1. Traditional Market Models

The assumption underpinning *perfectly competitive markets* is that consumers can choose not to buy goods and services from suppliers whose prices are not competitive with those of alternative suppliers. Hence, exit underpins consumer sovereignty since the individual consumer can exercise effective choice. The model of perfect competition is restricted solely to the power of exit, there being no provision within the model for use of voice if an individual is dissatisfied with a firm's output. Indeed, the assumption of homogeneous output assumes away the issue of quality, with the result that exit only occurs if price is high relative to alternative suppliers. In other words there is no quality elasticity of demand, only price elasticity.

However, *monopoly* power reduces consumer sovereignty because lack of alternative suppliers limits the consumer's power of exit. This is obviously the case when there is only a single supplier. It is also the case when *oligopoly* exists, since there are only a few suppliers and, furthermore, they may act collusively to share the market by adopting common prices and quality of output. Non-price competition via a proliferation of brands with otherwise very similar product characteristics may mislead consumers into thinking that they have considerable powers of exit when, in fact, they are unwittingly buying alternative brands from the same producer or from a small number of producers. In general, however, in oligopolistic and monopolistic markets, exit from a particular supplier occurs not only if price is higher than that charged by its competitors but also if quality of output is below that available elsewhere. There is therefore a quality elasticity of demand in these market forms.

The economist's preferred solution is to use anti-monopoly legislation to both break up and limit the accumulation of monopoly power in the private sector. In the public sector the solution is to abolish statutory monopolies through sale of assets, liberalization and encouragement of private sector provision through competitive tendering. These forms of privatization are less effective where *natural* monopolies exist at national, regional or local level. For example, public utilities such as water and sewerage services are usually a natural monopoly at the regional or local level (see Chapter 1). Regulation may therefore be required.

Scope for exit can be increased by splitting the production and distribution of such services in order to increase competition. For example, train companies could be required to compete to provide services on a separately-owned railway network or electricity producers could be required to compete to supply consumers on a separately-owned transmission grid. In addition, consumer sovereignty can be strengthened by requiring the regulatory authorities to consult statutorily-established *consumer representative bodies*. In this way consumers are given a collective voice through which to make representations about the cost, availability and quality of services.

Hirschman (1970) recognized that voice could be a valuable adjunct to the market mechanism in dealing with negative externalities such as pollution. Expression of voice may enable them to be contained or prevented altogether.

2. Transaction Costs

Hirschman (1974) later recognized that vertical integration by firms can be considered as an arrangement for institutionalizing and routinizing voice between units within a unified organization with a common goal. More generally, voice is an implicit characteristic of hierarchical control within organizations and is required where *transaction costs* are high (Williamson 1976, 1986). Exit and voice are mainly concerned with community and public policy issues, whereas transaction costs are narrowly concerned with the efficiency of contracts and corporate governance.

Transactions occur across a technologically-separable interface. The extent to which transactions occur externally through markets or internally within organizations depends upon the costs associated with the governance of contractual relations. If contracting between buyer and seller is costless, then transaction costs are zero and the market is the most efficient provider of a company's inputs, costs being minimized by competition. This is the case where inputs are not specialized so that buyers can easily find alternative suppliers and, likewise, sellers can easily find alternative buyers. Contracting becomes particularly costly when such substitutability is not possible such that buyer and seller become 'locked into' each other: that is, the transaction becomes idiosyncratic.

This mutual dependency between buyer and seller occurs when three conditions prevail *simultaneously*:

1. *bounded rationality* arising from imperfect information and imperfect decision-making;
2. *asset specificity*, occuring when resources used by the supplier in providing the output are so highly specific to the transaction that they are not easily redeployable to exchanges with other parties; and
3. *scope for opportunism* on the part of the buyer or seller, either or both parties exploiting contractual ambiguities and difficulties of contract enforcement to pursue their own advantage.

Transaction costs are zero in the perfectly competitive market model because of perfect information, homogencity of inputs and outputs, many buyers and sellers (or high market contestability) and so no scope for opportunism. In that case there is no dependency between particular buyers and sellers, the market being the most efficient governance structure. Transaction costs will arise in markets which are less than perfectly competitive, for example where the human and physical capital used to produce the commodity are so highly specialized that they are transaction-specific. The greater the transaction costs the more likely it is that firms will produce inputs internally (so as to minimize both production and transaction costs) rather than purchase them from the market. This will particularly be the case for recurrent (rather than one-off) transactions. Vertical integration is therefore a cost-minimizing response to high transaction costs.

Intermediate cases will result in *bilateral exchange* being the most efficient governance structure for recurrent transactions. In such cases the supplier depends heavily on the buyer making continuous purchases in order that the costs of the original investment can be recovered. Similarly, the buyer is heavily dependent on the seller in having sufficient supply of the output which is not readily available from elsewhere. Exit is not possible in such cases. Both buyer and seller must converse with each other (that is, express voice via contractual negotiation) in order to ensure that the precise specifications of the good or service being provided by the supplier are in accordance with the needs of the purchaser.

Hence, transaction cost economics *implicitly* incorporates exit and voice. Exit is the least costly option where transaction costs are zero. Voice is the least costly option where transaction costs are high and result in vertical integration or bilateral exchange. While exit remains the ultimate sanction where voice is ineffective, long-standing bilateral exchange may elicit loyalty. The buyer may be reluctant to exit immediately voice becomes ineffective, preferring instead to strive to reinstate the effectiveness of voice.

Hence, Hirschman overstated the schism between exit in economics and voice in politics. Economic theory relating to regulation of natural monopolies and to transaction costs recognizes the scope for voice to improve economic efficiency. Hirschman was arguably correct, however, in stating that economics is preoccupied with exit and politics preoccupied with voice, such that each discipline undervalues the preference-revelation mechanisms of the other. However, Mueller (1972) argued that many organizations can be disciplined by exit alone, and that voice not supported by the threat of exit is almost always impotent. He also claims that political scientists have been more neglectful of considering exit than economists have been in respect of voice. Where political scientists have examined exit it has been in terms of the splintering of political parties and revolutions.

CONSTRAINTS ON EXIT AND VOICE

Local government affords its service users potential for both exit and voice. Both exit and voice may be subject to diminishing returns. The returns to exit are clearly a negative function of transaction costs. The returns to voice can be expected to be subject to diminishing marginal returns, which may become negative if voice becomes so demanding of managers' time that it blocks their attention to remedial measures.

The increasing emphasis on the need to improve public accountability has gone hand in hand with a shift from government to governance (see Chapter 12). The effectiveness of measures to increase accountability and the shift from government to governance can be analysed in terms of the extent to which the opportunity for *both* exit and voice has been increased. The scope for exit rises with increased competition on the supply side. The scope for voice rises through increased public participation in local government decision making on the demand side. Both exit and voice have the potential to increase hierarchical control over service providers, ameliorate the principal –agent problem, and so improve the accountability of service providers to their users.

Hence, it would be inappropriate to interpret improved accountability solely in terms of increased scope for expression of voice, for example through more representative voting processes or increased use of consultation and other such administrative mechanisms. This, however, is the usual approach in the politics, public administration and public sector management literature.

Likewise, traditional methods of improving public accountability, such as expenditure audits and legislative reviews, are of limited effectiveness because they almost invariably exclude service users and citizens. They concentrate on inputs and processes rather than on outputs and outcomes. They enforce accountability in a top-down fashion, making use of politicians and bureaucrats as proxies for the public (see Chapter 13).

In practice, the public may have little effective capacity to demand and monitor good performance in delivering public services. In particular, there are a number of characteristics of services which limit scope for voice.

1. *Legal and institutional barriers* Totalitarian states curtail dissenting voice by prohibiting political opposition, a free press and so on. Democratic states give more scope for voice through pluralist political party systems and liberalized media but may still make inadequate legal provision for representation of user groups, public hearings, rights of redress in the event of service failure and so on.
2. *Information asymmetries* As already noted in Chapter 2, public service bureaux may restrict the public's access to information so that they can maximize their budgets, and hence their own welfares, at the expense of the public's welfare (see also Chapter 5). In so doing they engage in 'rent-seeking' activity, maximizing their own economic rents. Citizens' charters and publication of performance league tables for service providers reduce information asymmetries and strengthen voice.

3. *The degree of differentiation of public services* Where a service such as water supply is not differentiated, voice by a few (for example, objections regarding impurities in the water) benefits all. However, where a service is highly differentiated (such as where the quality of education varies between different schools), the benefits of voice by the few are necessarily restricted to fewer beneficiaries.
4. *The socioeconomic characteristics of the public* Higher income, better educated groups tend to be more articulate than poorly educated low-income groups and so can more readily express voice.
5. *The relative importance of a service* The more important a service to one's standard of living, the more likely one is to express voice (more so for municipal housing, less so for public libraries).

Rent-seeking activity, noted in point 2 above, diminishes the effectiveness of voice. Hence, accountability can best be promoted by increasing the scope for exit in order to limit the scope for rent-seeking by bureaucrats. However, public services differ in their amenability to use of exit because they exhibit different characteristics.

1. *Non-excludability* Pure public goods are characterized by non-excludability and non-rivalness in consumption. Non-excludability effectively prevents exit – unless the individual can move outside the geographical scope of the public good. National public goods such as defence and environmental protection are impossible to exit by definition, unless one emigrates. Exit from local public goods (such as local environmental protection) requires (perhaps expensive) relocation to other parts of the country. In contrast, exit from externalities (for example, noise pollution) can be achieved by more localized moves, possibly intrajurisdictional.
2. *Economies of scale* These are often so substantial for public utilities such as energy supply and water and sewerage that they lead to natural monopolies from which exit is severely limited by the high costs of alternative supply.
3. *Legal barriers to entry of alternative suppliers* Such barriers may mean that there is little or no scope for exit to alternative providers (such as school education).
4. *Spatial barriers* These occur where it is only feasible to have one school or health centre in a sparsely populated area and the costs (both monetary cost and the opportunity cost of time spent travelling) effectively curtail exit. Geographically large local governments also act as a spatial barrier.
5. *Imperfect information* Lack of perfect knowledge may lead to under-estimation of the benefits of exiting to another local government or service provider.

Hirschman (1970, p. 43) argued that an emphasis on exit can 'atrophy the development of the art of voice' because it is the most articulate quality-conscious groups who are most likely to exit. In this case substantial and rapid exit paralyses voice, a negative externality. Increased exit options may therefore have adverse impacts on democratic processes as the higher-income, vocal, middle classes selectively outmigrate to other local governments or choose to avail themselves of private sector alternatives for education, leisure and recreation, transport and so on.

The counter-argument is that the voice option may in fact be strengthened by the exit option since, without the latter, service providers may have little incentive to respond to voice. Even if exit is more costly than voice, individuals can ultimately resort to the former if the latter becomes ineffective. Removal of the exit upon may allow policy-makers to pursue their own interests rather than act in the public interest. Exit is therefore a means of dealing with the government failure (Brennan and Buchanan 1980). More generally, it allows taxpayers to avoid policies which they do not desire. Hence, exit and voice can, in some circumstances, be mutually supportive and so exit may not necessarily have the deleterious impact on voice that Hirschman supposed.

Moreover, Sharp (1984, p. 77) argues 'that exit without voice is an unlikely response to local government problems among the better-educated. Rather, exit is an option of last resort *after voice* for them.' This conclusion is based on the argument that better educated, higher-income groups are more likely than lower-income groups with lower levels of education to use *both* voice and exit. Use of exit and voice also seems to differ according to race, perhaps not only because many (but not all) ethic minorities have lower incomes and less advanced education.

Those who argue for substantial scope for exit, in order to create competitive fiscal structures, believe that governments have a tendency to grow too large and accumulate monopoly power. This is the preferred solution of *constitutional economics* whose recommendations are based on the assumed leviathan model of government. Those who argue for reduced scope for exit believe that governments act in the public interest, providing policies that are not directly demanded by taxpayers but which take account of market failure so as to achieve allocative efficiency. This is the preferred solution of *conventional economics* which assumes the despotic benevolent government model (see Chapter 1).

Marlow (1992) argues that the appropriate mix of voice and exit options depends on one's perception of the appropriate size of government. In the UK, the 'New Right' favours increased scope for exit via market mechanisms in order to stimulate competition and individual choice. The 'New Left' favours increased scope for voice via strengthened democracy, participation and collective control. The New Right champions the individual consumer whereas the New Left promotes citizenship, communities and collective consumer groups.

Rolling back the frontiers of the state through such measures as sale of assets, liberalization, competitive tendering and quasi-markets is built upon expanding the exit option. The constraints of exit noted above serve to qualify adoption of the competitive model for public services. Critics of the competitive model are as prone to assertion as its supporters. For example, Burns *et al*. (1994, p. 25) makes several unsubstantiated claims. First, that exit creates 'two-tier' systems of service where the affluent exit to higher quality services (whether in the public or private sector) leaving a declining resource base and so poorer quality services for the less well off who cannot afford to exit. Second, that contracted service provision leads to a highly centralist form of control (more so than previously) which diminishes innovation and local learning. Third, that the market mechanism fosters self-interested individualism which militates against public debate about collective needs. A priori arguments about the disadvantages (or benefits) of extending competition simply cannot be upheld without research. The same can be said about claims that voice is strengthened by extending democracy.

Not surprisingly, much of the public administration literature has a much more positive attititude towards the concept of citizen than to that of customer and so values voice more highly than exit as an empowerment strategy. ('Empowerment' is a sociological concept refering to individuals or communities being given choice, power and control over the services provided by their local governments.) Normative stances abound. Customers or consumers are regarded as selfish (by implication bad) whereas citizens are regarded as concerned with community (by implication good). Voice can be promoted through improved voting mechanisms (representative democracy) or through direct participation in local affairs (participative democracy). Quality of government is seen as just as important as quality of services and both are said to require promotion of a civic culture through a collectivist local polity.

In contrast, neoliberal economists and the public choice school (see Chapter 1) emphasize the maintenance of liberty as the key role of government. Choice is regarded as good since it underpins consumer sovereignty, the necessary condition for maximizing utility. This requires governments to stimulate competitive markets in order to facilitate individual choice through exit. The Tiebout model of competitive local governments typifies the presumption in favour of exit, voice having no place in that model (see Chapter 4). The scope for exit is also a constitutional matter, limiting the scope for exit perhaps being contrary to civil liberties.

Advocates of exit via competition may adopt too narrow an approach to local government, analysing it primarily in terms of a provider of services. Alternatively they may have an excessively inhospitable view of local government, regarding it as an institution whose worthy public interest objectives are too often frustrated by self-serving bureaucrats, politicians and narrow interest groups. However, advocates of local government as a crucial ingredient of the representative and welfare states may likewise over-generalize an idealistic view to areas where inefficiency, ineffectiveness and monopoly control are contrary to the public interest.

Though certain groups (low income, ethnic minorities, women and so on) are underrepresented at national and local government levels and may be more dependent upon the local welfare state, it is not self-evident that attempts to empower them by strengthening voice will always be successful. Nor is it clear that strengthening voice is necessarily exclusive of increasing the scope for exit. Both exit and voice may be positively related to the degree of decentralization (see Chapter 4). Decentralization has implications not only for efficiency, but also for equity (since it limits the feasibility of redistributive programmes) and constitutional rights (since it constrains the control governments have over people's lives).

Hirschman (1974) later acknowledged that, for some individuals, for some purposes, at some time, voicing is valued for its own sake. Those who advocate adoption of a particular public policy may derive a benefit (rather than incur a cost) from the time and effort spent in its advocacy, particularly where there is a strong public interest component such as public health or public safety. In such cases, the supposed cost handicap of voice relative to exit will be reduced or even eliminated. That handicap will also be reduced by a liberal sociopolitical environment characterized by a free press, widespread dissemination of information, established legal rights and so on.

Hirschman also acknowledged that he took the costlessness of exit too much for granted, costs only featuring if loyalty to the organization was present. This assumption greatly understated the costs of exit, particularly from a local government, in terms of disruption to employment, family, housing and so on. Nonetheless, it is allocatively inefficient to block exit at the local level since it would be contrary to the Tiebout model of competitive local governments (see Chapter 4). Such inefficiency is less likely at the national level, where blocking exit may be the only way in which public goods can be financed (that is, blocking exit prevents free riders benefiting from them whilst avoiding payment). Blocking exit may also be the only way of preventing unwise choices by (national) taxpayers; for example, making inadequate provision of merit goods such as health care or pensions. Similarly, it may be necessary to block exit at the national level if redistributive programmes such as social security are to be implemented. Such redistributive programmes would be inefficient at the local level, however, precisely because the scope for exit would thwart those programmes (see Chapter 1).

ILLUSTRATIONS OF EXIT AND VOICE FOR PUBLIC SERVICES

Figure 3.2 provides examples of public sector services graded by scope for exit and voice. Cell 1 includes services characterised by low scope for exit and weak voice, cell 2 those of strong voice and low scope for exit, cell 3 weak

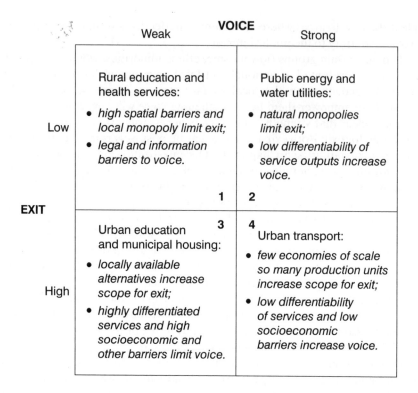

Figure 3.2   *Service examples of exit and voice combinations*

voice and high scope for exit, cell 4 high scope for exit and strong voice. Note that the allocation of the specified services to cells depends on the net result of the various characteristics (listed above) which influence scope for exit and voice. Hence, the appropriate cell into which a service is allocated may vary between different countries and between different regions within any one country. Bearing this caveat in mind, the reader should think of other local government services such as leisure and recreation and collection of domestic waste and attempt to fit them into the appropriate cell.

Any one service could appear in more than one cell. For example, school education may display high voice for the 'higher' socioeconomic groups (with higher incomes and more advanced education) but low voice for 'lower' socioeconomic groups, simply because the former tend to be more articulate and proactive than the latter. Moreover, the force of exit–voice characteristics may change over time, resulting in services shifting cell in Figure 3.2. For example, legal barriers to entry may be relaxed, causing a service to shift from a low exit cell (1 or 2) to a high exit cell (3 or 4). Similarly, a reduction of information barriers would cause a service to shift from cell 1 or 3 to cell 2 or 4. Clearly, therefore, there are many policy options for improving exit and voice.

THE SERVICE USER'S CHOICE BETWEEN EXIT AND VOICE

The main question is how to determine the optimal combination of exit and voice so as to improve accountability in public services (Paul 1992). The service user will choose to exit or use voice only if the expected returns (for example, from better quality of service) are greater than the associated costs. Assuming equality of benefits arising from use of exit or voice, the choice of which preference revelation mechanism to use depends on the cost of exit relative to voice and vice versa. The relative cost will vary according to the degree of market failure. This is demonstrated in Figure 3.3, the cost of and returns to exit and voice being measured on the vertical axis and the degree of market failure on the horizontal axis.

It would be invalid to combine all forms of market failure on the horizontal axis, since the costs of voice and exit can be expected to vary according to the type of market failure. For example, as already noted, the cost of exiting from a negative externality associated with a locally-provided service will be less than that associated with a national public good. For the purposes of exposition, the following analysis assumes that Figure 3.3 depicts market failure arising from any natural monopoly characteristics exhibited by different services.

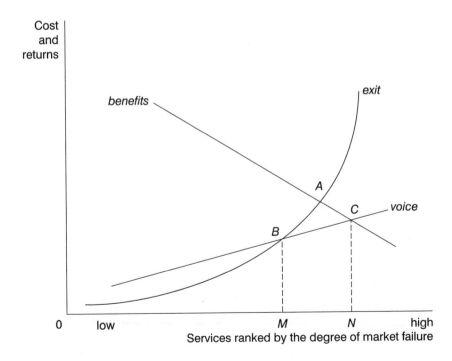

Figure 3.3 *The tradeoff between exit and voice*

Costs faced by individuals include not only the personal costs (such as the opportunity cost of time) of, say, making representations to local politicians and service managers but also the local tax costs of any institutional measures implemented to facilitate expression of voice. Clearly, the distributions of personal costs and of local tax costs are not full coincident if only because not all service users pay the same amount of local taxes.

Ignore the schedule marked 'benefits' in Figure 3.3 for the time being. The schedule marked 'exit' represents the cost of exit, and that marked 'voice' represents the cost of voice, incurred by the individual service user for each of the services ranked on the horizontal axis. The costs of exit are positively related to the degree of market failure, explaining the upward slope of the exit schedule. For example, a natural monopoly in electricity supply will impose considerable costs on a consumer seeking alternative supply. The schedule is non-linear because it is assumed that the costs of exit rise at an increasing rate as the degree of market failure increases.

It seems reasonable to assume that voice costs are unlikely to be as heavily influenced by market failure as exit costs. For the sake of analysis, the voice schedule assumes that the cost of voice rises at a constant rate as the degree of market failure increases.

Highly competitive markets are characterized by low degrees of market failure as a result of both limited monopoly power and high ease of exit to alternative suppliers. Hence, exit is nearly costless towards the origin, making voice relatively expensive. However, exit costs can be expected to rise more rapidly than voice costs as the degree of market failure increases. Hence, the exit schedule ultimately rises above the voice schedule as market failure increases.

Service users will resort to exit or voice as long as the resultant benefits exceed the costs. They will exit from public services whose degree of market failure falls within the range $0M$ (such as public transport), but use voice for public services whose degree of market failure exceeds $0M$ (such as municipal water supply). The switch from exit to voice reflects the lower marginal costs of the latter above $0M$.

Account now has to be taken of the monetary-equivalence of benefits arising from use of voice or exit, depicted by the schedule marked 'benefits'. Its downward slope assumes that the expected returns to exit or voice diminish as the degree of market failure increases. For example, the less the competition faced by a company the less responsive it can be expected to be to customer complaints. Similarly, in respect of exit, the fewer the number of producers the more likely they may be to act collusively and so reduce the benefits to be gained from exit from any one producer.

Given the position of the benefits schedule, exit will still be the preferred strategy between the origin and M. However, voice will only be used for services falling between M and N, since the costs of voice exceed the benefits for services with degrees of market failure in excess of N. Nonetheless, Figure 3.3 demonstrates that, under the cost and benefit conditions depicted therein, the switch from exit to voice in the range MN improves efficiency by the amount of additional net benefit measured by the area ABC. Hence, while exit is more efficient than voice in competitive market conditions, voice may be more efficient than exit for services with natural monopoly characteristics. However, voice can be analysed within a public choice framework (see Chapter 5). Neither exit nor voice is worthwhile for services with degrees of market failure in excess of $0N$.

Analytical Complications

1. *Though the return to exit is definite and immediate (assuming perfect information), the return to voice is less certain and perhaps longer term.* Hence, the future benefits of voice may have to be discounted both to present values (by the individual's rate of time preference) and to the probability of the benefits occuring (the risk factor). The former will depend not just on the discount rate but also on how important the service is in terms of the individual's standard of living. The latter will depend upon the influence and bargaining power of the consumer, perhaps aided by administrative mechanisms such as service charters and rights of redress.
2. *The likelihood of choosing voice rather than exit can be assumed to increase in line with the individual's assessment of his or her ability to influence the organization and with the degree of loyalty to the organization.* These two factors may be linked, suggesting that loyalty is not necessarily irrational. Loyalty presupposes the ability to exit and therefore does not apply in cases of unbreakable monopoly. Reneging on loyalty is one of the costs of exit.

EXIT AND VOICE STRATEGIES

Hirschman (1970) stresses the importance of institutional design in balancing the scope for exit and voice and notes that this balance is a crucial underpinning of the degree of internal democracy in organizations. By this he means that exit should not be so easy that it completely removes incentives for voice. Many public administration and political science academics would agree with this proposal, emphasizing the importance of voice for the deliberative role of local government. They argue that perfectly competitive market conditions simply cannot be achieved in providing the majority of public services. Furthermore, such costless exit would destroy the deliberative, policy-making role of local government.

However, Hirschman notes the tendency of institutions *and* those they serve increasingly to underestimate the less familiar mode of preference revelation (in this case exit) and to rely increasingly on that which is most familiar (in this case voice). Hence, it cannot be assumed that local governments necessarily achieve an optimal balance between exit and voice. Neoliberal economists argue that there are too many restrictions on exit in the public sector. It could also be argued that the scope for voice is more apparent than real, given the acknowledged limitations of voting mechanisms in terms of preference revelation (see Chapter 10) and the underdevelopment of other mechanisms for expressing voice. Institutions may seek to repress both exit and voice because they may be contrary to the self-interest of managers and bureau-crats.

Therefore, even if an optimal (in terms of the public interest) mix of exit and voice could be specified for a particular organization at any one point in time, that mix is not forever fixed, since forces will be instigated which, by design or default, change the scope for exit and/or voice. For example, self-serving managers could so emasculate voice mechanisms that expression of voice is simply 'blowing off steam'. Consultative mechanisms which lead to little or no remedial action are a case in point.

The conditions for an optimal and stable mix of exit and voice are there-fore unlikely to exist over the long term. Institutions may oscillate between voice and exit as the deficiencies of the current over-reliance on one or the other become apparent. This observation about the instability of exit–voice combinations should be borne in mind while considering measures to increase the scope for exit and voice. Those measures may be piecemeal or part of a radical reorganization of local government.

PIECEMEAL MEASURES

Where exit or voice are unnecessarily limited by legal, institutional and policy-induced barriers, the efficiency prescription is to remove them. Returning to Figure 3.2, the emphasis in cell 1 must be to improve voice, simply because it is not possible to increase scope for exit in the presence of high spatial barriers. In cell 2 the emphasis must also be on increasing voice, even though already strong, because natural monopolies severely constrain exit. In cell 3 both exit and voice can be increased by increasing the number of alternative suppliers and removing barriers to voice. Different policy prescriptions are required to enhance exit and voice.

1. Making Exit Easier

In theory, exit can be made easier by measures which serve to liberalize the supply-side of public service provision, enabling service users to choose between alternative suppliers.

1. *Migration* can be stimulated by having more small local governments rather than a few large ones (see Chapter 4 on Tiebout).
2. *Charging* for local government services use of which is discretionary means that people who do not wish to use a service no longer have to pay for it through compulsory local taxes, even if they remain within the local government's jurisdiction.
3. *Service vouchers* (for example, for school education – see Chapter 2) can enable service users (in this case the parents of school pupils) to 'shop around' for the service provider (school) most appropriate to their needs and preferences. In the education example, rather than the child being allocated to a particular school by a centralized planning system, the parents choose the school for their child.
4. *Competitive tendering* for public service contracts can facilitate choice between alternative providers (for example, of leisure facilities) as long as whole services are not let as single management contracts.
5. *Deregulation* of, say, public transport dissolves statutory monopolies.
6. *Privatization* can also increase the scope for exit as long as public sector monopolies are not simply reconstituted as private sector monopolies.

The first three initiatives *shift* the exit schedule downwards in Figure 3.3, since they reduce the cost of exit from any one municipality, service or school. The last three initiatives cause a leftwards *movement along* the exit schedule, provided they create a plurality of providers among which consumers can choose, so reducing the degree of market failure. However, competitive tendering is unlikely to increase consumer choice regarding which contractor collects domestic refuse (garbage) simply because it is not economical to have more than one refuse collector in a given neighbourhood.

Some of these exit strategies (such as deregulation) may involve no cost to local governments or their citizens, while others (for example school vouchers) may have high administrative costs. Others may have high administrative costs more than offset by efficiency gains through improved factor productivity (such as competitive tendering – see Chapter 13).

The efficiency of the alternative exit strategies can be expected to vary. For example, the cost reductions arising from competitive tendering depend upon the contestability of markets (see Chapter 13) and that contestability may vary for different services (for example, lower for domestic waste collection than for catering) and for different local governments (for example, higher for urban than for rural municipalities).

2. Making Voice Easier

Voice can be made easier by measures which serve to amplify the demand side.

1. The public and service users can be given *more opportunity to participate in decision-making*. Examples include increased use of referenda on specific issues and the election or appointment of parents to school boards.
2. *Increased consultation* with citizens and service users can be implemented. Examples include public opinion surveys (both before adoption of measures and for evaluation thereafter), public hearings and citizens' juries.
3. *Complaints procedures* can be implemented, for example by appointment of ombudsmen and/or by introduction of citizens' charters (which incorporate legally-specified minimum standards of service provision).
4. *Legal challenge* through the courts could be facilitated; for example if a local government's actions led to adverse outcomes for public health.

Voice strategies are likely to be costly to implement because of the high personal time costs and high local tax costs of administrative measures. This is assumed in Figure 3.3, the voice cost schedule lying above the exit schedule for services with low levels of market failure.

It explains the economist's preference for measures to increase competition rather than administrative measures, the former not only increasing choice but also having the potential to achieve savings in service costs. However, Figure 3.3 also makes clear that voice will be the most efficient option where market failure is substantial. Moreover, Hirschman (1974) argues that some element of voice is an important input into the development of local welfare state services in advance of real knowledge of how to satisfy new and evolving demands for a service. Put simply, voice can be as much about educating the producer as it is about protecting the consumer. Exit strategies assume that services are already established in policy terms whereas voice may be necessary before that policy can be determined. Voice can enable the public to demand something be done about a problem poorly understood by service managers (for example, in the area of social work), a reversal of the usual information asymmetry.

Perversely, the providers of public services may value exit in terms of their own personal utilities (rather than those of the users whom they are supposed to serve) because it promotes 'a quiet life' for them. This response is the result of non-existent or inadequate hierarchical management control systems. Hence, exit and voice strategies *on their own* may do little to improve the accountability of service providers to service users. 'Public service providers may remain as inefficient and ineffective as before if they do not get the right signals through an adapted hierarchical control' (Paul 1992, p. 1055). Private companies lose sales revenue whereas public sector bureaux do not necessarily lose subsidy. For example, research on exit within an urban school system found that loss of consumers (pupils) was not great enough to threaten the public organization's (school's) existence and so did not provide the required motivation (Matland 1995). Indeed, the UK school system has long been characterized by schools with surplus capacity (see Chapter 6).

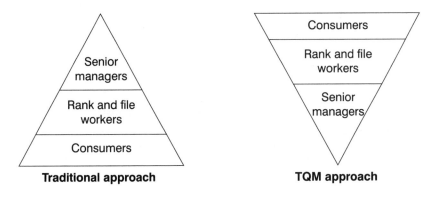

Figure 3.4   *Traditional and customer-orientated management philosophies*

Measures must also be adopted to make local government service managers more responsive to the wishes of service users. This goes beyond measures which simply increase scope for exit or voice. There are two main initiatives. First, performance review which relies on effective monitoring and reporting of results followed, as necessary, by any subsequent remedial action (see Chapter 5). However, service providers may act collusively to frustrate hierarchical control or dilute its effects. Second, adoption of a new institutional philosophy which emphasizes a change in political and management cultures away from service quality as a collectivist, 'take it or leave it' paternalistic and inward-looking, institution-based concept. Instead, the culture should be based on outward-looking responsive relationships with individual customers, meeting their individual needs.

Total quality management (TQM) is one such institutional or management philosophy. Drawn from the private sector, if successfully applied, it makes maintaining and improving service quality the responsibility of every member of an organization (Morgan and Murgatroyd 1994; Younis *et al.* 1996). In its pure form, it inverts the traditional 'top down' style of management as depicted in Figure 3.4.

The traditional approach shown on the left-hand side has hierarchical control focused on senior managers, to whom rank and file workers are primarily responsive. The TQM approach shown on the right-hand side makes rank and file workers primarily responsive to consumers, 'serving the customer' becoming the underlying philosophy of the organization. Hence, adoption of exit and voice strategies together with customer-responsive management philosophies can increase the welfare gains for users. However, economists prefer to trust in economic incentives, rather than management philosophies or altruism. Ultimately, service providers will only be made more responsive to service users if their revenues are directly dependent upon the volume of use of their outputs because exit then leads to the loss of revenues depicted in

Figure 3.1. Charges are one such means of linking remuneration to service takeup (see Chapter 7).

CONCLUSIONS

Although exit and voice are unfamiliar terms within mainstream economics, as concepts they underpin much of neoclassical economic theory. Exit is the fundamental underpinning of profit maximization within the theory of the firm because of its effect on revenue. Voice is implicit in transaction costs analysis for recurrent and highly idiosyncratic exchange. It is therefore mistaken to believe that only exit falls within the realm of economics, voice falling within the realm of political science.

Allocative efficiency can be improved by increasing the scope for exit (that is, by making supply of local government services more competitive) and by increasing the scope for voice (for services with significant degrees of market failure). However, Chapter 4 will conclude that the scope for exit is necessarily severely constrained by relocation costs and Chapter 5 will question the extent to which increased scope for voice will actually increase allocative efficiency because some groups of local citizens may use voice to pursue their own particular interests, rather than those of the local community.

In many cases, though service users will choose that method which is least costly to them, voice and exit are more complementary than mutually exclusive. In particular, the ultimate sanction of exit can increase the effectiveness of voice – provided always that the providers of public sector services lose revenue as a consequence of exit and that appropriate structures of hierarchical control are in place.

This exposition of the exit–voice typology provides a conceptual framework which will be referred to in later chapters. Although developed separately from fiscal federalism theory, and from the other areas covered by local government economics, in effect it underpins them. Voice is implicit in Oates' decentralization theorem and exit in Tiebout's 'voting with the feet' hypothesis (see Chapter 4). The differing financing arrangements for local government, reform of its internal structure, privatization of its activities, and other such reforms, can all be analysed by making use of the exit–voice typology to a greater or lesser extent.

4 Revealing Preferences via Exit and Voice

INTRODUCTION

Chapter 1 noted the problems created if local governments implemented programmes designed to achieve substantial income redistribution from high-income to low-income groups. It concluded that outward migration of high-income groups and inward migration of low-income groups would not only make such programmes ineffective but also create allocative inefficiency. This conclusion was based on the propensity for individuals and households to migrate to local governments providing their preferred mix of taxes and services. Chapter 2 provided the efficiency rationale for decentralized units of government and Chapter 3 demonstrated how allocative efficiency is underpinned by the ability of consumers to exit from suppliers whose outputs are of poor quality. These separate strands of analysis can now be combined to show that unconstrained migration between decentralized units of government has the potential to provide a solution to the long-recognized problems relating to revealed preferences for public goods.

The analysis of public goods leads to the rather pessimistic conclusion that the market will not achieve an allocatively optimal level of output. The non-rivalness and non-excludability of pure public goods leads to free-riding, whereby consumers of the public good understate their true preferences for it in order to avoid payment. Hence, it is not possible to determine the allocatively optimal level of output where, at the margin, willingness to pay equals the cost of supply. However, though true of public goods at the level of the national economy (such as defence), this theoretical dilemma may be solvable for local public goods provided by local governments. The resolution is achieved by unconstrained migration between different local governments.

This chapter examines the potential for interjurisdictional migration to reveal preferences for local public goods, paying particular attention to the constraints upon migration which may frustrate preference revelation. It then considers alternative solutions through intrajurisdictional decentralization (that is, within local governments). It will be demonstrated that whereas interjurisdictional migration relies solely on exit, intrajurisdictional migration can make use of both exit and voice and so facilitate fuller revelation of preferences.

REVEALING PREFERENCES THROUGH MIGRATION: THE TIEBOUT EFFECT

Individual citizens or households can be thought of as consumer-voters seeking to maximize their own welfares by matching supply with their prefered package of local government services, and the associated local tax costs. Given the set of expenditures and tax costs available, consumer voters will therefore migrate to that local government providing the optimal service/tax package. Hence, migration achieves an optimum allocation of resources. This is even the case for local public goods where revelation of preferences is blocked by free riders refusing to indicate willingness to pay for services from which they cannot be excluded and which are non-rival in consumption.

This model of consumer-voter choices is referred to as the Tiebout hypothesis (Tiebout 1956). Put simply it states that 'voting with one's feet' reveals citizens' preferences for local public goods and so provides a market-type solution to the problem of preference revelation. The greater the number of local governments and the greater the variations between their service/tax packages, the better the match between supply and preferences of the citizen-consumer and the greater the resulting welfare.

Citizens can exit local governments providing unsatisfactory service/tax mixes, moving to those providing their welfare-maximizing package. The Tiebout hypothesis therefore relies solely on the scope for exit, making no provision for expression of voice (see Chapter 3). Its assumptions are as follows.

1. *Consumer-voters have a set preference pattern* for local government outputs and tax liabilities.
2. *Consumer-voters are fully mobile*, moving to that local government which provides a service/tax package which most closely approximates their preference pattern. Otherwise, consumer-voters are indifferent about where they live.
3. *There is a large number of local governments* in which consumer-voters can choose to live.
4. *Consumer-voters have perfect information* about the service/tax packages on offer.
5. *Consumer-voters live off dividend income* (from shares) so that employment considerations impose no constraints on their mobility.
6. *Local government services exhibit no spillover effects*, there being no benefits or costs which spill over into other local governments' jurisdictions and which would affect locational decisions elsewhere.
7. *There is an optimum population size* which minimizes the average cost of services, provided according to the preferences of their current inhabitants (see Chapter 2). Optimum size may occur because land is in fixed supply, given current zoning laws relating to land use, type of dwelling and so on.

8. *Local governments try to attain the optimum size.* Those below it try to attract new residents in order to reduce average costs. For example, they may offer mobile firms investment and/or employment subsidies to attract inward investment and associated employment, relaxing zoning laws to allow any necessary housing developments. Those above the optimum size seek to deter new residents, for example by prohibiting further residential development in order to avoid congestion effects. Those at optimum size try to keep their populations constant.

This is therefore a 'pure theory' of local expenditures because, except for the service/tax packages provided by local governments, its assumptions make it devoid of all other real world factors which influence the decision to migrate. In particular, assumptions 2, 4 and 5 result in migration being costless. It is therefore a highly abstract model which necessarily results in preference revelation as consumer-voters decide in which local government to live.

Tiebout did, of course, recognize the highly abstract nature of his model. In particular, he recognized the restrictive nature of the assumptions, noting that preference patterns may vary (perhaps systematically as the household moves through its lifecycle), that knowledge is not perfect, mobility is costly, spillover effects may occur, and so on. Nonetheless, casual observation makes clear that households' decisions about where to live are based on preferences for particular local government areas (for example, the suburb versus the inner city). Just as people express preferences in terms of the shops to which they go to make private sector purchases, so they also express preferences for local public sector outputs. 'Spatial mobility provides the local public-goods counterpart to the private market's shopping trip' (Tiebout 1956, p. 422).

This model of residential location necessarily achieves equilibrium because of assumptions 1 (stable preference patterns), 6 (service technologies), 7 (stable service packages), and 8 (the behaviour of local governments). Note, however, that the model does not determine the number of local governments offering tax/expenditure packages. For welfare to reach its maximum potential, there would have to be as many local governments as there are different preference patterns. If all consumer-voters have different preference patterns there would have to be as many local governments as there are consumer-citizens. In other words each consumer-citizen would have to form his or her local government. This is, of course, an unrealistic scenario if only because of lost economies of scale (see Chapter 2).

Being indeterminate in the model, the number of local governments will be determined by historical, constitutional, sociological, political and other exogenous factors. The Tiebout model can therefore only demonstrate that the greater the number of local governments the greater the welfare of consumer-citizens, because they are afforded more choice between alternative tax/expenditure packages (see assumption 3). This is analogous to Oates' decentralization theorem (see Chapter 2). However, the Tiebout model goes further than Oates in theoretical terms, demonstrating how scope for exit (migration) facilitates maximization of consumer-voters' welfares within the resources available. An optimal outcome is possible.

The policy implications of Tiebout's model also go further than Oates' decentralist prescriptions in policy terms. First, merger of adjacent local government areas (for example central city and suburb) is justified in Paretian welfare terms only if more of any service can be produced at the same total cost without reducing the output of any other service. Second, allocative efficiency will be increased by policies which promote residential mobility and more fully inform consumer-voters about local service levels. Third, income redistribution from rich to poor at the local government level will not be a sustainable policy because migration will ultimately lead to its collapse (see Chapter 1).

The Tiebout hypothesis results in many testable implications, including the following.

1. *The greater the number of competing local governments, the greater the welfares of consumer-voters* because they can match services more fully with their preferences.
2. *The greater the number of local governments within the same metropolitan area, the greater the competition between them* because they try to attain optimum size, those below it attracting residents so as to minimize the costs of service provision.
3. *The greater the number of competing local governments, the more homogeneous each will be* because households will tend to sort themselves into segregated socioeconomic, racial, ethnic and other groups according to their preferences for services and their tax costs. Besides providing preferred services, local governments will adopt regulations to permit or restrict activities in their areas in accordance with local preferences (such as gambling, retailing of alcohol).
4. *Local government taxes as well as services influence residential mobility.*
5. *Migration patterns can be explained by differences in local government tax/ service packages.*
6. *The levels of services and taxes will be reflected in property values.* Higher service levels and/or lower taxes cause values to rise as inmigration drives up property prices. Poorer services and/or higher taxes cause property values to fall because they stimulate outmigration. These effects are known as capitalization – of taxes and of public expenditures (see Chapter 8).

There has been substantial empirical testing of these (and other) implications of the Tiebout model. Despite the many problems faced when testing the Tiebout model and the methodological criticisms of many of the studies, after surveying the evidence published in over 200 articles and books Dowding *et al.* (1994) conclude that, on the whole, there is evidence that tax and service levels affect locational decisions and so have some influence on property values (implications 4, 5 and 6 above). This is supported by the results of a sub-sequent survey, by the same authors, of household relocation in four local governments within London (John *et al*. 1995). It found that residential choices were 'Tiebout rational', households prioritizing low tax levels moving to low tax jurisdictions, those prioritizing better services moving to jurisdictions with a reputation for better services.

However, the generality of research finds that tax/service packages seem more influential in attracting people who, for whatever reason, are in the process of relocating. They seem less important in stimulating people to move and so are more influential on the 'pull' rather than 'push' side of deci-sions to move residence. In other words, assuming *ceteris paribus*, household migration only occurs at the margin in response to clearly visible and significant interjurisdictional variations in local tax levels and service provision (both level and quality).

Other reasons for moving are taken account of in broader economic models of housing and residential location choices. The most well-developed model is the *access–space tradeoff model* of residential location, which relaxes the Tiebout assumption that consumer-voters live off dividend income by taking account of accessibility to place of work and of other factors which influence the price of land and therefore of housing (Evans 1985; MacLennan 1982). The model assumes workers commute to a large city with a single central business district, all other factors being assumed away. Hence, the optimum cost-minimizing location can be determined for households of varying demo-graphic and occupational characteristics.

Figure 4.1 assumes that travel costs rise at a diminishing rate with increas-ing distance from the centre, reflecting the fact that transport fares and vehicle costs per kilometre fall with increasing length of journey. However, transport costs also include the opportunity cost of time spent travelling (conventionally costed as a proportion of the commuter's wage rate). It is also assumed that housing costs fall at a diminishing rate with increasing dis-tance from the centre because of high demand for central locations. This assumption is reflected in the diminishing gap between the schedules for travel costs and for total costs, that gap narrowing as distance from the centre increases. In deciding its optimal location, the household therefore trades-off travel costs against housing costs, minimizing the combined cost at location *L* in Figure 4.1. The model explains the tendency for households with children but only one working partner to live in the suburbs (to gain more space) and for childless working couples to live nearer the centre (both partners com-muting and needing less space).

Although relaxing the non-working household assumption of the Tiebout model, the tradeoff model is itself based upon highly restrictive assumptions and oversimplifies the multidimensional nature of the housing commodity. In particular, it ignores local government taxes and services, the investment value of owned housing, institutional constraints on the availability of mortgage

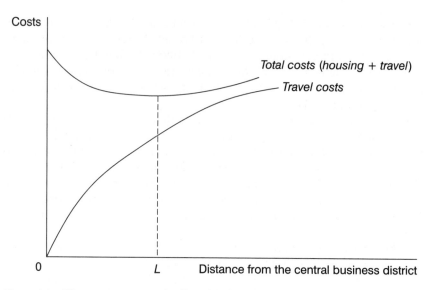

Figure 4.1   *The access–space tradeoff model of residential location*

finance, the segmented nature of housing markets, housing search costs, geographically restricted transport systems, and externalities arising from the agglomeration into discrete neighbourhoods of socioeconomic, ethnic and religious groups. Of course, the Tiebout model also ignores all but the first two of these variables. It is therefore not surprising that empirical tests of the Tiebout model find that local government tax/service packages are more influential on the 'pull' rather than 'push' side of decisions to move residence.

There is mixed but marginal support for the proposition that greater municipal competition increases welfare (implication 1 above). It is difficult to test the proposition that the greater the number of local governments, the greater the competition between them (implication 2). It is almost tautological that the more local governments there are, the more homogeneous they will be (implication 3). More generally, while empirical research results at the *aggregate* level provides many results attributable to the Tiebout's local market for public goods, at the *micro-level* there is little evidence that citizens-consumers possess high information levels about local services and the available alternatives (Teske and Schneider 1994).

The lack of overwhelming corroboration of the Tiebout model should not be surprising both because of its restrictive assumptions and because conclusions are usually tentative and disputable in the social sciences. In particular, the Popperian theory of knowledge holds that theories and hypotheses can never be verified, only refuted. If a theory predicts that event x will happen in response to a given change but x does not happen, then the theory is refuted. If, however, x does happen it does not prove the theory, since x may not happen on every such occasion in the future. The empirical research testing Tiebout's theory also demonstrates how very difficult it is to test the main hypothesis (that people vote with their feet). A series of secondary hypotheses have to be tested instead (that is, the six testable implications listed above). Falsification of any one of these six implications does not necessarily falsify the Tiebout hypothesis, nor does confirmation necessarily prove voting with one's feet. Tautological statements such as implication 3 simply cannot be used to test a theory.

The results of empirical research into the Tiebout effect are clearly complicated by factors other than local tax/service packages which influence location. Consumer-voters will tend to have better knowledge of local taxes than of local services in different local governments simply because information about the former is more easily obtained. The quality of services such as education are particularly difficult to assess. Moreover, empirical findings may vary over time and between different countries. For example, racial problems may encourage spatial segregation such that white and black groups respond differently to variations in local government tax/service packages. More generally, selective outmigration of different socioeconomic groups and resultant fiscal stress may lead to increasing disequilibrium in the 'market' for local government tax and expenditure packages (see Chapter 6).

Despite all the limitations and qualifications of the Tiebout model and its testing, it still improves understanding of urban political economy by specifying the micro-foundations of social and political divisions within metropolitan areas, by explaining variations in property values and in stimulating so much empirical research. Nonetheless, the Tiebout model also demonstrates that an allocatively optimum supply of local public goods is unlikely to be stimulated by an optimal level of migration because its assumptions have to be too restrictive for it to work. In stating what has to be the case for mobility to yield optimal results, the Tiebout model is actually making clear that migration cannot be relied upon to solve the theoretical dilemma of revealed preferences. Put simply, migration (exit) cannot be relied upon as the sole means of solving the revealed preference problem. Other measures are also necessary.

REVEALING PREFERENCES THROUGH DECENTRALIZATION

If migration cannot be relied upon fully to reveal preferences for local public goods then neither can it be relied upon to reveal preferences for the other service outputs provided by local governments and financed by collective means. It was noted in Chapter 1 that very few services provided by local governments are pure public goods; most are private goods, often with positive externalities. Moreover, because of the multifunctionality of local governments, their area of jurisdiction may not coincide with the geographic coverage of any local public good they do provide. Their areas may, instead, be determined by the minimum scale consistent with securing economies of scale for any public utility services they provide (see Chapter 2).

Hence, the problem of revealed preference is not just a theoretical issue relating to local public goods. It is also a practical problem arising from the non-market provision of the generality of local government services, many of which are private and mixed goods. Revelation of preferences for these outputs may be promoted by decentralization *within* local government (as distinct from the decentralization from central to local government considered in Chapter 2).

As already noted, the Tiebout model relies solely on the scope for exit, making no provision for expression of voice. Hirschman recognized that he had underestimated the costs of exit (see Chapter 3) whereas Tiebout explicitly assumed away those costs. However, given that the costs of migration can be high, citizen-consumers may in fact be more prone to resort to voice when they become disatisfied with the tax/service package offered by their local government. Loyalty to the municipality may also be a restraining influence on exit.

Tiebout emphasized the scope for policies to make exit less costly. Policies could also be adopted to strengthen voice. In the politics and public administration literature decentralization *within* local government is seen as a way in which voice can be strengthened by shortening the channels of communication between local governments and their citizens. However, it can also facilitate exit by removing spatial barriers to exit. It may therefore be possible to use decentralization within local government to reveal preferences for the generality of local government services. This can be illustrated by analysing decentralization within British local government.

Though their voice may be limited, there already are statutory forms of decentralization below what is generally regarded as the principal level of local government in Britain, for example elected community councils (Scotland and Wales) and parish councils in England (Chandler 1996). Moreover, local governments providing school education have long been legally obliged to co-opt representatives of teachers and churches onto education committees. Local governments are also statutorily required to consult the public in respect of local and structure plans, and community councils in respect of planning applications. They must also inform tenants about relevant aspects of housing management.

Many British local governments have themselves developed localized and integrated forms of service delivery with increased use of consultation and participation (Gaster and Hoggett 1993; Gaster and O'Toole 1995; Gaster and Taylor 1993). Hence, decentralization measures often reflect both central and local initiatives.

Large, centralized bureaucracies were created within British local government during the 1970s because central managerial accountability took precedence over decentralisation of services and decision-making. It is now generally accepted that British local governments became monolithic institutions, overly bureaucratic and paternalistic in their treatment of individuals and of the local communities in which they live. The old-style bureaucratic paternalism is alleged to have overridden the needs of individual citizens and their neighbourhoods in providing standardized services based on the premise that local politicians, bureaucrats and professionals know better than service users and local communities what is best for them, often leading to a 'take it or leave it' approach to service delivery. This is the despotic benevolent model of government (see Chapter 1). Hence, the democratic rationale for local government was increasingly brought into question in the UK (Hambleton 1988, 1992; Hambleton *et al.* 1994).

The main forms of decentralization within the UK are depicted in Figure 4.2. Although UK-centric and relating to the 1980s and 1990s, the general concepts and principles are applicable in many other countries. Reference to consumers and/or citizens recognizes that, except for purely private market transactions, service users are not the only people whose requirements are of relevance. Though a simplification of the true scenario, the situation before decentralization measures are introduced can be typified as one of bureaucratic paternalism, local government being the universal provider of services and having a producer culture in providing services to the public. Services are directly delivered by professionally-skilled staff in hierarchical structures overseen by functionally-based committees.

As an alternative to the direct service provision strategy, decentralization of local government services can take two main forms, either *outside* or *within* local government.

1. Decentralization Outside Local Government

During the 1980s and early 1990s, centrally-inspired decentralization measures *outside* local government included transfer of powers and responsibilities to quangos (quasi-autonomous non-governmental organizations) and to voluntary sector organizations, or privatization (see Figure 4.2).

(a) Quangos
The term 'quango' is used by political scientists to indicate the arms-length relationship between this type of public sector organization and central government. Quangos are appointed public agencies holding executive powers and discharging a small number of functions previously under the control of democratically-elected politicians. They are an example of *functional or administrative* decentralization. The UK's National Health Service, the former New Town Development Corporations and the Scottish and Welsh economic development agencies are long-standing examples. Public health services in other countries are usually part of the system of local government. More recently, there has been considerable growth in these government-appointed

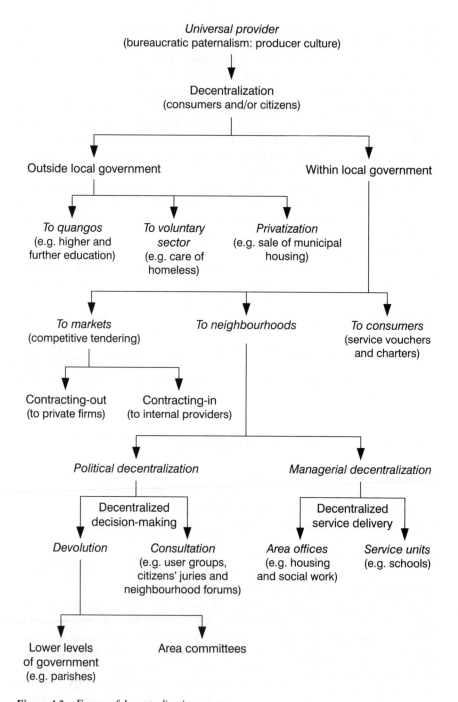

Figure 4.2   *Forms of decentralization*

agencies, including Urban Development Corporations (of the 1980s and early 1990s), Training and Enterprise Councils, Housing Action Trusts, and so on. Being single-purpose bodies, quangos are supposedly more flexible, less politicized, more efficient and more effective than multi-purpose local governments in providing their particular service.

However, they have been criticized as an unelected, anti-democratic means of delivering public sector services (AMA 1994; Grayson and Davis 1995; Lamb 1995; LGIU 1994; Mulgan 1994; and Nolan 1995). In sharp contrast with local government, the meetings of quangos are usually not open to the public and so the basis on which decisions are made is unknown. Critics argue that quangos reduce the influence that individuals have on decisions that affect their lives, a non-elected elite assuming responsibility for large parts of local public sector (Mulgan 1994). The scope for expression of voice is therefore reduced.

The counter-argument is that democratic accountability does not, in itself, ensure that services respond to users' needs. Single party political dominance may combine with low voter turnout at local elections to create limited accountability for local governments in providing services. Moreover, quangos may increase the scope for exit to the extent that competition is increased among a greater number of service providers. There are a number of examples relating to the 1980s and early 1990s in the UK, which are more fully analysed in Chapter 12.

1. Increased competition in the higher and further education sectors, brought about by conversion of that part of higher and further education previously provided by local governments into centrally-funded self-managing quangos. Subsequent alliances and mergers among these institutions (to achieve economies of scale) have not fully offset that increased competition.
2. Allowing schools to opt-out of local government control and allowing parental choice about which school to send their children. In fact, relatively few schools did opt out and they no longer can do so.
3. Diversification of the social rented sector through expansion of housing associations, allowing municipal tenants to opt for another landlord, and decentralization of management to the individual estate level. Again, as for further and higher education, some amalgamations of housing associations have subsequently taken place in response to potential economies of scale and other financial incentives. Hence, these reforms have the *potential* to increase scope for exit by breaking-up monolithic municipal provision. Whether they do in fact do so can only be determined by empirical research (see Chapter 12).

(b)   The Voluntary Sector
Voluntary sector organizations within the UK are increasingly participating within a 'mixed economy of care' based on the separation of purchaser and

provider functions (see Chapter 12). For example, though local governments remain responsible for assessing need for individual elderly people, residential care of elderly people is increasingly being provided by the private and voluntary sectors. However, it is by no means certain that such private and voluntary sector organizations are any more sensitive to voice than are local governments, nor does their provision of services necessarily increase the scope for exit. For example, large residential care establishments for elderly people may achieve economies of scale at the expense of both voice and exit.

(c)   Privatization

As part of their 1980s privatization programme, UK central governments required local governments to sell assets such as undeveloped land, bus companies and municipal housing. Privatization was part of a comprehensive strategy to roll back the frontiers of the state to its core functions (for example, policy-making), sometimes referred to as the 'dismantled state' or 'enabling state'.

However, privatization may not, in fact, increase scope for exit or voice. As already noted, individuals cannot exit local or regional monopoly providers of utility services such as the privatized water and sewerage companies in England and Wales. Use of voice requires skills and inputs of time which many consumers may not have or be able to afford. Political control of such services may provide stronger voice.

2. Decentralization Within Local Government

The three forms of decentralization outside local government increase the scope for exit but do not increase the scope for voice. In contrast, decentralization within local government has the potential to strengthen voice and can, in certain circumstances, also increase the scope for exit. It can strengthen voice by providing for needs to be defined locally at, say, neighbourhood level rather than at municipal level. It can increase the scope for exit by facilitating choice between alternative suppliers of a given service within the municipality. There are a number of options (see Figure 4.2).

(a)   Decentralization to Markets

The compulsory competitive tendering (CCT) regime required British local governments' own Direct Service Organizations (DSOs) to compete with private sector firms for contracts to provide an expanding range of services. Local governments increasingly work with external agencies (including quangos and voluntary organizations as well as private sector companies) to ensure the delivery of their services: a shift from government to governance (see Chapter 12).

Policies regarding service levels and standards are still determined by local governments rather than relinquished to private markets, such that this is not privatization. Depending upon which bidder for the contract is most efficient, provision of the service can be *contracted-out* to private firms or *contracted-in* to DSOs (Figure 4.2).

It is debatable whether CCT increases the scope for exit or strengthens voice. It has been claimed that CCT is leading to the specification and monitoring of service contracts at neighbourhood level (Gaster 1995a). However, current users have generally not been heavily involved in drawing up contract specifications (see Chapter 14). Moreover, it is difficult to exit neighbourhood services such as refuse collection.

(b) Decentralization to Consumers

Service Vouchers supposedly increase scope for exit (see Chapter 2), the threat of which may strengthen voice (especially in the case of small-scale service providers). They are not well developed in the UK but were piloted and subsequently briefly used for nursery education between 1996 and 1998 and are still used for certain post-school training schemes. They have also been proposed for other public sector services including housing and the arts. Within national or local policy parameters, holders of service vouchers can 'shop around' alternative service providers in order to secure the service most suited to their needs.

Service Charters, now well developed in the UK, include the UK central government's 1991 Citizen's Charter and the multitude of local charters issued by local governments themselves (Cm 2970). They supposedly strengthen voice by increasing the accountability of local governments to individuals as consumers of their services, as distinct from accountability to local communities or sectional interests. However, the Citizen's Charter has been criticized because it relates to individual voicing by consumers rather than collective voicing by citizens, confering few, if any, new statutory entitlements (Pollitt 1994). Increased users' voice only operates at the level of the individual through complaints procedures, rather than collectively through representation in the planning, management or evaluation of the service. Charters also do nothing to increase the scope for exit.

(c) Decentralization to Neighbourhoods

Decentralization to neighbourhoods has the potential to strengthen voice through increased decision-making inputs from local citizens. It may also increase the scope for exit by enabling individuals to move to preferred service providers by relocating *within* the municipality. This potential differs between the two alternatives (see Figure 4.2).

(i) Managerial Decentralization   This refers to the decentralization of service delivery to neighbourhood-based outlets. In the most advanced form of managerial decentralization, local government is effectively treated as a managerial system based on a core–periphery form of organization. Services and their staff are moved out of the local government's town hall headquarters and into local *area offices* to make services more physically accessible to service users (localization), and to meet their needs more effectively by devolving managerial decision-making to the lowest possible level in the management hierarchy. However, this initiative tends to be limited to housing and social services (Chandler *et al.* 1995). With the exception of schools and public libraries, which are decentralized *service units*, other services are much less decentralized.

In determining whether managerial decentralization improves allocative efficiency, any strengthening of voice or increased scope for exit has to be balanced against the costs of implementation. First, the more localised the service the more expensive it becomes to staff offices with the requisite range of professional expertize (for example, for social work services) and service specialists may be reluctant to become generic workers. Second, professionals may become isolated from the central policy-making structures of their local governments and monitoring and evaluation may become more difficult.

(ii) Political decentralization   Political decentralization refers to decentralized decision-making, as distinct from decentralized management processes. It can considerably strengthen local collective voice in the provision of services *for* and *with* (rather than *to*) the public. This is the empowering state as distinct from the enabling state or universal provider state, all three being common terms within the public administration and politics literature. However, the two forms of political decentralization differ quite markedly in terms of strengthening voice.

1. *Devolution* vests power to make at least some policy decisions in *area committees* (a subcommittee of the principal local government) or to *lower levels of government* (such as parish councils) and so facilitates a diminution of direct control from the centre. Though considerably strengthening voice, it has been adopted by very few UK local governments, only one having devolved the majority of its services (Chandler *et al.* 1995).
2. *Consultation* occurs when local governments seek comment and advice from other agencies, representatives of interest groups or the general public on a formal and regular basis but are not bound by their views. Many claimed forms of devolution are actually consultation, since they do not always vest in local residents the power to make at least some policy decisions. Consultation does not increase the scope for exit but can strengthen voice. It is most extensively developed in school education. Parents have

the right to information and to attend annual meetings reporting on school performance. These rights are in addition to their statutory rights regarding choice of school for their children. The composition of school governing bodies has been revised in order that they can be made more representative and responsive to the communities they serve. This may not necessarily be the result, however. While the educational policy-making role of headteachers has been enhanced, governing bodies generally do not provide a link with the community, nor do they act as a democratic counter-weight to their local government (Alaszewski and Manthorpe 1988).

For other services, *user groups* have been established to become involved in the day-to-day running of major facilities, for example in leisure and recreation and day nurseries. Their effectiveness in strengthening voice depends on increased participation by local residents, which in turn requires highly publicized meetings at times convenient for them rather than for local government officials and with open agendas and non-specialist explanations of service issues.

Neighbourhood forums have a much wider remit than user-group committees, attempting to build the neighbourhood perspective into mainstream services and professional practice. They may include local politicians, local government officials and representatives from tenants' groups, residents' groups, youth groups, church groups and so on. They may discriminate in favour of otherwise underrepresented groups by guaranteeing committee places for ethnic minorities (for race relations issues), women (equal opportunities), disabled people and so on. However, critics argue that though services have generally been made more responsive to service users, they have no greater say in determining priorities. This again illustrates the difference between consultation and devolution in terms of strengthening voice.

PUBLIC CHOICE PERSPECTIVES: USES AND ABUSES OF DECENTRALIZATION

Ideally, the overall objective of decentralization is to improve the welfares of local citizens by increasing scope for exit and strengthening voice. However, decentralization may be used for political purposes (Gyford 1987). Left-wing parties often believe that services must be operated at the local level to win political support for local government services and so create contervailing pressure against public expenditure restraints. Right-wing parties see decentralization as an opportunity to reduce bureaucracy, state interference and planning controls, facilitating a more individualized market relationship, consumers exercising market power (exit) instead of collective political power (voice).

Surveys of political participation have shown that local government is dominated by better educated, higher income, middle-aged white men, this group being more likely to participate than other groups and being more effective in public debate. Ethnic minorities, disabled people, women and both the young and elderly are relatively underrepresented. In this case, local democracy can supposedly be strengthened by infusing *representative* democracy with *direct* democracy through decentralization.

However, increased direct democracy may experience similar problems in terms of the lack of representativeness of area committees or of local residents co-opted onto neighbourhood forums or user-group committees. By definition, co-optees will only be concerned with their own narrow sectional interests and there is potential for consultation to be manipulated by well-organized political minorities. Alternatively, co-optees may become self-perpetuating and unaccountable to those whom they are supposed to represent, possibly becoming apologists for the policies of their local governments. Co-optees may become so incorporated into their local government's value set that they become distanced from the local communities they are supposed to serve. Hence, co-optees do not necessarily counteract the power of local politicians, particularly since they do not have voting rights, only having the opportunity to comment upon policy issues.

Decentralized services may become controlled by other municipally-patronized, self-serving local elites. This outcome is a strong possibility. First, in most services, decentralization initiatives have come from managerial and professional groups, rather than from consumers or local communities. While the supposed benefits to consumers and communities justify decentralization, there has been little attempt to assess the benefits (if any) subsequently accruing to them (Smith 1989). Evaluation has tended to concentrate on the views of managers and professionals, rather than on those of user-groups (see Chapter 14).

Second, area-based decentralization initiatives are often resisted by those groups who see them as a threat to their own interests, particularly bureaucrats and trades unions. Service bureaucrats and managers may be concerned about the effect on career structures if decentralization is intended to facilitate cost reduction by removing unnecessary layers of middle management, so flattening the traditional hierarchical management structure by giving greater autonomy to area and neighbourhood managers. Middle managers may have similar reservations about multi-service team work, even if it improves the quality of work for lower-level staff by giving them more opportunities for local initiatives, so raising their morale. Trades unions may be concerned with implications of decentralization for their members' conditions of employment; for example, more flexible working hours being required for the convenience of local area representatives.

Third, prioritization of deprived areas under area-based budgeting may be resisted by more affluent, relatively over-endowed areas, which would consequently lose service outputs. Similar resistance may result from prioritization of particular ethnic, demographic or other socioeconomic groups. Indeed, an affluent community may seek devolved powers in order to protect itself from pressures exerted by a majority within the local government as a whole. For example, it may use its powers to exclude ethnic minorities from access to services within its area or adopt other such discriminatory practices.

Fourth, chairpersons of service committees may fear loss of their traditionally dominant role. Any substantial degree of devolution of power will necessarily involve a diminution of direct control by the centre. For decentralization to improve the welfares of local residents, central decision-makers must be prepared to allow area committees having their own decision-making powers to adopt policies of which they may not approve. They must also be prepared to accept different policies in different areas, as well as the possibility that the majority party at local government level may not have a majority on the area committee. In practice, as already noted, local governments rarely adopt full devolution for all services and usually retain powers of intervention in respect of those which have been devolved. They may require the chair of the area committee to be a member of the local government's majority party. They may also draw the boundaries of area committees in such a way that they and the centre are likely to have the same party in majority. Alternatively, they may ensure this by using powers of co-option to area committees. The discretionary powers of area committees may be further reduced by restricting the amount of budgetary devolution, independent decision-making being difficult without independent budgets, such that what appears to be devolution is little more than consultation.

These issues are more consistent with the leviathan model of government than with the despotic benevolent model implied by bureaucratic paternalism (see Chapter 1). They demonstrate that decentralization is a necessary but not sufficient condition for promotion of the public interest through increased scope for exit and strengthening of voice. They make clear that an increased level of public participation in decision-making does not necessarily lead to more democratic outcomes. Much depends upon whether participative structures and processes are more or less representative (that is, whether participants are formally elected or not) and so upon their degree of democracy. There may, in fact, be too few candidates to hold contested elections, a small and stable group of activists may become dominant, or some sections of the community (for example, ethnic groups) may remain excluded from participation.

Hence, decentralization creates the opportunity for more responsive service delivery but does not necessarily secure it. The actual outcome resulting from decentralization will depend on the distribution of power among the various groups operating within and alongside local government institutions. While not denying the many benefits of decentralization, Leach *et al.* (1994) argue that it has not fundamentally altered political and managerial power in the

UK. British local government is still a bureaucratic organization, officers retain their professional power and local politicians retain their political power. Moreover, decentralization is limited by the advantages of a corporate approach to policy-making and service provision, for example child care and local economic development.

Unless there are overriding welfare arguments in favour of continuing local government provision of services, the possible abuses of decentralization provide the rationale for provision by markets so as to increase choices open to consumers. In this context, privatization is the preferred option. If it is not feasible, however, competitive pressures must be created by other means, such as service vouchers and competitive tendering. Other measures include increasing the voice of consumers by introduction of service charters. Increasing the voice of parents on school governing bodies to counterbalance teachers and other local government nominees is another example. However, the effectiveness of such measures ultimately depends on how they change the balance of (economic and/or political) power between service users and service providers. Many of the decentralization measures considered above may change organizational structures more than the structure of power.

EMPIRICAL EVIDENCE

Case-studies of decentralization, including the London Borough of Tower Hamlets are available in Beale *et al.* (1994), Blake *et al.* (1991), Burns *et al.* (1994), Chandler *et al.* (1995), Charters (1994), Gaster (1993, 1994), Haine and Keen (1994), Leach *et al.* (1994), Lowndes and Stoker (1992a, 1992b), Shepherd (1994), Stoker *et al.* (1991), Stoker and Lowndes (1991).

Although the analysis is ongoing (Lowndes 1994), the general consensus is that decentralization led to dramatically increased service volumes and to improved service quality, at least for those services provided directly to recipients and which can be localized. In Tower Hamlets service delivery improved because of a number of factors. First, the simple proximity of staff in different departments (such as leisure, landscape and planning staff) facilitates better working, as does the ease by which key groups of staff can be brought together to tackle particular tasks. Second, neighbourhood chief executives have a more intimate knowledge of the smaller areas for which they are responsible and are more susceptible to pressures from local organizations and from local politicians sitting on the neighbourhood committee. Third, local politicians were likewise made more accountable and had more intimate knowledge of their own neighbourhood. Fourth, increased political control at the neighbourhood level promoted a political vision for each neighbourhood that had previously not been possible within the officer-dominated centralized hierarchy.

Decentralization works well for housing repairs, physical planning, refuse collection, street cleansing, leisure and so on. However, some aspects of service policy and delivery determined by a single neighbourhood could have significant impacts on other neighbourhoods. For example, in theory, a neighbourhood could decide to stop providing a non-statutory service such as recreation regardless of the impact on borough-wide provision, possibly creating negative spillover effects. Moreover, decentralization blocked central policy-making in areas where it was needed, for example job training, economic development, equal opportunities and race relations, all of which are best dealt with at municipal level than by neighbourhoods. In other words, decentralization finds it difficult to cope with many of the new strategic issues facing local government, issues much broader than service delivery. Local politicians rarely see each other unless they sit on central committees. In effect, decentralization creates isolated pools of local government. Services with localized delivery benefit at the cost of loss of expertize for municipality-wide services. These losses are related to strategic policy-making, as distinct from economies of scale (see Chapter 2).

Although widely regarded as radical, decentralization within Tower Hamlets only increased the degree of public *influence* on the authority; it did not give neighbourhood populations substantive *powers* to direct municipal services. Decentralization extended traditional forms of representative (rather than participatory) democracy at local level. Management decentralization has occured more within than across departments. Decentralization has related more to access than to decision-making. Decentralization relates more to decision-making within the officer structure than to devolution of power to area committees. This is because decentralization did not fundamentally alter political and management power, contrary to the expectations of some advocates of decentralization.

CONCLUSIONS

Local governments clearly have the potential to increase scope for exit and voice, both via Tiebout's 'voting with ones' feet' (migration) and through decentralization both outside and within local government. However, whether that potential is achieved depends upon many factors. In practice, migration cannot be solely relied upon to match service delivery with citizen's preferences. Devolution is also required but likewise faces many problems. Many claimed forms of devolution are, strictly speaking, only consultation, since they vest no decision-making powers in consumer-representative bodies. Political decentralization seems mainly to take the form of consultation. This may be little more than listening, but not responding, to service users' comments. Voice is hardly strengthened in such cases, being little different from customer-orientated private sector management techniques.

The services that are most advantageously decentralized are those which relate to residential or business properties or their immediate environs and those which frequently necessitate interaction between local residents and their local government. Schools, libraries, housing and personal social services are the most commonly decentralized services. Planning, and environmental health are less frequently decentralized.

The benefits of decentralization have to be balanced against the costs of decentralized political and managerial processes, especially the possible loss of any economies of scale and of strategic policy-making. It is, however, difficult to measure the costs and benefits of decentralization. The difficulty of measuring the largely intangible benefits of single services, whether decentralized or not, was recognized in Chapter 2.

Many of the claimed advantages of decentralization are based upon expected outcomes rather than upon the results of empirical research. In practice, benefits may be captured by particular groups within local government. Expression of voice is ineffective if one lacks the *political power* to make it lead to change. It can be made more effective by increasing the scope for exit – that is, giving service users *economic power* so that the threat of exit strengthens (rather than replaces) voice. Hence, where it is not possible or acceptable to subject services to market provision through privatization, economists advocate forms of contestability which give service users more choice. Note, however, that internal markets may only improve X-efficiency. They will only promote allocative efficiency if they increase the scope for choice. For example, the competitive tendering of refuse collection contracts promotes X-efficiency but not allocative efficiency since it does not facilitate choice about service levels or standards (see Chapter 13).

Oates' decentralization theorem cannot be used to justify all forms of decentralization within local government. It only justifies devolution of decision-making within local government because only in that case can the varying preferences of local residents be taken into account. The main deficiency of Oates' decentralization theorem is that it does not take account of models of power within local government. This chapter has indicated some of the reasons why devolution may not have the effect envisaged by Oates in terms of securing a net welfare gain for the local community as a whole.

5 The Economics of Local Government Expenditure

Local self-government denotes the right and the ability of local authorities, within the limits of the law, to regulate and manage a substantial share of public affairs under their own responsibility and in the interests of the local population. ... Local authorities shall be entitled, within national economic policy, to adequate financial resources of their own, of which they may dispose freely within the framework of their powers.

(European Charter of Local Self-Government: Articles 3 and 9)

INTRODUCTION

Central governments may wish to control local government expenditures in aggregate both because they may impinge upon the former's management of the economy and they are usually part-financed by central government. Hence, there is a macroeconomic rationale for control of local government expenditure. However, central control would clearly limit local autonomy, as recognized in the above quotation.

Local autonomy would be severely limited if central government could control all the sources of revenue for each local government and, thereby, controlled spending of *individual* authorities. In effect, local governments would only have discretion about the *distribution* of a given level of spending across the range of services they provide.

Alternatively, central government may seek only to control the *aggregate* expenditure of local authorities, so maximizing the scope for local democracy at the individual local government level in terms of both the total of expenditure and its distribution.

Though the *macroeconomic* rationale for central control of local spending has long been recognized, the *microeconomic* rationale for control has appeared much more recently. During the 1980s, in particular, attention increasingly focused on the need to encourage greater managerial efficiency in service delivery. Efficiency and value for money studies have long been (and continue to be) undertaken for local government services, but more recently restrictions upon local government income and expenditure have been intended, in part, to force local authorities to achieve efficiency gains in service delivery. The differing macroeconomic and microeconomic rationales for control of local government expenditure are dealt with in this chapter.

81

It has to be recognized, however, that central governments may wish to control local government spending more for political and ideological reasons than for economic reasons. This is more likely to be the case where there are different political parties in control at central and local levels. For example, right-wing central governments generally want to 'roll back the frontiers of the state' while local governments controlled by socialist parties generally wish to expand municipal socialism via an enlarged local welfare state. Such a divergence of political control characterized the UK during the 1980s and early 1990s, ideological and political arguments becoming enmeshed with economic arguments.

THE COMPOSITION OF LOCAL GOVERNMENT EXPENDITURE

The precise mix of local government spending varies between countries reflecting differences in the service responsibilities attributed to them by their respective central governments. For example, whereas in many countries local governments provide water and sewerage services, energy supply and health care, they are not provided by UK local government. Moreover, the means by which services are financed varies, energy supply being predominantly financed by user-charges, while non-utility services are generally financed by a combination of local taxes, intergovernmental grants, charges and borrowing. Expenditure control may not be applied to self-financing public utility services.

As a broad average applicable over a run of years, local government expenditures in the UK are dominated by current expenditure on 'consumables' (accounting for four-fifths of local expenditure), the rest being capital expenditures on fixed assets. *Capital expenditures* were dominated by council house building programmes during the 1960s and 1970s, since when it has borne the brunt of severe capital expenditure controls. *Current expenditure* is dominated by education spending (about half) and by wages and salaries (about three-quarters). Unlike central government expenditure, dominated by *transfer payments*, local government spending is almost wholly incurred on *exhaustive expenditures* (goods and services). The main exception is that local authorities act as agents of central government in paying Housing Benefit (a national transfer payment assisting tenants' rent payments) to tenants of their municipal housing.

The predominance of labour costs in local government spending implies that any reduction in expenditure would entail substantial redundancies, to the extent that they cannot be achieved by natural wastage (retirement and resignations). Labour shedding will naturally be resisted by employees and their trades unions. Service levels are not necessarily reduced, however, since it may be possible to increase labour productivity. This will be the case if local governments have surplus capacity (for example, many half-empty schools in an area where rationalization is feasible – see Chapter 6), if capital can be substituted for labour (for example, in refuse collection and disposal – see Chapter 14), or if improved working methods can be adopted (for example, through more flexible labour contracts – see Chapter 14). However, the longer the period over which 'efficiency savings' are required of local governments the more likely it is that the levels and/or standards of services will have to be reduced. This can be expected to be unpopular with service users, though not necessarily with local taxpayers.

THE MACROECONOMIC RATIONALE FOR CENTRAL GOVERNMENT CONTROL

The rationale for central control of local government expenditure is based on its often substantial shares within total public expenditure and GDP. It is therefore inevitable that local government will be required to bear its share of any relative or absolute reductions in the size of the public sector. In the UK, for example, local government accounted for a third of public expenditure during the 1970s, falling to a quarter during the 1980s.

In fact, the level of local government spending varies significantly between countries. Table 5.1 shows that municipal expenditures in 33 member states of the Council of Europe accounted for more than 5 per cent of GDP in 21 countries and for more than 10 per cent of general government expenditure (GGE) in 28 countries in the early to mid-1990s. In general, however, municipal expenditures account for less than 15 per cent of GDP and less than 30 per cent of GGE in the Council of Europe. This suggests that many European countries still have a long way to go in applying the Council of Europe's decentralist principle of Article 4 (see Chapter 2).

Though UK local authorities have a considerable degree of autonomy, the view of the UK's central government, expressed in a consultative document in 1981 (Cmnd 8449, para. 1.11), is that

> the Government, however, has overall responsibility for all public services, including those provided by local authorities, and for national economic objectives. Neither local government nor local taxpayers are in a position to assess either the relative claims of local services as a whole to national resources or the overall economic impact of local expenditure. These are matters on which the Government must take a strategic view in the course of its management of economic policy. For these reasons it is essential that the Government should be able to influence local revenue-raising and local expenditure.

There are three main policy areas: demand management, resource allocation and the control of inflation.

Local Government Economics

Table 5.1   *Municipal expenditure relative to GDP and GGE*

Country	Year	% of GDP	% of GGE
Albania	1995	7.7	25.4
Austria	1993	12.7	20.2
Belgium	1993	4.9	10.9
Bulgaria	1994	9.0	20.0
Cyprus	1993	1.4	4.1
Czech Rep.	1994	9.3	20.9
Denmark	1994	19.9	31.3
Estonia	1994	7.1	17.6
Finland	1993	18.0	29.5
France	1992	5.5	27.2
Germany	1993	8.1	28.7
Greece	1989	3.3	5.6
Hungary	1994	17.0	53.0
Iceland	1994	9.1	22.3
Ireland	1994	4.9	13.8
Italy	1993	7.0	13.0
Latvia	1994	12.5	24.0
Lithuania	1993	13.1	58.8
Luxembourg	1993	9.9	32.3
Malta	1995	0.3	0.6
Netherlands	1994	13.3	23.1
Norway	1994	18.9	60.0
Poland	1994	7.0	21.6
Portugal	1993	4.6	9.7
Romania	1993	3.5	16.9
San Marino	1993	0.1	0.2
Slovakia	1994	4.8	11.8
Slovenia	1995	4.4	10.1
Spain	1994	4.9	12.2
Sweden	1994	27.5	38.0
Switzerland	1993	10.8	27.9
Turkey	1992	2.4	12.3
United Kingdom	1994	11.0	27.0

Source: Council of Europe (1997), reproduced with permission of the Council of Europe.
Notes:
There were 40 member states in 1998
GDP: Gross Domestic Product
GGE: General Government Expenditure

1. Demand Management

Chapter 1 noted that local governments should not attempt their own stabilization policy. However, central government may seek to manipulate aggregate local government spending in order to control the economy. It may also seek to manage aggregate demand at the regional level (for example, to stimulate depressed regional economies). The effectiveness of such manipulation depends upon whether the economy operates according to a Keynesian or a monetarist model.

(a) A Keynesian Model

A Keynesian model of the economy shows that aggregate local government spending can be manipulated to control aggregate demand and so control the levels and trends in any or all of national income, savings, investment, consumption, employment, inflation, output, the balance of payments and economic growth. In a recession, for example, local governments could be encouraged to create jobs *directly* by increasing their own employment and *indirectly* through increased infrastructural investments. In the latter case, building more roads, schools and municipal housing create multiplier effects which 'crowd in' subsequent rounds of private spending. In short, local authorities increase injections into the circular flow of income.

In the Keynesian model, increased capital expenditure (on physical assets) is more effective at stimulating aggregate demand than increased current expenditure (for example, on supplies and services or labour). Capital spending is generally financed by borrowing, whereas current expenditure is generally financed through increased local taxes. The latter is the case where local authorities have to adhere to a balanced budget rule (that is, current income = current expenditure). Unless the extra tax payments financing the increased current expenditure are completely financed from savings, there will be some offsetting reduction in current spending in the private sector. Hence, there will be a balanced-budget multiplier associated with increased current expenditure, although it will be small.

In contrast, borrowing represents a net addition to aggregate demand because it is financed from private sector savings and is repaid by higher future taxes, current tax levels remaining unchanged in the face of increased spending. Hence the multiplier will be smaller for current expenditure financed by taxation than for capital spending financed by borrowing. This Keynesian analysis justifies the usually tighter central controls on capital expenditure than on current expenditure. This explains the qualified statement in respect of borrowing in Article 9 of the European Charter of Local Self-Government which states that 'for the purpose of borrowing for capital investment, local authorities shall have access to the national capital market within the limits of the law'.

Table 5.2, again in respect of member states of the Council of Europe – this time for 1995, shows that though local government capital expenditures can account for large proportions of total municipal expenditure, they generally only account for 1 or 2 per cent of GDP. However, in a country where local government capital expenditures account for 3 per cent of GDP, a rise of capital spending by one-third world, if financed by borrowing, add one per cent to aggregate demand. Moreover, local government capital expenditures can account for substantial proportions of general government capital expenditure

Table 5.2   *Municipal investment expenditure relative to total municipal expenditure, GDP and GGIE[a]*

Country	% of total municipal spending	% of GGIE	% of GDP
Albania	14.4	3.1	1.11
Austria	16.8	70.3	2.13
Belgium[b]	17.8	28.0	0.87
Bulgaria	8.9	54.2	0.80
Cyprus	17.1	6.7	0.24
Czech Rep.	40.0	55.9	3.72
Denmark	5.7	51.4	1.26
Finland	7.0	47.7	1.26
Germany	19.4	64.3	1.57
Greece	27.9	3.9	0.93
Hungary	13.8	42.2	2.35
Iceland	25.3	25.1	2.23
Ireland	32.0	25.0	1.57
Italy	3.3	26.2	0.23
Latvia	0.6	7.8	0.08
Luxembourg	28.1	75.2	2.78
Malta	6.8	0.2	0.02
Netherlands	17.5	80.1	2.33
Norway	9.4	60.0	1.78
Poland	22.5	52.0	1.58
Portugal	41.4	41.5	1.90
Slovakia[c]	31.2	38.8	n.a.
Slovenia	43.0	11.2	1.89
Spain	24.4	29.4	1.19
Sweden	5.6	49.8	1.54
Switzerland	31.7	15.8	3.42
Turkey	22.0	16.0	5.53
United Kingdom	10.0	38.0	1.10

Source: Council of Europe (1997), reproduced with permission of the Council of Europe.
Notes:
GDP: Gross Domestic Product; GGIE: General Government Investment Expenditure
a: For the years indicated in Table 5.1.
b: The GGIE figure refers to Flanders region only.
c: Data relate to 1995 and n.a. denotes 'not available'.

– as high as 80 per cent in the Netherlands, exceeding 50 per cent in nine countries and between 25 and 50 per cent in 11 countries.

Hence, borrowing controls are necessary, not just for controlling aggregate demand, but also to prevent individual local authorities borrowing more than they can afford to repay. About half of the Council of Europe member states control local government borrowing by prohibiting their access to capital markets unless they have central government approval. Very few member states allow unrestricted borrowing in foreign currencies.

Given the variability demonstrated by Table 5.2, it is not surprising that borrowing as a proportion of total municipal funding was also highly variable in the mid-1990s, but equalled or exceeded 10 per cent in only seven member states (see Table 5.3).

Table 5.3   *Sources of municipal funding (%)*

Country	Exclusive local taxes	Fees and charges	Intergovernmental transfers[a]	Borrowing	Other
Albania	3	3	94	0	1
Austria	15	19	35	8	23
Belgium	32	5	40	13	10
Bulgaria	1	10	78	2	9
Cyprus	25	33	30	12	0
Czech Rep.	16	12	45	11	16
Denmark	51	22	24	2	1
Estonia[b]	0	1	91	2	6
Finland	34	11	31	3	21
France	36	2	26	10	26
Germany	19	16	45	9	11
Greece	2	22	58	6	12
Hungary	4	8	66	4	18
Iceland	12	16	53	5	14
Ireland	18	10	57	2	13
Italy	18	11	38	9	24
Latvia	6	1	68	0	25
Luxembourg	31	29	37	3	0
Malta	0	0	98	0	2
Netherlands	5	13	60	19	3
Norway	42	16	33	7	2
Poland	21	7	60	0	12
Portugal	20	19	38	6	17
Romania	5	16	79	0	0
San Marino	0	0	31	69	0
Slovakia	10	9	39	5	37
Slovenia	5	9	67	1	18
Spain	31	16	37	10	6
Sweden	61	8	19	1	11
Switzerland	46	24	18	3	9
Turkey	7	1	56	0	36
United Kingdom	11	6	77	0	6

Source: Council of Europe (1997), reproduced with permission of the Council of Europe.
Notes:
a: Intergovernmental transfers include shared taxes and grants (see Table 9.1).
b: Estonian municipalities raised 0.1 per cent of their funding from exclusive local taxes.
Funding sources may not total to 100 due to rounding.

(b) A Monetarist Model

A monetarist model of the economy emphasizes the impact of local government spending on monetary control. Monetarists argue that the attempt to achieve multiple objectives through the Keynesian approach is overly-ambitious and spuriously precise. Instead, monetarists argue that control of the rate of growth of the money supply in line with the rate of growth of the economy's output is both a necessary and sufficient condition for macroeconomic control. Local government debt is a near perfect substitute for central government debt (gilts and Treasury Bills in the UK). To allow local government freedom to create debt would reduce central government's control over interest rates and the money supply through its operations in the bond market.

In particular, local governments' capital expenditures lead to an increase in the public sector borrowing requirement (PSBR) which, in turn, has implications for the growth of the money supply, the management of financial markets and international confidence in the country's monetary policy. Provided that the market for borrowable funds was not previously experiencing an excess supply, the rise in demand for borrowable funds on the part of local governments leads either to an increase in interest rates on public sector debt or to an increase in the money supply (Bailey 1995, ch. 5). Either the excess demand created by the government's demands for borrowable funds drives up their price (the interest rate) or the central bank has to 'print money' in order to avoid flooding the market with government bonds.

Governments cannot control both interest rates and the money supply simultaneously. If the money supply is controlled, then interest rates must be allowed to rise (the excess suppy of government bonds driving down their selling price such that a given redemption value yields a higher rate of interest). Higher interest rates may 'crowd out' interest-sensitive private sector expenditures, so that multiplier effects are insignificant or even negative (that is, investment falls so much that economic growth is reduced). However, local government's capital expenditure is often complementary with private spending (such as roads and cars), so reducing any crowding-out effects caused by interest rates. Nonetheless, the resulting higher interest rates will cause a reduction of expenditure on private investment and private consumption (the size of those reductions depending upon their interest elasticities of demand), so justifying control of capital expenditure.

If central government tries to prevent the rise in interest rates caused by increased local government borrowing, it must prevent the excess supply of government stock, effectively arranging an overdraft facility for local governments from the central bank. Hence, bank deposits expand ('printing money') and so the government forgoes control of the money supply in order to control interest rates. An increase in the money supply causes inflation according to the Quantity Theory of Money $MV = PT$, M being the money supply, V its velocity of circulation (measured by dividing GDP by M), P the average price level, and T the volume of transactions. Monetarists argue that V and T are fixed so that a rise in M causes a rise in P (inflation). Inflation crowds-out private spending by reducing the real value of incomes. In effect, the public sector can always outbid the private sector for scarce resources. Keynesians dispute the causation from M to P (it could be reversed, for example, if rising input prices cause firms to borrow in advance of revenue from sales), question the relevance of P (since it is relative, not average, prices that determine demand), and use their 'liquidity trap' to argue that V varies to offset changes in M (that is, where all or most of the increase in M is held as idle balances).

While their models of the economy differ in predicting the impact of changes in local government spending, *both* monetarists and Keynesians provide a macroeconomic justification for central control of local government expenditures. Keynesians would not sanction increased or reduced local government expenditure in economic booms or slumps respectively, since that would exacerbate the economic cycle, increased spending in booms creating an inflationary gap. Monetarists would not sanction 'printing money' because of its inflationary impact, whether in a boom or a slump. Moreover, in monetarist terms, if higher local taxes reduce private savings there will be less funds available to purchase central government debt, *ceteris paribus*. Hence, for a given interest rate policy, the money supply will tend to increase.

Although the foregoing analysis justifies central control of local government spending, it does not necessarily justify its active manipulation to 'fine tune' the economy, namely attempting to stabilize the level of economic activity and employment by using public spending to offset the economic fluctuations of the trade cycle. There are practical and/or theoretical constraints which may make *Keynesian counter-cyclical policy* ineffective or even destabilizing.

At a *practical level*, time lags in the implementation of counter-cyclical measures may for example result in expansionary fiscal policy, decided during economic downturns, taking effect during periods of economic recovery, so becoming pro-cyclical and exacerbating the economic cycle. This may be because recruitment of labour with the requisite skills takes time and sharp fluctuations in recruitment and employment (especially redundancies) may be politically unpopular. Likewise, capital expenditures may also be difficult to vary in the short term because, by their very nature, they require long-term planning if they are to be undertaken efficiently. This is especially the case for new-build programmes as distinct from refurbishment of existing capital assets (for example, roads and municipal houses). Certainly, it will be more difficult to increase than reduce capital expenditure in the short term, although even in the latter case cuts in programmes already under way will be constrained by contractual obligations. If control is on borrowing, rather than on capital spending itself, local governments may accumulate borrowing approvals over a period of years so that central prohibition of further local borrowing is ineffective in the short term. In addition, local governments may frustrate control by using their often considerable balances to finance capital spending.

At a *theoretical level*, demand management may be made ineffective by the *permanent income/life-cycle theorem* (which holds that a change in current income thought to be transitory will have a negligible effect on permanent income and, hence, on current consumption) or by '*rational expectations*' (where the private sector anticipates and counteracts government policy with the result that it has no effect on economic activity). If, for example, increased government borrowing leads to expectations of future higher taxes to repay the debt then savings increase, with the result that aggregate demand is left unchanged.

Hence, whether on practical or theoretical grounds, local government spending should not be treated as a fine-tuning instrument by which to implement central government's stabilization policy.

It is arguable that, though central government does need to control *capital* expenditures financed by borrowing, it need not control *current* expenditures financed by local taxation. First, if substantial crowding out occurs for current expenditure, it means that there will be no net effect on aggregate demand of increased local government current spending and so no need for central government to control it. However, central government may still wish to control the growth of the public sector relative to the private sector if it believes that the latter is the primary source of economic growth (see Chapter 6, the 'relative price effect') Second, if local taxpayers regard additional local taxes as payments for additional local government services, there is no reason why they should reduce savings and so there will be no effect on aggregate demand. However, this argument is qualified if a substantial proportion of local taxation is borne by business rather than by voters and if adverse impacts on the local economy result (see Chapter 8). Therefore, some central control of local government expenditure is required for demand-management reasons.

2. Resource Allocation

Local government expenditure affects the allocation of resources between the public and private sectors (for example in reducing private consumption and investment) and within the public sector (that is, between central and local government). Whether local governments should have powers to affect resource allocation in their own areas is a political and constitutional issue. It is a question of whether central government priorities take procedure over local government priorities. A central government may be elected on the basis of a manifesto to reduce the size of the public sector whereas a local government may simultaneously be elected on the basis of a manifesto to increase spending. This contradictory state of affairs is almost inevitable because different political parties may form the majority at central and (some) local levels. Central governments may claim that only they are in a position to determine national priorities, the allocation of resources between public and private investment and consumption, exports and so on, as the Council of Europe's statement at the start of this chapter indicated.

The argument that central government should retain ultimate responsibility for resource allocation is strengthened if six conditions hold:

1. *if a substantial part of local government expenditure is undertaken to meet statutory obligations* imposed upon local government by central government, for example because of beneficial spillover effects. Given that it may be difficult to quantify the financial obligations relating to statutory (legally prescribed) duties, responsibility is ill-determined;
2. *if central government pays effort-related grants* which increase in line with total spending (see Chapter 9). In that cases, additional local expenditures would lead to higher central government taxes to finance those grants;
3. *if a large part of local taxes is paid by business*, tax incidence theory suggesting that potentially large proportions of such taxes may be passed on to consumers, many of whom may live outside the local authority in question (see Chapter 8). Hence, local tax burdens may be 'exported' to other jurisdictions, contrary to the assumptions of Oates' decentralization theorem (see Chapter 2);
4. *if a significant proportion of higher domestic local tax bills is passed on*: backwards to central government (through increased social security, that is transfer, payments) or forwards to employers (through higher wage claims). The former scenario is only likely to be the case for a few 'inner city' local authorities with a substantial proportion of low-income households with high needs for transfer payments (for example, large or single-parent families whose head of household is unemployed). The latter scenario will be of greater effect where local tax bills are included in the official measure of inflation upon which wage claims are based, as in the UK. In both scenarios local pressures for higher local government spending are not accompanied in practice by a genuine willingness on the part of voters to accept lower real disposable incomes;
5. *if a large part of present day spending will be paid by future generations of local taxpayers*, increased spending being financed by borrowing the repayment of which will fall in the future. Central government may wish to protect future local taxpayers from the spending decisions of current local taxpayers. If so it should only control borrowing, not actual capital spending which can be financed by other means; and
6. *most fundamentally, if local democracy does not work effectively*, being characterized by apathy, low voter turnout and self-serving pressure groups (see below). The less representative of local opinion local government is

judged to be, the less willing central governments will be to devolve to local governments a substantial degree of local autonomy. Such unrepresentativeness may provide the justification for central government of one political persuasion to control the spending of local governments dominated by another political persuasion.

The above six conditions break the link between voting in local elections and payment for consequent changes in local service levels. In its mid-1980s deliberations relating to reform of local government finance, the UK government went further in identifying 'too great a gap between those who use, those who vote for and those who pay for local services' (Cmnd 9714, para. 3.47).

Although such conditions strengthen the argument for central control, they do not necessarily justify it. Effort-related matching grants could be replaced by fixed lump-sum grants, locally-variable taxes on business could be replaced by a nationally determined tax rate uniform across all local authorities, and liability to pay local domestic taxes could be broadened to include all voters. This fiscal structure was introduced in Britain in 1990. However, though the first two reforms remained in place, the attempt to relate payment of local domestic taxes more closely to service use through the local poll tax was short-lived, a revised local property tax (the council tax) being reintroduced in place of the poll tax in 1993 (see Chapter 8).

Nonetheless, local voters in the UK arguably still bear the full costs of their voted-for *incremental* expenditures, there being no in-built tendency for central taxes or firms' prices to increase. Hence, the clear link between changes in a local government expenditures and the corresponding changes in local domestic tax bills remains under the council tax. On average, about 80 per cent of British local governments' income net of charges is financed by central government grants, the remaining 20 per cent or so being financed by council tax. This creates a *gearing effect* whereby, on average, British local governments would have to raise the council tax by 5 per cent or so in order to increase their net expenditure by 1 per cent. This can cause severe fiscal stress for local governments (see Chapter 6).

In increasing the marginal cost of incremental expenditures faced by local voters, such a high gearing effect may provide a sufficiently strong constraint upon local government spending such that further controls are unnecessary. However, that constraint will be ineffective if local governments blame central government for the high percentage increases in local tax rates brought about by relatively small incremental expenditures, as has been the case in the UK. Moreover, even if the high gearing effect caused local governments to contain council tax rises to 10 per cent (financing extra spending of just 2 per cent), spending rises by £1.5 billion (1995 values), such a substantial increase in spending being contrary to central government's attempts to control total public expenditure.

Having failed to match voting with tax liability and wishing to control both local tax levels and total public expenditure, the UK government introduced an expenditure-control system in which local authorities are given a spending limit each year. This replaced the earlier discretionary local tax-capping system which had allowed local governments to set their own budgets, tax-capping only having been applied to those local governments whose expenditure levels were considered to central government to be especially profligate. Now all local governments' budgets are effectively set centrally, rather than in their own locality, budget-capping having replaced tax-capping.

The UK situation demonstrates that, irrespective of the willingness of local voters to pay increased local domestic taxes, central governments may feel the need to control local tax levels in order to limit the overall tax burden on the economy. This may be because central government believes the economy's overall taxable capacity has been reached, local and central government taxes consequently competing for the same finite pool of tax revenues. The UK government has continued to emphasise the need to control the total tax burden despite the fact that, compared with other developed countries the UK has been a low-tax economy since 1980 (Bailey 1995, ch. 10).

This continuing restriction of central and local tax rates reflected three concerns:

1. a philosophical belief that the state should not 'requisition' the individual's income;
2. that high marginal rates of tax cause strong disincentive-to-work effects which reduce the taxable capacity of the economy (see Chapter 8); and
3. that high local tax rates combined with a narrow local tax base would cause severe distortion of expenditure patterns.

As already noted, UK local government's own revenue source is restricted to the domestic (residential) property tax. Taxes on housing which are high relative to taxes on other items of consumption could cause suboptimal consumption of housing services, perhaps contrary to central government policy to improve housing standards and offsetting its income tax reliefs on housing costs such as mortgage interest repayments.

There is no objective solution to the first concern, it being a normative issue. The second concern raises an empirical question about the strength of disincentive-to-work effects, if any. The evidence is not clear (Bailey 1995, ch. 4). The third concern regarding distortion of expenditure patterns could be allayed by broadening the local tax base, for example giving local government a local income tax in addition to a local property tax. However, Chapter 1 concluded that strongly redistributive tax and expenditure packages at the local level are probably not feasible because they encourage separation of rich and poor groups through interjurisdictional migration.

3. Control of Inflation

The possibly inflationary consequences of local government borrowing were explained above in terms of both the Keynesian and monetarist models. Increases in local government taxes may also cause inflation. Local government tax increases reduce *disposable* incomes and may stimulate claims for higher wages, leading to wage-cost-push inflation. Inclusion of the local property tax in the UK's index of retail prices (RPI), upon which wage claims are often based, provides the wage-push mechanism and there has long been evidence that money wages tend to keep up with prices. The inclusion of the property tax in the RPI is an anomaly since, though it is part of the cost of housing, it is not a retail price. Moreover, it conflates two separate effects: rising input costs and local decisions regarding service levels.

Although it may be regarded as valid for workers to seek to maintain their real wages by recovering through wage claims the higher costs of a given level of local services, it is invalid so to do if higher local taxes reflect democratic choices for increased service provision. In the latter case, *final* income (post-tax income plus the value of public services consumed) remains unchanged. Local voters have simply chosen to reduce their consumption of private sector outputs in order that they can consume more local public sector outputs. This is therefore not a legitimate reason why wages should rise, and yet the RPI-wages link will encourage such a rise. The local property tax may best be regarded as payment for local government services rather than as part of the cost of housing.

Wage-push inflation may also occur if generous local government wage settlements are used to justify pay increases elsewhere in the public sector and in the private sector, as other groups of workers try to maintain wage relativities. This tendency will be exacerbated by effort-related grants since, say, a 50 per cent matching grant would mean that half of the additional wage costs would be financed by central government through intergovernmental grants. Hence, central government may subject local government employees to a formal prices and incomes policy or, alternatively, control total local spending so that high wage settlements can only be financed by reducing local government employment.

Summary of the Macroeconomic Rationale for Central Control

While accepting that demand management is clearly a central government function, Jackman (1982) argues that it is not self-evident that local government spending actually affects aggregate demand (because of the possibility of crowding-out) and that, from a monetarist perspective, central government does not need to control the balance between private and local government spending (resource allocation).

The UK government recognized the force of this argument in that between 1990 and 1992 its public expenditure *planning* total related only to expenditures determined by central government, consistent with recommendations by Jackman (1988). Hence, while it included the value of intergovernmental grants, it excluded spending financed by local taxes, sales and capital receipts (which, nevertheless, still counted as public expenditure). The problem of how to match outcomes with plans is solved by capping local tax levels and grants or by adopting the 'marginal principle' whereby the full costs of increases in local government spending fall only on those who voted for them (or at least on local domestic taxpayers rather than on local businesses or on national taxpayers). Such direct matching of costs and benefits at the margin is the basis of economic optimization rules. It is considered more fully in Chapters 7 and 8.

THE MICROECONOMIC RATIONALE FOR CENTRAL GOVERNMENT CONTROL

The microeconomic rationale for central control of local spending is concerned with the efficiency with which local governments determine output levels and with their efficiency as service providers. The former concerns allocative efficiency, the latter X-efficiency. Allocative efficiency is concerned with the optimal allocation of resources between and within the public and private sectors (see Chapter 2). X-efficiency is concerned with the internal efficiency of local government operations (see Chapter 3).

The 1981 UK government quotation noted above, emphasized control of overall expenditure. By 1986 this objective had been supplemented by an emphasis on internal efficiency to become 'A concern to contain local government expenditure at affordable levels ... Encouragement to authorities to carry out services more efficiently, and to introduce private sector competition where possible ... A reduction in detailed controls over local government' (Cmnd 9714, 1986, para. 1.19).

Resource allocation has already been considered under the macroeconomic rationale for central control of local expenditure, but it is necessary to consider the microeconomics of local decision-making processes which lead to excessive production. It has already been noted that intergovernmental grants justify central government interest in controlling local spending. It was suggested that lump-sum (rather than effort-related) grants could secure the necessary expenditure restraint by ensuring that the full marginal cost of locally-determined expenditure increases are borne by local taxpayer-voters such that central control of the total of local government spending may be unnecessary.

However, it can be argued that even lump-sum grants may not remove the need for such control. First, local decision-making may be dominated by pressure groups whose preferences are not the same as those of the local community (represented by the median voter – see Chapter 10). Second, lack of competition may result in X-inefficiency. Third, bureaucrats may seek to maximize their own self-interest rather than the local public interest.

1. Pressure Group Influences on Spending

Organizations (in both the public and private sectors) can be thought of as distributional coalitions, seeking to promote the interests of their members and/or clients (Olson 1965, 1982, 1986). Olson's theory of distributional co-alitions focused on an explanation of national economic growth differentials. However, the concept can be extended to the local level. Local governments are distributional coalitions in themselves, seeking increased intergovernmental transfers for their citizens. In effect they are acting as 'rational economic agents' (Schott 1982, p. 45).

Local governments are also composed of distributional coalitions using particular services and making payments of taxes and/or user-charges. In terms of this public choice analysis, they will tend to overemphasize equity (that is, redistribution in their favour) or their constitutional rights to free (or heavily subsidized) services and, likewise, underplay any resulting inefficiencies. This is because the gain to themselves of any redistribution in their favour will be greater than any loss they incur due to any inefficiencies at the economy-wide level (for example, resulting from any disincentive-to-work effects caused by higher marginal tax rates). The same considerations apply to local authorities seeking to increase their claims on the nation's resources.

A major part of redistribution at the local level is through service provision (in-kind transfers) as distinct from differential local taxes. Hence, there is an incentive for subgroups within a local authority to seek to increase their share of service provision which is paid by the generality of local and national tax-payers. Such self-serving (rent-seeking) behaviour would be pre-empted if local government areas were populated by people with homogeneous prefer-ences, individuals being free to vote with their feet by moving to that authority providing the preferred package of local taxes and service outputs in accord-ance with the Tiebout hypothesis. However, as already noted in Chapter 4, local tax and expenditure packages seem to be a relatively small influence on residential location compared with, for instance, the availability of employ-ment or family ties. Moreover, the diversity of local tax and expenditure pack-ages tends to be limited by the equalizing objectives of intergovernmental grant systems (see Chapter 9), by rising property values in popular authorities and so on.

Given constraints on such interjurisdictional migration (exit), the largely non-voluntary nature of 'membership' of a municipality results in each local government area containing a number of distributional coalitions, potentially as many as there are discrete sets of preferences. Each coalition can be expected to express its preferences (voice) in an attempt to improve the welfare of its members. There is therefore an in-built incentive for service expansion and redistribution as an inherent outcome of the collective financing of services combined with rivalry between groups in their use, it having been noted in Chapter 1 that most local government outputs are private goods (that is, both excludable and rival in use). Their impact may be constrained through a series of debates (for example, concerning the public interest), compromises and vote trading, but such incentives can be expected to have a pervasive influence on local government service provision.

Local tax payments are largely fixed in that common rules apply regarding liability to pay (for example, a local property tax) and payment does not vary directly or immediately with the individual's consumption of services. Hence, the incentive is to seek either to vary the level of output or to change its distribution within a given tax cost. Voters will tend to resist increases in service levels if the marginal costs to themselves are greater than the extra benefits received. A minority of residents would prefer higher standards but have to accept the collectively determined standard. Attempts to achieve a redistribution of services in favour of their coalition members are constrained by any *ultra vires* rules (see Chapter 1), by statutory duties imposed on local governments (even if ill-defined), by budget constraints, and by resistance from those groups which would bear the costs of any redistribution in favour of other groups. Hence, attention tends to focus on the distribution of incremental expenditures and much attention is paid to annual budget changes which are usually small in relation to the overall budget total.

No coalition of largely self-interested people will be willing to see a cut in its service provision even if the balance between costs and benefits has deteriorated and resources could be more fruitfully employed elsewhere in promoting the authority-wide collective interest. This is because any reorientation of services (such as the closure of schools in areas losing population of the relevant age groups) would see a reduction in the benefits accruing to this group but no change in local tax liability. Hence the ability of a local authority to adapt to changing socioeconomic conditions is severely constrained by characteristics which are inherent in any system of service provision which requires a *fixed* financing commitment on the part of individuals.

Such an outcome creates allocative inefficiency and is in direct contrast to the rather simplistic model of local government decision making which underpins Oates' decentralization theorem (see Chapter 2). It explains the qualified conclusion in Chapter 3 that expression of voice can improve allocative efficiency in conditions of market failure. The analysis of voice failed to recognize that local governments are composed of competing distributional coalitions and so do not speak with one voice. The incentives facing differing citizen/consumer groups as they express their preferences for variable service levels but fixed tax liabilities tends to lead to allocative inefficiency. A similar outcome may result from the behaviour of service providers.

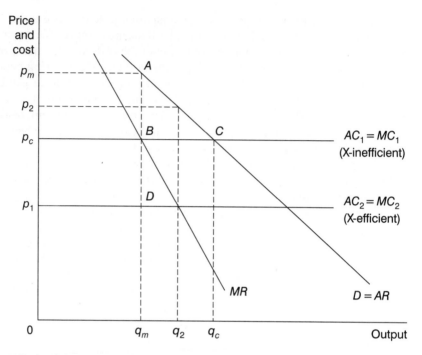

Figure 5.1   *Welfare losses of allocative and X-inefficiency*

2. X-inefficiency due to Monopoly

Lack of competition and the principal–agent problem (see Chapter 3) may allow organizational slack (X-inefficiency) to occur. This is illustrated by Figure 5.1, which uses a static partial equilibrium model to determine the potential welfare losses attributed to monopoly supply, ignoring problems of second best.

For simplicity, Figure 5.1 assumes constant costs within the relevant range of output so that MC equals AC, the lines $AC_1 = MC_1$ and $AC_2 = MC_2$ denoting alternative supply schedules. Ignore the latter for the time being. The profit-maximizing monopolist equates marginal cost and marginal revenues at point B and so produces q_m at the selling price p_m. Assuming identical cost conditions, the equilibrium point under conditions of perfect competition would be at C where $p = MR = MC$. Equilibrium is now $p_c q_c$. Hence the welfare loss to society as a result of the lower output under monopoly is the loss of consumers' surplus measured by the area ABC, referred to as the 'Marshallian triangle'.

The extent of this allocative inefficiency depends on the price elasticity of demand for the monopolist's product (that is, the slope of the demand schedule) and hence the mark-up of price over marginal cost. Pivoting the demand curve on point C to make it steeper increases the area ABC. Its relative import-ance in terms of the whole economy depends on the share of the monopolist's output in national output. It is generally accepted that, given normal demand and supply conditions, the welfare loss due to monopoly is very small, a frac-tion of one per cent of GDP. Allocative inefficiency may not be the only result, however.

A condition for profit maximization is that firms use inputs, solve their organizational problems and produce output at least cost. However, the costs of monopoly provision could be higher than the minimum as a result of organizational slack. X-inefficiency may occur if organizations are not subject to competition, so that more inputs are employed and/or they are paid more than is strictly necessary to produce the output of the organization. Hence, inputs enjoy economic rents, either in the form of remuneration in excess of their transfer earnings, or an easier working life.

X-inefficiency occurs because the relationship between inputs and outputs is not a determinant one. Contracts for labour are incomplete, not all factors of production are marketed, the production function is not completely specified or known and, to greater or lesser degree, organizations imitate each other with respect to technique. Some inputs, particulary labour, do not have a fixed specification. Pieces of capital equipment do have fixed engineering specifications but two organizations may use the same piece of equipment with differing results as a result of differences in the human element of labour applied to it. Much is left to custom and authority, as well as to individual dis-cretion and judgement. This is because it is extremely rare for all elements of labour performance to be specified in a labour employment contract. The more that remains unspecified the potentially more inefficient are labour contracts.

Assume that minimum achievable costs are depicted by $AC_2 = MC_2$ in Fig-ure 5.1. The X-efficient monopolist has a lower price (p_2) and higher output (q_2) than its X-inefficient counterpart (p_m, q_m). Hence, there is now an addi-tional welfare loss to society as a result of X-inefficiency which is clearly distinguishable from the loss of allocative efficiency. It relates to the unnecessarily high production costs per unit of output of p_c-p_1. The excess costs resulting from X-inefficiency would therefore be $p_1 p_c BD$. Such tech-nical inefficiency arises as a result of the failure to operate at the minimum attainable costs of production.

It is therefore immediately apparent from Figure 5.1 that the welfare losses due to X-inefficiency may be much greater than those arising as a result of allocative inefficiency under monopoly. Leibenstein (1966) argued that the magnitudes are so large that X-inefficiency is frequently more significant than allocative inefficiency. If so, then any reservations regarding the possibility of second-best problems virtually disappear and one can be more optimistic about the likelihood of an improved welfare position, especially where improved X-efficiency releases resources to be used elsewhere. Certainly, there are very wide international, national, regional and local differences in output per unit of labour for firms and organizations within the same industry, in both the private and public sectors. Management restructuring, sometimes following employment of consultants, often yields considerable increases in productivity and increased output. Hence, there is both a theoretical and an empirical rational for the introduction of measures to reduce X-inefficiency.

3. Niskanen's Model of Bureaucrats' Behaviour

The model of bureaucrats' behaviour (Niskanen 1968, 1971 and 1975) is based on the principal–agent model (see Chapter 3). It assumes that senior bureaucrats attempt to maximize their own utility rather than that of those they serve. The bureaucrats' utility function contains many variables, for example, salary, perquisites of the office, public reputation, power, patronage, ease of managing the bureau, and ease of making changes. Niskanen argues that all of these are a positive monotonic function of the budget, thus making budget maximization the goal for bureaucrats seeking to maximize their own welfares. The model has three key features:

1. Bureaucrats maximize the total output of their bureau, given the demand and cost conditions of the service(s) the bureau supplies, subject to the constraint that the budget must be equal to or greater than the minimum total costs of the equilibrium output (that is, that which maximizes the bureaucrat's utility).
2. The bureau exchanges a specific output (or combination of outputs) for a specific budget.
3. Assuming that the bureau has some degree of monopoly power, it presents the governing politicians with an all-or-nothing choice. The relationship between bureau and sponsor is one of bilateral monopoly in that each is heavily dependent upon the other for output and budget respectively.

Niskanen assumes that the bureau is in a superior bargaining position because of its exclusive knowledge of the production function, and hence of costs, of the service it produces. The sponsor is therefore unable to assess the efficiency of the bureau, whether in terms of X-efficiency or allocative efficiency. Hence, the bureau will be able to raise its budget to a level where *total* benefits equal the *total* costs to the community, this being in excess of the economic optimum based upon the equality of *marginal* costs and benefits. Moreover, those costs may not be the minimum attainable costs because lack of competition means there is no market policing mechanism. In other words, the bureau exploits high transaction costs (see Chapter 3).

A diagrammatic explanation of the Niskanen model and its effect on local government expenditure is provided in Chapter 11. However, the models of local government, and the relative power of the various stakeholders within each model, outlined in Chapter 1, clearly indicate that the Niskanen model gives too much monopoly power to the bureaucrat. Not surprisingly, therefore, Niskanen's model has been subject to further theoretical refinements and modification (for example, Peacock 1979 and 1983). Whether refined or not, it provides the theoretical justification for *output-control devices* to eliminate allocative inefficiency caused by oversupply and *shirking-control devices* to eliminate X-inefficiency. Both types of inefficiency dissipate consumer surplus.

Both control devices must be used simultaneously. If only output is controlled, the bureau will have an incentive to increase X-inefficiency in order to maximize its budget. Likewise, if only shirking-control devices are used, the bureau will have an incentive to increase its output in order to maximize its budget. Moreover, shirking-control devices such as performance-related pay for bureaucrats may be of limited effectiveness in reducing X-inefficiency because the sponsor may be heavily dependent upon the bureau in defining and measuring that performance. Clearly, bureaucrats will have an incentive to frustrate such control measures by advocating definitions and measures of performance that protect their positions.

It is arguable that it is costlier to police X-inefficiency than allocative inefficiency. The latter can be constrained directly by centrally-specified output levels or indirectly by the centre's allocation of budget. However, X-inefficiency requires detailed case studies of least-cost practice in order to eliminate organizational slack and minimize transaction costs. This explains the roles of bodies such as the UK's Audit Commission for local government (Palmer 1992).

Recognizing the limitations of shirking-control devices provides additional justification for output-control devices. Controlling output by controlling expenditure can eliminate excess production *and* put pressure on bureaucrats to reduce service costs in order to maintain output in the face of shrinking financial resources. In other words, central control over local government spending can be legitimized by the need to avoid *both* excess supply and excess costs. However, it does not remove the need for other control measures designed to reduce the monopoly power of the bureau, such as the stimulation of competition among service providers. Measures include competitive tendering for service contracts and service voucher schemes (see Chapters 4 and 13). Such measures increasing the scope for exit will be more effective than strengthening voice if such bureaucratic behaviour is endemic throughout local government and if information about service costs is asymmetric in favour of bureaucrats (see Chapters 3 and 4).

It could be argued that it is a local, not central, government responsibility to introduce output-control devices and shirking-control devices. Local government associations could identify 'best practice' amongst their members and recommend their other members adopt it for their own service provision.

The effectiveness of this approach depends upon the willingness of individual authorities to adopt cost-saving measures. Moreover, central government will be concerned to the extent that it pays grants to local authorities, those grants possibly being used contrary to central government's objectives.

Put simply, bureaucrats will use as much as possible of any increase in grants to maximize their budgets (and therefore their own welfares) rather than see any returned to voters via reduced local taxes. This may be contrary to the rationale underpinning payment of the grant, for example where it was intended to reduce local tax levels below those existing before payment of the grant. Instead, the outcome is that tax levels remain unchanged because all of the grant is spent on excessive levels of service provision. Central government may therefore wish to control local government spending in order to avoid such an outcome – referred to as 'the flypaper effect' (see Chapter 11).

Summary of the Microeconomic Rationale for Central Control

Lack of competitive processes in the supply of local government services, pressure group influences, the largely fixed nature of local tax liabilities in the face of falling service levels, and the Niskanen model together provide a compelling *microeconomic* rationale for central control of local spending in order to control costs.

There are two policy options on the *supply-side*: introduce competition (see Chapter 13) and/or introduce performance-related pay tied to a system of performance measurement (see below). These are not necessarily mutually exclusive alternatives, reliance on the latter being greater the less the scope for the former. The policing mechanism of competitive markets is preferred, in principle, simply because it is usually a costless spur to greater efficiency, the exception being when economies of scale are lost through fragmentation of the scale of production (see Chapter 2). Competition may eliminate monopoly rents (that is, the mark-up of price over cost) as well as lead to a reduction in unit costs due to improved X-efficiency.

In situations where there is little competition, managerial staff can be expected to trade the disutility of greater effort, search and control of subordinates for the utility of their preferences for less pressure, not trying so hard and better interpersonal relations. The strength of those preferences is ultimately the outcome of management culture and of historical tendencies to write vague labour contracts. Such cultural causes of X-inefficiency are probably at least as important as the degree of monopoly power, although the two may be interdependent. Introduction of greater competition will not, of itself, change the culture in quite the mechanistic way implied by economic theory. Nevertheless, competition and adversity create pressures for changed management practices and, in particular, for more precise and more useful kinds of contract and information (see Chapter 13).

Performance measurement is designed to reduce the degree of organizational slack or managerial discretion. In other words it attempts to remove the consequences of the separation of ownership from control. It may involve profit sharing, share options, work study, management audits and payment-by-results schemes. More generally it attempts to change the management culture.

Performance review is not costless and so should be treated like any other investment, as a means to an end (cost reduction) rather than an end in itself (driven by ideology). The optimal level of expenditure on performance review is where the marginal benefit derived from such measures equals their marginal cost. The possibility of demotivation of staff and employees should not be overlooked, namely where very close supervision of workers creates perverse outcomes of resentment and demotivation, leading to *increased* X-inefficiency (see Chapter 13). Ultimately, the emphasis should be on the efficiency of managers, since they determine not only their own productivity but also that of all co-operating units within the organization. Hence, the inefficiencies created by poor managers can be very large.

DOES PERFORMANCE MONITORING ACTUALLY REDUCE X-INEFFICIENCY?

In the classical market scenario consumers and producers make their own decisions about what to buy and what to produce. However, a common feature of economic life is that resources are often allocated by *delegated* decision-making. In this scenario the *principal* entrusts the *agent* with responsibility for making decisions intended to yield benefits to the former (see Chapter 3). In return the agent is remunerated by the principal. This is a common arrangement in modern companies, the agent being the managers who run the company in return for salaries and the principal being the shareholders who hope to receive dividends financed by profits.

Principal–agent relationships also characterize the public sector, governments deciding policy objectives then delegating to intermediate administrative structures (such as universities or health authorities) responsibilities for achieving them. Similarly, there will be other principal–agent relationships between superiors and subordinates within hierarchical organizations. For example, intermediate administrative bodies delegate day-to-day decision-making to bureaucrats and/or professional employees such as teachers and doctors.

Clearly, use of general terms such as 'the firm' or 'the government' are analytically unhelpful, since they do not recognise the complexity of hierarchical structures within such organizations and the possibility that the objectives of individual agents may differ substantially from those of their principal. There is no reason in principle to expect harmony of objectives between agent and principal. Hence, given the degree of discretion usually available to agents, there is no reason to expect that the principal will always be satisfied by the actions of the agents.

However, such delegated choices create the principal–agent problem whereby the agent may exploit the operational discretion afforded by the principal in order to pursue private objectives which may not be consistent with those of the principal. Ultimately, the issue is one of whether the incentives facing the agent are strong enough to ensure that discretion is always exercised in favour of the principal's interests rather than those of the agent. Hence, the principal has to agree a contract with the agent. That contract has to incorporate incentives which are sufficient to ensure that the agent's privately optimal strategy is in accordance with that of the principal.

This requires the principal to monitor the *outcome* resulting from the work of the agent and to vary the agent's remuneration according to its degree of conformity with the principal's objectives. Outcomes may be readily observable in the private sector, for example the profitability of the company and the size of the resulting dividends to shareholders. In the public sector, however, outcomes may be difficult both to conceptualize and measure. For example, is the role of universities simply to produce lots of employable graduates (a 'degree factory') or to provide a much broader experience of higher education (personal intellectual development or 'human capital') of which employability is one criteria amongst many?

In the event of it being impossible to measure outcomes accurately some proxy measure must be employed. Such proxy measures are referred to as 'performance indicators' and may be complemented by performance norms and output targets. Some or all of these may be set by the principal and linked to the agent's remuneration. For example, in school education the UK government introduced a service norm in the form of a national curriculum as well as performance indicators in the form of 'league tables' for pupil's examination performances and truancy rates. The government (principal) now remunerates individual universities (agents) according to the numbers of students they enrol.

Strictly speaking, however, for the principal–agent problem to be resolved it is necessary to monitor *all* outcomes and to tie them to incentives for remuneration (Whynes 1993). This requires a market-type solution where the principal contracts with the agent for provision of outputs on a fee-for-service basis, illustrated in Figure 5.2.

The principal instructs the agent to produce two outputs, X and Y. Assume the agent produces amounts x_1y_1. The agent is operating at maximum X-efficiency, combination x_1y_1 lying on the production possibilities frontier (PP). Nonetheless, the principal's welfare could be increased by producing combination x_2y_2 so shifting the principal from indifference curve I_{p1} to I_{p2}.

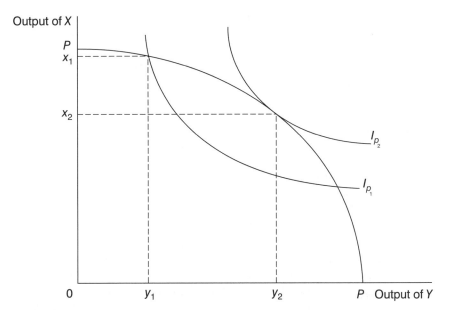

Figure 5.2 *The impact of monitoring*

The principal should therefore introduce either competition or a perform-ance-related remuneration scheme. Competition for contracts (see Chapter 13) would lead to agents producing on their production possibility frontier *and* offering that combination of outputs which maximizes the principal's welfare so as to win the contract, so shifting towards combination $x_2 y_2$. This requires competition also to be present at successive recontracting rounds, otherwise the monopoly confered by the contract may lead to a return to a non-optimal output combination. This will particularly be the case where there are only a few potential suppliers and where they act collusively to share the market between themselves.

Introduction of performance-related remuneration schemes is an alternative to competition. However, it is problematic because not all outputs are mon-itorable (for example, intangible human capital benefits derived from educa-tion). Hence, relating pay only to the performance of monitored tangible outputs (such as school examination results) is likely to cause distortions, services being reconfigured to maximize the rewarded tangible outputs at the expense of intangible outputs not subject to monitoring. Hence, adequate performance indicators must be available otherwise partial or incomplete monitoring may not improve on an absence of monitoring.

Both performance monitoring and competition face the problem that the measurement of quality for public services is extremely complex, if possible at all. Outcome objectives (for example, for health or personal social services) may simply not be measurable and/or quality may be influenced by many other (such as environmental) factors outwith the control of the agent. In such cases, agents' levels of remuneration are often fixed (for instance, annual salary), the principal perhaps requiring provision of at least a minimum level of service set with reference to professional norms.

EUROPEAN EXPERIENCE

Frequent reference has been made to the UK to illustrate the various attempts to control local government expenditures. However, such control has long been a feature of many other countries (Council of Europe 1986). The Council of Europe adopted a three-part classification of countries based on their characteristics in the early 1980s:

1. *No initiatives*: countries where central governments had not pursued an active policy of controlling local government spending. This category included Cyprus and Turkey (where limited local government service responsibilities resulted in little expenditure such that central concern with spending was obviated) and France and Greece (where central governments were committed to maintaining public expenditure and local autonomy). The positions of France and Greece have since shifted to increased central control over local government spending because of the need to meet the Maastricht criteria for economic and monetary union within the EU, originally scheduled to culminate in the adoption of a single currency in 1999.
2. *Limited initiatives*: countries where there had been only limited attempts to influence spending. This category included two subgroups. First, the Scandinavian countries of Denmark, Norway and Sweden where local government spending is substantial but where voluntary agreements between central and local government made detailed controls unnecessary. Second, Austria, Germany and Switzerland, whose federal constitutions enshrine the autonomy of local government and so limit the scope for central control. By the early 1990s Sweden had local tax rate freezing (Oulasvirta 1992) and Germany's Länder system became subject to greater control in bearing a substantial part of the costs of reunification of East and West Germany.
3. *Extensive initiatives*: countries where there had been detailed attempts to influence spending. This category also included two subgroups. The first was a group of countries where central governments had to intervene in order to alleviate impending local fiscal crises (Belgium, Italy, Luxembourg, Portugal and Spain). The second subgroup was comprised of countries which sought to control local spending. In Ireland, central government not only controlled grants, it also abolished the local tax on domestic

dwellings in 1978. The Netherlands and the UK central governments sought reductions in public expenditure and so subjected their local governments to increasingly detailed financial controls. The UK and Ireland represent extreme cases in that their central governments went beyond controlling the aggregate of local government spending, instead controlling the budgets of individual local authorities.

The degree of central control has increased in many European countries since the mid-1980s. This is because of the demands of monetary union within the EU, because of the admission to the EU of countries with tight controls (such as Sweden), because of rising budget deficits in many countries (Bailey 1995, ch. 11), and because the increasing global openess of economies limits the scope for divergent public expenditure patterns.

The European Charter of Local Self-Government gives the impression that a given degree of local autonomy can be determined at a specific point in time. However, local autonomy is as much an outcome of historical processes as it is of a charter published at any particular point in time. In the UK for example, central government has granted powers to local government over a considerable period of time through innumerable general and local acts. This has resulted in local government service expenditures

> being determined not by formal requirements alone nor by free local choice but by a complex mixture of pressures and influences. Informal advice and exhortation from government departments, inspection, nationally accepted standards, accumulated past practice, professional attitudes, political influences and actions by various pressure groups, national and local, all play a part in determining local government expenditure, along with the statutory provisions. (Cmnd 6453, Annex 12, para. 4)

The fact that the newly-elected Labour Government signed the European Charter in 1997 is unlikely to change this scenario. Although the charter enshrines the principle of local democracy, the degree to which it is implemented in practice is determined by the interaction of institutional, cultural, political, economic and other factors.

CONCLUSIONS

The rationale for central government control of local government spending is based upon both macroeconomic (demand-side) and microeconomic (supply-side) considerations. While constraints on aggregate supply are many and varied, local government spending will constitute a supply-side constraint if it crowds out private consumption and investment or if it wields significant monopoly power. Local government revenues and expenditures may be subject to central control for macroeconomic purposes, whether the rationale be

Keynesian or monetarist. They may also be subject to central control in order to eliminate allocative inefficiency and X-inefficiency arising from microeconomic distortions of decisions regarding output levels and production methods.

While the macroeconomic rationale for central control of local government spending has long been recognized, the microeconomic rationale has emerged much more recently, during the 1980s in particular. In combination, the macro and micro rationales severely qualify Articles 3 and 9 of the European Charter of Local Self-Government reproduced at the beginning of this chapter. In recognizing that local autonomy can only be exercised 'within national economic policy' the charter effectively makes indeterminate the degree of local autonomy. Moreover, local autonomy is as much an outcome of historical processes as it is of a charter published at any particular point in time.

Central government faces inherent difficulties in attempting to control local government spending. This is not just because it is technically and administratively difficult to control all sources of local government income. It may also be politically difficult to institute such control because local governments are major providers of public services underpinning the welfare state. Hence, notwithstanding a financing system which is technically capable of controlling local government expenditures, central government may lack the political will to do so. This may explain the increasing attention given to performance appraisal in some countries as a means of reducing organisational slack and so improving X-efficiency.

Ultimately, central government may decide that the most effective way of restraining local government expenditures is to reassign responsibilities. It could take some services out of local government and provide them directly from the centre (for example, health) or reassign their provision to non-elected public sector bodies or quangos (for example, higher education). Transfer of responsibilities may be more likely for services the provision of which is a statutory duty (such as education), and less likely for those provided on the basis of purely permissive powers (such as leisure). Central government could also transfer some services to the voluntary sector (for instance, social care) or privatize them where feasible (for instance, municipal housing). Those remaining within the local government sector could be made more cost-effective by introducing competition via external and internal markets. Given the possibility of distortion of performance monitoring, competition is to be preferred, perhaps in association with performance monitoring. The options for competition were briefly considered in Chapter 4 and will be returned to in more detail in Chapter 13. In total, these measures imply a radical change in the operations of local government (see Chapter 12). The next chapter examines the dynamics of local government expenditures in terms of the inherent tendency to fiscal stress.

6   Fiscal Stress

The financial systems on which resources available to local authorities are based shall be of a sufficiently diversified and buoyant nature to enable them to keep pace as far as practically possible with the real evolution of the cost of carrying out their tasks.

(European Charter of Local Self-Government: Article 9)

INTRODUCTION

Attempts by central governments to control local authority spending for the macroeconomic reasons identified in Chapter 5 may create tensions between central and local government. The greater the disparity between central and local government expenditure objectives, the greater the potential for central–local conflict. This is especially the case where central government preferences require local authorities to spend less on services than they wish, because it implies central restrictions on the various sources of local government income. This may create severe budgetary problems for local governments, whereby they find it extremely difficult, if not impossible, to finance all their expenditure needs. This would be contrary to the spirit of Article 9 of the European Charter of Local Self-Government, indicated by the above excerpt.

While such fiscal stress can be endemic to local government in general, it is usually regarded as being restricted to a relatively small number of authorities within any given country. It arises because of the coincidence of an unusual concentration of expenditure needs and a diminishing resource base (whether from grants and/or local taxes). The result is inadequate levels and standards of service relative to local preferences and/or sharply rising local taxes.

DEFINITION AND CAUSES OF FISCAL STRESS

Fiscal stress occurs when there is a tendency for the costs of a given level of service provision to rise faster than the revenue required to finance it. This necessitates either higher local taxes and/or reductions in real expenditures and in service levels. Put simply, fiscal stress is caused by the unbalanced growth of revenues and expenditures leading to a *structural gap* in the local public finances. There are a number of possible explanations, progressing from those which refer to public expenditure in general to those which refer to local government spending in particular.

1. The Crisis of Capitalism

Neo-Marxists see fiscal stress as the necessary outcome of the crisis of capitalism whereby the profits arising from economic growth are held by private individuals whilst the state has to bear the costs of promoting that growth (for example, provision of education and health care services). Hence the structural gap opens up between increasing public expenditures and constrained tax finances, the private sector being reluctant to provide the latter (O'Connor 1973; Hill 1977). O'Connor's legitimation thesis is that the state has to legitimate profit-seeking activities by using public expenditures to address the resulting social and economic problems relating to the unacceptable inequalities in standards of living and quality of life.

2. The Crowding-Out Thesis

At the opposite end of the political spectrum to Neo-Marxists, right-wing theorists argue that growth of the public sector is at the expense of the wealth-creating private sector. The former supposedly 'crowds out' the latter and so results in lower economic growth than would otherwise be the case. Crowding out can be direct (where the public sector employs factors of production, such as skilled labour, that would otherwise be employed in the private sector) or indirect (caused by high interest rates or inflation resulting from government borrowing) – see Chapter 5. Once again, a structural gap opens up as public spending grows whilst crowding out simultaneously inhibits economic growth and the tax revenues which it provides.

3. The Failure of Local Collective Choice

Fiscal stress may be the inevitable outcome of the failure of collective choice for the reasons discussed in Chapter 5, in particular the divergence between those who vote for, those who pay for and those who use public sector services. Benefits are concentrated on service users, many of whom may not be liable to pay local taxes. The lack of matching of benefits and costs may create the structural gap between expenditures and income. Walsh (1988, p. 49) argues that a durable solution to fiscal stress requires 'a reappraisal and reaffirmation of the nature of citizenship and local democracy'. In other words, the economist's model of the utility-maximizing selfish individual as consumer is rejected in favour of the individual as democratically-enlightened citizen.

4. Fiscal Illusion

The public choice perspective argues that intergovernmental grants and low visibility taxes fool voters into thinking that services are cheaper than they really are. Intergovernmental grants reduce the apparent tax cost of additional service levels and so stimulate demand for provision in excess of the economically optimal level where marginal tax cost equals marginal benefit. This is an explanation of 'the flypaper effect' (see Chapter 11). Low visibility taxes are those for which the amount paid is not obvious, for example local sales taxes (see Chapter 8), again creating demand for spending in excess of the economically optimum level. Hence, demand for services outstrips the abilities of local authorities to supply them, creating the structural gap. This is exacerbated by rising expectations of improved local government services, because they lead to mounting demands for expenditure increases (Jackson *et al.* 1982). Add to this the self-interest of pressure groups (who receive a disproportionate share of the benefits of local services whilst costs are spread very widely over all taxpayers), of politicians (who 'buy' votes with more services) and of bureaucrats (more services mean bigger empires, reward and status) and the conditions are created for over-supply of public services compared with what people are willing to pay (see Chapter 5 and Bailey 1990a).

5. Chronic Instability in Fiscal Systems

Referring to the British case, Newton and Karran (1985) argue that 'the fundamental source of instability is the fact that the system tries to balance a wide range of heavy and expensive duties on a remarkably narrow local tax base' (p. 126) and 'the fact that Britain seems set to preserve this state of affairs is not so much a comment on what is often termed the local fiscal crisis, but a reflection on British democracy' (p. 129):

> Altogether exogenous forces are the principal determinants of about 83 per cent of local government expenditure ... the power to raise revenue is also substantially outside local government's control ... local spending can be reduced more quickly and effectively by central government measures, which are more important influences upon wages, inflation or interest rates, than by measures immediately within the practical determinants of local authorities. (Rose and Page 1982, pp. 223 and 227)

In other words, fiscal stress at the local government level is created more by the actions of central government, than by the failure of local collective choice or fiscal illusion.

6. The Relative Price Effect

Baumol (1967, p. 423) argued that

> a large proportion of the services provided by the city are activities falling in the relatively non-progressive sector of the economy...[which]...offers very limited scope for cumulative increases in productivity [and]...the upward trend in the real costs of municipal services cannot be expected to halt; inexorably and cumulatively, whether or not there is inflation, administrative mismanagement or malfeasance, municipal budgets will almost certainly continue to mount in the future, just as they have been doing in the past. This is a trend for which no man and no group should be blamed, for there is nothing that can be done to stop it.

Baumol assumes that private sector wage increases are matched by improved labour productivity such that unit labour costs remain constant in the private sector. He also assumes limited scope for improved labour productivity in the public sector, and that it has to match wage levels in the private sector in order to attract workers, causing unit labour costs to rise in the public sector. Hence, the price of municipal outputs rises relative to those of the private sector. These assumptions have been questioned elsewhere, most notably that the public sector has less scope for productivity improvements than the private sector and that public sector pay increases match those of the private sector (Bailey 1995, ch. 3). Nonetheless, as long as the relative price effect is positive, technological conditions create pressures for increased spending. The resulting fiscal stress cannot be blamed on self-interested pressure groups, central or local politicians or local bureaucrats.

7. The 'Big City' Factor

As a general rule that applies throughout the developed world, larger cities tend to spend more per capita than other local authorities. While some of this higher spending may be incurred voluntarily, it is arguable that urban government is generally more expensive than non-urban government. Higher costs occur because urbanization itself requires higher levels of service provision (for example, spatial planning, refuse collection and disposal, public works and so on); services are more costly to provide than in non-urban areas because of the higher costs of land; and the larger the city, the greater the range of highly specialized and expensive recreational, cultural and special educational facilities and services it must provide to its hinterland. Such hinterland services are not usually fully financed by user-charges (see Chapter 7), such that city governments have to subsidise them – perhaps in recognition of their positive spillover effects (see Chapter 1). In combination, these factors mean that city governments will tend to experience greater fiscal stress than non-urban authorities because of the pressures on their expenditures (Newton 1988).

8. Selective Outmigration

Even without the big city factor, Bradbury *et al.* (1982) argue that selective outmigration of the more affluent groups in less need of local government services (such as those in employment and with their own housing and transport) reinforces fiscal stress in cities because the need for local government expenditure does not decline as fast as population. However, they suggest that fiscal stress is the necessary outcome of desirable trends such as rising real incomes, rising car ownership, rising home ownership and a desire to live in new, low-density suburbs. Hence, rather than seeking to reverse demographic and economic decline, public policy should help cities to adjust to that decline and to avoid negative impacts, especially on the poor.

9. Declining Economic Base

In addition to their rising expenditures, Bahl (1978, p. 8) argued that metropolitan central cities experience a declining economic base, serving to reduce taxable resources. The relative (if not absolute) shift of manufacturing investment and the associated jobs and population from urban to rural areas is common to large cities throughout Europe and North America (Fothergill and Gudgin 1982; Gudgin 1995; Champion *et al.* 1998; and see Chapter 8). In general, the greater the urban scale, the greater the urban–rural shift. In such cases the structural gap between income and expenditure becomes profound and long-lasting. Economic and social deprivation results in inner urban areas.

The first two causes of fiscal stress listed above are clearly mutually exclusive of each other. The other causes of fiscal stress could occur simultaneously with one or other of the first two causes, interacting with each other to cause severe fiscal stress. Many apply to local government in general but the last three apply to cities in particular. Indeed, Newton (1980b, p. 182) argued that 'cities are at the leading edge of the local resource squeeze in that they display, in magnified form, most of the symptoms of financial constraint which affect the larger systems of local government'. Bennett (1980, p. 74) notes that 'it is in urban areas that there is the greatest disparity of expenditure needs and benefits, of revenue burdens and abilities and of financial needs and revenue resources; and hence it is in the city where most concern is focused on the equity of the public fisc.' Boyne (1988) suggests that the amount of 'lever-age' (that is, public subsidy) required to attract private sector investment may be greatly increased in areas experiencing a *'fiscal stress syndrome'* whereby fiscal stress and economic and social deprivation reinforce each other in reducing real incomes through higher local taxes and/or lower service levels.

Severe fiscal stress is more likely if individuals and households choose local government service/tax packages in accordance with the Tiebout hypothesis (see Chapter 4). In particular, fiscal stress may lead to outward migration, citizen-consumers 'voting with their feet' by moving to local governments not experiencing fiscal stress. Nonetheless, the outmigrants may continue to use free or heavily subsidized central city services as they commute back in to their jobs and to leisure and cultural facilities provided by central city author-ities. Hence, it has been argued that residents of suburban municipalities 'exploit' central cities, although American evidence suggests that this has typ-ically been of minor quantitative importance (Bradford and Oates 1974).

More generally, the average costs of services may rise as people move out of the jurisdiction, either because of indivisibilities in service provision or because the groups left behind are those most in need of local government expenditures (for example, those who are unemployed, require provision of municipal housing and assistance with rent payments, and who depend upon public transport). The resulting rise in local tax rates may cause the tax base to shrink as more people and companies move to other jurisdictions (see Chapters 4 and 8), with the effect that the tax rate has to rise even further, stimulating more outmigration, and so on in a self-reinforcing spiral of causa-tion and interaction.

Local governments experiencing spiralling fiscal stress clearly do not con-form with the Tiebout hypothesis in that they fail to attract sufficient res-idents to minimize the average costs of their services (see Chapter 4). This outcome is a specific example of the instabilities created if local authorities pursue highly redistributive policies (see Chapter 1). In effect, the market for local government tax/service packages fails to reach an equilibrium. This has adverse outcomes for welfare and efficiency.

First, welfare losses occur if reductions in service levels as a result of fiscal stress lead to *'multiple deprivation'*, whereby economic and social disadvantage becomes self-reinforcing and increasingly concentrated upon particular socioeconomic groups in particular geographical areas. The characteristics of multiple deprivation include unemployment, low incomes, poor housing, poor educational attainment, lack of vocational skills, racial and ethnic discrimination and so on (Atkins *et al.* 1996). Employers may choose not to locate their businesses in areas of multiple deprivation because of low labour skills, high incidence of crime, for instance. This can lead to further deteriora-tion of skills, further losses of employment, deteriorating housing conditions (since the poor cannot afford to maintain their properties in good repair) and so on.

Second, local authorities experiencing substantial population losses will have considerable spare capacity whilst those experiencing substantial in-migration will increasingly face problems of congestion. There may be market or administrative limits to increasing congestion. Examples, respectively, are where deterioration of service quality stems further inmigration, or where local authorities use their physical planning powers to prevent further housing or other developments. There may, however, be no such limit to excess capacity since it drives up service costs and hence local taxes, leading to further out-migration in a process of cumulative causation. Property values would fall (at least in relative, if not absolute, terms) but inmigration will not be stimulated if there are few if any jobs to attract potential residents. This would be an allocatively inefficient use of a nation's productive capacity.

The near bankruptcy of the New York city government in the mid-1970s was seen as a prime example of fiscal stress but Nathan and Adams (1976) warned of the dangers of overgeneralizing from this case. In particular they stressed that every city is different and that other American cities faced much more serious social and economic problems than New York and yet had avoided such catastrophic fiscal stress (see, for example, Alcaly and Mermelstein 1977; Wolman 1982; Rubin 1985; Gramlich 1976; Sharp and Elkins 1987; Morgan and Pammer 1988; and Hoggart 1991). Glassberg (1981, p. 165) announced that 'the urban fiscal crisis becomes routine' and that 'fiscal stringency has become more the norm than the exception'. Nonetheless, more recently, Orange county went bankrupt in 1994 and Los Angeles county was on the verge of bankruptcy in 1995.

Fiscal stress seems to have been less pronounced in the UK because

by transferring the greater part of the financial responsibility for local services to central government, Britain largely avoided the urban fiscal crisis that hit the United States. [There was]...a genuine concern to improve the identification of the needs of the cities and to meet the particular circumstances of metropolitan decline. (Kirwan 1980, p. 98)

The UK central government attempted to protect local governments with high per capita expenditure needs and low per capita resources (so-called 'inner city authorities'), paying them intergovernmental grants accordingly (see Chapter 9). Nevertheless, 'the available evidence indicates that the poorest areas tend to remain relatively poor, even though they are very considerably better off with the existing grant system than without it' (Newton 1981, pp. 219–20).

The main problem is that, although well developed as a concept, attempts to measure precisely fiscal stress faced by individual authorities have proven unsuccessful because of methodological difficulties in objectively assessing need to spend and because of interrelationships between expenditures and effort-related grants (Gibson *et al.* 1987).

Kirwan (1980, p. 99) had noted rather prophetically that impending public expenditure restraint and cuts in national taxes would lead to the very fiscal crisis that the UK grant system had been so successful in avoiding. Bennett (1982, pp. 246–8) found early evidence of this effect with cuts in grant and rising local tax rates being particularly marked in London and some Metropolitan Districts. The 1970s were pervaded by a political commitment to discriminating in favour of the UK's inner city authorities through payments of public money. This had largely evaporated by the mid-1980s (Mouritzen 1991). The subsequent adoption of central controls of local budgets (see Chapter 5) served to shift the balance of fiscal stress from high local tax increases towards lower service levels.

It is, of course, possible to ameliorate such fiscal squeeze by providing city governments with an adequate local tax base and a system of intergovernmental grants which compensate such local authorities for relatively high per capita needs and/or relatively low per capita resources (see Chapter 9). However, this may exacerbate both fiscal illusion and the failure of collective choice which, as noted above, are hypothesized causes of a structural gap between incomes and expenditures. Moreover, the narrower the local tax base, the greater the importance of the adequacy of the grant system, and so the greater the potential for chronic instability of the fiscal system.

FISCAL STRESS AND SYSTEMS OF FINANCE: THE GEARING EFFECT

Chronic instability of fiscal systems results from the high 'gearing' between expenditures and local tax levels. The 'gearing effect' measures the proportionate impact of changes in expenditures and/or intergovernmental grants on local tax levels. The gearing effect can be illustrated by the system of local government finance introduced in Britain in 1990/91.

As already noted in Chapter 5, the three main changes were the replacement of domestic rates (a property tax) by the Community Charge (dubbed 'the poll tax'), nationalization of the local business rate and a new system of central government grants. The contributions from both business and national government became fixed lump-sum payments, this arrangement continuing after replacement of the Community Charge by Council Tax (a modified local property tax) in 1993. Hence, the local domestic tax has had to finance all of any locally-determined marginal discretionary expenditure since 1990.

A high share of fixed lump-sum payments (that is, intergovernmental grants and business rates) within total revenue makes it very expensive in local tax terms for individual authorities to increase service levels. A small proportionate increase in total spending requires a disproportionately large increase in the local tax. A study of British local authorities experiencing urban stress during the late 1980s and early 1990s found that their gearing effects had increased substantially as a result of the new system of finance

(Bailey 1991). Chapter 5 noted that the Council Tax has to rise by 5 per cent in order to increase net expenditure by 1 per cent, given that the tax only raises about 20 per cent of local government income.

A high gearing effect also means that the local tax level will have to rise by a substantial amount to make up for a relatively small revenue shortfall. This is the case if central government grants are cut or, alternatively, displays such significant inertia that they fail to compensate fully for increased expenditure needs. The latter is a particular problem where central government's funding model is unresponsive to the dynamics of social, economic and demographic change. Hence, chronic instability of fiscal systems results when the local tax is constrained to a small proportion of total revenue. This is one of the causes of fiscal stress listed above. It is particularly the case when local governments dominated by left-wing parties wish to increase spending contrary to central government's policy to reduce public expenditure. The critical importance of the fiscal structure in generating fiscal stress through a high gearing effect qualifies the argument that 'the roots of the crisis are political in nature' (Derrick 1988, p. 239). The roots may, indeed be political, but the extent of crisis reflects the fiscal structure, namely the small proportion of finance coming from the local tax base.

The root cause of this increased fiscal stress was not the nature of the local tax itself, nor the political differences between central and local government, but rather the increased dependence on funds from central government. This conclusion would apply to any local tax restricted to such a small share of total income. The reduction in the share of spending financed by the local tax combined with payment of a fixed lump-sum grant increased the gearing effect. This led to anomalies both in the exercise of local discretion and in the redetermination of grants. The very high gearing effects led to substantial percentage increases in local tax rates. Where central government underestimated need to spend for authorities experiencing urban stress, the result was a coincidence of multiple deprivation and high percentage increases in local tax rates from year to year.

These distortions were made unnecessarily severe simply because the local tax base was (and still is) inadequate to finance the wide range of local government services. As a result, the grant system has had to 'overfund' local government expenditures, paying local authorities more than is necessary to equalize for differing per capita expenditure needs and differing per capita local taxable resources, simply to constrain local tax rates within politically acceptable upper limits (see Chapter 9). However, this overfunding itself created the high gearing effects. As noted in Chapter 5, central government ultimately felt obliged to set limits on the increases in local tax rates from one year to the next and, subsequently, on their budgets. Local autonomy was therefore severely constrained, this being inconsistent with the European Charter of Local Self-Government (see the quotations at the start of Chapters 5 and 7). The result is that, in the UK, the manifestations of fiscal stress have been redirected from upward pressures on local tax levels to downward pressures on service levels.

A CASE-STUDY OF THE COSTS OF DEMOGRAPHIC DECLINE

Eversley (1972) and Stone (1978) argued that local authority costs do not decline pro rata with declines in population and economic activity so that local authorities in the declining conurbations are particularly disadvantaged. This could be due to supply rigidities (indivisibilities) which prevent steady progressive reductions in service levels in line with falling population, or because selective outmigration of the more self-sufficient population groups leaves behind those people who make above-average demands upon local services. In both cases the per capita costs of service delivery will rise. Furthermore if population declines faster than the local tax base then the subsequent rise in per capita taxable resources results in a loss of any resource-equalizing grant, which compensates for inadequate per capita taxable resources (see Chapter 9), putting upward pressure on local tax rates. Kennett (1980a, 1980b) found UK evidence supporting these hypotheses.

The UK school education service provides a useful case-study for assessing whether demographic decline exacerbates fiscal stress. School education is by far the largest single local government service in the UK (approaching half of expenditure) and recently experienced major declines in pupil numbers as the effect of falling birth-rates worked through the demographic age-structure. It provides an example of just how difficult it is to achieve expenditure reductions and/or efficiency gains.

Uncertainty relating to future pupil numbers may constrain adjustment to current falls. While the present supply of educational inputs is known (for example, numbers of teachers and school places), future demand for those resources is subject to considerable uncertainty. This uncertainty may inhibit the efficient rationalization of the service. National projections of future pupil numbers are subject to increasing uncertainty the further into the future those projections are made, error margins typically being around 20 per cent of the principal projection. This is because forecasts of future female fertility rates are subject to considerable uncertainty. Fertility rates cannot simply be extrapolated on the basis of past trends since the economic, social and other factors determining the birth-rate at any one point in time are not susceptible to accurate forecasting. Indeed, there have been unexpectedly sharp reversals of trends in the numbers of births during the past five or six decades.

Projections of secondary school pupils (compulsory age range 11–16) are subject to less uncertainty than those for primary school pupils (compulsory age range 5–11) simply because the effects of changing fertility rates take longer to feed through to the older age group. However, even secondary school pupil numbers can vary unexpectedly as the staying-on rate for pupils beyond compulsory school age (ages 16–18) varies. Hence, the potential for unanticipated changes in pupil demand for secondary education is both real and substantial.

These uncertainties at national level are exacerbated at the local level. Birth-rates tend to differ between local governments in reflection of their differing demographic and socioeconomic structures, perhaps being higher in deprived inner-city areas than in affluent suburbs. Moreover, pupil numbers are heavily affected by population migration. The postwar shift of population from city to suburbs has recently been complicated by the regentrification of some inner cities (as young, childless, affluent groups rehabilitate former working-class areas – see Chapter 4) at the same time that de-urbanization has occured in many Western countries.

Hence, in planning educational provision, local governments must allow a substantial safety margin in order to cope with uncertainties about the size of the school-age population, about the timing of peaks and troughs in pupil numbers, and about the spatial location of demand within their jurisdictions. Intrajurisdictional demand for school places will be further complicated by the need to maintain home-to-school travelling distances within acceptable bounds (especially for primary school pupils) and the need, if any, to make provision for schools of differing religious denominations.

Although uncertainty about future pupil numbers inhibits service rationalization, it affects the provision of school places more than the recruitment of teachers, the latter not being site-specific. In principle, local authorities can vary their teaching forces in line with pupil numbers. More binding constraints are imposed by the need to provide a full curriculum of academic subjects and the resistance of teacher unions to compulsory redundancies.

In these cases, the resulting smaller class and school sizes (in terms of number of pupils) would lead to short-run average costs rising above long-run average costs (see Chapter 2). However, considerable savings can still be achieved, since school education has a high proportion of labour costs (about three-quarters) within total costs. Nonetheless, it will be difficult to maintain teacher costs per pupil constant in the face of falling pupil numbers for three reasons:

1. *Natural wastage* of teachers will be of limited effectiveness. Teachers retiring, leaving to take up employment elsewhere, leaving to start a family, or dying in service are not replaced. However, this measure is limited because of the need to provide a balanced range of academic subjects in each school and because wastage rates will fall as other education authorities also reduce their recruitment of teachers, assuming a national fall in pupil numbers.

2. *Early retirement* is of limited effectiveness and is expensive. The effectiveness of this measure depends upon the age profile of teachers and is severely limited if most teachers are in the younger age groups and older

teachers are concentrated in academic subjects experiencing teacher recruitment difficulties. Early retirement is also expensive since the public sector (if not local governments themselves) has to make up the pension contributions that would have been paid by both employee and employer had the teacher not taken early retirement.

3. *Compulsory and/or voluntary redundancies* are costly. A programme of redundancies would facilitate the planning of the teacher profile but is costly in terms of redundancy payments. It would cost less if younger teachers were made redundant since they have had less time in employment to build up entitlement to compensation. Teacher costs per pupil would rise nonetheless because 'grade drift' would occur as the proportion of promoted posts in total teaching posts rose, as would 'incremental drift' as the average age (and therefore average salary) of teachers rose. Hence, average teacher costs per pupil is likely to increase even if pupil–teacher ratios (PTRs) are kept constant.

The inevitable rise in costs is illustrated in Figure 6.1, which shows that a fall in pupil numbers from Q_2 to Q_1 causes an increase in per pupil costs from C_2 to C_1, because staff and buildings are under-utilized, because shedding staff is costly, and because of grade and incremental drift. In contrast, an increase in pupil numbers from Q_2 to Q_3 would reduce unit costs from C_2 to C_3 since, while the supply of teachers can be assumed to be highly elastic, the fixed costs of buildings are spread over a larger number of pupils. The diagram is drawn to demonstrate that, for a given change in pupil numbers (that is, $Q_2 - Q_1 = Q_3 - Q_2$), a fall in pupil numbers causes a larger proportionate change in costs per pupil than a rise (that is, $C_1 - C_2$ is greater than $C_2 - C_3$). This is based on the usual assumption that capital is fixed in the short run (see Chapter 2).

In practice, local authorities often argue that falling pupil numbers provide the opportunity to increase educational standards by maintaining total spending constant so that PTRs fall. Expenditure per pupil therefore increases but spending per pupil does not necessarily equate with educational standards. First, spending may be used to maintain surplus capacity (such as school space) which does little to improve educational standards. Second, beyond a point, further reductions in PTRs may result in little or no improvement of pupils' education or achievements. In other words, diminishing marginal educational returns to falling PTRs may be experienced.

Falling PTRs are also likely because of the resistance of teacher unions to job losses and the strong obstacles to service reduction in the decision-making machinery of local government. Local politicians may have spent many years promoting the expansion of the school education service and be reluctant to introduce cuts. Education may predominate the committee-based system of local government and be unwilling to see financial resources freed by falling pupil numbers diverted to other services, a public choice perspective (see Chapters 1 and 5). The advantageous position of education may reflect its

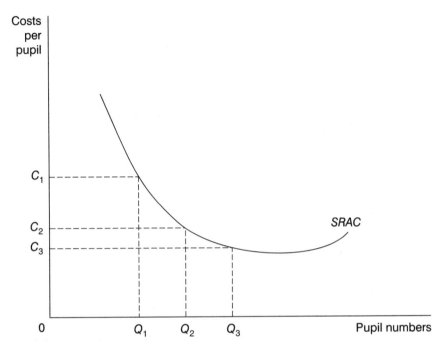

Figure 6.1 *Declining pupil numbers and unit costs*

long-established role within local government, its stronger research and planning function compared with other services, and the greater clarity of its service base (that is, pupils versus ill-defined clients for other services such as community care). There will also be resistance on the part of users to service reductions not directly matched by reductions in their liability to pay taxes (see Chapter 5) and the uncertainties relating to future pupil numbers.

In the UK case, during the 1970s and 1980s costs per pupil rose much further than they necessarily had to because major British city education authorities were slow to respond to falling pupil numbers. They adopted *ad hoc* or piecemeal responses to falling school rolls rather than a more systematic, radical city-wide strategy. Even allowing for a 10 per cent fall in PTRs, on the grounds that education authorities took the opportunity to improve educational standards by having fewer pupils per teacher, it appears that major city authorities achieved less than two-thirds of potential savings, and in some cases not much more than half (Bailey 1982a, 1982b).

Government figures for subsequent years showed increasing amounts of surplus school accommodation. Figures relating to 1994 revealed that state *primary* schools still had more than 1 million surplus school places, about 13 per cent of their total capacity. This resulted in wasted costs for heating, maintenance and other services costing local authorities at least £140 million per annum, more than doubling after taking into account unnecessary teaching costs arising as a result of half-empty schools. State *secondary* schools had a further 600 000 surplus places. Pupil numbers continued to fall in major British city education authorities during the 1990s and some continued to have surpluses in excess of a third of school places.

This scenario has been complicated by two factors. First, increased parental choice of school for their children may require or result in some surplus places. Nonetheless, the UK government announced in 1998 that it would close schools judged to be underperforming in educational terms and which had substantial surplus pupil places (for example, over 25 per cent of total places). Second, the earlier ability of schools to 'opt-out' of local education authority control meant that those threatened with closure by the authority had more incentive to opt-out of its control and become directly funded by central government (see Chapters 4 and 12).

Local education authorities can no longer redraw school catchment areas to match demand with the supply of school places in a particular locality. Hence, any economies of scale at the level of the local education authority may have been lost. Nonetheless, a large proportion of surplus school places in 1998 (nearly 10 per cent of total places in England's schools) reflected the unwillingness of local authorities to act swiftly to reduce excess school accommodation. In turn, this led to unnecessarily high staffing levels and accommodation costs.

Even before the onset of falling pupil numbers, Peacock and Wiseman (1964) argued that the near monopoly position of UK local education authorities gave little impetus to the achievement of cost savings. Whilst decentralization of budgets to individual schools (under the early 1990s Local Management of Schools initiative) has provided an incentive for head teachers to make surplus teachers redundant, this applies at the school level rather than at the education authority level. Further substantial savings in teaching and accommodation costs could be achieved, either by authority-wide rationalization of school education or by the introduction of more effective competition between schools (such as a voucher scheme, see Chapter 2).

The foregoing analysis has been in terms of cost per *pupil*. However, fiscal stress will arise on the expenditure side only if school education costs rise per head of *population*. If pupils fall faster than population, educational costs per head of population fall, provided that declining pupil numbers does not impose such high costs on local authorities that the rising costs per pupil more than offset the gains otherwise obtained. School education costs per head of *population* will rise where the proportion of pupils in total population rises (whether total population is declining, constant or rising), even if the costs of educating *pupils* remain constant. Hence, educational costs can rise on two fronts. First, the rising costs per pupil brought about by declining pupil numbers. Secondly, the rising costs per head of population brought about by rising proportions of school children within total population.

In summary, the education case study demonstrates a general conclusion that

> only if local authorities produce under conditions of constant returns to scale, have no contractual obligations, can forecast precisely future demands for their services, lose population in a balanced way and can avoid economic decline spilling over into poverty creation, then, and only then, can they avoid some adverse fiscal effects. (Cameron and Bailey 1987, p. 213)

Where these technological, legal and demographic conditions do not prevail, there can be no precise mathematical relationship between loss of population and expenditures per head of population. In particular, it cannot be concluded that if population falls by x per cent per capita expenditures will rise by y per cent. This is because decline will not affect all demographic groups equally. It is not even possible to derive a formula for a specific service delivered to a specific demographic group, such as school education, because the policy response of local governments has a much greater impact than the technological characteristics of services in terms of any indivisibilities within the production function. Policy responses relate not only to the acceptability of compulsory redundances amongst teaching staff. They also reflect educational philosophies and theories regarding maximum class sizes, breadth of curriculum, organization of post-compulsory school education and so on. Costs are highly sensitive to the precise form of reorganisation undertaken by each local authority. For example, tertiary colleges can make the most efficient use of teaching staff in providing a given curriculum by avoiding unnecessarily small class sizes in schools (Bailey 1984).

CONCLUSIONS

Though fiscal stress is a well-developed and clear concept, it is impossible to quantify it in such a way that it can be used to determine the amounts of financial allocations from central to local governments. Fiscal stress seems to be endemic in the public sectors of many countries. It may be the result of the lack of matching of decisions to spend with liability to pay the resulting costs. If so, it is the inevitable outcome of the collective financing of public services. It may be exacerbated by technological factors, if there is limited scope for productivity improvements.

At the local level, fiscal stress will be exacerbated by demographic and economic decline because of the resulting impact upon local revenues and expenditures. The local effect is further exacerbated if selective outmigration from cities causes revenues per capita to fall faster than need to spend per head of population. Payment of intergovernmental grants which attempt to take account of differing per capita taxable resources will be reduced to the extent that population falls faster than the local tax base. A fiscal gap will therefore open up between need to spend and the available resource base.

Particularly severe fiscal stress is confined to individual local authorities which lose population such that the unit costs of their services rise faster than the ability of their revenue sources to finance them. In this case, Tiebout's voting with the feet leads to disequilibrium in the market for local government tax and service packages. Ultimately, local authorities experiencing economic and demographic decline may verge upon bankruptcy.

The case-study of the impact of demographic decline on the school education service illustrated the resulting unavoidable rise in educational costs per pupil arising from long-term indivisibilities in education inputs. However, in the UK case, educational unit costs also rose because of improvements in the standard of service, in part made possible by falling pupil numbers releasing the necessary finance. Moreover, inertia on the part of education authorities meant that unit costs rose because they did not act fast enough to dispose of surplus school premises. Since it is difficult in practice to measure separately the influence of each of these three factors on the rising costs per pupil, it is also difficult to determine how much finance should be paid to individual local governments in order to compensate them for the unavoidable costs. Hence, in a period of general financial restraint on the public sector, any tendency towards fiscal stress will be exacerbated for those local authorities experiencing demographic and economic decline. Fiscal stress will be further exacerbated by high gearing ratios between spending and local taxes, particularly in that they create chronic instability in fiscal systems.

This demonstrates the need for a system of local government finance which does not widen any emergent structural gap in the local public finances. This is the essence of that part of Article 9 of the European Charter for Local Self-Government reproduced at the beginning of this chapter. Assessment of the adequacy of local government income sources requires a more detailed examination of local government charges, taxes and intergovernmental grants in Chapters 7, 8 and 9 respectively. The analysis of this chapter has shown just how difficult it may be to fulfil the principles of Article 9.

7 The Economics of Local Government Charges

*Part at least of the financial resources of local authorities shall derive from local taxes and **charges** of which, within the limits of statute, they have the power to determine the rate.*

(European Charter of Local Self-Government: Article 9)

INTRODUCTION

Many texts dealing with local government finance either ignore charges or deal with them only after considering intergovernmental grants and local taxation. This reflects the perceived greater importance of the alternative methods of financing local government and the emphasis, within the economics literature, on fiscal federalism. Charges are often perceived as the financing instrument of last resort. However, within conventional economic analysis, it could be expected that local taxes and grants would only be used to part-finance those services (or parts of services) which could not be wholly financed by charges because of market failure (see Chapter 1). Otherwise, the achievement of allocative efficiency relies upon consumer sovereignity being safeguarded through market mechanisms that rely on suppliers and consumers responding to product prices.

When analysing exit and voice in Chapter 3, it was concluded that service providers will only be made more responsive to service users if their revenues are directly dependent upon the volume of use of their outputs. Such a financing arrangement provides incentives for service providers since, as in the private sector, poor quality leads to loss of revenue from sales. This provides the rationale for substitution of variable for fixed financing methodologies for service providers. Rather than being guaranteed revenue from local taxes or from intergovernmental grants, service providers could be made heavily dependent upon revenues directly related to service use. Those revenues could be generated by direct charges on users, provided they were compatible with service objectives and with notions of equity.

THEORETICAL PERSPECTIVES

Use of the term 'charge' rather than 'price' recognises the administrative, rather than market, determination of payments. The Organization for Economic

Co-operation and Development (OECD) provides a standardized definition of user-charges, namely *requited* payments. The link between payment and service provided may vary considerably in terms of the degree of cost recovery. At least part of such variations can be justified in theoretical terms where the objective is to maximize allocative efficiency. A full explanation is provided elsewhere (Bailey 1995, ch. 2), only a brief exposition being provided here.

Pure public goods have to be provided free at the point of use because their non-excludability means that payment cannot be secured from 'free riders' and any one person's use of the service is not rival with that of other users. In contrast, pure private goods are both rival and excludable and charges should fully reflect the costs of their provision if allocative efficiency is to be secured. As already noted in Chapter 1, very few local government services qualify as public goods, most being categorized as mixed goods with positive externality or merit good features. These characteristics justify only *partial* subsidy. For services generating positive externalities or spillovers, the amount of subsidy should be directly related to the monetary value of the benefits bestowed upon others by the consumer's use of the service. Likewise, in respect of merit good characteristics, the value of the subsidy should be directly related to the degree of undervaluation (in terms of willingness to pay) of a service by myopic consumers.

These theoretical considerations make clear that there are limits to the amount of subsidy that should be paid to support the provision of local government services. Nonetheless, they also justify subsidy in allocative efficiency terms, quite separately from equity issues based upon ability to pay. The amount of subsidy which must be paid if allocative efficiency is to be maximized is an empirical question. In respect of the UK, Foster *et al.* (1980) argue that these market failure characteristics would justify completely free provision for no more than a tenth of local authorities' service outputs. Other services would also be partially subsidized but, in practice, it is difficult to derive monetary values for positive externality and merit good characteristics. While the proportions of subsidy are debatable, it is clear that charges could be levied on the majority of local government services, although only if allocative efficiency considerations prevailed over social considerations.

Hence, reference to economic theory would lead one to expect that local governments make use of charges for the majority of their services and, further, that charges are based upon the usual long-run marginal cost criteria (Bailey 1995, ch. 6). However, economic theory seems to have had little impact on the charging practices of local governments in developed countries. For both the USA and UK respectively, Bird (1976) and Prest (1982) pointed to the sharp contrast between the economic theory of pricing and the lack of its application in practice. There are two charging concepts.

1. Charging in Relation to Costs

Public sector pricing theory recommends that prices be set equal to long-run marginal costs (that is, long-term incremental capital and running costs) so as to achieve allocative efficiency. This pricing rule both maximizes the output derived from finite productive resources and matches the distribution of that output with willingness to pay the incremental costs of its production. By definition, it also maximizes economic welfare. Variation from this rule is only sanctioned during periods of excess capacity (where output demanded is less than available supply). In such cases price should equal short-run marginal cost (essentially just running costs) but, if overcapacity is permanent, the productive facility should not be replaced upon its economic exhaustion.

The optimal two-part tariff has both a fixed component (to recover capital costs) and a variable component (to recover running costs). It is particularly suitable for public utility pricing, being able to differentiate between the costs imposed by peak and off-peak patterns of demand. However, there are both theoretical and practical problems associated with marginal cost pricing. First, the assumptions on which the theory of allocative efficiency is based generally do not hold and, second, implementation may not be feasible.

The theory requires there to be no external effects in consumption or production (that is, no impacts on those other than the producer and the consumer) and competitive forces operating throughout the economy. Neither of these is the case in practice. Services such as education have profound, though intangible, effects on both society and the economy and monopoly power is certainly more widespread than are perfectly competitive forces. Moreover, the theory assumes that the Paretian criterion for welfare is the objective (in particular that the individual is the best judge of personal welfare) and that the distribution of income and welfare resulting from marginal cost pricing is acceptable. These assumptions are invariably invalid in the local government context, since services are often provided free at the point of consumption specifically because the market distribution is deemed unsatisfactory (for example, because the fixed component or standing charge is effectively a regressive tax) and collective/objective decisions often override individual/subjective rationality (compulsory school education is an example). Hence, difficulties in strictly adhering to economic pricing rules in the public utility industries are magnified by profound equity and constitutional factors for non-industrial municipal services.

It has long been recognized that marginal cost pricing is only one of a number of imperfect possibilities because the relevant information is simply not available (Bird 1976). Local authority cost data is often grossly deficient, predominantly identifying sources and uses of funds rather than current replacement costs or opportunity costs. Such figures are also influenced by the esoteric accounting practices noted in Chapter 2. For example, straight-line depreciation would initially result in lower reported costs (and therefore charges) than accelerated depreciation (Frenckner 1989). Overheads and loans pooling, 'creative accounting' techniques and other arbitrary measures serve to highlight the irrelevance of local government accounts in identifying true economic costs (Elcock *et al.* 1989; Cmnd 9714).

Moreover, if marginal cost pricing is to mimic the first-best allocation of resources, account has to be taken of the interrelationships between both substitutes and complementary goods and services (such as public and private housing and roads and cars respectively) and the impact of price changes on real incomes and therefore on demands for goods and services (Baumol and Bradford 1970; Feldstein 1972). Hence, it is now recognized that marginal cost pricing is not an efficient pricing rule but simply a way of recovering costs: it is a concept, *not* a pricing policy.

The efficiency ideal of marginal cost pricing can only work in mechanistic mathematical models where agents are programmed automatons operating within clearly defined utility and cost functions within competitive markets. This is obviously not the case for municipal services, charges being determined as the result of the politico/bureaucratic process.

2. Charging in Relation to Benefit

The identification of benefits is even more difficult than the identification of true economic costs. Output, consumption and benefit received are all difficult to identify and measure. Output is not necessarily the same as consumption – for example, over-capacity in schools facing falling pupil numbers (see Chapter 6). Politicians and bureaucrats may value services more highly than the actual recipients of those services. It is also not clear what the benefits of some services will be prior to their consumption by individuals (for example, public library information services). Net and gross benefit will differ, the gross valuation exceeding the net valuation by the monetary value of travel costs, say, to a sports facility, this being the transport fare plus the value of time spent travelling (Losch 1954; Bennett 1980; Sharpe and Newton 1984). Free-rider problems will exist for local public goods such as street lighting, refuse disposal and law and order. Besides, experience with discriminatory fares (positively related to willingness to pay, a proxy for benefit received) suggests that they are only practical for broad groups of users and, even then, can lead to complex fare structures and confusion and resentment on the part of consumers such as rail passengers (Trotter 1985).

These caveats serve to qualify the UK government's assertion that 'Realistic charging policies help to improve the efficient use of resources' (Cmnd 9714, para. 7.3). The government's claim that 'effective pricing policies help to make more explicit the extent of the subsidy that is provided and to whom' (Ibid., para. 7.6) would appear to have greater validity, in that increased use of charges would ideally require the accurate identification of both service costs and service take-up by prioritized and other groups of user, so aiding the more effective targeting of both service provision and subsidy.

Charges and the Collective Provision of Services

Most advocates of the increased use of service charges see them as an *altern-ative* to collective action in that they are intended to replicate free market forces and are part of an overall strategy to roll back the frontiers of the state (for example, see Harris and Seldon 1976). This scenario is the logical out-come of an overwhelming emphasis on economic efficiency to the near com-plete exclusion of the institutional, constitutional and liberal democratic context of local government. In that sense it is a highly blinkered approach to local government as a regulatory response to the problems caused by market failure. Moreover, it takes the view that government failure is likely to be of greater significance than market failure. It makes a methodologically invalid comparison of free markets with government provision, failing to recognise that modern corporations exist in the private sector because of market ineffi-ciencies arising out of transaction costs (see Chapter 3). The methodologically valid comparison is government provision versus provision by private sector companies. Nonetheless, government failure is a serious problem arising from the failure of collective choice.

Chapter 5 noted that the major part of redistribution at the local level is through service provision and, further, that liability to pay the local tax does not vary with service use. Hence, it was concluded that there is an incentive for subgroups within a local authority to seek to increase their consumption of those services of particular benefit to themselves, knowing that the extra tax payments required to finance increased service consumption are paid by the generality of local and national taxpayers. Hence, there is an in-built incentive for service expansion and redistribution as an inherent outcome of the collective financing of services combined with rivalry between groups in their use.

It is here that user-charges (even theoretically imperfect ones) have a poten-tial role. Note, however, that the immediate introduction of charges is *not* an effective way of achieving efficiency savings. Their more immediate effect is simply a redistribution of income either in cash terms (if demand is unaf-fected) or in kind (if demand collapses), or a combination of both. Efficiency cannot be improved at a stroke. Moreover, introduction of charges may simply lead to a reformation of distributional coalitions in much the same way as changes in market conditions can lead to a redistribution of corporate power and influence without actually destroying it. Put simply, public choice theory has failed to integrate charging policy and practice into its own analytical frame-work. It only gets as far as the simplistic maxim that charging for previously or otherwise free services does not buy votes or encourage service expansion.

It is too simplistic to believe both that allocatively efficient user-charges could be introduced and that they would lead to a significant improvement in efficiency. The Niskanen model of bureaucratic empire-building (see Chapter 5) makes clear that, unless a user-charge reduces the ability of the bureau to capture some of the economic rent that its output creates, there is no reason to believe that a charge will increase efficiency.

The bureau's ideal charge would not affect its ability to produce an excessive output at excessive cost. In particular, the charge would not reduce demand and would guarantee additional earmarked income (over and above tax-financed income) to expand the bureau's output. Coercive levies are more acceptable to service providers because they do not put their jobs or promotion prospects at risk. Perhaps this explains the predominance of property-related charges noted below. More widespread use of charges would therefore not dispense with the need for efficiency studies. Indeed, user-charges should also be examined in terms of the extent to which they promote the interests of dominant groups (Wagner 1991).

To sum up, the conventional argument for user-charges, that there will be excess demand for services provided free at the point of use (a demand-side explanation), is too simplistic in that it ignores the decision-making mechanism which determines supply. It also leads to over-optimistic conclusions about the efficiency gains resulting from the increased use of user-charges. Synthesis of the theories of transaction costs (Chapter 3) and distributional coalitions (Chapter 5) within a collective choice framework provides a coherent means of integrating both demand-side and supply-side influences. Charges intended to maximize allocative efficiency may be manipulated by those who administer them, both to maximize bureaucrats' utility and to secure gains for distributional coalitions.

More generally economists often fail to consider implementation theory and fail to recognize that a methodology for user-charges must seek more than just allocative efficiency. It must also ensure X-efficiency. The latter can be achieved by making sure that payment of charges is directly related to the volume of services consumed and that there is considerable scope for exit (see Chapters 3 and 4). In that case service providers will be provided with incentives to minimize the costs and maximize the quality of their outputs. Payment of the charge effectively becomes compulsory if payment is not directly related to consumption and if exit is not possible, allowing bureaucrats to exploit consumers. Both allocative and X-inefficiency result.

ACHIEVING EQUITY VIA EXEMPTIONS AND CONCESSIONS

As well as being used to achieve economic efficiency in the broad sense, charges also have to be consistent with notions of equity, particularly in terms of ability to pay. Put simply, charges for local government services may severely disadvantage low-income individuals and households in need of service provision but who are unable to pay charges related to their use of services. Hence, exemptions and concessions are a corollary of user-charges, facilitating a pragmatic political compromise between the conflicting efficiency case for charges and the equity argument against them. There are two main forms of exemptions and concessions:

1. *Categoric exemptions and concessions*, which fully or partially relieve from user-charges whole groups of people with given characteristics relating to age, employment status, physical disabilities and so on;
2. *means-tested exemptions and concessions*, which allow account to be taken of the user's income and therefore ability to pay, sometimes on a sliding scale of personal subsidy. The principal means-test in Britain is the eligibility for Income Support, receipt of which provides the recipient with a 'passport' to receipt of other benefits such as Housing Benefit and free school meals for children (see Chapter 14).

Means-testing is more efficient than categoric exemptions in targeting subsidy (for example, not all retired people qualifying for categoric exemption from charges are poor) but also more intrusive of personal privacy (in requiring details of personal financial circumstances) and of greater administrative cost. However, the related criticisms of the complexity and the demeaning nature of claiming (which are said to lead to low rates of takeup in Britain) seem less important in practice than the level of benefit (value of exemption). This is especially where the progressive reduction (tapering) of subsidy in line with rising income results in low cash values of benefit, itself deterring their takeup.

Despite the possibility of categoric and means-tested exemptions, subsidies are almost invariably paid in respect of facilities rather than people and little or no attempt is made to ration service use on the basis of socioeconomic, demographic or other eligibility criteria (for example, use of leisure and recreation facilities). Subsidizing facilities benefits the most advantaged groups if their takeup of services is greater than that of disadvantaged groups. This perverse outcome is exacerbated if national and local taxes (used to finance those subsidies) are not particularly progressive as, for example, in the UK (Bailey 1995, ch. 10).

Hence, pursuit of increased equity also requires a much more sophisticated managerial approach towards service delivery. It is not necessarily counter-productive in social policy terms to use charges in particular cases. Nonetheless, in the UK at least, extensive use of charges would have to be 'part of a deliberate national policy applied to other publicly-provided services as well as to local government services, not least because the required redistribution of income would be a government responsibility' (Cmnd 6453, ch. 9).

ALTERNATIVE CHARGING METHODOLOGIES

Charging for services has to serve many different functions, not just allocative efficiency. These include raising revenue, covering costs, the need to meet financial targets or required rates of return on assets, checking abuse of service, the need to target subsidy and the pursuit of equity. Use of the term 'charge' rather than 'price' implies politico-administrative rather than market control in such a way that charges (and related subsidies) secure the publicness of the service. As already noted, economic theory consistently uses 'price' and restricts its role to the pursuit of allocative efficiency.

Where levied, charges are usually based on *accounting* costs, the deficiencies of the latter having already been noted. The options are '*variable-cost charging*' (covering all or part of running costs), '*partial-overhead charging*' (covering all variable costs and a proportion of fixed costs, either as a conscious political decision or as the largely arbitrary outcome of financial pressures) and '*full-cost charging*' (covering all fixed and variable costs). The reader will recall that it was noted above that these accountants' measures of costs are not measures of true economic costs. Other charging rules based loosely on benefits rather than on costs include '*going-rate charges*' ('copy-cat' charges set at the same levels as in other local authorities irrespective of any differences in costs, in client groups and so on) and '*demand-orientated charges*' (set by reference to private sector alternatives). All or a combination of these methods may be followed, modified by concessionary schemes for particular types of service user.

Fixed and variable costs may be financed simultaneously through a combined charge levied at the point of service use, for example the two-part tariff noted above. Alternatively, those costs may be financed through separate charges at different stages in the provision of a service. For example, some local authorities in both the UK and the USA levy separate 'up-front' charges for the provision of physical infrastructure (to cover fixed costs) in addition to charges when the infrastructure is actually used (to cover ongoing variable costs). For example, the infrastructure charge can be used to recover the costs of installing water and sewerage systems, while a charge per cubic metre of water supplied can be used to cover the ongoing costs of supplying water and treating sewage. The infrastructure charge may be related to costs (a legal requirement for 'impact fees' in the USA) or to benefit (as may sometimes be the case for the UK's 'planning gain'). These forms of payments are considered in more detail in the USA and UK case-studies below.

A prior choice has to be made regarding which services are chargeable, which should continue to be fully financed from local taxes and intergovernmental transfers, and which should be financed by various combinations of charge and subsidy. This choice requires a clear charging philosophy. It has already been noted that the technical and financial information required for the introduction of charges is often grossly deficient, but the main problem is in fact 'the complete absence of any coherent philosophy about their role' (Heald 1983, p. 305). There are a number of alternatives.

1. *The 'distribution of benefits' approach* which, based on economic theory, categorizes services in terms of the degree of 'market failure' caused by externalities and other spillover effects in consumption and production. Services benefiting the community exclusively (pure public goods) are fully funded by subsidy and services benefiting users exclusively (pure private goods) are fully funded by user-charges. Respective examples are non-excludable and non-rival public goods such as local street lighting and refuse/garbage disposal, and excludable and rival private goods such as golf facilities and personal photocopies of library materials. As a crude rule of thumb, services where the community benefits more than users may receive 75 per cent subsidy. Similarly, services benefiting users more than the community receive 25 per cent subsidy and those where the benefits are equal receive 50 per cent subsidy (Smith 1986, p. 84).

2. *The 'categorization of services' approach*. Although based more in terms of social policy analysis, this approach is similar to the first alternative in that it defines services as 'need' 'protective', 'amenity' or 'facility' services. The 'need' services (such as social care) would be wholly financed from taxation and so free at the point of use whilst the 'facility' services (such as photocopying materials at public libraries) would be wholly financed by charges. In between these extremes, the 'protective' services (for example, meals-on-wheels for elderly people) and 'amenity' services (for example, keep-fit classes) would be financed by a combination of taxes and charges, income from subsidies exceeding charges for the former and the reverse for the latter. Both approaches are over-simplistic as well as essentially arbitrary and subjective in that they are based on practitioners' impressions of the nature of benefits derived from individual services. The examples given reflect the author's own subjective impressions of service benefits.

3. *The 'subsidy-by-default' rationale*. Here, the rule is to charge fully for services unless there are good reasons to the contrary. This approach is based on a presumption in favour of charging so that subsidies are only paid by default. It was followed in the UK by the 1976 Layfield Report (Cmnd 6453), by Glasby (1981), and by a consultative document in 1986 (Cmnd 9714). Good reasons to the contrary relate to control of access; the acceptability, incidence and administrative cost of charging; the nature and extent of benefits; the ability to pay; demand and cost factors; and, finally, to efficiency and effectiveness.

4. *The minimum standards approach* uses taxation to finance collectively-determined minimum service levels, charges thereafter financing discretionary increases in service provision. A variant of this approach was

recommended in two notes of reservation (by Day and Cameron) to the 1976 Layfield Report (Cmnd 6453, pp. 302–15).

5. *The basic and non-basic services approach*. Different services and/or their components could be classified as *basic* (and therefore provided free) and *non-basic* (and therefore chargeable at full cost). This approach assumes that there are some service components which are germane to the service and others that are not essential. This is questionable but was recommended by the UK government in respect of public library services (Cm 324). For example, it suggested that book borrowing should be a free basic service while specialist information services and non-print materials (such as those emanating from computers) should be chargeable non-basic services. There are no clear principles upon which such a distinction can be based. The proposed distinction between books and computer printouts is technology-driven and, as information in electronic form increasingly replaces that in book form, user-charges would be extended by default (Bailey 1989a).

6. *The customized value-added services approach*. Here, charges are only levied where there is substantial real discretion on the part of service users to customize the levels and mix of service outputs themselves. In other words, either local governments have no monopoly power or they do not exercise it by restricting output. This is distinct from the other approaches in that it does not require definitions of minimum standards nor of basic and non-basic services, nor an assessment of the balance of benefit between the individual user and the community. It is incremental in approach and relates to the development of both new services or variants of existing ones, but only those that are specifically designed to be providing customized value-added services at the discretion of the individual user. It is a *demand-side* approach to service provision which can complement the other *supply-side* methodologies as necessary.

There are several key points for the customized value-added approach:

- this methodology seeks to promote access to improved services, enabling rather than restricting service development;
- it recognizes the potential compatibility between individual/subjective (consumer rationality) and collective/objective (democratically determined) preferences: they are often complementary, not necessarily mutually exclusive;
- it integrates economic and political concepts relating to service delivery in that it modifies the structure of incentives without destroying the nature of the service;
- while there is an increased emphasis on demand-led developments, only those services would be provided which are consistent with broader service objectives. Hence, the demand-led element of service determination

is constrained by supply-led decisions so that outcomes are not comparable with those determined by markets.

None of the first five charging methodologies is based on a *coherent* philosophy about the role of charges in the provision of local government services. Decisions relating to supply and finance are seen as independent of each other rather than as part of an integrated decision-making process. The *minimum standards* and *basic services* approaches assume a clear delineation between collective/objective interests and individual/subjective interests. Collective/objective interests are those defined by despotic benevolent local governments acting in the public interest and knowing what is best for the individual. Individual/subjective interests reflect consumer sovereignty under a fiscal exchange model of government (see Chapter 1).

Such a delineation leaves little role for local government in that such a scenario would only require a local agency receiving a lump sum from national and local taxes, thereafter pursuing output maximization subject only to the income constraint imposed by individuals' willingness and ability to pay charges. Hence, decision-making criteria are assumed to be fundamentally different: arising out of the political process in the minimum/basic case and out of a market process in the higher standards/non-basic case. It is not self-evident why such a dichotomy should be necessary. It assumes that the political and market resource allocation processes are mutually exclusive and cannot operate jointly and simultaneously in determining the particular standard for a particular service. In that sense it is not an organic process but rather a disjointed one which fails to integrate a variety of decision-making procedures in a dynamic interactive process.

Local or central governments issuing vouchers for pre-school nursery and play-groups for children aged between three and five years (see Chapter 4) provide an example of a combination of political and market processes. The political decision to finance collectively consumption of the service is a collective/objective decision, while the decision to use the service (which is not compulsory), and the choice of school at which to trade the voucher for a place, is the individual/subjective decision of the child's parent.

Under the *service categorization* approach, the balance between charge and subsidy is rigidly determined by bureaucrats and politicians acting independently of service users. It adopts a crude paternalistic approach to the assessment of individual and community benefits and leaves unresolved the question as to why local authorities should provide services providing purely private benefits. This is because it fails to consider how services providing purely personal benefits can be used to promote service objectives other than cost-recovery through marginal cost pricing.

Similar comments apply to the *subsidy-by-default* methodology in that there is no opportunity for service users to influence service specifications. In practice, neither votes nor political representation are sensitive enough to allow subtle respecification of service characteristics to suit user preferences. The *minimum standards* approach adopts the opposite extreme in that it allows for no collective input into private decisions regarding the takeup of services above the minimum. Local authorities would most probably be unwilling to forgo all control over how their resources are being utilized for purely private ends (if such a distinction could be made).

As already noted, whilst the economic argument for the increased use of charges for service outputs relates to both allocative and X-inefficiency, charging rules must take account of the possibility that charges can be manipulated by bureaucrats. Payment of charges must therefore be for services whose consumption is at the discretion of the service user and must relate to increments of service consumption. They must also be consistent with service objectives and management incentives. These often relate to accessibility to and expansion of services whilst satisfying economy (of input costs), efficiency (in the transformation of inputs into outputs) and effectiveness (in fulfilling service objectives and satisfying service users).

Just as economists must allow for market failure in their policy advice to governments, so they must also allow for government failure. Their prescriptions must be made situationally relevant. However, it has been noted that

> few economists devote much time or effort to studying the mechanisms by which economic writings and research are translated into public policy... Economists tend to view their professional role in the governing process as that of experts separate from politics, value judgements, and other subjective and normative factors. (Nelson 1987, p. 49)

Nelson argues that, despite their claims to be neutral, economists are partisan advocates of efficiency and he argues that they should accept that fact.

Hence, an economist's charging rule which is intended to improve efficiency also has to fit within a broader philosophy of service provision and, in particular, must take account of both the institutional framework and the behavioural characteristics of service providers. It must recognize the incentives which bureaucrats face and be capable of modifying them in ways which promote efficiency. It must recognize the distortions caused by government failure and introduce an offsetting incentive structure.

Adopting the economist's preference for efficiency, the objective of service provision should be to provide services which are highly valued by consumers (rather than by producers) and as cheaply as possible. It has already been noted that charges highlight costs of production and therefore provide incentives to increase economy and efficiency. If charges also allow an increased input by consumers as regards both the quantity and quality of output, then charges can also promote effectiveness. However, as already noted, output is the result of both collective/objective and individual/subjective decision-making processes.

A fundamental question is what methodology guides the differentiation between those services (or parts of services) which must be provided to meet collective needs from those which can be personalized, adding customized value-added characteristics? This is both a political and a management issue. It would be naïve to expect that all services would be reviewed and reclassified as customized value-added (and therefore chargeable) and 'other' services (and therefore not chargeable). In practical policy terms, charging could only be introduced for completely new services or new variants of existing services. Initial endowments relating to service use would have to be recognized for the theoretical microeconomic reasons outlined in Chapter 5.

Local authorities would have to set clear service objectives which explicitly allow for differentiation (rather than uniformity) of service levels, standards and mixes, subject to them being consistent with those objectives. Managers have both an administrative and a developmental role. The latter can relate not just to changing service characteristics but also to their financing. In other words decentralization of budgetary responsibility should also allow for delegation of an element of revenue enhancement through new service developments which managers will have to justify in terms of service objectives. Such developments will generally have to promote rather than restrict service evolution and its takeup, avoid discrimination against proritized groups, avoid dilution of service characteristics or displacement of objectives and, at all times, avoid any element of compulsion regarding payment for service or exclusion of those who currently use it simply because of the changing financing arrangements.

The major disadvantages of the other charging methodologies is that rules are both static and mechanistic, services have to be both specified in advance and allocated to unchanging categories (such as 'need', 'minimum' or 'basic'). This hardly fits the dynamic concept of service specification and delivery where practitioners are usually at the forefront of service evolution. The customised value-added approach extends this professional input into service financing as well as its method of delivery. Each service has to be considered separately in terms of which service component can be given customized value-added characteristics. Takeup would then depend on the willingness of service users to pay for incremental consumption of those service components. A more detailed discussion of the pros and cons of this charging methodology, and its charging structure, is provided elsewhere (Bailey 1994). The essential point is that the customized value-added charging methodology facilitates both exit and voice (see Chapters 3 and 4).

INTERNATIONAL CHARGING PRACTICES

The Council of Europe figures reproduced in Table 5.3 (p. 87) show that fees and charges accounted for as much as a third of municipal funding in the

Table 7.1   *The growth of local government revenues, 1980–90[a]*

Country	Increase in grants received[b]		Increase in user-charge revenues		Increase in local tax revenues	
	%	rank	%	rank	%	rank
Australia	128	4	449	2	178	2
Austria	92	7	100	10	83	8
Canada	101	6	166	5	123	6
Denmark	59	9	165	6	133	4=
France	145	3	250	4	220	1
Germany	32	11	74	11	47	11
Ireland	125	5	280	3	120	7
Netherlands	34	10	102	9	82	9
Norway	212	1	576	1	154	3
UK	196	2	133	8	60	10
USA	80	8	146	7	133	4=

Source: OECD (1997) Tables 144–201 and the respective tables of earlier volumes.
Notes:
a: The data specifically excludes state and national government figures and refers to increases in cash amounts. No adjustment is made for inflation.
b: Grants received by local governments include those paid by other levels of government and by international or supranational authorities.

mid-1990s. However, there is considerable variety of experience, fees and charges accounting for 3 per cent or less of municipal funding in seven countries. In general, transfers from central to local government were the largest component of municipal funding (see Chapter 9), followed by local taxes (see Chapter 8).

The growth of user-charges since 1980 is described in Tables 7.1 and 7.2. The tables only include those OECD countries for which a consistent data set was available for the whole of the 1980s and for the early 1990s. The OECD definition of user-charges, noted above, includes payments in exchange for *non-capital* goods and services which are *not* of an industrial nature, for example charges for education and health, for entry into museums, parks, cultural and recreational facilities, and rents for housing. During the 1980s, in almost all countries there was a clear and consistent trend for user-charge revenues to grow substantially faster than other income sources, the only exception being the UK (Table 7.1).

The scenario for the early 1990s is much less clear than for the 1980s. Nonetheless, revenue from user-charges still rose faster than grants and local taxes in half of the countries (Table 7.2). Grants received from upper tiers of government grew faster than charges in the UK (Table 7.1) as a result of the reform of the system of local government finance in 1990 (see Chapters 8 and 9), this being particularly marked during the early 1990s (Table 7.2).

Table 7.2 *The growth of local government revenues, 1990–latest year*[a]

Country	Increase in grants received		Increase in user-charge revenues		Increase in local tax revenues		Latest year's data[b]
	%	rank	%	rank	%	rank	
Australia	24	6	42	2=	20	8	1995
Austria	21	8	41	4	28	3	1994
Canada	23	7	16	9	26	5=	1993
Denmark	32	4=	42	2=	31	2	1995
France	34	3	26	7=	27	4	1995
Germany	n.a.	—	n.a.	—	n.a.	—	1990
Ireland	56	1	27	6	26	5=	1994
Netherlands	17	9=	64	1	32	1	1995
Norway	17	9=	26	7=	18	9	1994
UK[c]	49	2	9	10	−29	10	1995
USA	32	4=	32	5	25	7	1994

Source: As for Table 7.1.
Notes:
a: As for Table 7.1
b: The latest year is common to all three income sources in any one country.
c: The UK local tax revenues figure is negative because the local business property tax was taken over by central government in 1990 and became an assigned revenue, effectively an intergovernmental grant (see Chapters 8 and 9).
n.a. denotes not available.

The differential growth in income sources resulted in some substantial increases in the ratios of both charges to grants and charges to local taxation during the 1980s and early 1990s (Table 7.3). Nevertheless, revenues from user-charges exceeds that from grants in only two countries: Australia and Austria. Likewise, revenues from user-charges exceed local taxation in only two countries: Ireland and (only recently) the Netherlands. With the exception of Australia, Austria and Germany none of the other countries sees the ratio of charges to grants exceed 50 per cent but more countries exceed this ratio for charges against local taxes (Australia, Austria and Germany again, plus Ireland and the Netherlands).

Comparing Tables 7.1 and 7.3, during the 1980s some countries experienced large increases in user-charge revenues which nevertheless remained small relative to grants (Denmark, Ireland, Netherlands and UK) and relative to local taxation (Denmark, Norway and UK). This suggests large proportionate increases on a low base. Germany experienced the lowest increases in all three revenue sources (Table 7.1) but also the third highest ratio of charges to grants and the third highest relative to local taxes (both in 1990). This suggests modest proportional increases on a large base.

In general, during the 1980s, the countries with the highest percentage increases in user-charge revenues also have the largest proportionate increases in

Table 7.3 *Ratios of income sources, 1980, 1990 and latest year*

Country	Ratio of user-charges to grants (%)			Ratio of user-charges to local taxes (%)		
	1980	1990	Latest year	1980	1990	Latest year
Australia	63	152	175	27	53	63
Austria	157	163	191	48	52	57
Canada	20	26	25	26	31	29
Denmark	8	13	14	11	12	13
France	31	45	42	31	43	34
Germany	65	85	n.a.	54	64	n.a.
Ireland	10	17	13	92	160	161
Netherlands	5	8	11	77	86	106
Norway	15	33	35	11	29	30
UK	13	10	7	20	30	46
USA	21	29	29	25	26	28

Source: As for Table 7.1.
Note:
Latest years as for Table 7.2 and see notes to Tables 7.1 and 7.2

grants and local taxes. Australia, Norway, Ireland and France had the largest relative increases in both grants and user-charges, with a remarkably close matching of ranking (Table 7.1), and also had the largest increases in local taxation (except for Ireland). As already noted, Germany had the slowest increases in all three sources of revenue with identical rankings (11th) for each. Rankings for the Netherlands were also nearly identical.

Rankings become much less consistent during the early 1990s (Table 7.2). This may be due to a number of factors. First, the provisional nature of the latest data for some countries. Second, the different years for which the latest data is available. Third, reform of systems of local government finance serving to make difficult comparisons between the beginning and end of the period, in the UK's case the reclassification of the former local business property tax as an intergovernmental grant (see Table 7.2, n. c).

Though conclusions are qualified for the early 1990s, this analysis suggests that user-charges were *not* simply replacing local taxes or grants – certainly not during the 1980s. However, the increasing ratios of charges to grants were generally more consistent and more marked during the 1980s than the increasing ratios of charges to local taxation (Table 7.3). The explanation of these results is rather more complex than a simple *fiscal substitution strategy* (that is, the replacement of grants and local taxes by revenues from user-charges). A mixture of cultural, organizational, constitutional and other factors underpin these changes and can only be appreciated by case-studies of individual countries. The above data only provides a superficial appreciation of events. Case-studies of the USA and UK follow, more detailed analysis country-by-country being available elsewhere (Paddison and Bailey 1988). The conclusions then bring together the main factors.

USER-CHARGES IN THE USA

California's Proposition 13 (Netzer 1983) and Massachusett's Proposition $2\frac{1}{2}$ (Flynn *et al.* 1981), both in the late 1970s, created a popular picture of a massive switch to user-charge financing of local government services in the USA. These propositions were local property tax cuts which, because upper-tier grants were limited, necessitated a re-evaluation of the role of user-charges for a variety of services. For cities, 'parks and recreation, engineering, subdivision and zoning are the four divisions (in order) with the greatest number of charge increases' (Mercer *et al.* 1985, p. 76). For large counties, health, planning, engineering, parks and recreation, and institutional care services saw the greatest increases in user-charges. However,

> it is erroneous to interpret the increased reliance on user-charge revenue shown in the aggregate data to mean that hard-pressed local governments as a general rule turned to user-charges to solve their financing problems, thereby relieving the pressure on their revenue from general taxes. The popular picture of a massive switch to user-charge financing to replace local tax revenue is unsupported by the evidence. (Netzer 1983, pp. 12–13)

The restrictive nature of the OECD's definition of user-charges (discussed above) qualifies direct comparison with national accounting data but this conclusion remained valid throughout the 1980s. Table 7.1 shows that the USA was below middle-ranking in terms of the percentage increases in each of user-charge revenues and grants, and just above middle ranking for local tax revenues. The ratio of charges to local taxes was virtually static during the 1980s, rising somewhat by 1994 (Table 7.3). Indeed, if charges replaced anything it was grants, not local taxes (Table 7.3). This is perhaps not surprising since local government taxes grew faster (113 per cent) than federal and state taxes (84 per cent) during the 1980s (OECD 1992). Most other countries experienced much greater increases in the ratio of charges to local taxes than did the USA, almost all having higher ratios than the USA by 1990 (Table 7.3).

User-charges increased from about a quarter to a third of all own-source revenue in the USA during the 1970s and 1980s and came from three sources:

1. There was increased spending on functions for which reliance on user-charges has changed little but which therefore has led to an increase in the associated user-charge revenue: examples are local government-operated electricity and gas utilities and airports which saw a tremendous increase in expenditures during the period and which have traditionally been self-supporting from user-charges.

2. Some functions experienced rapid rises in spending and increases in the extent to which user-charges finance that spending: examples are sewerage, hospitals (via medical insurance and so on) and local government-operated higher education institutions.
3. There were functions where the increase in expenditure was not particularly rapid but where there is now greater dependence on user-charges (such as recreation and refuse collection and disposal).

User-charge financing actually declined for some services, for example transit. Utility charges, from water, electricity, gas and transit accounted for almost half of user-charge revenues during the later 1980s.

More generally, user-charges in the USA have been predominantly related to *property-based* services and these, together with transportation, were the major targets for increased use of user-charges for the 1980s. The fastest growth in the late 1970s and early 1980s was in zoning and subdivision fees, which vary by size of building, type of use and time taken for inspection (Johnson 1980; Toft and Warnecke 1980; Morgan and Mercer 1981; TACIR 1981; Logalbo 1982; CML 1983). The popularity of property-based charges persisted into the early 1990s (Osborne and Gaebler 1992).

For sewers, street maintenance, solid waste collection and inspections, the norm has been *full-cost* recovery. For services such as recreation, charging to cover operating costs has been common, that is *variable-cost* recovery. Police and fire rely negligibly on charges: no police department obtained even 5 per cent of operating funds from user charges on private individuals or organizations. Those that were levied were for fingerprinting, record copying, parade permits, accident reports and extra services for special events. No fire department used fire suppression fees. Where charges were levied they were for fire inspection, enforcement of fire codes, building permits and permits for potentially dangerous activities.

Parks and libraries are characterized by political resistance to a heavy dependence on user-charges. Libraries make the least aggressive use of user-charges. Parks have a very limited scope for user-charges, usually only parking fees and any franchise fees paid by concessionaires. Recreation departments were probably under the most pressure to adopt some form of benefit-based charge, recovering between a quarter and two-thirds of operating costs. 'Seldom do public or merit good services recover as much as 10 per cent of costs through consumer charges' (McCarthy *et al.* 1984, p. v). For example, art museums and galleries raised only 5 per cent of their revenues from admission charges in the late 1980s (Luksetich and Partridge 1997).

Sanitary sewer systems were (and still are) more likely to be supported by user-charges than any other local government service. Together with solid waste disposal, sewers have usually been run as enterprise funds (the public sector equivalent of a private business) with costs covered by user-charges. They may also be organized on a special district basis (which involves performance

of a single function) because of the dearth of viable general purpose governments, especially in suburban areas (Sachs and Andrew 1975).

Benefits from sewer provision are clearly identifiable, charges are easy to
administer (added to the water bill) and there is little public opposition. (By
contrast, there is considerable public opposition to user-charges for solid
waste disposal.) Fees can be set as monthly service charges, waste-water quality
surcharges, hook-up and development charges, and inspection and permit
fees. There is, however, considerable opposition to user-charges for storm
drainage systems, probably because of difficulties in establishing a link between
usage and the user-charge so that the latter is regarded as 'a tax on rain'.

Charges for *new* infrastructure have increasingly been financed by means
of 'impact fees' and 'in-kind' contributions (Bailey 1990b; Brueckner 1997).
Impact fees are levied on new residents to pay for the cost of incremental
off-site infrastructure such as water supply. In-kind contributions occur
when developers install and pay for on-site infrastructure such as streets,
sidewalks, kerbs, and so on. There is also an increasing use of special assessments whereby those areas benefiting from a particular improvement to
existing infrastructure (such as the street) pay a surcharge on the local property tax or a front-footage charge, directly related to length (or sometimes
area) of the abutting properties (see Chapter 8). Finally, inspections, licences
and permits charges are most important for building permits and inspection
fees.

The (non-utility) services generating the highest operating cost recovery rates
from user-charges have generally been sewers and solid waste disposal (close
to 100 per cent), streets and traffic services, inspections, permits and licences
(generally over 50 per cent) and recreation (usually less than 50 per cent):

> Among the remaining service areas, few of the governments we contacted
> recovered more than 10 per cent of their costs through fees and many
> raised less than 5 per cent. The one exception to this general finding was in
> the fire prevention area; several departments were able to cover more than
> 10 per cent of total costs. (McCarthy *et al.* 1984, p. 45)

A study by Criz (1982) also found that the greatest revenue is realized from
those services that are least discretionary, including sewerage and refuse collection, functions that the average household or business is not likely to do
without because of charges. However, revenue–cost ratios were generally
lower than those reported by McCarthy *et al.* (1984), probably because they
excluded education, welfare services, hospitals, corrective facilities, public
utilities and local government-operated liquor stores. These results confirm
the conclusions reached by Netzer (1983), reported above, that there was *not*
a massive switch to user-charges.

Variations in the use of user-charges, and the revenues so obtained, occur
among cities of different sizes and in different regions. 'Cities with medium
sized and small populations tend to rely more on charges and utility revenue

than do cities with larger populations' (Criz 1982, p. 1). This reflects both differing service responsibilities (with property-based, non-discretionary service being relatively more important for smaller than for larger cities) and the fact that larger cities have a more diversified range of revenue sources than do small cities (being largely confined to a residential property tax base). Other geographic variations in the use of user-charges for specific services have no such rational explanation, except presumably differing regional preferences. However, fees for sewerage services are almost universal in geographic coverage. Mushkin and Vehorn (1977) provide an overview of the types of fees, charges and licences levied in the USA, ranging from those for junk dealers and dogs through recreation and transportation to police and health user-charges.

The US experience clearly demonstrates that substantial user-charge revenues can be generated from utility type, non-discretionary services such as water and sewerage. The growth of separate capital property-related charges (that is, for infrastructure) has also been substantial and, together with the exclusion of services of an industrial nature from the OECD's definition, helps to explain the discrepancy between the popular picture of substantial increases in the use of user-charges and the much more modest picture painted by the data in Tables 7.1, 7.2 and 7.3. The remaining discrepancy appears to be created by a few highly-publicized special cases such as California and Massachusetts.

USER-CHARGES IN THE UK

Unlike the USA and some other countries, UK local governments do *not* provide electricity, gas, hospital, higher education, or water and sewerage services. As noted earlier, these services accounted for about half of user-charge revenues and much of their increase in the USA during the 1980s. Hence, a different evolving charging pattern can be expected.

There are about 600 individual services in Britain for which user-charges (including licence fees and sales) are levied but information is generally difficult to obtain, even from official sources (Heald 1990; Rose 1990a). Levels of charge are largely at the discretion of local governments but national government adopted powers in 1989 to set regulations for the introduction of charges where not specifically excluded by law. Exclusions relate to school education, core public library services, fire fighting, electoral registration, elections and police functions.

Despite the so-called 'unitary state' in the UK, charging practice is highly variable amongst local governments (Bailey *et al.* 1993). The popular view is that severe fiscal constraints on local government finances were caused by restrained intergovernmental grants and the inelastic nature of the revenues financed by local taxation, including the former poll tax (Bailey 1991; Bailey and Paddison 1988). However, this failed to bring a substantial shift in favour of user-charges, the UK ranking eighth in terms of percentage increase (Table 7.1). Local tax revenues were not in fact as inelastic as popularly perceived. Indeed, local government tax revenues grew faster (138 per cent) than central government tax revenues (127 per cent) during the 1980s (OECD 1992).

The low UK figure for tax revenues in Table 7.1 is explained by the reform of local government finance noted above. This reform also explains the falling ratios of user-charges to grants and the rising ratios of user-charges to local taxes in the UK (Table 7.3). In fact, UK local governments were generally reluctant to increase existing charges or to extend charging practice. By the end of the 1980s, sales, fees and charges only accounted for just over a seventh of the total revenue income of local government, having risen from an eighth at the start of the decade (DOE 1981 and 1991).

Of the main services in the late 1980s, education only covered 7 per cent of accounting costs, the main user-charges being for vocational college courses and for consumable items taken home by school pupils after cookery and woodwork classes and so on. Social services covered 11 per cent of costs, mainly charges for residential care of the elderly but also for meals-on-wheels, day nurseries, aids and adaptations and so on. Roads and transport financed 13 per cent, mainly parking fees but also charges for, for example, lighting, transportation surveys. Local environmental services financed 12 per cent of costs, mainly from cleansing and burial/crematoria charges but also for public toilets and so on. Libraries, museums and galleries covered 6 per cent of costs, mainly from photocopying and entrance charges respectively. Police services covered 4 per cent of costs (for example, from charges for crowd control at major sporting events) and fire services 1 per cent. School meals charges covered 39 per cent of costs in 1988/89, planning and economic development 33 per cent and leisure and recreation 20 per cent but each service only accounted for 7 per cent of total income from sales, fees and charges (DOE 1991). These major 'revenue fund' services account for four-fifths of current expenditure and about half of all current revenues from user-charges.

Local government housing recovers two-thirds of costs from user-charges but only accounts for 17 per cent of current expenditure and a third of user-charge revenues. Nonetheless, rents for municipal housing have long accounted for the largest single source of user-charge revenue and, of all charges, experienced the most notable increases during the 1980s. While the national government accepts that rents for local government housing will frequently be below market levels, they are increasingly being expected to cover housing costs without the need for external subsidy and to reflect capital values within their area (see Chapter 12).

Trading services include airports, harbours and ports, road bridges with tolls, slaughter houses, ferries and local transport undertakings. They also recover two-thirds of costs from user-charges but only account for a seventh of current revenues from user-charges because they account for only about 2 per cent of current expenditure. Hence, the services which offer the greatest scope for charging only constitute relatively small proportions of revenue expenditures (compare the USA).

Though legislation prohibits user-charges for domestic refuse collection and disposal, local governments are allowed to charge for collection of trade wastes. Most of the larger urban municipalities do charge for non-domestic refuse but usually allow for the domestic element of mixed domestic and commercial premises such as hotels. Most also allow a free bin as for domestic properties and there seems to be little if any relationship between the levels of charges and the costs of service provision.

Less than one-third of local governments levy a general admission charge for their museums and galleries, and a tenth levy admission charges for access to special temporary collections, usually on loan from other museums at home and abroad. The proportions charging remained largely unchanged during the 1980s and 1990s, although the proportion asking for voluntary donations rose sharply from an eighth during the mid-1980s to almost half by the later 1990s (Bailey *et al*. 1993 and 1998). Admission charges are low and concessions (discounted charges and exemptions for children, the elderly retired people, family groups and so on) are high, both relative to other museum providers in the UK.

Municipal theatres and halls usually attempt (but often fail) to recover running costs from admission charges but not the fixed overhead costs of the venue. As a very broad generalization, the average level of subsidy per visitor for theatres and halls is therefore only two-thirds that of museums and galleries. On average, the latter only recover an eighth of revenue expenditures whilst the former recover 60 per cent from admission charges.

User-charges for sports facilities are well developed but, on average, they cover less than a quarter of the debt charges and running costs of outdoor activities and less than half of those for indoor activities. Swimming pools have generally only covered a fifth of costs from charges and sports centres barely a third. Copy-cat charging leads to a broad uniformity of user-charges which, combined with substantial variations in operating costs and debt charges, leads to a greater dispersion in the range of subsidy between municipalities. Other facilities are not charged for simply because they are not financed from the sport's account. For example football and other pitches in public parks are charged to the 'parks account' since they are deemed to form part of the open space, use of which is free.

User-charges for residential care of the elderly typically accounted for up to four-fifths of income from charges for social work services while accounting for only about a quarter of gross expenditure during the 1980s. The levels of charges depended primarily on the levels of state welfare payments which underwrote them. This led to relatively small variations between local governments in charging levels, certainly in comparison with user-charges for home-helps, meals-on-wheels and so on. The shift towards private sector provision of residential care during the 1990s is leading to a greater diversity of charging levels as, increasingly, they vary between local authorities in reflection of regional and local variations in the costs of property and labour. Charges have to be paid by elderly residents themselves (unless they are supported by their relatives or by a charity) if they are ineligible for national welfare payments and if their local authorities are unwilling or unable to help with costs.

Education user-charges have changed substantially following greater local discretion over charges and given local government's loss of responsibility for further (vocational) education in 1993/4. The UK government relinquished control over school meals charges in 1980 and introduced enabling powers for schools to charge for provisions other than school meals and milk in 1988. Meals charges rose by more than 60 per cent in real terms during the 1980s (Rose and Falconer 1992). The absolute aggregate level of subsidy also fell along with falls in the numbers of pupils taking school meals (see Chapter 14). Schools can now levy charges on parents for a specified range of ('non-essential') items or on activities which take place wholly or partly outside school hours. These include charges for materials or ingredients used in practical subjects where the finished item is retained by the pupil, for wasted examination fees, for board and lodging costs, for individual instrumental music tuition which is not required by the National Curriculum and for day-trips and overnight visits to sporting and cultural venues and so on.

Police forces charge for crowd control at commercial events, accompanying abnormal loads on roads and motorways, housing remand prisoners and providing prison escorts (recharged to the Home Office) and for providing training in emergency and other procedures. Some fire services also charge for emergency training and some charge for non-emergency services.

Of particular potential for urban municipalities, charges for city road use have been actively considered by the UK government during the 1990s (DTp 1993). If introduced, they may be in the form of real-time route congestion charges using 'smart card' technology rather than the timeless area-charges levied by licences in Hong Kong and, formerly, in Singapore. They would raise an estimated £600 million per annum in London and tens of millions in other large British cities. Ideally, city municipalities would collect the revenues and reinvest them in public transport improvements.

There is also increasing use of hybrid user-charges for *capital* expenditures in the form of 'planning gain'. The charge can be in cash or in kind. The latter occurs where developers of real estate build capital facilities not strictly required for their own development and then donate them to the local municipality. An example is a road by-passing the site so as to reduce traffic congestion which is neither directly nor solely a consequence of the development.

Similar to the US and Canadian experiences (Bailey 1990b), this capital charge is used mostly in areas of rapid urbanization, particularly East Anglia and the South East of England. It is not strictly a user-charge, since it is levied at the construction stage rather than at the point where individuals use the facility. Nonetheless, it is an important source of revenue for highways improvements in some local authorities.

Besides the by-pass roads example, development charges are also being used in the UK to finance the provision of playing fields, community halls, sites for schools and libraries and even nature reserves and managed woodlands. The UK national government has recently formalized development charges into 'planning obligations' which allows planning gain to be formally incorporated into land development controls.

The UK experience demonstrates the endemic nature of user-charges for local government services. However, despite some movement towards 'economic' charges for services ranging from housing rents to entry fees at swimming pools, the UK experience also demonstrates the limited importance of charges in terms of cost-recovery and total spending. At the time of writing this book, the latest research demonstrated that Scottish local governments raised an average of only £1.20 per head of population per week from service charges (1.7 Euros), exclusive of rents for municipal housing (Accounts Commission 1998). Only parking and property enquiries fully covered costs from user-charges and very few Scottish authorities had a corporate approach to charges, or even to subsidies.

DOES POLITICS MAKE MUCH DIFFERENCE TO CHARGING PRACTICE?

Despite the apparently contradictory value stances taken by the main socialist and conservative political parties in the UK, the evidence (reviewed in Bailey *et al*. 1993) is that politics does *not* make a substantive difference in the decision to charge or not to charge. The normative prescriptions of both market and collectivist groups tend to be dismissed in the face of the practical necessities of government. Political parties differ more in what they articulate or say about user-charges than in what they do. Programmes and policies are inherited upon changes of office, as are the methods of their financing (Rose 1990b).

Differences in charging practice are marginal rather than absolute. Charging issues are dealt with by the ethic of responsibility and tradeoffs between competing ends, rather than in accordance with absolute principles. Principles are priceless but services are not costless. Governments inherit before they choose, the inertia of commitments being a significant practical constraint on charging practice. The same considerations seem to apply to local authorities' use of concessionary charges or exemptions from charging for different groups (see above).

CONCLUSIONS

A major criticism of proposals for the increased use of charges by local governments is that they usually take little or no account of the context and broader objectives within which local government operates. The deadlock in the charges debate is attributed to the apparent conflict between equity and efficiency but, in fact, the major problem is the failure to adequately theorize the nature of 'public' within which user-charges must operate. Rather than analysing user-charges solely in terms of efficiency or equity, it may be more productive also to analyse them in terms of whether or not they promote the publicness of services by enhancing their quality and accessibility.

The economists' prescription of efficient pricing failed to be implemented because of its lack of subtleness in terms of taking account of collective interests. It fails to make fine distinctions at the level of implementation or to have any delicate perceptions of the reality of service provision. Though it is a standard by which all other charging arrangements can be judged, it is disingenuous in terms of its applicability within the local government context. Like other abstract economic constructs (such as the perfectly competitive market model) it is an ideal, non-implementable in practice but nonetheless a valuable benchmark against which all feasible charging arrangements can be judged.

The relevant question is not whether any particular set of charging arrangements maximizes efficiency, because in this case all practical arrangements would be condemned as failures. Rather, given the situational context, it is a question of whether or not the charging system promotes efficiency *as far as possible*. This approach to the question of efficiency recognizes the constraints imposed by both equity and service implementation.

The pursuit of increased economic efficiency requires a much more sophisticated approach than simply the introduction of user-charges based on incremental service costs, even when adjusted to take account of any wider social and economic benefits which they confer. Charges will do little to reduce X-inefficiency (thought to be of much greater magnitude than allocative inefficiency) where local governments have effective monopoly power. User- charges will also have little impact on allocative efficiency where service users have little real discretion over service provision, for example for property-related services. Their contribution is potentially greater when consumers are genuinely free to vary service use and payment (that is, they have the power of exit). This requires a completely variable user-charge free of any standing charge. An example would be choosing whether or not to use private (rather than public) transport on congested city roads and so whether or not to incur the congestion charge.

The essential point is that charging policy has to be compatible with the institutional framework within which it is applied. Charging rules cannot be transfered unamended from market to non-market systems of provision. At the very least, public choice theory has to incorporate charges within its own rent-seeking assumptions. More generally, charging policy will be fashioned by political economy, recognizing the existence of distributional coalitions operating within the political system. Charges for public sector outputs will inevitably be fashioned more by political and institutional factors than by economic prescriptions. Charges must be consistent with service objectives regarding access to and quality of service. They must also be capable of being determined within the interactive, sequential and incremental environment of policy-making.

The international evidence is that charges yield substantially less revenue than grants or local taxes and that there is no significant tendency for charges to increasingly replace the other income sources. The future role of user-charges will depend on constitutional change (for example, service responsibilities); changes in the delivery of services (for example, whether provided in-house or contracted out); changes in service dynamics (such as demographic change); changing technology (for instance, for road charges); spatial dynamics (such as changing patterns of urbanization and interaction with infrastructure charges); collective choices (the priority given to differing services with different rates of cost recovery through charges); managerial initiatives (such as charges for emergency training); and consumer (or citizen?) responses to different chargeable services. Compared with the aggregate of these other influences, the state of public finances appears to have little if any impact on the extent to which user-charges are levied for local government services.

That charges do not, and cannot, fully fund local government services is reflected in the quotation at the opening of this chapter. Much the same conclusion is reached after studying local taxation in the next chapter. By this means the rationale for payment of intergovernmental grants is derived.

8 The Economics of Local Government Taxation

Part at least of the financial resources of local authorities shall derive from **local taxes** *and charges of which, within the limits of statute, they have the power to determine the rate.*

(European Charter of Local Self-Government: Article 9)

INTRODUCTION

In demonstrating the allocative efficiency gains resulting from decentralization of democratic decision-making regarding service levels, Oates' decentralization theorem assumed that the resulting service costs are matched by willingness to pay on the part of local voters (see Chapter 2). In principle, this should be the individual service user paying user-charges, unless markets would fail to achieve allocative efficiency in the local government jurisdiction. In that case, local government intervention is required to deal with market failure, (see Chapter 1). Such intervention does not necessarily preclude use of charges, only partial subsidies being justified except in the case of local public goods (see Chapter 7).

Local government taxes must be levied in order to finance the subsidies paid in respect of local positive externalities, local merit goods and local public goods. The question then is how to decide what types of local taxes should be levied (direct and/or indirect) upon whom and upon which levels of subcentral government (that is, region or muncipality).

A large number of criteria must be considered when deciding what taxes to levy at the local level. Allocative efficiency considerations take account of any crowding-out effects caused by high marginal rates of local income taxes. Equity is also an important criterion, namely whether the tax is regressive or progressive. Article 9 of the European Charter of Local Self-Government emphasizes the need for a diversified and buoyant resource base (see above and Chapter 6). This implies a local tax with an elastic revenue base.

151

DEFINITION OF A LOCAL TAX

A local tax can be defined as one where the local authority:

- *determines the tax revenue* by setting the tax rate and/or defining the tax base, and
- *retains the resulting proceeds* of the tax for its own purposes.

This is clearly implied in Article 9 of the European Charter of Local Self-Government. The local authority need not necessarily collect the tax itself. Nevertheless, it is usually more efficient for local authorities to collect their own local property tax, since they usually hold registers of properties within their own jurisdictional areas. In the case of local income taxes and local sales taxes, however, it will often be more efficient for local authorities to 'piggy back' them onto the national taxes collected by the central tax collection authorities. Such an arrangement would minimize the costs of collection and enforcement by avoiding the need to administer two separate tax collection systems. In this case, local and central taxes share the same tax base. Nonetheless, they are still local taxes as long as the local authorities can themselves determine the tax revenue by being free to vary their tax rates.

Local and central government share the proceeds of income tax, VAT and other taxes in many of the member states of the Council of Europe (see Chapter 9) and in many of the transitional economies of central and eastern Europe (Bird *et al.* 1995). Almost invariably, however, this *tax-sharing* allows local authorities to determine neither the tax rate nor the tax base, these being decided by central government. The revenues resulting from such centrally-determined tax arrangements cannot be regarded as local taxes. Indeed, they are a form of *assigned revenue*, where the central government decides what proportion of revenue raised from a particular national tax should accrue to local government. This does not necessarily guarantee that a particular amount of revenue will be received by local government: it only guarantees a particular *share* of tax proceeds. The actual amount of money received will vary as the tax base shrinks or expands in economic recessions and recoveries respectively. Such variation may, however, be limited if central governments undertake counter-cyclical fiscal policies (but see Chapter 5).

A local income tax is also used in some western European countries, most notably in Scandinavia (Karran 1988). They are, however, best used to finance regional, not local, governments and limits are usually set on the degree to which local and regional authorities can vary tax rates. This is consistent with the fiscal federalist principle that local authorities should not undertake highly redistributive policies (see Chapter 1 and below).

Council of Europe data for the mid-1990s, reproduced in Table 5.3 (p. 87), show that truly (exclusive) local taxes accounted for over 50 per cent of municipal funding in only two of the Council's member states, and for less than

20 per cent in 20 member states. The major source of funding in general is transfers from central to local government (see Chapter 9). Local government tax revenue as a percentage of total local authority income was greatest in Sweden (61 per cent), reflecting its use of a local income tax. The two most common local taxes within the Council of Europe are property taxes, on both residential and business properties, (used by three-quarters of member states) and personal income taxes (used by two-fifths of member states). Sales taxes and taxes on business incomes are also sometimes used (Council of Europe 1997).

Local income taxes predominate in Scandinavian countries, whilst local property taxes are of greatest importance in English-speaking countries. Local sales taxes are common in North America, being feasible because the large size of US states and Canadian provinces serves to limit cross-border shopping (see below).

THE BENEFIT MODEL OF LOCAL GOVERNMENT FINANCE

The benefit model of local government finance requires those who benefit from local government services to bear the costs of their provision. It underpinned much of the analysis of the earlier chapters and so is only briefly summarized in this section. Direct payment for service use occurs automatically in the market context for individualized exchanges between buyer and seller.

In the case of collectively-financed services, an optimal area is one which matches the geographic spread of benefits with liability to pay local taxes. Optimal areas were considered in Chapter 1 in relation to internalizing spillovers. They also underpin Oates' decentralization theorem and King's model of optimum population size (see Chapter 2).

It was noted that the potential tradeoff between Oates' decentralization theorem and economies of scale means that each function should be assigned to the lowest tier or level of government only as far as is consistent with achieving efficiency in service provision. Therefore, the only public sector services that should be provided by central government are those for which there are no local variations in willingness to pay. This decentralization rule is qualified where there are substantial spillover effects between jurisdictions, but only where they are so substantial that they cannot be corrected by payment of intergovernmental grants or by other means such as central government contracting with local authorities for provision of such services. This led to the conclusion in Chapter 1 that only national defence, foreign policy and other such national pure public goods should be provided by central government.

There are, however, a number of criticisms of the benefit model of local government finance. First, the emphasis on allocative efficiency may ignore equity considerations, in that poorer individuals and poorer local authorities may be unable to finance provision of the service for which they would otherwise be willing to pay. This has implications for the structure of local taxation (considered below) and for intergovernmental grants (considered in Chapter 9). Second, benefit areas would have to be formed for each separate service if willingness to pay is to be determined. This could lead to very complex and costly local government structures, making more difficult the development of strategic policies, for example to combat multiple deprivation using an array of local services (see Chapter 6).

PRINCIPLES OF LOCAL TAXATION

The standard principles of taxation are as applicable at the local government level as at the central level, even if their application differs somewhat. However, there are also a number of other principles which apply at the local level:

1. *Equity* The usual notions of horizontal and vertical equity apply, i.e. that, within the local authority, taxpayers in similar financial situations should pay similar amounts of tax and that taxes should not take higher proportions of income from low-income groups than from high-income groups.
2. *Efficiency* Local taxes should promote allocative efficiency. This requires local voters to pay local taxes so that use of service reflects willingness to pay.
3. *Visibility* The accountability of service providers to taxpayers depends on voters knowing exactly how much they are paying in taxes. Local accountability is therefore enhanced by highly visible local taxes.
4. *Local autonomy*   If the allocative efficiency gains of Oates' decentralization theorem are to be achieved, it is essential that local governments and their voters are free to determine the rates at which local taxes are set. Central control of local tax rates would be tantamount to imposition on local government of a nationally uniform standard of services.
5. *Economy* From the local authority's point of view local taxes should not be so costly to collect that much of the revenue raised is lost on administration of the tax system. From society's point of view, the local tax should not create such high levels of default that expensive legal processes must be incurred to enforce payment or punish those who will not pay. From the taxpayer's point of view, the tax should be simple to understand and easy to comply with.
6. *Revenue sufficiency* The tax yield should be sufficient to finance the levels of services for which local people vote. The local tax should therefore have an easily adjustable tax rate and/or an elastic tax base, the latter being buoyant over time, expanding as fast as expenditures in order to avoid severe fiscal stress (see Chapter 6).

7. *Revenue stability* It would be difficult to find a tax not affected by adverse long-term economic trends, but it should be possible to find one which does not experience short-term instability in tax revenues. Such instability would create discontinuities in the availability of local government services, especially as many central governments do not allow local authorities to borrow to finance current expenditure. This may be regarded as undesirable if those services are crucial components of the welfare state. In that case, the most suitable local tax is one whose revenue yield is largely unaffected by *cyclical* variations in the local economy.

8. *Immobile tax base* Relatively high rates of local taxation in one authority should not lead to erosion of the local tax base, otherwise the revenue sufficiency and stability rules will be breached. Hence, local taxes should not be levied upon highly mobile tax bases because tax-base migration could result.

These eight principles make clear that the local tax should not allow '*tax exporting*' whereby the economic incidence of the tax falls outwith the jurisdiction of the authority which levies the tax. This is particularly likely to be the case where local taxes are levied upon the production value of natural resources (such as crude oil), upon wholesale (or other pre-retail stage) prices, on business properties (at least levels of local taxation in excess of those warranted on benefit grounds), and on tourist accommodation.

ASSESSMENT OF ALTERNATIVE LOCAL TAXES

The eight principles of local taxation can be used to determine which taxes are appropriate for local government. Those principles therefore provide a solution to the *tax-assignment problem*, namely determining which level of government should control the major taxes. It will be demonstrated that a substantial proportion of the major taxes should be assigned to national government, especially highly redistributive taxes on income, profits and wealth.

1. Local Taxes on Incomes Profits and Wealth

Such taxes would be more closely related to ability to pay than to the use made of services. They would therefore satisfy equity criteria more than efficiency and accountability criteria. Furthermore, it was made clear in Chapter 1 that highly redistributive taxes are not suitable as local taxes if it creates incentives for highly-taxed groups to exit jurisdictions discriminating in favour of lower-income groups. The smaller the scale of local government the greater the potential for migration. Hence, the conclusion is that both horizontal and vertical redistribution through taxation is best left to central government. In particular, the base of taxes on income, profits and wealth are probably too mobile to provide revenue sufficiency and stability for local (and perhaps regional) authorities.

In addition, the first two tax bases are substantially dependent upon the state of the local economy and so, again, may fail to satisfy the sufficiency and stability principles. Local control of these three taxes may also make more difficult central government's management of aggregate demand and frustrate any policy to reduce the national aggregate level of taxation (see Chapter 5). Finally, collection of income tax at the place of work will not necessarily correspond with the place of residence in that they may be in different local authorities, this being particularly the case in large metropolitan areas with many local governments.

2. A Local Sales Tax

A local sales tax would experience many of the same cyclical problems as taxes on incomes, profits and wealth. Moreover, relatively high tax rates levied by one authority within a metropolitan area would encourage people to shop in neighbouring jurisdictions, this cross-border shopping being more marked the smaller the geographical area of the 'high tax' authority. This would have two effects. First, falling tax revenues in the relatively highly taxed authority. Second, tax exporting by the other authorities whose local sales tax would now be increasingly paid by non-resident shoppers (those resident in the highly taxed authority). Allocative inefficiency results in all cases because, in not having to bear the full costs of their decisions, local voters vote for excessive levels of services.

Hence, local sales taxes are more suitable for regional than for local government. Nonetheless, like a local income tax, a local sales tax is generally not highly perceptible, the tax payment being 'hidden' in the retail price of the commodity. Even if the amount of sales tax paid is printed separately on the till receipt, it is unlikely that the shopper calculates the total amount of tax paid each year. In addition, it would be administratively complex to levy the tax (that is, to monitor purchases at all sales outlets), the yield would be 'lumpy' (if decimal points in the rate of tax are to be avoided) and unevenly distributed across households (large families perhaps spending more, single persons perhaps spending less) and across commodities (some exempt, others not).

3. A Local Property Tax

Land and buildings are generally referred to as immovable or real property. An early 1990s survey (Youngman and Malme 1994) found that land and property are almost everywhere taxed jointly by local governments and these taxes are usually jointly referred to as 'the property tax'.

Compared with the alternatives, a local tax levied upon land and property best fulfils the eight principles of local taxation set out above. It satisfies the *efficiency* criterion in that the incidence of the tax cannot easily be passed outwith the authority (but see below). It is a *highly visible* tax in that, unlike a local sales tax, it is not 'hidden' in the final price of a commodity. Instead, in many countries, land owners and householders are presented with a written demand for payment of the local residential property tax. This enhances the accountability of service providers to voters. It promotes *local autonomy* in that, unlike income and profits taxes, it does not have to be shared with central government or with other local authorities. It satisfies the *economy* criterion, being relatively cheap to collect, property being easier to identify, define and measure than taxable incomes or profits. It can provide *sufficient revenue* since, while the tax base may be inelastic between periodic revaluations (which may be costly in administrative terms), the tax rate can readily be increased.

Local politicians and bureaucrats often challenge this, claiming that it is politically difficult to raise the rate of the residential property tax. Such resistance on the part of property tax payers to higher tax rates is the inevitable result of the high visibility of the tax: without it accountability would not be ensured. Otherwise, distributional coalitions and budget-maximizing bureaucrats would find it too easy to increase spending in their own interests (see Chapter 5).

A property tax has a *stable yield*, being largely unaffected by short-term fluctuations in economic activity since it is not based upon incomes, expenditures or profits. The residential property tax base is virtually *immobile*, in that land and property cannot easily be moved from a high tax to low tax jurisdiction.

The only principle which the property tax has difficulty in satisfying is that of *equity* based on ability to pay the tax. Company profits are not directly related to the taxable value of company property. Similarly, for residential property, while there is usually a fairly strong positive correlation between a person's (or household's) income and the value of the property occupied, there are many anomalies. Ownership of an expensive house may reflect past (rather than current) income, especially in the case of retired owner-occupiers. Similarly, some affluent households may prefer to inhabit low value (purchased or rented) housing, either prefering to spend their income on other commodities or choosing to save instead of spend. Hence, both horizontal and vertical equity are difficult to satisfy. While, almost all countries assign property or real-estate taxes to local government, these equity considerations limit the financial burden which can be placed upon the property tax. No European country has raised proportionately substantial local tax revenues without a local income tax.

Nevertheless, the whole tax system (both central and local taxes) must be considered when judging progressivity. Criticizing the property tax for its lack of consistency in promoting vertical and horizontal equity adopts a highly partial view of the tax system. Central government may choose to improve vertical equity by giving property tax reliefs to those on low incomes and by allowing the tax to be offset against other company taxes (for example, on profits).

However, it is inherently difficult for a residential property tax to achieve horizontal equity. This is because the relative values of different types of property (such as houses and apartments) tend to change over time, as do the relative values of a given type of property in different neighbourhoods within a single jurisdiction. These changes will be incorporated in periodic revaluations of the tax base. The resulting horizontal inequities may make it difficult for local authorities to levy high tax rates, so compromising the revenue sufficiency criterion. This revenue constraint is quite separate from any imposed on local authorities by central government's need to control local tax rates for macroeconomic purposes (see Chapter 5).

Despite the broad commonality in terms of the joint taxation of land and buildings, there is considerable variation among countries in the way the local tax is imposed. The main variations relate to the taxable subjects in the tax base (land, buildings, other business assets and so on), the valuation of that base (capital or rental valuations), which tier of government (central, regional, or local) determines the tax base and tax rate, exemptions of various classes of property (agricultural, government buildings, charities and so on), and the frequency of revaluation of the tax base.

Of the 14 countries surveyed by Youngman and Malme, only in Australia is land alone the primary legally-prescribed tax base. Capital values form the tax base in Canada, Indonesia, Japan, Sweden, and the USA. Annual rental values are used in France, whereas area is used in Israel. The UK generally uses rental values for non-residential property (although less so in Scotland – see Mair and Laramie 1992) but capital values for residential property, property here referring to buildings not land. In Sweden, only residential land and buildings are subject to local taxation, commercial properties having been removed from the tax base in 1993.

Instead of becoming bogged down in the details of different property tax regimes, suffice it to say that in terms of its global usage, a property tax almost invariably taxes *both* the value of a building and the value of the land upon which it is situated. However, it is useful for conceptual purposes to clearly distinguish between the value of land and the value of property on that land. Those two values can diverge quite substantially.

For example, the property may be of a form of which there is an excess supply, perhaps because it is structurally unsuitable for modern business uses. Modern manufacturing processes require single-storey, open-plan buildings such that there is little demand for old multi-storey factories with heavily partitioned spaces. Such obsolete industrial properties therefore command low rents, even though they may be occupying highly valued sites. A given tax rate on the market value of use of the property would therefore raise less revenue than a tax on the market value of the land determined by its most profitable alternative use.

(a) A Land Tax

A land tax differs from a property tax in that it taxes the market value of the land upon which the property is located, not the property itself. A land tax could therefore improve allocative efficiency in land use by stimulating re-development of the site to its most profitable use. However, redevelopment of the site may be constrained by the planning authority or because fragmented ownership of land results in any one site being too small for modern uses. Both of these are institutional factors. For example, the planning authority may have designated the site for a particular use which is not its most profit-able use (for example, central city land to be used for housing rather than for offices and other commercial uses). Fragmented ownership of land is a feature of many European cities and has been identified as one of the causes of the urban–rural shift (see Chapter 6) because it makes difficult the aggregation of many small sites into one large site.

A tax on the rise in land values not attributable to improvements by the proprietor has been advocated for centuries, for example by Ricardo, J. S. Mill and Henry George (George 1966). In particular, the granting of plan-ning permission by a local authority can result in a huge increase in the market value of a piece of land. Examples are a site previously used for agriculture but now to be used for a hypermarket, or a site previously alloc-ated for housing but now available for office construction. Local authorities provide considerable inputs of infrastructure (such as water and sewerage systems or local roads) which further adds to the value of a development site.

The relevant policy distinction is whether to *tax the increase in land values* resulting from the local authority giving permission for the redevelopment to go ahead and/or to levy an *infrastructure charge* to recover the costs incurred by local authorities in providing roads, schools and other community facilities required by that redevelopment (Bailey 1990b). Chapter 7 noted that various infrastructure charges are currently in use in the USA and Britain. The tax is generally referred to as a *betterment tax*, 'betterment' being the rise in the value of the site to be redeveloped consequent upon receiving planning permission. A betterment tax would raise revenues in direct proportion to the rise in land values rather than simply recover the costs of infrastructure provided by the local authority.

There are a number of means by which betterment can be recovered.

- *A betterment tax*, which taxes the rise in land values not attributable to improvements by the land owner at the time planning permission is given for redevelopment of the site: the betterment tax would be a one-off tax and could be used alongside an ongoing property tax.

- *Site-value rating*, where the capital value of the site forms the tax base, not the rental value of the property on it: whereas the betterment tax would tax the rise in land values at the time planning permission is given for redevelopment of the site, site-value rating would tax rising land values on an ongoing basis.
- *Auctioning*, the efficiency of which assumes a highly competitive market for land, which is obviously not the case where developers act collusively in agreeing not to compete with each other for every piece of land.
- *Land nationalization* – this is the polar opposite to auctioning sites within a free market, but not acceptable in most countries.
- *Planning gain* (used in the UK and now called 'planning obligations' – see Chapter 7) whereby developers build capital facilities (e.g. roads) or provide amenities not required for their own schemes and then dedicate them to the local authority: this is a form of pseudo betterment tax in that it is financed out of the developer's profits consequent upon receiving planning permission and/or infrastructural investment by the local authority.

The post-1947 attempts also to tax increases in UK land values consequent upon the granting of planning permission caused controversy and inhibited development. In recent years a betterment tax was attempted spasmodically in Britain up to 1985 through betterment levies and development land taxes. Problems of site valuation resulted in the tax being regarded as an 'arbitrary fee' subject to haggling between developer and district valuer. Similar problems had been experienced before 1947, when attempting to tax betterment resulting from specific infrastructural improvements as distinct from the general rise in land values. Betterment taxes create significant resource disparities among local authorities, raising more revenue where there are pressures for development (for example in the South East of England) than where there is general underdevelopment (as in parts of the North of England). Capital gains tax is the only national tax on such gains in the UK today.

(b) A Local Residential Property Tax

Whilst the local residential property tax scores poorly in terms of ability to pay, it does well in terms of the other principles of local taxation (although the supposed matching of benefit and payment is questioned below). The equity principle relates to the fiscal transfer model of government, whilst the other principles relate to the fiscal exchange model (see Chapter 1). This illustrates the potential conflict between efficiency and equity. The *benefit model* of local government finance conforms with economic analysis since it equates willingness to pay for, and benefit received from, the last (marginal) unit of service consumed. The *ability to pay* model may be preferred by those who value equity above efficiency.

(c)   A Local Business (Non-residential) Property Tax
It is arguable that a local business property tax satisfies the principles of visibility, local autonomy, economy, and revenue sufficiency and stability. However, a local business property tax fails to satisfy the other three principles, namely equity, efficiency and an immobile tax base.

As already noted, a business property tax suffers the same equity problems as the residential property tax because it is not related to profits. It is also susceptible to tax exporting to other jurisdictions through higher product prices. This should be avoided because of the resulting allocative inefficiencies. Inefficiency also results because local businesses usually have no vote. Firms whose business is specific to the locality are largely immobile and therefore susceptible to excessive taxation by their local governments. Even where local authorities consult with local business, voice remains weak because consultation may not affect decisions (see Chapters 3 and 4). The tax base is potentially highly mobile. Companies whose business is not tied to local markets or to local inputs (such as natural resource deposits) have considerable scope for exit from authorities levying relative high business property taxes.

The benefit principle of local taxation means that the amount of property tax paid by local businesses should equal the value of the services from which they benefit. That benefit clearly relates to services provided directly to local business, for example the collection and disposal of waste from office blocks. It also includes some of the indirect benefits provided by other services, for example if education provides a skilled work force. Direct benefits are easy to measure relative to the value of indirect benefits. For example, the direct benefits of waste collection and disposal can be measured by comparison with charges by commercial waste collection and disposal companies. Indirect benefits cannot legitimately be used to justify the open-ended taxation of local businesses by local governments.

(d)   Subjurisdictional Property Taxes
Other forms of local property taxes are available which are consistent with many of the eight principles of local taxation set out above:

(i) Special Assessments   As already noted in Chapter 7, special assessments are used in a very limited way by municipalities in the USA to finance improvements of local streets, sewers, water systems and sidewalks (pavements) above basic standards and of benefit to specified properties. They are not used to finance general community-wide expenditures such as schools. Nor are they used to finance new infrastructure being provided for the first time.

Where they are used the special assessment payable per property is usually assessed on a crude rule-of-thumb basis, usually front footage (that is, length) or acreage (that is, area) of properties since these determine the lengths of street, sewer and water lines, and so on, and therefore their cost. Hence, the approximation is between cost and financing rather than between benefit and financing.

They must be approved by, say, referenda, voters having the choice to forgo infrastructural improvements if they judge the costs to be greater than the benefits. This is consistent with efficiency and the other principles of local taxation. The drawback is that, if approved, the current generation of voters in the locality in question commit their successors to ongoing payments without necessarily considering whether or not they can bear the cost.

This problem was highlighted in the USA by the 1930s Great Depression. People (and businesses) simply could not afford to pay these additional annual tax liabilities during a period of mass unemployment and reduced demand. Similar liquidity problems would apply today, although these could be overcome by combining special assessment with tax deferment (at market interest rates) whereby owners of residential properties would pay them when they sell the benefited property or die, whichever occurs first. In holding a large portfolio of deferred assessments, city authorities could receive a predictable flow of repayments by which to amortize the debt on their issues of special assessment bonds used to finance the cost of the infrastructure.

(ii) Other Neighbourhood/District Property Taxes   There has been a dramatic growth of private government in the USA, in the form of 150 000 or so *residential community associations* (RCAs) and 1000 or so *business improvement districts* (BIDs). RCAs and BIDs are groups of private property owners agreeing by majority voting for additional municipal-style services to be provided in their own areas (neighbourhood, commercial centre, office complex or town centre) and for which charges or property-based taxes are levied on their members.

These broadly democratic but private organizations take collective decisions for provision of municipal-style services such as security, leisure and recreation, street cleaning, refuse collection, grounds and roads maintenance and local economic development in residential areas (RCAs) and in city or town centres (BIDs). They have developed out of a context of significant involvement of non-profit organizations and voluntary action (Broom and Wild 1996; Dilger 1993; Houston 1996; Lavery 1995; Travers and Weimar 1996). They are an example of the shift from government to governance (see Chapter 12).

Charges or property-based taxes are levied on their members to finance these services. These payments are additional to those paid to their true (constitutional) local governments. Although this may be regarded as a form of double payment, and therefore in some sense inequitable, it matches additional service benefits with additional property tax payments and therefore satisfies the benefit principle of taxation. Given the clear link between payment and direct benefits, the tax base can be expected to be much less likely to move out.

4. A Local Poll Tax

A local poll tax is a flat-rate, locally variable, tax payable by all adults resident within a local authority's administrative area. Liability to pay a local poll tax mirrors eligibility to vote in local elections much more closely than liability to pay a residential property tax. Hence, a poll tax should bring about a much closer correspondence between those who vote for, those who pay for and those who receive local government services (see Chapter 5). If so, accountability is greater under a poll tax than under a property tax.

In theory, a poll tax also promotes economic efficiency. Compared with an income tax, a poll tax provides a stronger incentive to work because it has an income effect but no substitution effect (an income tax has both) in terms of the tradeoff between work and leisure. Hence, a poll tax does not lead to allocative inefficiency through any disincentive-to-work effects. This result is well known and an explanation is provided elsewhere (Bailey 1995, ch. 4). This assumes that people fulfill their legal obligations to pay both taxes and that there is work available for them as they seek to regain their original level of welfare. Although better in terms of allocative efficiency, economists have traditionally accepted that a poll tax fails to satisfy equity criteria, notably because it is a very regressive form of taxation.

As already noted in Chapters 5 and 6, a local poll tax was introduced in Britain for a short period in the early 1990s as a replacement of the former local residential property tax. The substitution of one local tax for another was part of a broader reform of local government finance, including nationalization of the local business rate and changes to the system of central government grants.

The *raison d'être* of the local poll tax was to secure improved local accountability in the provision of services. 'Local accountability depends crucially on the relationship between paying for local services and voting in local elections' (Cmnd 9714, para. 1.52). Only householders were liable to pay the former domestic property tax, meaning that non-householders could vote for more spending without necessarily having to bear the financial consequences. Similarly, about a third of householders received full or partial property tax rebates during the mid-1980s. Moreover, local businesses financed more than half of total property tax income (up to three-quarters in some authorities) and yet had no vote.

Hence, the UK government believed that local accountability was not being achieved. It argued that there was an in-built tendency for local electorates to vote for ever higher levels of local government spending. Local politicians were in a position to 'buy votes' with service expansion at little or no cost to the majority of voters, and were therefore too easily inclined to give in to pressure groups demanding more services specifically targeted to their needs (see Chapter 5).

Introduction of the poll tax meant that the constitutional axiom of 'no taxation without representation' had been turned on its head at the local government level – 'no representation without taxation'. This could be regarded as the ninth principle of local taxation, in addition to the eight listed above. The very limited rebate and exemption scheme meant that voters had more of a financial incentive (though perhaps still not strong enough) to be better informed of the budgetary options offered by competing local political parties:

> In addition to bringing the tax base more closely into line with the electorate, however, the new arrangements must also ensure that taxpayers see a clear link between changes in their authority's expenditure and the corresponding changes in local tax bills. (Cmnd 9714, para. 4.3)

This could be regarded as the tenth principle of local taxation.

Conversion of the former effort-related intergovernmental grant into a lump-sum grant (see Chapter 9) further enhanced local accountability because the full cost of any increases in service provision, over and above those supported by central government grant, were borne by the local poll tax. The poll tax had to finance expenditure fully at the margin while only partially financing total spending.

As already noted in Chapter 6, the poll tax financed such a small proportion of total spending that it created some very high gearing effects in particular authorities. It was (and still is) arguable that the new system of local government finance created too strong a link between voting and local taxes, the result being excessive restraint on local spending. Elsewhere it was argued that 'the aim of the reform therefore appears to be to increase accountability in order to reduce spending – objectives which cannot necessarily be achieved simultaneously' (Martlew and Bailey 1988, p. 76). Certainly, the UK government felt it necessary to continue to 'cap' local tax increases and, ultimately, to cap local authorities' budgets. Given the continuing rises in local tax levels above what the UK government considered appropriate, the poll tax apparently failed to achieve local accountability.

The poll tax was predestined to be unpopular since, while there were roughly as many households paying less tax as those paying more (the reform being 'revenue neutral'), the losing households contained more voters. Hence, although the domestic property tax had been unpopular, its replacement was even more so. The reaction of academics and other commentators was also overwhelmingly hostile to the reform, even before its implementation. The negative response reflected its distributional consequences (Smith and Squire 1986; Bailey 1987; Smith 1988), its deleterious effects on local government and local democracy (Jones *et al.* 1986; Midwinter and Mair 1987; Bailey and Paddison 1988), its impracticability (Quirk 1986), and the high administrative costs, especially those of trying to trace all adults in order to raise tax payments from them. It was estimated that collection costs were about 5 per cent of total poll tax revenue compared with 1 per cent for the former domestic local property tax (Bailey 1988b, 1990c).

Table 8.1 *Distributional effects of the former UK poll tax*

Characteristic	Gainers	Losers	Causation
Individuals	High income	Low income	Regressive flat-rate charge
	Employed	Unemployed	Every adult had to pay at least 20 per cent
Households	One adult	Several adults	Property tax paid per household, poll tax paid per head
	House-holders	Non-householders	Non-householders pay poll tax but not property tax
	Owner-occupiers	Non-owner-occupiers	Owner-occupiers experienced a capital gain following the abolition of property tax
Areas	High rateable value	Low rateable value	Poll tax bears no relation to an area's amenities – property values do
	Suburbs	Inner city	,,
	Urban	Rural	,,
Authorities	London and SE England	Northern England	Resources equalization ended[a]
	Growing	Declining	Loss of population reduces grant[a] and business tax revenues[b]
	Small % grant	High % grant	Grant-gearing[c]
	Low need	High need	Grant-gearing[c]
Taxpayer	Non-domestic	Domestic	UBR increases limited to inflation[d]
	National	Local	Grant-gearing[c]
	Urban business	Rural business	UBR raised tax rates in rural areas and reduced them in urban areas[b]
	Dishonest	Honest	Tax evasion increased the average poll tax

Notes:
a: See Chapter 9.
b: See below.
c: See Chapter 6.
d: UBR denotes the Uniform Business Rate (see below).

The early evidence subsequent to the introduction of the poll tax suggested that the UK government underestimated the impact on tax levels (Bailey 1989b, 1990c, 1991; Midwinter and Monaghan 1991). Such underestimation may have occured because the government failed to realize the implications of high gearing effects. Local authorities could blame central government for sharp increases in local tax levels, on the grounds that intergovernmental grants were inadequate.

The British experience of the poll tax made clear that equity issues were much more complex and multifaceted than simply its regressive nature. This is demonstrated in Table 8.1, a fuller explanation being available elsewhere (Bailey 1987).

The impacts of the poll tax package of reforms were clearly multifaceted. In combination they seriously disadvantaged the residents of inner cities who typically have relatively high rates of unemployment, relatively low incomes, relatively large household size, relatively high needs for local services and relatively high dependence on central grants.

The poll tax also had unforeseen implications for ethnic groups. The average number of adults per UK household was then 2.0 for whites, 2.3 for West Indians and 2.7 for Asians. In fact 22 per cent of Asians and 17 per cent of Afro-Caribbeans lived in households with more than three adults, compared with only 6 per cent of whites (Brown 1984). Furthermore the ethnic groups were (and still are) much more likely to live within the inner city than are white households. Hence, the increases in local tax bills for many inner city households were substantially underestimated. Even if one takes the view that such households had made inadequate local tax contributions in the past, the financial consequences of the poll tax were nonetheless severe, particularly for ethnic groups which already experienced relatively high unemployment and relatively low incomes.

Such was the unpopularity of the poll tax that it was replaced by a new form of local residential property tax (council tax) in 1993 (see Chapter 6). While the council tax resurrected all the criticisms of a property tax, the reform had demonstrated the advantages of a property tax in terms of the principles of local taxation. Nonetheless, the incremental principle was retained.

The council tax has three components:

1. *A property component*, the amount of tax payable depending upon the *capital* value of the house or flat. (The residential property tax prior to the poll tax was based upon the imputed *rental* value of each property.) Under the council tax, residential properties are allocated to 8 broad bands of valuation. Rates of council tax increase for properties in successively higher bands of valuation but properties in the highest band pay no more than 2.5 times the amount paid by properties in the lowest band.
2. *An individual component*, with a discount of 25 per cent where the property is occupied by only one liable person aged 18 or over and of 50 per cent where the property is not a liable person's sole or main residence. Residents not liable for the tax include students, apprentices, those on youth training programmes and long-term patients in hospitals.
3. *An income-related component* whereby a means-tested graduated system of rebates (of up to 100 per cent) provides financial support for council taxpayers with low incomes. Hence, compared with the former poll tax, the new residential property tax reinstates a broad correspondence between

income and ability to pay (Gibb 1992; O'Hare 1993). Put simply, there-fore, the poll tax was allocatively efficient but not very equitable. The council tax is broadly equitable, if not allocatively efficient.

A CLOSER LOOK AT TAX INCIDENCE AND MIGRATION OF BUSINESSES

The formal or legal liability for tax may not coincide with the economic (or effective) incidence of that tax. Variations in tax incidence between local authorities can be expected to influence the location of firms in much the same way as interjurisdictional differences in tax and service packages affect the location of households (see Chapter 4).

1. A Local Sales Tax

It is well established within the theory of tax incidence that if a firm has some degree of market power, it will be able to raise the selling prices of its products and so pass on to its customers some or all of a commodity tax such as a local sales tax (Bailey 1995, ch. 4). This *forward shifting* is greater, the greater the degree of monopoly power (because customers are less able to seek alternative suppliers) and the less the availability of substitute products. Alternatively, the firm may reduce the prices it pays for its inputs of land (rent), labour (wages and salaries) and capital (interest). This *backward shifting* is greater the greater the degree of monopsony power, for example where the firm is the sole or main buyer of a particular input such as a particular labour skill. It could also reduce the amount of dividends paid to shareholders, *lateral shifting*.

Consider, in isolation, a local authority which increases local sales tax bills. All businesses *in that authority* face an increased tax bill, so any firm knows that it can pass the tax forwards or backwards to the same extent as other firms in the same jurisdiction. There may be short-lived problems caused, for example, by fixed-term contracts for the supply of goods or rent levels but, assuming all firms seek to maximize profits, these firms will seek to pass on the increased tax bill in the medium to longer term.

Now consider *all* local authorities, the competition between firms in different authorities and the extent of forward-shifting into price. If a local authority levies a higher local sales tax bill than other authorities, the firms in that area will only be able to pass on as much of the tax in higher prices as is incurred by firms in other areas, assuming a highly competitive market for their out-puts. The result is that firms in the higher taxed area become less profitable. This may be compounded by cross-border shopping (see above). Some firms at the margins of profitability may go out of business altogether, resulting in job losses. Others may decide to move into lower-taxed areas, taking jobs with them. Most will remain in the higher-taxed authority since it will cost more to relocate than the present value of the extra tax paid in years to come.

However, these firms will have less after-tax profits either to reinvest in the business or for distribution of dividends to shareholders. Reduced dividends will make it harder for firms to raise further external finance for investment and there will also be less retained profits for reinvestment. Reduced investment leads to fewer jobs than would otherwise have been the case. Moreover, new firms seeking a location will be more likely to decide not to set up business in the higher taxed area, 'pull' factors probably being greater than 'push' factors when relocating (see Chapter 4). In combination, these various factors mean that gradually, over time, the local authority experiences a decline in business investment and a loss of jobs, always assuming *ceteris paribus*.

Consider now the ability of firms to pass the tax backwards into lower input prices. Over time, as contracts become due for renewal, firms may be able to renegotiate lower wages, lower rents and so on. The extent to which this is possible depends on the elasticity of supply of inputs, the greater that elasticity the greater the proportion of the tax borne by the firm itself.

Tax exporting occurs where the incidence of the tax falls outwith the local authority and is therefore a variant of tax incidence. Tax exporting in the form of *forward shifting* can only occur for commodities traded outwith the jurisdiction and will not apply to purely local services such as hairdressing and local legal, accountancy and other services supplied only to local businesses. It is only likely to be significant where local firms have sufficient monopoly power in regional and national markets that they can raise prices paid by consumers both within and outwith the jurisdiction in which they are located. Similar conclusions apply to tax exporting in the form of *backward shifting*, where lower prices are paid for inputs drawn from outwith the locality. This would be the case, for example, where workers commute from surrounding jurisdictions and where alternative employment was not available such that the business had considerable monopsony power. Tax exporting via *lateral shifting* occurs when owners of the firm are not resident in the jurisdiction. This would lead to existing shareholders incurring capital losses due to falling share values and lower market valuation of the company.

2. A Local Business Property Tax

A local business property tax can be expected to have effects similar to those outlined above in respect of a local sales tax. Like the analysis of incidence of a local sales tax, the theory of property tax incidence is also based on a set of assumptions that firms maximize profits and that, in the long-run equilibrium, the net returns to mobile factors of production are equalized across alternative locations. It is also assumed that firms set prices in relation to variable costs. The key difference is that it is assumed that property taxes are a component of fixed costs whereas local sales taxes are assumed to be a component of variable costs. Hence, unlike a local sales tax, a property tax has no impact on price, instead being borne out of profits. Tax differentials between alternative business locations will therefore lead to corresponding differences in short-run net profits. In the long run, capital will move out of the relatively highly-taxed areas into relatively low-taxed areas in order that profits be maximized.

Tax capitalization theory suggests that landowners would bear a large part of the economic burden of the local business property tax through lower land prices and rental values. Tax capitalization refers to the impact of a tax change on the capital value of an asset. That value falls if a tax is levied (or increased) and rises if the tax is reduced (or abolished) assuming *ceteris paribus*. Equilibrium is regained when the rate of return on the asset is restored to the level before the increase or decrease in tax. The capital value of the asset is therefore inversely related to the change in the tax levied on it. For example, an increase in tax reduces the post-tax rate of return represented by a given level of earnings divided by the capital value of the asset. Hence, that capital value must fall in order to restore the rate of return to its former level since no one will buy the asset until its relative rate of return is restored, the returns on other assets being unchanged due to the *ceteris paribus* assumption (see Bailey 1995, ch. 10). Landowners would therefore bear a large part of the economic burden of the property tax at the time it is introduced or increased.

Chapter 4 noted evidence of capitalization in terms of property values as a result of Tiebout-style migration. Other research results in the UK, where many business properties are rented rather than owned by the occupier, suggest that increases in the rates of the local business property tax reduce commercial property rents – although data deficiences meant that it was not possible to estimate precisely by how much (Bond *et al.* 1996). However, landowners are unlikely to bear *all* of the economic burden of the property tax since, whilst total physical area is fixed, land does have alternative uses in urban areas (for example, housing instead of industrial uses). Hence, the supply of land is not perfectly inelastic. Therefore, given the limited scope for forward and backward shifting of the local business tax, higher-taxed jurisdictions may experience a loss of economic activity, leading to relatively high unemployment.

The foregoing analysis is partial in approach in that it focused on business activity to the exclusion of the knock-on implications for local government spending in the high taxing authorities (that is, the demand-side effects). Some of the increased spending financed by relatively high levels of local taxation can be expected to benefit local businesses whether directly (for example, collection of waste from business premises) or indirectly (for example, through a better-educated work force). Furthermore, local authorities make direct purchases of supplies and services from local firms, as well as from those outwith their jurisdictions. However, the bulk of local government spending benefits local people rather than local firms and, while real income levels may be increased by the provision of local services, the resultant multiplier effects are probably quite small because of leakages outwith the jurisdiction (see Chapter 1).

Consistent with the law of diminishing marginal returns, the increased supply of capital in the lower taxed areas ultimately leads to a fall in the marginal productivity of capital and so profits fall at the margin, cutting off further inward investment. Similarly, the reduction in the supply of capital in the high taxed area leads to increased marginal productivity, the rise in profits at the margin stemming further outmigration of businesses. Long-run equilibrium is restored once sufficient capital has migrated to equalize the net of tax returns to capital in all local authorities. Given that capital and labour are complementary in production, the redistribution of capital will be associated with a similar redistribution of employment. No such redistribution would occur if local business property taxes were uniform across all local government jurisdictions. Hence, it is not the *level* of property taxes but rather *differentials* in tax bills between local authorities which induces capital movements.

The foregoing analysis is based on a partial equilibrium analysis of the theoretical impact of the business property tax. While justifiable at the level of the local authority, it has to be recognized that the final impact can only be analysed by means of a general equilibrium analysis at the level of the whole economy. The results of the latter will differ depending upon whether a neo-classical or post-Keynesian theoretical framework is adopted. Ultimately, a comprehensive model of the effective incidence of the business property tax must incorporate a theory of business pricing (that is, marginal revenue equal to marginal cost versus mark-up pricing), a theory of tax incidence, a theory of the distribution of income between the factors of production, and a theory of income determination (that is, classical versus Keynesian). Much more detailed formal treatments of the incidence of the local business property tax demonstrate the difficulties in coming to a clear a priori conclusion about the effective incidence of a business property tax (Mair 1984, 1987; Mair and Laramie 1992; Laramie and Mair 1993, 1996).

3. Empirical Evidence at the Local Authority Level

Considerable research has been undertaken in respect of the UK's local business property tax. There have been two main approaches:

(a)   *Econometric Analysis of the Local Impact*
If relatively high local tax bills were associated with relatively low profits, relatively low investment and relatively high unemployment, then there would be empirical evidence to corroborate (but not necessarily prove) the crowding-out

thesis. The problem with empirical research is that there are many factors which affect local economic activity besides the local business property tax (Gudgin 1995).

Manufacturing industry, for example, has tended to move out of urban areas, the so-called 'urban–rural shift' of manufacturing investment and jobs (see Chapter 6). In general, the greater the urban density the greater the job loss (*the urban structure variable*). In addition, an urban area may have a concentration of industries experiencing declining employment at both a national and local level (*the industrial structure variable*).

Only after all other factors influencing employment levels (for example, industrial structure, urban structure and regional policy initiatives) have been taken into account, can the residual employment pattern be statistically tested against differences in local business tax bills per square metre of floor space.

Differences in local tax bills would have to be significant and sustained over a period of years to offset costs incurred in moving. The optimal time to move would be when any major reinvestment in premises and or plant and machinery is required. Existing firms may endure relatively high local tax bills for years before operations become unprofitable and they close down or move elsewhere. Newly emerging firms take into account all business costs (of which local business taxes are usually a very small proportion) in choosing their location so that the impact of differences in local taxes will be muted and take years to become apparent.

Hence, studies using short time periods for their analysis will tend to underestimate the impact on employment. Time lags cannot be determined *a priori* and aggregative statistical analyses have to experiment with varying time lags until the 'best fit' (statistical correlation) occurs between differences in local tax bills and the emerging differences in unemployment (assuming the unemployed do not migrate in the meantime).

During the 1980s, urban areas as a whole in the UK experienced sharp declines in the real levels and shares of grant paid to them by central government. They tried to make up the loss of revenue by increasing their rates of local business property taxation. Hence, relatively high levels of unemployment could become statistically associated with relatively high business rate bills without there necessarily being a direct causation from one to the other. Much the same could be said about a statistical correlation between relatively high local business taxes and relatively low investment and/or low profits.

An empirical study which attempted to take account of structural factors (industrial and urban structure in particular) concluded that 'after one of the most extensive studies of local employment change to have been undertaken in Britain...we are able to detect little if any influence of [local business property tax] rates on the location of jobs' (Crawford *et al.* 1985, p. 92). However, this study was heavily criticized by Damania (1986).

First, it ignored the time lags (noted above) between changes in local tax rates and any resulting changes in employment. Second, it neglected theoretical issues by concentrating on tax *levels* and the temporal *changes* in tax rates whereas, as noted above, the location of business capital (and therefore employment) depends upon tax *differentials* between areas. Third, in driving businesses out of an area, relatively high local business property taxes may themselves influence urban structure. Allowing for urban structure before deriving the residual of employment change would therefore underestimate the impact of local taxation on business location. Hence, multi-collinearity could exist between the property tax variables and the structural explanatory variables. Put simply, the dependent and independent variables are not clearly separable.

Damania concluded that the Crawford *et al.* model was theoretically misspecified and econometrically deficient, leading to a set of implausible empirical results which do not accord with the theory of tax incidence.

(b)   Micro-level Surveys of Individual Businesses

Bennett and Fearnehough (1987) undertook a very restricted micro-level survey of British firms engaged in hand tools manufacture. Because of the close similarity of firms in terms of size, production methods, capital intensity and product range, the authors claimed a tightly controlled sampling framework. A third of these firms were located in Sheffield, the remaining two-thirds being widely distributed throughout Britain. They concluded that 'the paper does provide considerable objective, as well as subjective, evidence of major distortions to competitiveness and to rates of return to capital in one highly [taxed] locality' (p. 35). However, the authors do point out the smallness of the industry (approximately 105 firms), the low response rate to their survey (29 replies) and the caution necessary in generalizing from their results.

Their analysis focuses on tax rates and tax bills in total, relative to profits, to other production expenses and per employee. There are a number of caveats. First, consideration only of tax rates is of little value since the total tax bill depends on both the tax rate and the tax base (rateable values). It is known that rateable values vary widely between different areas because of differing property values. Second, total tax bills also vary according to the size of the premises and the amount of equipment they contain, since both are positively related to rateable value. Third, it is misleading to use number of employees as an indicator of firm size, because employees are not taxable capital. Fourth, a high proportion of tax bills to profits can indicate high taxes or low profits.

Profits will tend to be low if productivity per employee is low, and that depends upon the degree of capital intensity and the age of plant and machinery (new equipment usually incorporating technological improvements which boost productivity). This, in turn, may be related to tax bills. However, those bills are not the only influence upon capital intensity. A high proportion of local property tax to other production expenses may simply reflect backward-shifting of the tax, for example through to lower property rentals. A high proportion relative to employees may simply reflect high capital intensity.

Bennett and Fearnehough's conclusions are therefore highly qualified. Even without these qualifications, they are strictly only valid for this one industrial sector and not necessarily applicable to other business sectors where market conditions (particularly the degree of competitiveness) vary. Nor does their evidence specifically prove that local business property taxes were the primary influence on these firms' locational decisions. Hence, once again, the empirical evidence is inconclusive.

Overview of Theory and Evidence

Bennett (1987) notes that whilst there is a large amount of theoretical literature regarding the final incidence of local government taxes, empirical studies are relatively limited both because of the lack of good quality data and the restrictive assumptions which must be employed to obtain operational models. Bennett suggests that the final incidence of any local tax is unpredictable because it depends on the details of local markets, individual firms' behaviour and the structure of the tax:

> For local profits and property taxation incidence appears, from limited empirical evidence, to fall chiefly on profits. However, for given localities and businesses there are likely to be great differences in the effects observed. The general conclusion is, therefore, that with taxation which is not based on the benefit principle, considerable, and unpredictable, distortions to economic behaviour can result which include important impacts on businesses themselves as well as other actors. This conclusion holds at the level of both formal and final incidence. (1987, p. 67)

Combined with the equity issue (that business property tax liability bears no relation to profits), this conclusion provides strong counter-arguments to the advantages of the tax in terms of visibility, local autonomy, economy and revenue sufficiency and stability. Nonetheless, King (1993, p. 174) notes that 'property taxes have been widely used as subcentral taxes without any special regard to their incidence. This is no doubt the result of some special advantages as a local tax.'

In summary, given the robust theoretical implications of relatively high local taxes, and some limited evidence supporting that theory, it seems that the larger part of the local business property tax is borne by profits. In that case, it would be unwarranted to claim that interjurisdictional differences in property tax bills had no impact at all on the location decisions of firms.

This conclusion may justify central government intervention to constrain local business property taxes within acceptable limits, in particular ensuring that local business property (and other) taxes cover no more that the benefits accruing to local businesses from the municipality's provision of services. However, this does not necessarily legitimise the transformation, in the UK, of the local business property tax into a nationally standardized uniform business rate.

THE UK'S UNIFORM BUSINESS RATE

Despite the lack of clear empirical evidence about the impact (if any) of locally-variable business property taxes on the location of firms, during the 1980s and early 1990s, the UK government believed that relatively high tax rates for the local business property tax caused significant crowding-out at the local level by detering investment by locally-indigenous firms, by causing local firms to exit the locality, and by detering inward investment by firms from outwith the jurisdiction.

Much of the UK government's economic policy during the 1980s had focused on the removal of *supply-side constraints* (see Bailey 1995, ch. 8). Relatively high local business taxes were perceived as a supply-side constraint on the efficiency of local economies. Hence, the UK government considered business taxes unsuitable as a locally variable tax. This was seen as a particular problem in central city authorities, many of which had been characterized by the Conservative (that is, right-wing) central government as high-spending, high-taxing bastions of extreme left-wing Socialist authorities hostile to capitalism and actively pursuing a new economic order.

Consistent with this microeconomic supply-side policy, a single uniform business rate (UBR) has been levied upon business properties since 1990 in England and Wales, extended, after transitional arrangements, to Scotland in 1996. This transformed the local business property *tax* into an *assigned revenue*, central government now controlling both the tax rate and the tax base. The UK government accepted the argument that high local business property tax rates crowded out local businesses. Local authorities still collect the tax, acting as agents of central government. The revenues are paid into a national pool and redistributed as an equal amount per head of adult (aged 18 and over) population. Hence, any local distortions of economic activity caused by differential rates of local business taxation were removed. Nevertheless, tax bills still vary between jurisdictions because rateable values vary. These variations will continue as periodic revaluations reflect differential change in rental values between areas (as regional and local economic growth varies) and between types of business property (for example, retail, industrial, warehousing, and office premises).

The pooling and redistribution arrangement diverts finances away from local authorities with a relatively large amount of business premises per capita and/or a relatively large proportion of children within total population, to authorities with a relatively small amounts of business and small proportions of children (that is, with a high proportions of adults). In general, financial resources have been shifted away from central city authorities at the cores of large urban areas (conurbations) to suburban and rural authorities. That shift is exacerbated by declining urban populations since, as population falls, the per capita incidence of business properties rises and selective outmigration tends to leave behind a high incidence of single-parent families. These outcomes exacerbate any tendency towards fiscal stress (see Chapter 6).

In principle, it is possible to offset these effects through the distribution of central government grants designed to compensate for differing per capita expenditure needs (see Chapter 9). However, the method for assessing the expenditure needs of local authorities (and thereby making payments of grants) was simplified in 1990 and, by implication, was made less sensitive to differing needs. Furthermore, a population-based distribution of business property tax revenues bears little relationship to the distribution of local authorities' services to local businesses.

One is prompted to question whether such an administratively cumbersome procedure as the UBR is really justified. Since business property taxes are now an assigned revenue from central to local government, there is little real distinction between this and the other grants paid to local authorities (also largely on the basis of population). The tax is still unrelated to profits and so still a burden on the marginal firm on the edge of profitability. Indeed, introduction of the UBR pushed up tax bills in those areas where bills were previously below the national average and reduced those in areas whose bills were previously above the national average, in both cases because rateable values (the tax base) remained constant (see Table 8.1).

This can be expected to have brought about the very migration of firms that the UK government had sought to prevent. Similarly, subsequent revaluations of the tax base will lead to marked redistributions of relative tax liabilities between geographic areas and between business sectors (retail, office, industrial and warehouse premises). These redistributions reflect changing relative rental values as local and regional economies and/or business sectors boom or stagnate between revaluations. Either the local authorities' freedom to vary the rates of the local business property tax should be reinstated or it should be merged with central government's corporation tax. Merger would achieve administrative savings and more clearly relate tax payments to profits and, therefore, to ability to pay.

However, abolition of the business tax would lead to huge increases in the local residential property tax (it would more than double on average in order to make up the revenue shortfall) and/or necessitate large increases in central government grants (likewise increasing by about half on average). The former outcome may not be acceptable because it would lead both to unacceptably high local tax levels and exacerbate the horizontal inequities of the residential property tax noted above. The latter outcome could have unacceptable implications for other central government taxes. Hence, the solution was to nationalize the local business property tax.

An assigned revenue is difficult to justify in efficiency terms because it is not self-evident that the equilibrium of the taxed activity will necessarily ensure precisely that amount of revenues sufficient to finance the particular level of local government services where their marginal social cost equalled their marginal social value. If, however, an assigned revenue was still deemed necessary, then a fixed proportion of corporation tax revenues could be turned over to local authorities. The apparent disadvantage of this arrangement is that the monetary value of that proportion would vary as profits varied with the state of the economy. However, this variability could be compensated for if local authorities held sufficient financial balances from one year to the next.

The outcome will be largely the same for central government finances irrespective of whether the assigned revenue is derived from the uniform business rate or from corporation tax. Other than the fact that it was previously a locally-variable tax, there appears to be little if any rationale for separately identifying local business taxes within total business taxation. The current arrangements incur unnecessary administrative costs and place a regressive tax burden upon business.

AN OVERVIEW OF LOCAL GOVERNMENT TAXES IN THE UK

As already noted in Chapter 2, local authorities in Britain tend to be larger (in population terms) than those in most other developed countries, probably reflecting the widespread use of regional governments abroad. In terms of service responsibilities and expenditures, British local government has been fairly average during past decades (Gould and Zarkesh 1986; Karran 1988).

More recently, central government has taken major services out of local government, funding them directly from the centre (see Chapter 12). Such reduction in functions relieves the burden on the local tax. Nonetheless, Britain still differs quite radically from other developed countries in terms of the narrowness of its local tax base. Prior to the introduction of the former poll tax and with the exception of Ireland, British local government stood alone in having no income from direct taxation. Council of Europe data reproduced in Table 5.3 (p. 87) show that local authorities in most other Western European countries derive a third or more of their income from local taxes, the larger percentages generally reflecting use of local income taxes. British local authorities receive a much higher proportion of income from central government grants than most of their foreign counterparts and have been much more reliant on property taxes.

Elsewhere diversity is the norm, with local governments generally using four or more local taxes (Britain has one). The most common are the local income tax, property tax and commodity taxes. Karran (1988) noted that the local income tax is used in 14 OECD countries providing on average 55 per cent of local tax revenue. The property tax is used in 18 countries, accounting on average for 40 per cent of local taxation. Local commodity taxes are used in 18 countries, but raise only 4 per cent of local tax proceeds on average. Britain is unusual in having been solely dependent on the local property tax. Assigned revenues were last used in Britain 60 years ago, are uncommon elsewhere today, and certainly do not appear in the form of the UBR system.

The poll tax was even more unusual, being previously tried in Britain almost 300 years ago, being almost unheard of in developed countries and appearing in developing countries only to be subsequently abandoned. In the USA poll taxes had been phased out in most states by the 1920s (they had been used to deliberately disenfranchise black voters in the southern states). Canada abolished its poll tax in 1970 (it had raised 4 per cent of local taxation). The poll tax in Japan raises only 0.1 per cent of local taxation and has both a flat-rate and an income-related element (with complete exemption for social security recipients).

Hence, the British system of assigned revenues is highly unusual, while the poll tax was almost completely unheard of anywhere. In combination they were unique to Britain. Replacement of the poll tax by the modified property tax (council tax) does not alter the narrowness of the local tax base. There is considerable evidence that a plurality of local taxes does provide a workable system of local and regional government, especially local income tax together with a supplementary property tax.

CONCLUSIONS

The economic rationale for local governments to have their own tax raising powers is grounded in Oates' decentralization theorem (see Chapter 2) and the concept of benefit areas outlined above. Local governments without tax-raising powers are effectively agencies of central government rather than autonomous local governments. Even if they had powers to decide the distribution of a given centrally-determined sum, allocative inefficiency would result. This scenario is developing in many European countries, given the increasing tendency of central governments to set maxima on the levels of local governments' tax rates.

The residential property tax best satisfies the eight principles of local taxation but is generally regarded as unable to levy significant proportions of local governments' revenues because of equity problems. Although the evidence is by no means conclusive, migration may be a feature of a local business property tax, this possibility explaining nationalization of that tax in the UK. Other forms of property taxation offer limited revenue-raising potential, except possibly a land tax. The UK's experiment with a local poll tax was shortlived and almost unique. Local income taxes are used in Scandinavian and some other countries but are best levied by regional rather than local governments in order to avoid tax exporting.

The Council of Europe quotation at the beginning of this chapter emphasized the need for diversified and buoyant financial resources for local governments. Chapter 7 suggested that inadequate attention had been given to charges, especially in the UK. This chapter has demonstrated that there has been a misguided preoccupation in the UK with a search for a single local tax rather than looking for a combination of two or more taxes. A plurality of local taxes is the norm elsewhere. The result is that UK local governments are overly dependent upon intergovernmental grants which, in turn, are subject to centrally-imposed public expenditure restraints. This is the subject of the next chapter.

9 The Economics of Intergovernmental Grants

*Local authorities' financial resources shall be commensurate with the respons-
ibilities provided for by the constitution and the law. The protection of financially
weaker local authorities calls for the institution of financial equalisation procedures or equivalent measures which are designed to correct the effects of
unequal distribution of potential sources of finance and of the financial burden
they must support. Such procedures or measures shall not diminish the discretion local authorities may exercise within their own sphere of responsibility. As
far as possible grants shall not be earmarked for the financing of specific
projects. The provision of grants shall not remove the basic freedom of local
authorities to exercise policy discretion within their own jurisdiction.*

(European Charter of Local Self-Government: Article 9)

INTRODUCTION

Chapters 7 and 8 demonstrated the allocative efficiency case for user-charges
and local taxes. However, revenues from those two sources may be insufficient to finance an allocatively efficient level of local government expenditures. In particular, there will tend to be inadequate provision of local
government outputs that spill over jurisdictional boundaries to benefit non-
residents (see Chapter 1). This provides an efficiency rationale for national
government to pay grants to local governments in respect of such services. If
it did not pay grants to local authorities, there would either be suboptimally
low levels of provision of those services, or local tax levels would be suboptimally high.

In practice, central government may also pay grants to local authorities for
reasons other than allocative efficiency, most notably equity. First, it may
wish to restrain the level of local taxes, especially if their impact is regressive.
Similarly, it may wish to expand that part of the welfare state provided by
local government for reasons of equity, especially of services specifically
benefiting low-income groups. More generally, it may wish to compensate
local authorities for relatively high expenditure needs per capita and/or relatively low taxable resources per capita in order to avoid fiscal stress (see
Chapter 6).

INTERGOVERNMENTAL GRANTS TO ADJUST FOR MARKET FAILURE

In terms of economic theory, central government should only pay grants to local governments to adjust for any remaining market failures which persist despite local government intervention, for example where there are substantial spillover effects. However, rather than pay intergovernmental grants, it may be possible to adjust local government boundaries in order that they encompass benefit areas (see Chapters 1 and 8). In principle, adjustment of boundaries is the preferred efficiency response since intergovernmental grants have to be financed by taxes which may themselves create allocative inefficiencies, for example any disincentive-to-work effects caused by high marginal rates of national income taxes (see Chapter 8).

Given that local governments are multifunctional, however, it may not be possible to match benefit areas with areas of jurisdiction, either at any one point in time or over time. In particular, the development of local government over time has often involved changing service responsibilities. Changing service technology and improvements in public and private transport may also reconfigure the geographical spread of benefit areas. Hence, although benefit and jurisdictional areas might have matched at the outset, there is no guarantee that they will continue to do so over time. Adjustment of local government boundaries may be difficult because of constitutional or practical matters. Hence, even if benefit areas could be determined, it may be difficult to match administrative boundaries with them. In that case, spillover effects occur and so justify the payment of central government grants to local authorities, specifically to deal with this cause of market failure. In most countries, however, intergovernmental grants probably far exceed the levels required to deal with positive spillovers (see below).

A TYPOLOGY OF INTERGOVERNMENTAL GRANTS

A typology of grants is provided in Figure 9.1. It is assumed that the grants are paid by central government (the grantor) to local government (the grantee) in order to stimulate the provision of services. Hence, the term 'grants-in-aid' is used below.

Specific grants are paid in respect of specific services and can only be spent on that service. They are therefore also referred to as conditional, categorical or earmarked grants. They may be used to finance services which local authorities provide on behalf of central government, to encourage provision of services with substantial spillover effects, or to finance a minimum standard of service required by central government.

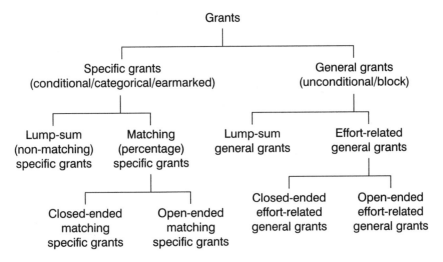

Figure 9.1 *A typology of intergovernmental grants*

General grants can be used to finance the broad range of services provided by local authorities as long as their activities are not *ultra vires*. They are therefore also referred to as unconditional or block grants. They are often used to achieve horizontal and vertical equity through financial equalization schemes (see below).

Both general and specific grants are sometimes paid to local governments, for example, where a specific grant is paid in respect of municipal housing and a general grant is paid in respect of education, personal social services, leisure and recreation and so on.

Specific grants can be lump-sum (that is, of fixed amount) or matching (where the grant forms a given percentage of the local government's spending, for example, 35 per cent). There may, however, be an upper limit on the amount of grant that can be levered by the local government, in which case it is a closed-ended grant. If there is no such limit it is open-ended.

Similarly, general grants may be lump-sum or effort-related. While a matching specific grant matches expenditure on the specified grant-aided service, the effort-related general grant is related to the revenue effort of the local authority. Revenue effort is usually measured in terms of tax effort: the greater the revenue raised from local taxes, the more grant the local authority receives. Again, grant may be open-ended or closed-ended, according to whether or not central government wishes to avoid too stimulatory an impact on local government expenditure. Article 9 of the European Charter of Local Self-Government, reproduced at the start of this chapter, clearly expresses a preference for general grants because they are not earmarked to specific projects. However, it expresses no view as to whether they should be lump-sum or effort-related.

Table 9.1 *Intergovernmental transfers*[a]

Country	Shared taxes (% of total municipal resources)	General grants (% of total municipal resources)	Earmarked grants[b] (% of total municipal resources)	Other (% of total municipal resources)
Albania	1	59	29	5
Austria	26	1	0	8
Belgium	0	25	5	10
Bulgaria	34	37	7	0
Cyprus	0	7	22	1
Czech Rep.	23	8	10	4
Denmark	2	12	0	11
Estonia	60	27	4	0
Finland	1	28	1	0
France	0	24	0	2
Germany	17	15	13	0
Greece	25	25	0	8
Hungary	7	52	5	2
Iceland	43	7	1	2
Ireland	0	11	46	0
Italy	2	8	24	5
Latvia	23	35	6	3
Luxembourg	24	2	0	11
Malta	0	91	0	7
Netherlands	0	20	38	3
Norway	0	17	14	2
Poland	23	15	22	0
Portugal	1	31	4	2
Romania	33	25	21	0
San Marino	0	31	0	0
Slovakia	30	1	8	0
Spain	0	8	29	0
Sweden	0	11	8	0
Switzerland	1	3	14	0
Turkey	3	0	3	51
UK	17	32	27	0

Source: Council of Europe (1997), reproduced with permission of the Council of Europe.
Notes:
a: For the relative importance of all transfers in municipal funding, see Table 5.3.
b: Also known as specific grants

Central government grants and transfers accounted for substantial proportions of municipal funding within the Council of Europe's member states
during the mid-1990s. Table 5.3 (p. 87) shows that they accounted for two-
thirds or more of municipal funding in nine countries and between half and
two-thirds in a further six. While it is difficult to derive monetary values, these
proportions are probably greatly in excess of those which could be justified by
positive spillovers.

Table 9.1 distinguishes between the type of intergovernmental transfers, showing that general grants are usually (and often considerably) greater than specific grants and, separately, shared taxes. General grants accounted for at least a tenth of municipal revenues in 21 countries and at least a quarter of revenues in 13 of those countries. Specific grants accounted for a tenth or more of municipal revenues in 13 countries. Similarly, shared taxes and assigned revenues (see Chapter 8) accounted for a tenth or more of municipal revenues in 13 countries.

ALTERNATIVE MODELS OF INTERGOVERNMENTAL GRANTS

The traditional models of the effects of intergovernmental grants on a community are based on standard indifference curve analysis (Wilde 1968, 1971; Bradford and Oates 1971a). There are three approaches.

1. Mapping the Preferences of the Decision-Making Body

In principle, mapping the preferences of the decision-making body of the grantee authority is the procedure best able to predict how grants are spent, simply because that body is the final decision-maker. This approach was used by both Scott (1952) and Wilde (1968). However, Scott concedes that in his model movement to a higher indifference curve 'means greater satisfaction to this body, not to the community at large' (1952, p. 394). In addition, using this method still requires value judgements and interpersonal comparisons where grants have redistributive effects, as is almost invariably the case. Moreover, since both Scott and Wilde assume that the decision-making body fully reflects the preferences of the community, the positive predictions of this model are similar to the those of community indifference mappings.

2. Mapping Community Indifference Curves

Community indifference curves were used by Oates (1972), Boadway (1979) and King (1984) because they can be used to make both positive and normative predictions. Once again, however, the redistributive effects of a grant may cause problems because they may cause community indifference curves to cross and so give no clear indication of the desirability of the resulting outcomes. Use of community curves therefore has to assume that there are no redistributional effects. However, many grants-in-aid programmes are quite explicitly intended to have redistributive effects. Hence, the validity and usefulness of analysis of grants-in-aid using community indifference curves is open to serious question, a criticism recognized by those who use them.

3. Mapping the Preferences of the Median Voter

The median being the value above and below which there are an equal number of observations, the median voter is the pivotal voter whose preferences are decisive for local government. In effect, the median voter is the representative voter of the community. There may, in fact, be little comparison between the median voter and the community (see Chapter 10). Alternatively, those who live in the community may have identical tastes and preferences. These alternative assumptions are the basis of Oates' decentralization theorem (see Chapter 2). It is further assumed that the identity of the median voter is not affected by the payment of grants, and that the local authority acts in accordance with the median voter's preferences. Despite these limiting assumptions, the median voter model is most commonly used to analyse the effects of grants-in-aid.

The next section adopts the median voter model for simplicity and assumes a fiscal exchange model of local government; that is, that local governments act in accordance with the preferences of local voters (see Chapter 1). In so doing, the local authority seeks to maximize the utility of the median voter in the same way as would the individual in accordance with neoclassical economic theory. The validity of this model will be examined more fully in Chapter 11.

THE IMPACT OF INTERGOVERNMENTAL GRANTS

Inter alia, intergovernmental grants stimulate provision of local government services either by increasing the real incomes of local voters (the *income effect*) and/or by reducing the relative price of the services in question (the *substitution effect*). In both cases, local voters will demand more of the service according to their income and price elasticities of demand respectively. Since real incomes have been increased, there will also be an increased demand for private sector goods and services, as long as the income effect exceeds the substitution effect (the relative price of private sector outputs having risen). Hence, while a grant is paid to stimulate local government spending, it may also stimulate spending upon private sector outputs. It could also induce a reduction in local government taxation. There are three key concepts:

1. *Direct net additionality* occurs where grants-in-aid (general or specific) finance spending on local government services that would otherwise not have occured. This is almost invariably the main objective of grants.
2. *Indirect net additionality* occurs when a *specific* grant induces spending upon local government services other than the one supported by that grant. This can be assumed to be an unintended consequence of the specific grant.

3. *Displacement* occurs when a grant-in-aid of additional service expenditures is used instead to finance reductions in current or future levels of local government taxation. General grants may be paid to restrain local tax levels, especially where local authorities depend upon a single local tax whose impact is broadly regressive and not widely spread across all residents.

A mixture of all three outcomes is possible at any one point in time as long as direct net additionality is less than 100 per cent but more than zero. Hence, it is clear that if central government pays grants to local governments, it cannot be sure that all of the grant is actually spent on the local government services for which it is intended. It makes no difference to the predictions of this particular neoclassical model of grants-in-aid whether a *lump-sum grant* is paid to the median voter or to his or her local government. This is because the decisions of the local authority are assumed to reflect fully the preferences of the individual voter. Paying the lump-sum grant to the local government simply means that it is paid indirectly, rather than directly, to the median voter. In both cases, it is the voter who will decide upon the balance of consumption between public and private sector outputs.

It does, however, make a difference to the predictions of the model if a *matching or effort-related grant* (whether specific or general) is paid to the local government. Clearly, the more the median voter decides to spend on local government outputs, the more will be the grant-in-aid paid to the local authority.

The following sections demonstrate that open-ended matching specific grants boost spending on the grant-aided service by more than a lump-sum specific grant of the same amount. The analysis closely follows that of King (1984), Brown and Jackson (1990) and Cullis and Jones (1998).

1. Lump-sum Grants

Lump-sum grants have only an income effect, since they do not change the relative price of the grant-aided service. A set of pre-grant and post-grant equilibria is drawn in Figure 9.2, which demonstrates the impact of both a lump-sum *general* grant and a lump-sum *specific* grant. The grant-aided local government service is denoted by X and all other goods and services are denoted by Y.

The latter are effectively the disposable income of local citizens exclusive of taxes paid to their local government. The indifference curves show alternative combinations of the two commodities (X and Y) yielding the same level of utility (their shape reflecting diminishing marginal utility) and, therefore, between which the consumer is indifferent. Indifference curve I_2 represents a higher level of welfare than I_1 because it represents larger combinations of X and Y (compare combination e_2 with e_1). Lines AC and BD are the local government's alternative budget lines, showing the maximum amounts of X and/or Y that can be purchased from its income. They are linear for simplicity,

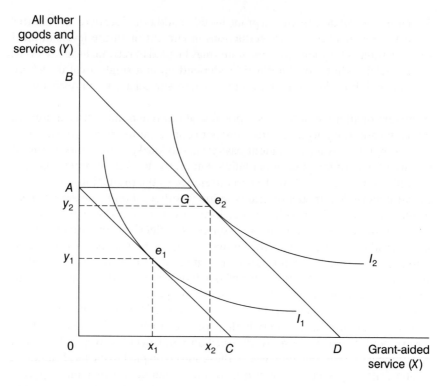

Figure 9.2   *Lump-sum grants (general and specific)*

that is prices of X and Y are assumed constant. Equilibrium occurs where the slopes of budget lines and indifference curves are the same at the point of tangency between them (that is, the marginal rate of transformation equals the marginal rate of substitution respectively).

Assume that a *lump-sum general grant* of AB or CD (which represent the same amount of grant measured in Y and X respectively) is received by the local government. This causes the budget line to shift from AC (pre-grant) to BD (post-grant), the two lines being parallel since there is no change in the relative prices of X and Y. In turn, the equilibrium shifts from e_1 to e_2. The median voter can now afford more of both X and Y (x_2y_2 rather than x_1y_1).

The *lump-sum specific grant* would have exactly the same result as a lump-sum general grant of the same amount since it would produce the budget line AGD (A still being the maximum amount of all other goods, since the grant can only be spent on X) with equilibrium again at e_2. Note that spending on the grant-aided service increases by less than the amount of grant (x_1x_2 being less than CD) because some of the grant is used to finance increased consumption of Y (of amount y_1y_2). This will be the case as long as the goods are normal goods (that is, with positive income elasticities of demand).

Assume for a moment that the vertical axis in Figure 9.2 represents all other services produced *only* by the local authority and that a lump-sum specific grant is paid to the local authority. The resulting increase in consumption of Y from y_1 to y_2 represents *indirect net additionality* because some of the specific grant is, in effect, deflected to support the other services, whose consumption increases from y_1 to y_2.

Now assume that the vertical axis in Figure 9.2 represents goods produced *only* by the private sector and that either a lump-sum specific or general grant is paid to the local authority. The result is now a reduction in local government taxation from By_1 to By_2, in other words *displacement* (in this case less than 100 per cent because consumption of X has increased).

Now assume that the vertical axis in Figure 9.2 represents all other goods produced by *both* the private and public sectors. In that case the increase in Y from y_1 to y_2 conflates both a reduction in local government taxation and an increase in the other outputs produced by the local authority: that is, both displacement and indirect net additionality.

It would only be possible to differentiate and quantify such displacement and indirect net additionality if price and income elasticities of demand were known for all goods and services, again assuming that local governments seek to maximize the utility function of the median voter. If, in fact, a *Niskanen-type leviathan model of local government* were the case, then the outcome would be different, since the local government is maximizing the bureaucrats' utility function rather than the median voter's (see Chapter 11). In that case the degree of displacement would be reduced but the degree of indirect net additionality would rise. Additionality and displacement can be illustrated by three extreme cases:

1. *Direct net additionality (of X) will be zero if the income elasticity of demand for X is zero.* In that case consumption of X would remain at x_1 and all of the grant would in fact be used to purchase additional amounts of Y. This is shown graphically in Figure 9.3, where the grant of AB (or CD) is used solely to increase the spending on all other goods and services (Y), resulting in a shift from y_1 to y_2, as the equilibrium shifts from e_1 to e_2. The income-consumption curve (*ICC* shows that the income elasticity of demand for X is zero between e_1 and e_2, resulting in zero direct net additionality for the grant-aided service. This seems unlikely if a general lump-sum grant is paid because middle-class groups can be expected to have positive income elasticities of demand for most local government services, for example education and leisure. It could occur when a specific lump-sum grant is paid if bureaucrats, operating within the Niskanen-type model, derived no marginal benefit from increased provision of the service, and were free to restructure other spending programmes at will. This also seems unlikely.

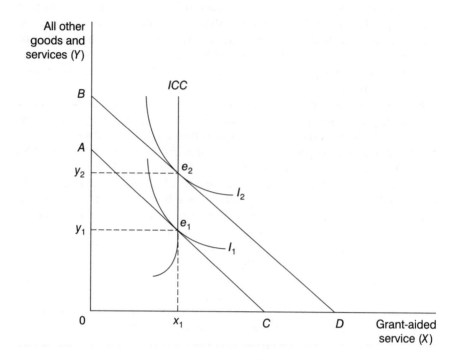

Figure 9.3 *Lump-sum grants yielding zero net additionality*

2. *Displacement of grant-in-aid will be 100 per cent if the grant-in-aid fully sub-stitutes for revenue from local taxation.* This will only be the case if the income elasticity of demand is zero for all local government outputs, again unlikely.

3. *Direct and indirect net additionality and displacement will be zero if an increase in lump-sum grants does not represent an increase in community income.* Brennan and Pincus (1996) argue that lump-sum grants from higher to lower levels of government are matched by a reverse flow of tax payments (they assume the higher level of government does not borrow to finance the grant). Hence, grants are not manna from heaven and do not represent increases in community income. Their argument applies specifically to a federal system because the grant has to be financed from within the federation by payment of higher federal taxes. It does not necessarily apply to intergovernmental grants in other constitutional types and does not apply to international grants.

Hence, on the basis of this theory, it can be expected that lump-sum grants (specific or general) will yield a combination of direct additionality (in terms of *X*), indirect net additionality (in terms of increased spending on other local government services) and displacement (that is, in terms of reduced tax payments).

2. Open-ended Matching Specific Grants

Matching grants reduce the absolute and relative cost of the grant-aided local government output and so encourage consumption by the median voter. In other words there is a reduction in the gradient of the local authority's budget line as the marginal rate of transformation of Y into X is increased. Hence, there is now a substitution effect (movement to the right along the indifference curve) as well as an income effect (shift to a higher indifference curve).

Figure 9.4 shows the effect of an open-ended matching specific grant paid at the rate $CF/0F$. Ignore BD and l_3 for the time being. The reduction in the relative price of the grant-aided good causes the budget line to pivot on point A (the price of Y being unaffected), since the maximum amount of X increases as a result of the grant from $0C$ to $0F$. Hence, the equilibrium shifts from e_1 to e_2 and production of the grant-aided commodity rises from x_1 to x_2. The production of Y has also increased as a result of the income effect (not marked, but visualize horizontal lines from e_1 and e_2 to the vertical axis).

This outcome can be compared with payment of a lump-sum grant (general or specific) of the same amount by drawing budget line BD such that it

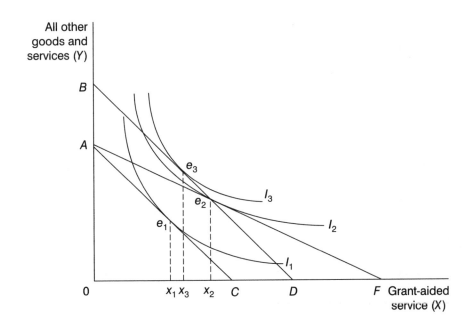

Figure 9.4 Open-ended matching grant versus lump-sum grant

cuts through e_2 (The equivalent line AG in Figure 9.2 is omitted from Figure 9.4 for simplicity.) In this case the outcome is e_3, demonstrating that a matching grant is much more effective in stimulating provision of X (to x_2) than a lump-sum grant (to x_3). The lump-sum grant leads to much greater indirect net additionality and/or displacement than the matching specific grant, the production of Y being much greater for the former than for the latter (not marked, but visualize horizontal lines from e_2 and e_3 to the vertical axis). In each case, whether for the matching grant or the lump-sum grant, the increased spending on X is still less than the amount of grant, $x_1 x_3$ and $x_1 x_2$ both being less than CD.

This analysis can be used to judge the effectiveness of the UK's National Lottery, whose *modus operandi* is to find *additional* finance for sports, the arts, national heritage, charities and celebration of the millennium (the five 'good causes'). Local authorities have been involved in some bids for lottery money. Awards of lottery money which are conditional upon contributions from local authorities can be categorized as open-ended specific matching grants. This is because they are paid in support of specific projects, the value of the grant ultimately depending on the cost of the project because the percentage rate of support is fixed. Lottery grants to local authorities are therefore not lump-sum grants. Furthermore, they cannot be used for the generality of local government services and are therefore not general grants.

Hence, in attributing to lottery grants the characteristics of open-ended matching specific grants, it is clear that expenditure on the 'good causes' is stimulated as much as possible, certainly by much more than would be achieved by giving the same amount of money to local authorities with no conditions attached. This can be illustrated in Figure 9.4, where the grant-aided service now refers to one of the good causes and the foregoing analysis relating to Figure 9.4 is repeated.

It would, however, be too simplistic to conclude that net additionality will necessarily be guaranteed by the mechanics of the lottery grant system. Much also depends on the behaviour of politicians, local authorities, other interest groups, and the distribution boards which decide the allocations of lottery funds (Bailey and Connolly 1997).

If it wishes to stimulate spending on a particular service (for example, because of beneficial spillover effects), central government will prefer a matching grant to a lump-sum grant. Note, however, that the latter may increase the welfare of the local authority residents by more than the former. This is illustrated by Figure 9.4, the utility of the median voter being greater (on I_3) for the lump-sum grant than for the matching grant (on I_2). This illustrates the imposition of the government's preferences (the grantor) on the median voter (the grantee). This seems to be the case for the National Lottery in that public opinion surveys have found less support for additional spending on the arts than on public health services, the latter not being supported by lottery funds.

FINANCIAL EQUALIZATION

In the absence of central provision of public sector outputs, central governments are obliged to enhance the fiscal capacity of local governments with relatively low per capita locally-taxable resources or relatively high per capita local expenditure needs. Otherwise, inequalities in the abilities of local governments to raise revenues and in their need to spend, each per head of population, may result in severe fiscal stress as affluent groups vote with their feet and exit poor needy authorities to relocate in prosperous authorities, and as businesses do likewise. This outcome may be unacceptable to central governments for a number of reasons:

1. It creates horizontal inequity, in that people in similar circumstances living in *different* local authorities will have to pay differing amounts of local tax for the same standard of service. Central governments may find this scenario unacceptable, particularly in respect of high profile local taxes such as a local property tax (see Chapter 8).
2. The horizontal and vertical inequities of the local property tax *within* a given jurisdiction will be exacerbated by very high tax levels (see Chapter 8).
3. High local tax levels could restrain local expenditures so much that beneficial spillover effects are lost (see Chapter 1).
4. The local welfare state could collapse in authorities experiencing severe fiscal stress (see Chapter 6).
5. Central governments may be trying to restore the local economies of cities with adverse industrial structures, on the grounds of both equity and efficiency. High levels of local taxation may lead to cumulative decline as selective outmigration of population and outmigration of business activity occurs (see Chapters 4 and 8).

It may not be possible to remedy relatively low per capita taxable resources by increasing the number of taxes under local government control because the small size of many European local governments (see Chapter 2) means that those who ultimately pay the tax may not live within the jurisdiction of the local government levying the tax. Such tax exporting would frustrate local accountability and cause allocative inefficiency. Likewise, there may be only very limited scope for additional revenues from user-charges because of adverse social impacts, high collection costs, the need to avoid monopoly exploitation of service users and so on (see Chapter 7).

There is therefore both a social and an economic rationale for the payment of intergovernmental grants to authorities with inadequate local taxable resources per capita and/or with high per capita expenditure needs. The need to compensate for such relatively low resources and high needs per capita is encapsulated in the quotation from the European Charter of Local Self-Government at the beginning of this chapter.

1. Equalization of Local Taxable Resources Per Capita

Variations in the abilities of local governments to raise local tax revenues per head of population largely reflect the uneven distribution of economic activity, some authorities having relatively large business sectors. This particularly affects the per capita revenues raised from given rates of local income taxes and local property taxes. In order to raise the same amount of local tax revenue per head, rural authorities would have to levy much higher tax rates (on both incomes and properties) than city authorities. In particular, central city authorities usually have central business districts yielding relatively high per capita business property tax revenues for a given rate of tax. Hence, where only a local property tax is levied, the business property tax is the main cause of inequality, Sweden and the UK being notable exceptions because only residential properties are subject to locally-variable taxes (see Chapter 8).

Equalization of the resulting differences in the potential per capita tax revenues requires measurement of the local tax base and often takes account of 'fiscal effort' (that is, the rates of local taxation applied to that base). The extent to which equalization is necessary depends upon the size of disparities in the the local tax base per head of population and so in the amount of potential local tax revenue per head for a given tax rate.

2. Equalization of Local Expenditure Needs Per Capita

Differences in the need to spend per head of population reflect differences between local governments in their demographic, socioeconomic, geographic and other structures. The variables affecting expenditure needs per head of population are wide-ranging, including the proportion of population of school age and of retirement age, the proportion of households headed by unemployed or single parents, urban density or rural sparsity, demographic and economic growth or decline, and so on. For example, local authorities with high proportions of children and elderly people in their populations, the two groups to which the most expensive services are directed (school education and personal social services), would have to spend more per head of total population than authorities with low proportions of those two groups, even if they spent the same amount per child or per elderly person as those other authorities.

While these factors can generally be considered 'objective criteria', Chapter 6 noted that the costs of service rationalization in response to economic and demographic decline are particularly difficult to quantify, and depend – perhaps in substantial part – on the policy responses of individual local authorities. Hence, the robustness of 'objective factors' is subject to qualification. Moreover, to accept that local government expenditures are determined by objective factors such as demographic and socioeconomic structures (the 'traditional approach' to expenditure determination) leaves no role for the median voter. Nonetheless, to the extent that such factors create a higher need to spend per head of population than would be desired by the median voter, they provide a possible explanation of the 'flypaper effect' (see Chapter 11).

Three main difficulties have to be faced by equalization schemes:

- Data inaccuracies and inadequacies mean that it is difficult to measure accurately the differences in the levels of need to spend created by each factor.
- It has to be recognised that actual expenditures reflect local discretion and so per capita spending cannot be taken as a measure of expenditure need. As noted above, it is difficult to allow for the expenditures determined by local policy discretion and so also difficult to calculate a standardized per capita expenditure needs figure for each government.
- Perhaps most crucially, a decision has to be made about which factors enter into the calculation of expenditure needs. In principle, all factors relevant to provision of the full range of local government services should be included in the assessment of per capita expenditure needs, and especially those causing significant differences in the need to spend per head of population.

The calculations would be enormously complex and suffer severe data problems. A more manageable model necessarily has to exclude some indicators of expenditure needs. Judgement therefore has to be exercised about which expenditure needs factors should be included or excluded, with the result that the process loses much of its objectivity. Even though countries such as Britain, Norway and Sweden use large numbers of 'needs indicators', the measurement of need to spend per head of population remains highly political. This is especially the case where some needs indicators favour a particular type of authority (such as urban or rural) predominantly controlled by political parties other than the one in power at national level. Accusations of political bias within expenditure needs assessment then become commonplace.

In the UK, for example, rural local authorities predominantly controlled by right-wing political parties accused the left-wing national government of bias against them in the mid to late 1970s, and left-wing urban local authorities subsequently complained of bias against them on the part of right-wing national government during the 1980s and early 1990s. This led to increasing tension between central and local government because, as already noted in Chapter 5, ideological and political arguments because enmeshed with economic arguments. These tensions provide the contextual background for the reforms discussed in Chapter 12.

This disjuncture between urban and rural local governments arises if only because the former provide urban core (or metropolitan) functions to residents of the latter – for example, social and cultural services (see Chapter 6).

National governments often compensate central cities for the costs of providing such beneficial spillover effects, in the UK case by taking account of the
cost of local government services provided to commuters. However, the true
costs of providing such services are very difficult to calculate and so may be seriously underestimated, leading to claims of bias against major urban authorities.

More generally, even if the total costs of service provision by each and
every local authority were correctly assessed at any one point in time, any
inertia in expenditure needs assessment would mean that the intergovernmental grant system would increasingly fail to take full account of the dynamic nature of change. For example, the fiscal stress syndrome of Chapter 6
demonstrates the cost-intensive dynamics of multiple deprivation combined
with selective outmigration. Hence, the disparity between the actual and assessed costs of service provision can apply in respect of *total* costs and/or *marginal* (that is, incremental) costs. Such a disparity may be enhanced by grant
mechanisms which seek to increase the marginal local tax cost of incremental
expenditures in an attempt to control the growth of local governments' expenditures (see below).

Despite the possibility of subjectivity, the conditions for an objective system
of expenditure needs assessment and consequent distribution of intergovernmental grants can be identified (Blair 1993):

1. Needs indicators should be common to all local governments at any point
    in time or over a short period of time.
2. They must be capable of being easily and objectively measured.
3. There should be a clear link between each indicator and both the need to
    spend and variations in the level of expenditure.
4. The needs indicator should not be susceptible to manipulation by either
    central or local government.
5. Like local government expenditures, the indicators should not be subject to
    cyclical change, nor be susceptible to large fluctuations from year to year.
6. Needs indicators should generally not display a high degree of inter-
    dependence.

The major outstanding problem is one of deciding the relative weights of
needs indicators, since these crucially influence the subsequent distribution
of grant between different types of local government (especially between
urban and non-urban). The choice of multiple regression analysis, 'client
group' or other means of weighting indicators is essentially subjective.
Hence, at best, an objective system of expenditure needs assessment can only
control, rather than eliminate, the degree of subjectivity in the distribution of
needs-equalizing grants. Some subjectivity and political influence is inevitable. Blair (1993) concludes that the substantial variations between European
countries in systems of expenditure needs assessment are explained by the
inherent subjectivity of the exercise.

3. European Practice

The degree of financial equalization between local governments has long varied greatly between countries throughout the world (Paddison and Bailey 1988; Page and Goldsmith 1987; Gibson and Batley 1993; Ahmad 1997; Gramlich 1997a). Some European countries have sought full (or nearly full) equalization through the grant system, even though this makes local government more dependent upon central government. Examples are the UK, Denmark and Norway. Other countries have sought partial (or even no) equalization, either in order to preserve local autonomy and/or because central government lacks the financial resources for full equalization. Examples are the Netherlands, France, Ireland, Italy and Switzerland.

Of those that do seek equalization, almost all seek to equalize *per capita taxable resources*. However, few adopt the 'Robin Hood' approach which involves taking resources from relatively rich local governments and giving them to relatively poor authorities. Instead, most countries give general (block) grants to the relatively poor authorities, financing them from national taxation rather than from other, richer, local governments.

As noted above, few countries make substantial use of specific grants, because they cannot achieve the same degree of equalization as general grants. They also restrict local autonomy. Specific grants used to finance services undertaken by only a few authorities (for example, coastal defence) would not be suitable for equalization purposes since they would be in breach of the first criterion for objective needs indicators listed above. Moreover, there is a general trend throughout Europe to replace specific grants by block grants. Most Council of Europe member states opt for lump-sum general grants because they are simpler to administer than effort-related grants and easier to control (see the UK case-study below).

The equalization achieved by block grants is necessarily restricted in countries where a high proportion of local government finance comes from local taxation, usually local income taxes (for example, Sweden). Nonetheless, small grants could be highly redistributive, especially if part of a 'Robin Hood' redistributive arrangement (such as in Denmark). The 'Robin Hood' arrangement is rare because it is politically very difficult to tax 'rich' local authorities and so is likely only to be used in exceptional circumstances. For example, inter-state equalization occurs in Germany between *regional* governments (Länder), financial transfers from the richest regions in West Germany to the poorest in East Germany being used to facilitate reunification of East and West during the 1990s, following the collapse of the former Soviet regime.

Nonetheless, compared with a high level of dependency on central funds, the 'Robin Hood' system of redistribution better preserves local autonomy. Moreover, large block grants may not be very redistributive, for example if they are based on total population only.

An argument against 100 per cent resource equalization financed by financial transfers from richest to poorest local governments is that it may discourage them from attempting to maximize their tax base. In effect, the pursuit of equity would negate the Tiebout model of competition between local governments, which states that they compete for residents in order to minimize the average costs of service provision (see Chapter 4). This is an example of the tradeoff between equity and efficiency. However, the significance of that tradeoff remains to be determined and substantial differences between local governments in their abilities to provide an adequate level, range and quality of services may simply be politically unacceptable.

Just as equalizing *per capita taxable resources* may cause inefficiencies by discouraging local authorities from seeking to expand their own per capita tax base, so might equalizing *per capita expenditure needs* lead to inefficiencies in service costs. High per capita costs of service provision may arise due to extremes of population density and population sparsity, high costs of labour and of land and so on. Again, on the grounds of horizontal equity, it would seem reasonable to compensate authorities for such higher costs, as long as those costs are outwith their control (so satisfying the fourth criterion for objective needs indicators listed above). Such compensation could not be justified, however, if those higher costs are due to X-inefficiency (see Chapter 5). Hence, countries such as Denmark, the UK and the Netherlands use standard costs in their calculations of expenditure needs so that X-inefficiency is not rewarded.

Equalization objectives are also necessarily tempered by the need to control local government spending in aggregate in order to achieve macroeconomic objectives (see Chapter 5). If there was no need to restrain local government spending, central government could pay open-ended effort-related general grants to local authorities (see Figure 9.1). Such grants would maximize local autonomy by leaving local electorates (or their local governments) to decide for which services those grants should be used to finance increased provision. However, if central government wishes to avoid imparting an excessive stimulus to local government expenditures it will use either lump-sum general grants or closed-ended effort-related general grants. The differences between these two types of grant can be illustrated by referring to the UK, where both types of grant have recently been in existence at different times.

THE ROLE OF GRANTS IN ACHIEVING ACCOUNTABILITY: THE UK CASE

A Council's powers to raise taxes locally, and the grant it gets from the national government, should be designed to ensure that the Council can provide adequate services. They should also be designed to ensure that local electors know what the costs of their services are, so that armed with this knowledge they can influence the spending decisions of their Council through the ballot box. (Cmnd 9714)

This quotation from the UK central government's 1986 Green Paper 'Paying for Local Government' qualifies Article 9 of the European Charter of Local Self-Government in emphasizing local accountability as well as local autonomy. The quotation illustrates the importance of both grants and local taxes in achieving improved accountability. As already noted in Chapter 8, the former UK local residential property tax (domestic rates) was criticized by the then Conservative government because eligibility to vote and liability to pay local taxes were poorly matched, for both the residential and non-residential property taxes. Attempts to match eligibility to vote with liability to pay the local poll tax were shortlived and a revised residential property tax (council tax), subject to the same criticisms as its earlier form, was reintroduced. However, the conversion of non-domestic (business) rates into an assigned revenue was maintained, along with the reformed system of intergovernmental grants.

Even if a closer match could be achieved between representation and local taxation, such a match is a necessary but not sufficient condition for the improvement of local accountability. The local tax level must also vary in direct response to local discretion in expenditure policy. This could most easily be achieved if the local tax financed 100 per cent of the costs of local government services net of income from charges, there being no intergovernmental grants or local business taxes. This is a situation of full local autonomy *in extremis*. However, uneven geographical distributions of per capita expenditure need and of per capita taxable resources would mean that poor authorities with high expenditure needs would have to levy much higher local taxes than other less needy, more prosperous authorities.

1. Closed-ended Effort-related General Grants in the UK

The grant system prior to 1990 comprised a combination of specific grants and general grant (Bailey 1988a; King 1988). The general grant was called the Rate Support Grant (hereafter referred to as 'old RSG'), because it was paid in support of domestic and non-domestic property tax rates. It was a closed-ended effort-related general grant (see Figure 9.1) since, although individual authorities could attract more grant by increasing their spending, if the aggregate of local authorities overspent against central government plans, the overspend was 'clawed-back' by reductions in grant paid to each and every local authority.

Introduced in 1966, its objectives were variously to:

1. reduce the fiscal burden of the local property tax;
2. constrain current expenditures;

3. bring the actual pattern of service expenditures more into line with central government's own priorities (particularly through payments of specific grants);
4. equalize for differing per capita rateable resources and expenditure needs;
5. maximize local discretion subject to points 2 and 3 above;
6. be comprehensible to local voters and their political representatives so as to improve accountability for local service provision.

This is a rather ambitious set of multiple objectives and they clearly conflict, as recognized in objective 5 above. Moreover, achievement of the equalization in objective 4 may be so complex as to frustrate achievement of objective 6. The balance between these six objectives changed over time, reflecting the changing political complexion and economic policies of central government. Hence, the mechanism for grant determination and distribution was subject to continual modification, both as the priorities of objectives changed and as the defects within successive grant regimes became apparent. One such modification was the introduction of the 'Block Grant' in England and Wales in 1980. This was an unhypothecated general grant paid in respect of major services such as education, personal social services, leisure and recreation.

The former structure of old RSG had been criticized for providing too strong an incentive for high-spending authorities to increase their spending further so as to gain more grant (Rhodes and Bailey 1979). Although the details varied between England and Wales, the new block grant was designed to increase financial pressure on local authorities to conform with the expenditure levels deemed appropriate by central government. Central government assessed each local authority's need to spend taking account of the various demographic, geographical, social, environmental and other factors thought to affect need to spend. This assessment was made for individual services but then aggregated to derive the Grant-Related Expenditure Assessment (GREA) for each authority.

Local authorities were not obliged to conform with either the distribution or total of spending over services, the GREA being used only to distribute the grant – at least initially. However, expenditure in excess of the GREA attracted extra block grant at a diminishing (or tapered) rate, the so-called 'taper system' of diminishing *marginal* grant rates. Most authorities received more block grant the more they spent (because the marginal grant rate was positive), but a larger proportion of incremental expenditure had to be financed by local taxation. The marginal grant rate could ultimately become negative if expenditure was far in excess of the GREA. The block grant system therefore increased the cost to local taxpayers of marginal increments in expenditure in excess of an authority's own GREA. This is illustrated in Figures 9.5 and 9.6.

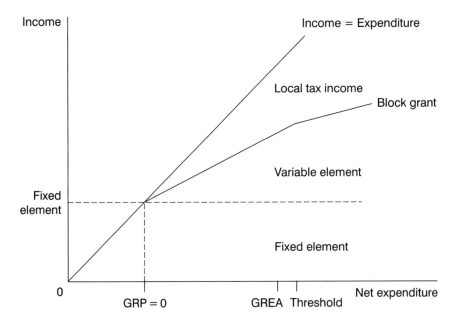

Figure 9.5   *Financing net expenditure*

Both Figures 9.5 and 9.6 show how net expenditure (that is, gross expenditure minus income from charges) was financed under the block grant. The 'income equals expenditure' line refers to expenditure relevant for block grant (largely expenditure financed by all grants minus that financed by specific grants). The difference between block grant and total relevant expenditure was financed by the local property tax.

Figures 9.5 and 9.6 show that the taper was only introduced above the threshold level of expenditure, set at 10 per cent above GREA in recognition of the difficulties in accurately assessing need to spend. The block grant comprised both a fixed element (which depended on the GREA) and a variable element (related to total spending). These elements are shown in Figure 9.5. The fixed element was the amount of grant received when the local tax rate related to the range of services financed by the block grant was zero. That local tax rate was called grant-related poundage (GRP). Thereafter, as local authorities increased their local tax rates (in other words their GRP), the grant they received either increased or decreased.

Figure 9.6 shows how block grant could vary for three authorities with differing expenditure needs and differing local taxable resources. The fixed element is highest for authority A (feA), lowest for authority C (feC) and intermediate for authority B (feB).

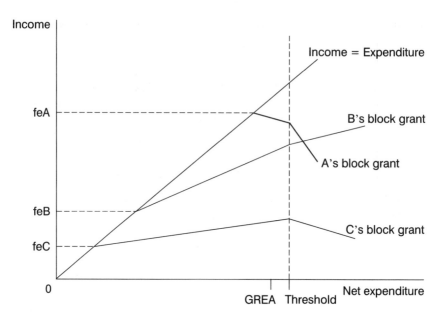

Figure 9.6 *Examples of grant versus expenditure*

Authority A has high expenditure needs per capita but also high taxable resources per capita. Hence, though receiving the largest fixed element of grant, it can raise a given sum with a lower tax rate than other authorities. It therefore has that advantage removed by means of the negative marginal grant rate for all levels of expenditure above where GRP equals zero. Authority B has a positive marginal grant rate throughout, lower above the threshold than below it. Authority C (the authority with the lowest expenditure need) has a positive marginal grant rate below the threshold but a negative one above it.

The result of the block grant was that each local authority could finance the same level of per capita spending as other authorities for a given local tax rate and also provide the same standard of service in relation to expenditure needs (that is, interjurisdictional horizontal equity was achieved). Those authorities with high per capita taxable resources had that resources advantage removed (through negative marginal grant rates), while other resource-deficient authorities had their resources augmented (through positive marginal grant rates).

This outcome satisfied several of the objectives listed above, namely horizontal equity between authorities ('equalization'), leaving local authorities free to determine the distribution of the block grant over services, and constraining total expenditure. The government could adjust the rate of taper of

marginal grant rates in order to provide financial incentives for local authorities to constrain spending such that macroeconomic control would be
achieved.

This grant arrangement was clearly in accordance with Article 9 of the
European Charter of Local Self-Government (see above). Moreover, the use
of marginal grant rates within the block grant mechanism were clearly in
accord with the economist's emphasis on equating both the marginal benefits
and marginal local tax costs of service provision. Local voters would supposedly be made aware of the incremental collective costs of voting for
additional service levels. However, as already noted in both of Chapters 7
and 8, there was still no correspondence between voting, payment and use of
local services. No matter how economically sophisticated the grant system,
it will be ineffective if only a minority of local voters are local taxpayers. Local
residents could vote for additional service levels knowing that someone
else would pay most, if not all, of the additional costs.

Not surprisingly, the financial incentives provided by the *taper system* of diminishing marginal grant rates were not strong enough to constrain local governments' aggregate expenditures in line with central government's objectives.
Hence, the block grant was accompanied by a separate and supplementary
target system of expenditure restraint whereby each local authority was noti-
fied of an expenditure guidance target, usually below its expenditure in the
previous year and consistent with central government's overall expenditure
plans. Authorities exceeding their expenditure targets were penalized, their
block grant allocations being reduced on a sliding scale related to the level of
overspend against target.

The target system compromised the equalizing objectives of the block
grant, for example where an authority underspent its GREA but overspent
its target. Recognizing these anomalies, central government abolished the
target system in the mid-1980s and, instead, increased the severity of the
reductions in the marginal grant rates. By the later 1980s, as central government was trying even harder to implement cuts in local government spending, these marginal grant rates were becoming negative for many authorities,
so that grant was actually withdrawn as spending increased. While this is a
description of the system in England and Wales, the separate Scottish grant
mechanism had the same effects.

The analysis in the previous paragraphs having demonstrated the implications of the partial coverage of the local tax, it is not surprising that central
government eventually abandoned the block grant system altogether.

2. Lump-sum General Grants in the UK

A new grant system was introduced into Britain in 1990. This was part of a
package of reforms which also abolished the residential property tax, replaced

it with a poll tax (the Community Charge) and which also transformed the non-residential property tax into an assigned revenue (see Chapter 8). The new grant system comprised four elements:

1. specific grants, largely unchanged from previous years;
2. the standard grant, paid as an equal fixed sum per head of adult population in all local authorities in support of the generality of services;
3. the needs grant, again lump-sum but varying between local authorities in accordance with differences in the assessed need to spend per head;
4. assigned revenues from non-domestic rates paid as an equal sum per head over all authorities.

The standard and needs grant are the new Revenue Support Grant (hereafter referred to as 'new RSG') which is a lump-sum general grant (see Figure 9.1).

With the possible exception of one or two matching specific grants (for example, for police), payment of grant is no longer related to incremental expenditures. This conclusion applies to both the new RSG and to business rates and represents a major departure from the previous system. The old RSG system achieved equalization at *all* levels of spending chosen by local authorities. Except when it had been compromised by the target system, those authorities spending at a given level or standard had to raise the same local rate poundage (because central government made grant adjustments to take account of differing per capita expenditure needs and resources). The new RSG system abandoned this form of equalization.

The highly sophisticated but increasingly modified old RSG system had failed to implement local accountability. Even for the small proportion of local voters that actually did pay the residential property tax, accountability was blurred by the complexity of the grant system. There was, in fact, no clear and simple relationship between increased spending and increased property tax rates. This link was destroyed not only by targets and penalties but also by cuts in the overall share of local government spending funded by grant. The same outcome was the case in Scotland.

It must be emphasized that the changes to the grant system and to the business property tax could have taken place independently of the local poll tax and within a system that retained the domestic property tax. Protection of non-domestic ratepayers from the unreasonable tax demands of local governments required neither the local poll tax nor the new RSG. The separability of these initiatives was made evident when the poll tax was replaced by the reintroduced domestic property tax (council tax).

The conversion of the UK's local business tax into an assigned revenue distributed as an equal amount per head of adult population effectively eliminated interjurisdictional differences in property tax revenues. This is because 'the biggest cause of variations in rateable resources is differences in the size of the non-domestic sector' (Cmnd 9714, para. 4.21). The local poll tax completely eliminated interjurisdictional differences in local per capita domestic taxable resources since, under a local poll tax, it is heads that are taxable not property, incomes or sales. In combination, the local poll tax and the uniform business rate completely eliminated the need for interjurisdictional equalization of per capita local taxable resources.

While *interjurisdictional* equalization had been achieved, *interpersonal* equalization had not because the poll tax was highly regressive. Although this was criticized as inadequate, central government achieved its desired degree of interpersonal equalization through the national social security system, rather than through the system of intergovernmental grants. This shift from indirect to direct subsidies was also adopted elsewhere in local government. The most notable example was the shift from 'bricks and mortar' subsidies, distributed to municipal tenants via low rents for council housing, to personal subsidies paid directly to individuals through the Housing Benefit component of social security.

The return to a domestic property tax (council tax) reintroduced into the local tax base relatively minor interjurisdictional inequalities. However, local authorities with relatively high domestic rateable values (the tax base) can set lower rate poundages (the tax rate) to raise the same total revenue as authorities with low tax bases and high tax rates. Council tax bills are therefore not necessarily higher in authorities with high tax bases. Equalization within the old RSG had been in terms of property tax *rates* (rate poundages) not property tax *bills*.

The shift from local domestic property tax ('domestic rates') to poll tax and back to property tax may have had little impact on local accountability. One of central government's own investigations concluded that

> the linkage between voting and paying rates might not be quite as poor as the figures ... would suggest. When asked whether or not their household pays rates 94% of electors said 'yes' and only 4% 'no'. This indicates two things. First, most electors who do not themselves pay rates are members of a household that does. Second, many electors perceive of themselves as 'ratepayers' even where their rates are partially or wholly rebated. (Cmnd 9797, p. 40)

It would seem that, psychologically, they were ratepayers irrespective of rebates (a form of fiscal illusion). If so, there is little difference between the local residential property tax and the local poll tax in terms of local accountability.

This suggests that the major cause of blurred local accountability was the grant system itself (old RSG). The question remains as to whether or not the new RSG improves accountability. In some respects, it is a great improvement compared with the old RSG.

- It is certainly less complex because it avoids use of targets and grant penalties. These were incomprehensible to the ordinary voter.
- In combination with the uniform business rate, it also avoids the need for resources equalization, also incomprehensible to voters.
- It is paid in accordance with the number of local taxpayers (adult residents) so that it directly influences local tax levels irrespective of local budgetary decisions.
- Local authorities face much less uncertainty about grant receipts, which are paid as a given sum, irrespective of the expenditure policies of themselves and of other authorities. As noted above, under the effort-related old RSG any projected aggregate overspending against central government plans, was 'clawed-back' by reductions in grant paid to each and every local authority. Hence, an individual authority's final grant allocation was uncertain until the rate of clawback against the initial allocation had been determined. This could not be done until all local governments had set their local property tax rates. New RSG is a lump-sum grant and such grants dispense with the need for clawback.

On the other hand any grant must necessarily blur local accountability, for a number of reasons.

First, it will reduce the apparent cost of local government services and lead to expansion beyond the level that would pertain if the full costs were borne locally. This may, of course, be what the grant is designed to achieve, if it is paid in support of market failure and spillover effects.

Second, the level of standard grant paid to local government depends upon central government's desired overall standard for local services. If this desired standard changes from year to year, then so will grant payment – and it may not be readily apparent to local voters what caused the consequential change in local tax levels. This would especially be the case where a local decision had simultaneously been taken to increase spending. How is the local voter able to separate the relative influences of locally and centrally determined changes to local tax levels and to service levels?

Third, if neither the minimum standard of service is rigorously specified nor are the costs of meeting it, there is a possibility that increases in grant from year to year may be insufficient to compensate for increases in costs. Even if grants and assigned revenues are index-linked to retail prices, a revenue shortfall may occur, since local authority costs tend to increase faster than retail prices. This is because labour costs are a significant proportion of total costs (see Chapter 5) and local authorities may be susceptible to the relative price effect (see Chapter 6). Moreover, central government will naturally tend to adopt its target for inflation in adjusting grants from year to year, rather than the actual level of inflation if higher. In such a case the local tax will have to increase even if local authorities are maintaining constant service standards. If both under-provision for inflation and the costs of higher standards occur together, local voters will be unable to separate out these two effects.

Fourth, the expenditure needs of local authorities invariably change from year to year, reflecting changes not just in the socioeconomic and demographic characteristics of their populations but also in the precise methods of expenditure needs assessment employed by central government. There is a long experience of continuous changes in the methodology and in the accuracy of data used in these assessments, changes which can have profound impacts upon grant payments and so on local tax levels in individual authorities. This problem applies with just as much force to the assessment of relative expenditure need, even accepting that absolute need is impossible to measure (Cmnd 6453, para. 36, p. 221).

Fifth, while the lump-sum nature of the grant system results in the local tax having to finance the whole (but not more than 100 per cent) of discretionary increments in local spending, local accountability may still be frustrated by high gearing effects. The local tax is such a small share of total income that large proportionate increases in local tax bills finance only very small proportionate increases in total spending. Local voters may fail to appreciate how this gearing effect promotes local accountability rather than simply restraining it. Inner-city local authorities which are most heavily dependent upon intergovernmental grants face particularly severe gearing effects (see Chapter 6). Hence, the relative tax price attached to the exercise of local accountability varies dramatically between local authorities. Because they are less heavily dependent upon grants, less needy affluent authorities find it less expensive at the margin to finance discretionary increases in service provision because of the lower gearing effects. Hence, highly differentiated gearing effects introduced horizontal inequity for *incremental* expenditures.

Sixth, rather than promoting accountability, the new system of intergovernmental grants transfers more of the responsibility for deciding the level of service provision into bureaucratic decision-making mechanisms operating at national level. The level of local tax and service provision in any one authority more than ever depends upon the levels of specific and revenue support grants, the method of expenditure needs assessment used for the needs grant, the index-linking of the national non-domestic property tax and the capping of local taxes and budgets. This strengthens national choice mechanisms, not local accountability.

These caveats demonstrate that traditional fiscal federalist conclusions about the merits of different types of grants in the USA's federal system of government cannot simply be applied to a unitary state such as the UK. It is not simply the differing constitutional arrangements that matter: the wider institutional and political context is also radically different. Fiscal federalism tends to focus on the *mechanics* of the grant system, ignoring the wider context within which grants must operate. That wider context may lead particular types of grants to have unforeseen effects. For example, Chapter 11 notes the case where lump-sum grants may have results more akin to those of effort-related grants because of the behaviour of bureaucrats who distribute them.

Notwithstanding the above criticisms of the new RSG, it may still be an improvement on old RSG. The new RSG could only be made simpler by abolishing the needs grant and paying all local authorities an equal lump-sum per head of population, irrespective of differing expenditure needs per capita. Nonetheless, changes in the expenditure needs assessment methodology and its data input, changes in central government's policies regarding public expenditure in general and local government spending in particular, and changes in the degree to which centrally-determined finances compensate local authorities for the rising costs of service delivery, all have the potential to cause marked instability from year to year in financial allocations.

As already noted in Chapter 5, political will is more important than the nature of the intergovernmental grant system and the arrangements for local taxation. On the one hand, central government may feel obliged to increase grants so substantially from one year to the next that their precise form (whether lump-sum or effort-related, general or service-specific) and the gearing effect upon local tax levels becomes irrelevant. On the other hand, central public expenditure restraints may severely curtail the exercise of local autonomy. In both cases, decentralization of service delivery to local government is not accompanied by decentralization of local decision-making and the allocative efficiency of decentralization is not achieved. In particular, Wilson *et al.* (1994) are highly critical of the increased central control afforded by the new RSG.

THE IMPACT OF EXPENDITURE NEEDS ASSESSMENT ON LOCAL TAX LEVELS

As already noted, social and economic influences on local government spending are particular difficult to identify and cost. Even changes in the number of clearly identifiable service users can be difficult to cost, as was made evident in Chapter 6.

Even more problematical is the concept of collective (or area) needs where the overall need (over all services and individuals) is greater than the sum of its parts. Hence expenditure need rises disproportionately. 'Where certain adverse social and environmental features are present in combination in a certain community, then social processes operate which have a negative impact on individuals. Examples include crime, vandalism, social isolation' (Bramley *et al.* 1983, para. 4.12). Whereas the old RSG used a very sophistic-ated method of expenditure needs assessment, the new RSG needs grant incorporates a simplified method of expenditure needs assessment which can hardly be expected to take full account of the requirements of inner-city authorities.

Note that the high levels of grants relative to local government spending in the UK are *not* required for equalisation of differing per capita expenditure needs or taxable resources. The national non-domestic property tax revenues and the new RSG standard grant are paid as a fixed sum per head of adult population. Only the needs grant is intended to be redistributive, reflecting differing socioeconomic and demographic conditions between authorities:

> It is perfectly possible to achieve a higher degree of equalisation with a much smaller grant, provided that local authorities are reasonably provided with adequate revenue-raising capacities of their own . . . The British public often makes the mistake of assuming that a huge grant means a redistribution on a huge scale. (Newton 1980a, p. 111)

The high gearing effect caused by the small proportionate contribution of local taxes to total spending will also magnify the impact on local tax levels caused by inaccuracies in central governments' assessment of need to spend (Ritchie 1989). It has been calculated that, if assessed expenditure need increased by 10 per cent, the poll tax would have fallen by between a quarter and a third for 10 authorities, reflecting the importance of the needs grant to those authorities (LGIU 1988, p. 34). Similar effects could occur for other authorities but it is arguable that the assessed expenditure needs of urban authorities are more likely to be strongly affected by minor changes in assessment methodology (such as the inclusion and/or weighting given to the effects of economic and demographic decline, to multiple deprivation, or to single-parent families). At the very least, it seems unwise to devise a system that creates such a high level of gearing between a central judgement of local expenditure needs and local tax levels.

CONCLUSIONS

In general, grants can be expected to stimulate spending on services and/or enable reductions in the levels of local taxes. Assuming *ceteris paribus*, a number of conclusions are drawn from the grants-in-aid theory developed above. First, general lump-sum and specific lump-sum grants have the same effects on grantee spending because they have only an income effect. Second, open-ended matching grants have a greater stimulatory effect on grantee spending than equivalent lump-sum grants because they have both income and substitution effects. Third, general lump-sum grants have similar (or the same) stimulatory effects on grantee spending as an equivalent rise in income in the community.

However, grant systems often have multiple and sometimes conflicting objectives, of which boosting expenditures may be the least prioritized. Despite the economist's preference for the matching of local expenditure decisions and local tax levels (in order to promote allocative efficiency), it is extremely unlikely that changes in local tax levels from year to year will ever reflect only changes in local spending. That could only be achieved if grants were to be completely abolished.

If equalization objectives are abandoned completely (or are so limited as to be insignificant in terms of the totality of spending), one is left to question why any grant should be paid at all. Specific grants would still have a function promoting expansion of particular services in order to offset market failure. Otherwise, the only justification for payment of grants is that they have always been paid and that the local tax is inadequate as the sole source of funding for the present array of services. This in turn suggests that the solution to the problem of local accountability lies not in the form of grant but, instead, in the form of local taxation.

Complete funding by local taxation would be pursuing local accountability for its own sake, since it would ignore the market failure and spillovers rationale for payment of grant. It would also be at the expense of ensuring socially-acceptable standards of public services in all parts of the country. However, Britain has now reached the stage where the ratio of grants to local taxes is so high that it is arguably the reverse of what is required to promote accountability. In addition, the British standard grant and assigned revenues regime illustrates the observation that more grant should not be confused with greater equalization of per capita expenditure needs and resources. In the British case, more grant means less local accountability and severely constrains the exercise of policy discretion by local authorities. Whereas the grant regime prior to 1990 accorded fairly well with Article 9 of the European Charter of Local Self-Government, the post-1990 grant and tax arrangements are contrary to it, especially in respect of local authorities' freedom to exercise policy discretion. This re-emphasizes the caveat, expressed towards the end of Chapter 5 (p. 107), that the UK government's ratification of the European Charter does not necessarily secure a high degree of local democracy in practice.

Ultimately, the neoclassical economist argues that the true test of local accountability is through freedom of choice within a competitive market system, rather than through the enforced consumption of and payment for local government services. Service charges combined with considerable scope for exit are preferable in efficiency terms to voice combined with intergovernmental grants and local taxes. Increasing the scope for voice (see Chapter 4) may be largely ineffective in treating the symptoms, rather than the cause, of inefficiency.

The next chapter examines in more detail the legitimacy of using the median voter's voice, expressed through the system of political representation, as representative of the collectivity of voters.

10 The Median Voter Model and Hypothesis

INTRODUCTION

Frequent reference has been made in previous chapters to the median or representative voter. As already explained in Chapter 9, this is the voter whose preferences lie precisely in the middle of the range of preferences of all voters and are therefore decisive. Median voter demand schedules and indifference curves were used, in Chapters 2 and 9 respectively, to demonstrate allocative efficiency and the impact of grants on collective choices. They will be used again in Chapter 11 to determine whether local governments habitually spend more than voters wish to be spent on local government services. Such acceptance and use of the concept of the median voter is the conventional neoclassical approach to the analysis of collective decisions concerning the supply of public sector outputs.

The reader may have questioned why economists have become involved in the analysis of political decisions and whether the median voter analytical framework is the most appropriate means of undertaking such analysis. The answer is that just as economic theory has developed a rigorous theory regarding the allocation of resources in private markets, so it has also used some of the traditional tools of economic analysis to develop a comparable theory for the distribution of public sector resources. Such a theory is necessary if only to explain government provision of public goods. In such cases, allocative decisions have to be undertaken by political rather than by market processes.

It is inevitable therefore that, though the analysis of voting concerns political science, economists have also sought to theorize voting outcomes. Indeed, it is arguable that economists have contributed at least as much as political scientists over the last half century or so in the development of a pure theory of voting. In analysing the preferences of the median voter, economic theory ignores the influence of party politics on local government decisions, and this despite a general belief in countries such as the UK that party politics have been the predominant feature of local government over the last two or three decades (see Chapter 1). So does party politics actually predominate over individual voters' preferences?

DOES POLITICS MATTER?

In hypothesizing that the output of local government services reflects the preferences of the median voter, economists are effectively saying that politics does not matter. This is because the median voter's preferences reflect only price, income and cross elasticities of demand. However, some political scientists argue that politicians adopt policies on the basis of *party ideology* rather than in accordance with median voter preferences, there being some empirical evidence in support of this alternative hypothesis that politics and political parties do matter (Boyne 1996a, 1996c; Castles 1982; Sharpe and Newton 1984).

However, other political scientists argue that politics has little, if any, influence on spending. Some argue that expenditures are instead determined by simple auto-regressive *incrementalist rules* such as last year's budget plus x per cent (for example, Lewis-Beck 1977). Incrementalist rules would, however, be consistent with maintaining equilibrium in the 'political market' for local government services, the question being what determines the size of increment? Yet other political scientists argue that service provision and its financing are tempered by the *institutions of government*, the *inheritance of past programmes* and *pragmatism* (Rose 1984, 1990a).

The apparent lack of influence of local politics on expenditures in cross-sectional studies may simply reflect the fact that political cultures differ across localities such that local parties set their expenditures in accordance with local (rather than national) political party values. Nevertheless, there are other potential explanations of the spectrum of service provision, *socio-economic factors* traditionally being used to derive the presumed wants of local electorates (Davis *et al.* 1966). Indeed, socioeconomic factors underpin the distribution in many countries of intergovernmental grants attempting to equalize differing per capita expenditure needs (see Chapter 9). Increasing central control of local government spending (for the reasons identified in Chapter 5) may mean that local service provision is primarily determined by *centrally-imposed preferences*. For example, the statistical relationship (r^2) between local government spending (by type of authority) in England and Wales and central government's spending guidelines rose from around 50 in the early 1980s to well over 90 in the early 1990s (Boyne 1996b). This was because of the increasing level of central control of local government spending in the UK (see Chapters 8 and 9).

In short, the various hypothesized determinants of public sector expenditures include median voter preferences, political parties and party ideology, incrementalist rules, institutional factors including the inheritance of past commitments and pragmatism, socioeconomic factors, and the imposition of central government's preferences on local governments. While the debate among political scientists about what determines local government expenditures rages on, this chapter is concerned only with the first determinant, namely the median voter.

If the median voter's preferences are to determine service levels, democratic *processes* must reflect those preferences and democratic *institutions* must translate them into service outputs. The earlier analysis of the principal–agent problem (Chapter 3) and of bureaucrats' self-serving behaviour (Chapter

5) questioned whether public sector institutions do actually act in accordance with democratic choices. A number of steps are necessary in order to determine whether or not they do:

1. Demonstrate voter sovereignty.
2. Demonstrate the primacy of the median voter's preferences.
3. Model the median voters' choices.
4. Develop the median voter hypothesis that spending matches those choices.
5. Test the median voter model and the median voter hypothesis.

This is the approach followed during the rest of this chapter.

VOTER SOVEREIGNTY

Models of resource allocation in both the private and public sectors assume primacy of the individual: consumer sovereignty in private markets, voter sovereignty in the public sector. In respect of the local public sector, the standard economic model assumes that local authority services are supplied in accordance with voters' willingness to pay the resultant local tax costs. This fiscal exchange model of government is a microeconomic model of public expenditure growth (Bailey 1995, ch. 3). Like the model of perfect competition in private sector markets, this model may seem overly simple (for example, in assuming perfect information) and naïve in its appreciation of local political processes (effectively ignoring them). Nonetheless, it has considerable explanatory power and helps us to understand both how the relative size of the public and private sectors is determined and how resources are allocated between services within the public sector.

Given the complexity of public sector decision-making processes, it is not obvious whether voters, their political representatives or some other agent is the primary decision-maker. This indeterminacy is encapsulated in the different and conflicting models of local government (Chapter 1) and the models of bureaucratic empire building (Chapter 5). Nevertheless, the basic assumption is of a democratic system in which political decisions reflect the collective preferences of voters who vote in accordance with their own self-interest, each seeking that level of expenditure and taxation which would maximise their utilities.

Aspiring and elected politicians must reflect voter preferences about levels of expenditures and taxes if they are to be elected to, and subsequently remain in, office. If they do not become vote-maximizers they will be replaced by political rivals who satisfy more fully voter preferences. Hence, competition among rivals for local political office (the competitive political process) is the public sector equivalent of perfect competition in private markets (the competitive market process). The discipline of the competitive political process in the public sector is directly analogous to the discipline of market forces in the private sector. An efficient allocation of resources results, as will be demonstrated below.

The economic analysis of voting decisions takes the form of a standard constrained maximization model. Comparable with the demand for private sector goods and services, a voter's demand for services is assumed to be a positive function of his or her income and a negative function of the corresponding tax price. Individual voters are assumed to act in a calculatively rational way in voting for that level of spending which equates the marginal cost of local government services *that he or she has to pay* with the marginal benefit *that he or she receives* from the additional consumption of those services. In perfectly competitive private markets, the equation of marginal cost and benefit is achieved by the *invisible hand of market forces*. Willingness to pay (dependent upon marginal benefit) is reflected by the market demand curve, which interacts with supply to achieve equilibrium conditions. No such invisible hand exists in the public sector, preferences having to be recorded through the voting system before public sector resources can be allocated. In effect, notwithstanding secret ballots, the public sector employs the *visible hand of democratic procedures* to allocate resources.

Voter Sovereignty under Representative Democracy

Chapter 2 noted the increasing size of local governments throughout Europe. Over historical time the increasing size of local governments caused direct democracy to evolve into representative (indirect) democracy. *Direct democracy* exists when voters are offered alternative levels of spending on a particular service and vote in accordance with their preferences. Referenda could be used where local authorities are too large for meetings of the whole electorate. In practice, however, most countries adopt *representative democracy* whereby electorates vote for politicians who act on their behalf in determining the economically optimal level and service distribution of local expenditures.

There is a great variety of representative systems throughout the world. Within Europe, Britain alone has a *'first-past-the-post'* voting procedure which allows each voter to vote for only one alternative. This majoritarian electoral rule means that the alternative with the most votes at the first and only round of voting 'wins' and so is adopted. France has an electoral system involving two rounds of voting, Ireland employs the single transferable vote, Germany and Italy have mixed-member proportional systems, the rest having various types of proportional representation. The particular type of electoral system is of no great concern to economic theory as long as citizens' votes only reflect their preferences for service provision and the related local tax costs. It can then be assumed that any political party which does not supply services in accordance with the wishes of its local electorate will be voted out of office and replaced with one which does.

However, there are institutional differences between direct and represent-ative democracies. Political parties and special interest groups become more in-fluential in decision-making under representative democracy, Sweden seeming to be a case in point (Nelson 1992). Therefore, assuming *ceteris paribus*, expend-itures may be higher in the latter than in the former. Higher spending under representative democracies would occur if monopoly power is acquired by elected officials or if distributional coalitions exercise disproportionate political power (see Chapter 5). By definition, this would not occur under direct demo-cracy, although public sector bureaucrats may still acquire monopoly power.

Under representative democracy the elected politician becomes the agent of the principal (see Chapter 3), in this case the median voter. However, voting decisions of elected representatives may also be influenced by political par-ties and other factors. Moreover, the economic approach to analysis of voter behaviour assumes that votes are restricted to specific issues influencing con-strained utility maximization. In contrast, in the political approach, votes on different issues are underpinned by ideology. Hence, while economic analysis of voting patterns can yield unstable voting patterns characterized by cyclical majorities (see below), political analysis recognizes that votes on different issues are linked by ideology which generates stable party coalitions through vote trading and so stable voting patterns and non-cyclical majorities. How-ever, ideology may simply be a reduced form of preference that incorporates economic interests, such as redistribution of income from high-income to low-income groups.

THE PRIMACY OF THE MEDIAN VOTER'S PREFERENCES

The main problem for the economic analysis of voting processes is the lack of information about the willingness to pay of each and every voter for successive marginal increments in service output. There is, however, an apparent solu-tion to this problem. The standard approach of neoclassical economics is to model the preferences of the *median voter*, rather than those of the com-munity, in analysing local government expenditures. This approach was adopted in Chapter 9 after recognizing the problems faced when mapping community indifference curves.

The argument is that, under a majority voting procedure, the median voter's set of preferences are decisive. This is because, considering the dispersion of all voters' preferences for local tax/expenditure mixes, there are an equal number of votes on either side of the median voter's. In effect, the median voter has the casting vote on every occasion. The median voter is therefore the pivotal voter. In effect, it is assumed that the objective of the political pro-cess is to enact the preferences of the median voter.

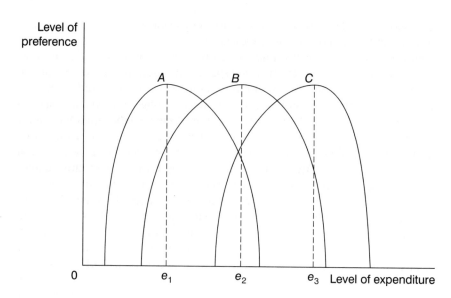

Figure 10.1 *Single-peaked preference schedules*

A very simple example illustrates this hypothesis. Assume there are only three voters resident within a local authority. The voting problem is to select, in accordance with the declared preferences of the three individuals, only one option from a set of alternatives. Voter A is willing to pay only a small tax bill because only a limited level of service outputs is desired. At the other extreme, voter C is willing to pay a high local tax bill for a high level of local government spending. In between A and C, voter B is willing to pay a moderate tax bill to finance a moderate level of service provision. B is the median voter because there are an equal number of voters on either side of B's set of preferences.

If the three alternatives (high, moderate and low levels of local spending and taxation) are put to the vote, B's preference will have a majority of votes (that is, two out of three). The moderate budget prefered by B will command most support in a choice between the low and moderate budgets (B and C in favour of the moderate budget, A in favour of the small budget). It will also receive a majority of votes in a choice between the high and moderate budgets (A and B in favour of the moderate budget, C in favour of the high budget). *Ultimately, therefore, the local authority's tax and spending decisions reflect the preferences of the median voter.* This is illustrated in Figure 10.1.

Individuals A, B and C each have *single-peaked preferences*. Single-peaked preferences arise if each individual's preference pattern results in indifference curves of the usual shape; that is, those drawn in Figures 9.2 to 9.4 above. Individual A most prefers a level of local government expenditure of amount e_1, while B most prefers e_2 and C most prefers e_3. This is the same preference

Table 10.1   *Single-peaked preferences*

Preferences	Voter A	Voter B	Voter C
First	e_1	e_2	e_3
Second	e_2	e_1	e_2
Third	e_3	e_3	e_1

pattern as in the last example. The further away any proposed level of expenditure from e_1 the less it is favoured by individual A, and likewise departures from e_2 and e_3 for individuals B and C respectively. B is the median voter. If three levels of spending are proposed corresponding to e_1, e_2 and e_3 then e_2 will gain a simple majority against every other proposal, as explained above. The median voter's preferences are therefore adopted by this decision-making rule.

This can also be illustrated by Table 10.1, the preference pattern of which corresponds with Figure 10.1. Specifically, voter A most prefers e_1 (which, by definition, maximizes that voter's utility), derives a lower level of utility from e_2 (see Figure 10.1), and none at all from e_3 (which lies on the horizontal axis to the right of A's preference schedule in Figure 10.1). Likewise, voter C gains maximum utility from e_3, a lower level of utility from e_2 (in this case greater than the utility derived from e_2 by voter A in Figure 10.1) and no utility at all from e_1 (which lies on the horizontal axis to the left of C's preference schedule in Figure 10.1). Voter B gains utility from all three alternative levels of expenditure, that from e_3 being less than that from e_1. Hence, the rankings of preferences would be as indicated in Table 10.1.

It can be seen that the voters' declared preferences in Table 10.1 satisfy the single-peakedness condition, e_2 being the alternative that no one ranks last. By comparison, the preference pattern depicted in Table 10.2 (which does not correspond to Figure 10.1) does not meet the single-peakedness condition because each alternative is ranked last preference by at least one voter and also ranked first preference by at least one voter. This is 'the Arrow problem' which creates cyclical majorities whereby no single option is preferred outright (Arrow 1959, 1963).

Assume expenditure level e_1 is offered by the local political party in control. Though it is favoured by voter A, both voter B and C prefer e_3 to e_1 and therefore e_1 will be voted out. Similarly, if expenditure level e_2 were proposed, it would be favoured by voter B but opposed by A and C (who prefer e_1). Likewise, e_3 would be defeated by e_2. Hence, no single alternative is preferred outright, such that majorities change (that is, they follow cycles) as alternative policies are put to the vote.

In Table 10.1, however, e_2 receives a majority of votes. If e_1 is offered (voter A's first preference) it is defeated by e_2 (since both B and C prefer e_2 to e_1). If e_3 is offered (voter C's first preference) it is defeated by either e_1 or e_2 (since

Table 10.2 *Cyclical majorities (the Arrow problem)*

Preferences	Voter A	Voter B	Voter C
First	e_1	e_2	e_3
Second	e_2	e_3	e_1
Third	e_3	e_1	e_2

both are preferred over e_3 by voters A and B). If e_2 is offered it will be voted for by both voter B (first preference) and by voter A if the alternative is e_3 (since A prefers e_2 to e_3). Alternatively e_2 will be voted for by both voter B and voter C if the alternative is e_1 (since C prefers e_2 to e_1). Hence, e_2 is always the outright winner, such that the median voter's preference is adopted under majority voting. The problem of cyclical majorities does not occur (that is, the Arrow problem does not exist) for this pattern of preferences. The same result will occur for all other alternative levels of expenditure, Tables 10.1 and 10.2 showing discrete alternatives, whereas Figure 10.1 represents a continuum of alternatives.

Mueller (1993) provides a more comprehensive analysis of voting. However, the crucial condition for a stable majority, and so a determinate voting outcome, is that voters' preferences are single-peaked. Voters may, in fact, have preference patterns displaying more than one peak, in which case there may be no proposed level of spending which can obtain a simple majority over all other levels and so a stable equilibrium outcome may not be achieved. Multi-peaked preferences may occur when voting on multidimensional issues. Alternatively, voter preferences may be asymmetrical, preferences not being normally distributed around a moderate level of expenditures. For example, voters may prefer either very small or very large expenditures on a particular service (such as local policing) but not levels in between.

THE MEDIAN VOTER MODEL

It is important to stress at the outset that the median voter model is strictly only a model of *voter choices*. It is not necessarily a valid model of *political decision-making* since factors other than the preferences of the representative voter may influence political decisions (for example, distributional coalitions). Furthermore, it is not necessarily a valid model of *public expenditure*, both because the median voter's preferences may not determine political decisions and, furthermore, because those decisions may not be fully implemented in practice. Failure to implement decisions could occur because of principal–agent problems between politicians and bureaucrats acting as service providers. Many of the criticisms of the median voter model reflect a confusion between the *model (per se)* and the related *hypothesis*, namely that public expenditures are in accordance with the median voter's choices.

The median voter model has a long pedigree, originating in the 1920s, and being further developed in the 1940s and 1950s and used in the 1960s to analyse local government expenditures (Hotelling 1929; Bowen 1943; Downs 1957; Black 1948 and 1958; Barr and Davis 1966). Developed into a powerful model to analyse political decision-making, it concludes that the median voter's most preferred tax and service package will be chosen under a majority rule because the median voter is the pivotal voter, as demonstrated above. Hence the name: the median voter model. This conclusion applies as much for committee-type majority-rule decisions and for referenda as it does for representative democracy, thus demonstrating the robustness of the median voter result.

As already noted, the median voter model has the great advantage that, in allowing economists to focus on the preferences of a single individual (the median voter) rather than consider the preferences of the entire electorate, the median voter model greatly simplifies the economic analysis of majority voting outcomes.

Widely accepted and used for several decades, it was not until the 1970s that the median voter model was subject to severe criticism and increasingly seen as a special case, applicable only under certain highly restrictive conditions. The median voter model has become one of the most criticised tools of public sector economists because, in reflecting the preferences of the median voter, local government fiscal decisions are explained and determined by received *consumer* theory. Effectively a microeconomic model of resource allocation in the local public sector, its level of abstraction and use of limiting assumptions is comparable with that of the model of perfect competition used to analyse resource allocation in the private sector.

As in most economic models of consumer and producer decision-making, the assumptions are often considered unrealistic and too abstract. In particular, the assumptions of the median voter model omit the complications of strategic or rent-seeking behaviour by voters (see below). The response of neoclassical economists is the standard one that the validity of the model is to be found in how well it explains local fiscal choices, rather than in terms of the realism of its assumptions. In practice, it is difficult to disprove or to corroborate the predictive accuracy of the model (see Chapter 11).

Assumptions of the Median Voter Model

There are several explicit and implicit assumptions of the median voter model:

1. *Single issue decisions* Voting takes place on a single issue with two alternatives (for example, two alternative levels of spending on school education).

2. *Single-peaked preferences, tastes for service outputs being distributed normally* This means that the alternatives can be arrayed along a single dimension (that is, the horizontal axis in Figure 10.1); for example, for alternative levels of expenditure. As was demonstrated by the examples above, the assumption of single-peaked preferences has two implications:

- For each voter, there is one level of spending that is preferred over all alternative levels and the voter's level of preference decreases as expenditures rise above or fall below the most preferred level. In other words, there are no voting intransitivities.
- Considering all voters, a median level of spending can be identified such that fewer than half of the voters have preferred levels below it and no more than one half have preferred levels above it. Given a choice from (at least) 3 options, there will be one alternative that no voter ranks last, namely that in the centre.

3. *A majority voting rule is in place, whereby the alternative winning the most votes is adopted.* Given assumption 1 above, this means that the median preferred level of spending will never lose if it is put to the vote (but it may tie). However, as noted above, some European local governments have proportional representation, not a first-past-the-post system of political representation where only the winning candidate takes up political office. The form of political representation, first-past-the-post or (the various forms of) proportional representation, may affect the validity of this assumption.

4. *All voters do, in fact, vote (that is, declare their preferences), there being no abstentions.* However, many elections experience less that full voter turn-out, sometimes less than half of those eligible to vote actually vote. If some of those eligible to vote fail so to do, then it is conceivable that the median preference of the totality of those eligible to vote can differ from the median preference of those who do actually vote. Elected officials may genuinely misinterpret voter preferences, particularly if voter turnout is less than 100 per cent in elections and if there is asymmetry of preferences between those who do vote and those who do not. Some groups may not vote because of alienation and/or indifference (Mathis and Zech 1986).

5. *The cost to the local electorate of producing alternative levels of services is known.* This is the standard assumption of perfect knowledge, there being no fiscal illusion on the part of voters.

6. *Utility functions are separable between private and public sector expenditures* – so that direct comparability between private and public choices is possible and so that preferences expressed through voting reflect only the marginal costs and benefits to be derived from local government services. This is valid if private and public sector expenditures are mutually

exclusive substitutes but may be problematic for complementary goods and services.

7. *Individual voters vote for their most preferred alternative.* However, voters do not always declare their preferences honestly, it being well known that strategic voting can occur. Individual voters may vote for a less favoured alternative in order to block adoption of the least favoured alternative where the Arrow problem of cyclical majorities occurs. For example, returning to Table 10.2, voter A may vote strategically for e_2 rather than e_1 in the *first* vote, with the result that e_2 is selected. Voter A may vote strategically in order to prevent adoption of e_3 (which would otherwise defeat e_1 but is the least prefered alternative of voter A).

8. *The political process is competitive and politicians seek to maximize the votes allocated to them.*

9. *A menu of distinct alternative policies and programmes is offered to voters.*

10. *The median voter is the pivotal voter.*

The limitations of the assumptions of the median voter model have been widely acknowledged (Sorensen 1995). Nonetheless, the model provides a powerful tool for empirical analysis and has become one of the most used models of public sector economists in seeking to explain local government expenditures. However, it must again be emphasized that the median voter model is a *demand* aggregation model. A further hypothesis is required if it is to be used as a model of public sector *supply*.

THE MEDIAN VOTER HYPOTHESIS

The median voter *hypothesis* is that local government service expenditures reflect median voter demand. The crudest version of the hypothesis assumes that the median voter has the median income of the local community, so that local government expenditures should correlate with median income. In effect, this is a reductionist form of the argument that expenditures are determined by socioeconomic factors (for example, Davis *et al.* 1966). The median voter hypothesis is illustrated in Figure 10.2.

The line *AC* is the community's original budget line depicting the combinations of the single local government service and the single private sector commodity which are available given their prices and the community's income. Assume an increase in income creates the new budget line *BD*, parallel to *AC* because the relative prices of the two commodities have not changed. Assuming a positive income elasticity of demand, spending on the local government output rises along the income–consumption curve (or line) *RS*, the points at which the budget lines are tangential to the median voter's indifference curves (not shown, but see Figure 9.3 above for comparison).

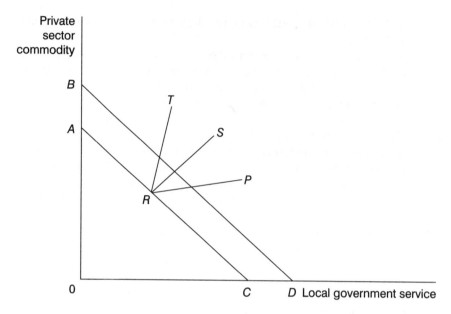

Figure 10.2   *The income–consumption locus*

The median voter hypothesis would be corroborated if empirical research revealed that the actual locus of consumption choices of the local government and private sector commodities did lie along *RS* as the median voter's income changed. If, however, the actual income–consumption locus were to lie above (such as *RT*) or below (such as *RP*) locus *RS*, then the median voter hypothesis would be refuted. In both cases, it would be evident that the local government service provision no longer matched the preferences of the median voter.

Locus *RP* results if local government's service expenditures are greater than the level predicted by the median voter's income elasticity of demand. Likewise, locus *RT* results if spending is less than that prediction. If spending does conform to *RS*, then the median voter model allows economists to explain local government spending without reference to politics, simply by applying the standard neoclassical microeconomic individual utility-maximizing theory. Such explanation is not possible if the result is other than *RS*.

In fact, the results of empirical research suggest that local government expenditures are higher than would be expected on the basis of median voter income elasticities of demand (that is, *RP* rather than *RS*). *RP* is evidence of the so-called 'flypaper effect' (see Chapter 11) and suggests failure either of the median voter model, or of the median voter hypothesis, or both. Alternatively, the empirical evidence could be flawed because either the data is deficient and inaccurate and/or because the econometric analysis of that data is flawed.

Each of these possibilities is examined in the remainder of this chapter and in Chapter 11. Having already considered the assumptions of the median voter model, the next step must be to consider the assumptions of the median voter hypothesis.

Assumptions of the Median Voter Hypothesis

1. *There is voter sovereignty* – so that the decisions of the median voter's local government concerning the supply of its services match voters' willingness to pay local taxes. As already noted, this assumes the *fiscal exchange model* of local government but elected politicians may not always serve the interests of the median voter. Elected politicians may have their own utility functions in which voter preferences are not the dominant component. For example, Democratic and Republican senators representing the same US state display very different voting patterns in respect of federal bills. Since they supposedly represent the same set of voters, such differences constitute a rejection of the median voter hypothesis (Poole and Rosenthal 1984). The explanation is that senators vote on bills in accordance with their own utility functions, in which voter preferences are not the predominant components, the others being the national 'party line', the senator's own ideology and the need to cater for specific constituencies as well as the overall electorate (Poole and Rosenthal 1984; Levitt 1996). If they seek government office they may ascribe more closely to the party line.
2. *The preferences of the median voter can be matched with those of a candidate for political office.* This is less likely the fewer the candidates for political office.
3. *There are no principal–agent problems.* This assumption means that bureaucrats act in accordance with the instructions of politicians who, in turn, reflect voter preferences. However, bureaucracies may exercise monopoly power, resulting in excessive levels of spending (see Chapters 5 and 11).
4. *The full marginal cost of voting for changes in the levels of service provision is reflected in the median voter's liability to pay local government taxes.* This will only be the case when government grants are exogenous lump-sum payments and when the only other source of revenue is the local *residential* property tax. In fact, grants are often not lump-sum, instead being conditional effort-related (endogenous) payments (see Chapter 9). Moreover, the local residential property tax is not usually the only source of revenue (see Chapter 8). Constitutional constraints can be assumed to require the budget to be balanced annually.
5. *The median voter is the person with median income, the median housing value and the median residential property tax bill.* This assumption is required to

calculate the income–consumption locus in Figure 10.2. It may be a less valid assumption under some forms of proportional representation than under first-past-the-post systems of electoral representation. Moreover, not all voters pay the local property tax (that is, those who are not heads of household and are therefore not legally liable to pay) or may not pay it in full (because they receive rebates and reliefs). Assuming the benefits of service provision are distributed equally among voters, those who do not pay the tax can be expected to regard local government expenditure as a free good. They therefore demand a higher level of local government expenditure than property owners, making the usual assumptions of diminishing marginal utility and *ceteris paribus*. These assumptions ignore any effects on property values through tax capitalization (so that the tax shares of voters are fixed). In practice, even non-payers of the property tax may take account of the financial consequencies of their voting behaviour on the budgets of the households in which they live and which do pay the tax (see Chapter 8).

6. *The tax reduction or, alternatively, the services that could be financed by an unconditional grant, is of equal value to the median voter.* However, the income in cash and in kind will only be of equal value if the median voter's tax share is the same as his or her share of service provision. The greater the median voter's local tax share, the greater that voter's tax reduction which can be financed by the unconditional grant. Eligibility criteria for service takeup will not automatically equate the value of service consumption with tax payment. Early versions of the median voter model took no account of the distribution of tax share. This deficiency was later remedied, for example by Borcherding and Deacon (1972).

7. *The median voter's budget constraint is represented by the median income within the local community.* However, expenditure data alone cannot confirm that the median income earner is the pivotal voter.

8. *Local governments have full autonomy regarding local tax levels and service provision.* However, in many countries there are central government constraints on local government expenditures.

These assumptions are highly restrictive. For example, Sorensen (1995) argues that the preferences of political representatives do influence local government expenditures. He presents evidence suggesting that politicians' preferences for higher or lower expenditure levels are influenced by their occupational background (those in the public sector or professions generally preferring higher levels of, say, education expenditures than those in the private sector and non-professional occupations); the political party to which they are affiliated (left-wing socialist parties generally favouring higher expenditures than right-wing conservative parties); and the committee on which they sit (those sitting on a particular service committee perhaps preferring higher expenditures than those sitting on finance and general purpose committees). There are elements of both self-selection and socialization (for example, other committee members inculcating new members with their own values) here which may result in committees being biased subsets of the full council, seeking to promote their own particular policy areas. Some occupational groups and social classes are overrepresented in local governments (see Chapter 1).

Given that the median voter is assumed to vote for that candidate or programme maximizing his or her personal welfare, it follows that the voter is, in effect, voting for that party which maximizes his or her final income (that is, income after payment of all direct and indirect taxes plus the value of public services consumed). Hence, the median voter will follow two strategies which contravene the 'equal benefits' and 'fixed tax shares' points within assumption 5 above. First, the median voter will seek to maximize his or her share of the benefits derived from the provision of public services. Second, the median voter will seek to minimize the tax price which he or she has to pay.

Both strategies can be promoted by forming distributional coalitions (see Chapter 5) which seek to control governments so that they focus the benefits on coalition members but divert the tax costs more generally onto non-coalition members. These strategies can be implemented, first, by increasing provision of those services most heavily used by coalition members and, second, by persuading the government to introduce a highly progressive tax structure which takes proportionately more from those whose incomes are above the median. Such redistribution is limited in practice because income is not the sole criterion underpinning the formation of distributional coalitions and because of competition among coalitions with opposing interests.

TESTING THE MEDIAN VOTER HYPOTHESIS

The following analysis specifically relates to testing the median voter hypothesis within a first-past-the-post system of electoral representation. As already noted, a system of proportional representation makes application of the median voter hypothesis methodologically difficult. There are two approaches to testing the median voter hypothesis:

1. *Cross-sectional estimation of demand functions for local government output*
   This approach requires all the assumptions of the median voter model to hold. It is by far the most common approach, although the precise details vary, particularly in terms of the number and variety of independent variables used to explain econometrically the dependent variable (that is, local government expenditures). For example, some studies of school education in the USA seek to explain demand as a function of the median voter's income, the tax price per unit of output, the median voter's tax share, size of population (to estimate the impact of congestion) and a set

of socioeconomic variables that reflect differences in tastes (Borcherding and Deacon 1972; Bergstrom and Goodman 1973). To these Inman (1979) adds the median voter's share of intergovernmental aid. This approach is considered in detail below.

2. *Micro-level surveys of voters' preferences for local government services*   None of the assumptions of the median voter demand model need hold. Micro-level surveys are rarely used but one such analysis, again of school education, found that more than half of voters in separate jurisdictions prefer no change in expenditure levels (Gramlich and Rubinfield 1989). This result is consistent with both the median voter demand model and incrementalist rules noted above.

Cross-sectional Estimation of Demand Functions

Use of cross-sectional estimation of demand functions for local government services is popular because it would seem that the median voter hypothesis can easily be tested as an explanation of local government spending using econometric techniques.

First, *alternative service levels can be readily identified*. It is, as already noted, difficult to measure the output of services such as school education and this may be thought to create difficulties for the expression of voters' preferences. Increased output could relate to additional pupils (for example, by raising the school-leaving age, increasing school hours or extending pre-school nursery provision); smaller class sizes requiring additional teachers and more school buildings; better qualified (and presumably more expensive) teachers; improved curricula and so on. If, however, there is a clearly established set of priorities regarding which services and which components of those services will be expanded (or contracted) if more (or less) spending is voted for, then quantity can be measured by levels of spending. Second, *there are usually large numbers of local governments in any one country*. This makes viable the use of empirical research methods. Third, *the characteristics of the median voter can be expected to vary from one local government area to another* because local populations tend to be more homogenous than national populations, population shorting being aided by Tiebout's voting with one's feet (see Chapter 4). Hence, differences in per capita spending can be correlated with, and explained by, differences in median voter characteristics. Fourth, in the USA at least, *educational expenditures can be studied in isolation* since, as noted earlier, this service is provided by unidimensional school boards which are independent taxing and spending authorities. Hence, voters in school referenda are restricted to single-issue voting and preferences are likely to be single-peaked.

A number of steps are required in order to utilise the median voter model in order to test the median voter hypothesis.

1. *Identify the median voter.*
2. *Determine the median voter's income.* The median voter's budget constraint is represented by the median income within the local community. This is only valid if voters consider only purely individual issues when casting their votes. If they take account of family or household interests then median family income or median household income respectively should be used rather than median individual income (Turnbull and Mitias 1995).

   Median household income is a broader measure than median family income, the former including the incomes of all persons within the household, not just those related to the head of household. Hence, the term 'median income' is ambiguous. All three definitions of 'median income' have been used in the empirical research, although it is not always clear which measure has been used. In practice, the measure of median income is often determined by data availability. This in turn will be determined by the taxable unit for income tax purposes: the individual, family or household. Where school education is tested, the median voter is by definition not the school pupil (who is not old enough to vote). Therefore the median voter is voting for services used by his or her family. So median family income is the correct measure.
3. *Calculate the median voter's liability to pay the local tax.* The voter's local tax price is calculated by multiplying the tax share by the unit cost of the local government service.
4. *Apply the relevant measures of both the price and income elasticities of demand for the local government service(s) whose expenditure(s) are being subject to econometric modelling.* As usual, a voter's preferences for different levels of expenditure depend upon tastes, income, the tax price of the service and any of the other factors noted above. The usual relationships can be expected to exist, namely that demand is a positive function of income (assuming that local government services are normal goods) and a negative function of price.

The majority of empirical studies find that median income is an important explanation of local government spending, differences in spending between local authorities being closely correlated with differences in median voter's incomes (and the tax price of service outputs). There is some evidence that the median voter model performs better, in terms of modelling local government expenditures, under direct democratic processes than under representative institutional arrangements (Pommerehne 1978; Santerre 1986). While this corroboration has not been replicated elsewhere (Chicoine *et al.* 1989), political parties and special interest groups clearly become more influential in decision-making under representative democracy (Nelson 1992). Politicians may seek a balance between adopting a spending programme which is likely to win the election and one which is more in tune with their own (or their party's) preferences (Hansson and Stuart 1984). Elections give majority parties mandates rather than commit them to specific decisions. However, there are a number of criticisms of the various studies.

CRITICISMS OF THE APPLICATIONS OF THE MEDIAN VOTER MODEL

There are two categories of criticism of the empirical applications of the median voter model to test the median voter hypothesis.

1. Theoretical Criticism

The theoretical basis of the median voter model can be challenged. First, as already noted, the major advantage of the median voter model is that it reduces collective decision-making to a question of solving an individual maximization problem, treating collective decisions as if they were the demands of the median voter. In effect, the median voter model bypasses the aggregation (of voters' individual preferences) problem. Since, in practice, there is a considerable degree of individual heterogeneity, the median voter model therefore *ignores distributional factors*, making it difficult to interpret the results of the model. Second, *the identity of the median voter may change* as a result of changes in the progressivity of the city's tax structure and associated tax capitalization effects, because disposable income will change as a result. The same effect would occur if receipt of a lump-sum intergovernmental grant were used to reduce local tax levels, since it too would change disposable income.

2. Empirical Criticism

Empirical criticism relates to inappropriate uses of the median voter model and to data problems in its application.

(a)   Challenging the Use to which the Median Voter Model has been Put
Turnbull and Djoundourian (1994) note that the large majority of studies have analysed data for single-service schools districts. Sorensen (1995) argues that the median voter model is not generally applicable because it is inappropriate in multi-party systems that provide multiple government services (the most common local government structure). It is applicable in the case of school boards in the USA because they manage only one service, they have tax-raising powers and their budgets have to be approved by local voters.

In most other countries, however, local governments provide a range of services, budgets for which are not submitted to voters for their approval, and their revenues may be determined at the central level. They may not have powers to raise local taxes. Even if they do, there may be central controls in the form of maximum tax rates or rates of increase year-on-year. Intergovernmental grants also distort tax prices to voters, as do any local taxes paid by non-residents or local businesses. In the extreme case, local government revenues are exogenous, rather than being endogenous to local decision-making by voters. In such a case, local governments can only decide the distribution of their revenues over the range of services, as distinct from deciding the total level of revenue. Hence, the median voter hypothesis is very unlikely to hold in multi-party, multi-issue settings, often characterised by political compromises, coalitions and voting cycles.

(b) Data Inadequacies

Mueller (1993) notes that the results of a large number of empirical tests support the median voter hypothesis but advises caution in interpreting the empirical results because data problems impose limits on the extent to which empirical models can match the theoretical model. Data inadequacies invariably require compromises and additional assumptions which serve to distort the application of the theoretical model.

1. *It is difficult to identify the median voter.* The difficulty of determining the willingness to pay for each and every voter has already been referred to. The privacy of the ballot box compounds this difficulty. Public opinion surveys regarding service preferences and willingness to pay the associated tax costs are limited in their coverage of the voting population, are sporadic in nature and do not necessarily provide accurate estimates of voting patterns. This effectively means that voters cannot be ranked according to their preferences and so the median voter cannot be identified.

   The solution, as noted above, is to make heroic assumptions, namely that the median voter in each local authority is the one with the median income, occupying the median-valued property (where local authorities heavy a local property tax). These assumptions allow identification of the median voter, data on incomes and property values often being readily available on a local authority basis. Even if this assumption were valid, there are further problems.

2. *If voter participation rates are less that 100 per cent, then one cannot be certain that the median income of those who do vote is the same as that for the total population of eligible voters.* This uncertainty is increased if the propensity not to vote is a function of social class or of income, ethnic, racial or religious group and so on. The more asymmetrical is the pattern of voting and of non-voting, the less likely the match between the median incomes of voters and all eligible to vote.

3. *It is not possible to know whether expenditures correspond to those desired by a voter with median income.* Expenditures could be some multiple of the level desired by the voter with median income. Though it would still be possible to calculate accurate estimates of the price and income elasticities of demand, it would not be possible to determine whether expenditure levels were too high or too low relative to the median voter's preferences. Moreover, the local government expenditure figures necessarily exclude voter expenditures on private sector alternatives (such as for school education and leisure and recreation). Substantial alternative private provision could lead to preferences for lower levels of provision by local governments.

4. *Local government expenditures may not only be positively related to median income*, but also to other measures of income such as the mean income or per capita income. This is to be expected if local government services are normal goods (Romer and Rosenthal 1979b).

5. *Local government expenditures may be inversely related not only to median tax price*, but also to other measures of tax price such as the mean (Romer and Rosenthal 1979b).

6. *Correlation between the median and mean incomes*   The contribution of the median voter model is to demonstrate how demand for local government services may be related to *median* income rather than *mean* income. There is, of course, a link between the mean and median income; they are not unrelated. Frequency distributions depicting the distribution of income are usually skewed to the right due to the relatively large incomes of a few individuals. In such cases, the mean income exceeds the median income. The gap between the mean and median disposable income will increase over time if the distribution of disposable income becomes less equal, whether because of increased unemployment or increased numbers of low-paid workers (often women and young people) in the labour force, or because of more regressive tax regimes (Rice 1985).

    Cross-sectional data can only be used to test the median voter hypothesis by assuming proportionality between the distribution of voters across jurisdictions in order that the output demanded by the voter with median income equals the median output demanded in each jurisdiction (Bergstrom and Goodman 1973). This may not be the case in practice but, in assuming that it is, the median and mean will correlate with each other such that it will not be possible to distinguish between them for the purposes of the empirical research.

After reviewing a number of studies, Romer and Rosenthal (1979b) concluded that there was no strong support for the median voter hypothesis. They have three main criticisms of empirical studies. First, they do not confirm that the median voter is the pivotal voter. Second, they fail to identify whether actual expenditures correspond to the level desired by the median voter or are some multiple (for example, twice or one-third) of that level. Third, the median voter model is rarely tested against competing models and so it is not possible to demonstrate the superiority of the median voter model over other models. There are two alternative approaches.

The first approach is to *use alternative statistical models*. The 'traditional approach' sought to explain government spending with reference to urbanization, population size and density, mean community income and other *socioeconomic variables* deemed relevant to the service in question. It was noted above that some political scientists attempt to use socioeconomic variables to explain spending without reference to political factors. Socioeconomic variables have also been identified as causes of fiscal stress (see Chapter 6). However, the likely response from economists is that these socioeconomic variables may be subsumed under a 'tastes' variable within the median voter model.

Alternatively, spending could be correlated with the *mean income or some other fractile*, instead of the median income. However, there is some evidence that median income outperforms other income measures (Mathis and Zech 1986), although this may only apply to US school boards' education expenditures (which are unidimensional). Nevertheless, adoption of a particular fractile is invalid if local governments are likely to differ in terms of that part of the income distribution in which the decisive voter's income is to be found (Aronsson and Wikstrom 1996).

The second approach is *to develop an alternative formal model of political institutions*. Todo-Rovira (1991) rejects the median voter model, arguing that local government expenditures are not solely dependent upon the characteristics of the median voter, whoever that may be. He readdresses the aggregation problem by developing a general model in which local government expenditures depend on a vector of city characteristics (such as the progressivity of the tax structure in the city) and on the distribution of individual characteristics. He finds that distributional characteristics do influence local government spending with the result that the level of local expenditures is unlikely to correspond with that preferred by the voter with median income.

He argues that his results are consistent with the hypothesis that local government weights the preferences of higher-income groups more than those of middle-income and lower-income groups when aggregating individual demands for local government service provision. This is because higher-income groups have relatively high voter turnout – and perhaps higher scope for voice and exit (see Chapter 3). Local politicians are therefore under greater pressure to satisfy the demands of higher-income groups than of middle-income and lower-income groups. The result is that the income elasticity of demand estimates of the median voter literature are likely to be underestimated because relevant explanatory variables have been omitted, especially the distribution of income.

CAN THE MEDIAN VOTER MODEL BE IMPROVED?

The above discussion of cross-sectional estimation of demand functions for local government output clearly demonstrated that the model can take account of more than just median income and, indeed, numerous studies have done so over the past several decades. Other possible modifications to the traditional utility maximization model are examined in detail in Chapter 11. Nevertheless, Poole and Rosenthal (1996) argue that the median voter, issue-by-issue approach to the analysis of public expenditure decisions is inadequate as a model of the political process. It assumes that preferences on specific issues or alternatives are directly linked to votes on those issues, failing to recognize that votes are traded across issues within political parties. Hence, while economic interests do have an influence on voting, they work in such complex ways that Poole and Rosenthal (1996) regard purely economic theories of voting as a failed idea. In effect, they are saying that the median voter demand model cannot be improved.

Holcombe (1989) argues that the median voter hypothesis is stronger than the model warrants. He argues that the model *is* a valid description of how demands are aggregated under majority rule in many situations. Though the empirical evidence does not show that local governments produce what the median voter prefers, this should not be misinterpreted as a refutation of the model. The questioning of the median voter model is a result of its over-zealous use in attempting to explain the real world.

The Need for a Supply-Side Model

If empirical evidence suggests that supply is not in accordance with demand, then either the model is deficient as a model of *demand* conditions, or the model is valid and it is *supply* conditions which must be considered. Just as the model of private sector markets was subsequently adjusted by adding elements of monopoly, so the median voter model can be adjusted by incorporating various complications such as multi-peaked preferences. However, improving the modelling of demand, while a useful exercise, is unlikely to provide a complete solution to the problem because it is now generally recognized that politicians and bureaucrats do not only serve voters' demands (that is, the fiscal exchange model of government is not valid).

There were no generally accepted models of public sector supply at the time the median voter model of public sector demand was developed. It took another three or four decades for one to be developed, namely Niskanen's model of budget-maximizing bureaucracy. Niskanen's contribution was to provide a supply-side model. However, Niskanen's model has also been subject to much criticism. Hence, with hindsight, it is not surprising that the median voter hypothesis was formulated in the absence of a well-developed theory of public sector supply.

Clearly, a more general model of public sector output has to incorporate both demand-side and supply-side factors. Attempting to use the median voter model of demand aggregation to explain equilibrium in the 'market' for public sector outputs would be like trying to determine equilibrium in private sector markets using only the market demand curve. Market supply curves are required in both cases.

Incorporating a supply side does *not* refute the median voter model of demand aggregation. It only recognizes that the model is not a valid explanation of public sector supply. The model would only be rejected, for example, if it could be demonstrated that political issues are not unidimensional, as assumed, but instead are multidimensional (McKelvy 1976, 1979). Altern-atively, it could be shown that majority voting rules will not produce a deter-minate equilibrium under certain quite plausible conditions (as in the Arrow problem case). This would make the median voter model less generally applic-able than had previously been thought – the view of public choice theorists.

Various attempts to build in supply-side relationships have been made. They are considered in Chapter 11. It is sufficient for now to note that one of the most well-developed approaches is to consider how bureaucrats may seek to control agendas in order to promote their own interests (through budget maximization) such that there is no unique and stable outcome of majority rule.

CONCLUSIONS

The questioning of the *validity* of the median voter model has to be distin-guished from *inappropriate uses* so the model. The proponents of the model have attempted to use it to explain fully local government outputs through the median voter hypothesis. Nonetheless, most of the evidence (reviewed in Chapter 11) is consistent with the *model*, if not with the *hypothesis* drawn inappropriately from it.

Use of the median voter model to explain local government spending is methodologically invalid if the objective of the political process is *not* to enact the preferences of the median voter. Like the neoclassical theory of the firm, the model fails to take account of institutional details which may influence spending, as well as ignoring the distribution of political power (by assuming voters are sovereign). The reply to this 'lack of realism' criticism is much the same as that for the theory of the firm; that is, that the validity of a model does not depend upon its descriptive reality but, instead, upon the accuracy of its predictions. Nevertheless, this chapter has made clear the methodolo-gical and other problems which make it extremely difficult to test the validity of the model. Suffice it to say that politics has a much more complex role than that attributed to it by the median voter hypothesis.

Formal models of political institutions would incorporate institutional power and bureaucratic influences on expenditure decisions. They could result in spending greatly exceeding the expenditures desired by the median voter (see Chapter 11). However, the explanation of the primacy of the median voter model may be that there is no alternative political theory which has comparable analytical advantages.

11   The Flypaper Effect

INTRODUCTION

Chapter 9 set out the traditional theory of grants-in-aid which shows how, in terms of the stimulatory effect on local government spending, a *general lump-sum grant* has the same effect as an equivalent increase in the disposable incomes of the individuals in the community (represented by the median voter).

However, Chapter 10 noted that, contrary to the theoretical outcomes, empirical studies have shown that a general lump-sum grant paid to a community has a greater stimulatory effect on local government spending than the equivalent increase in the income of the median voter. Local citizens appear to spend less on local public sector goods and services if their collective disposable incomes increase than if their local government receives an additional lump-sum general grant of the same amount from central government. It appears that additional money tends to remain in the sector into which it is paid. In other words 'money sticks where it hits', hence the term 'the flypaper effect'.

The flypaper effect therefore contradicts the traditional theory of grants-in-aid of exhaustive expenditures. It is inconsistent with the traditional neoclassical model because the balance between spending in the public and private sectors should only reflect the various income elasticities of demand of the median voter. Hence, the additional public expenditures generated by an increase in local voters' disposable incomes or, alternatively, by an increase in a general lump-sum grant of the same monetary amount received by their local government, should be identical. The fact that these measured outcomes are not identical casts doubt on the traditional theory. This chapter examines the possible theoretical and empirical explanations of the flypaper effect.

TRADITIONAL THEORY OF GRANTS-IN-AID

One of the conclusions of traditional grants-in-aid theory drawn from Chapter 9 was that general lump-sum grants have the same stimulatory effects on grantee spending as an equivalent rise in income in the community. This conclusion, demonstrated in Figure 11.1, is based on the median voter model which was much more fully developed in Chapter 10. Figure 11.1 is essentially the same as Figure 9.2, except that the notation of the axes has been changed slightly. The horizontal axis now represents the goods and services provided by the local authority and the vertical axis now represents

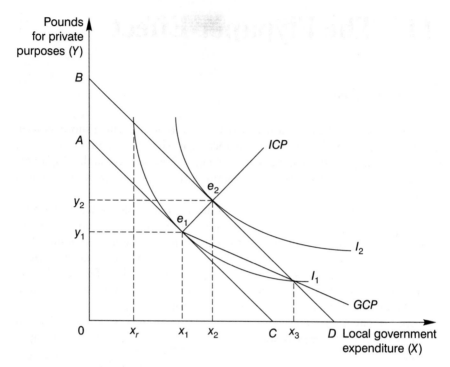

Figure 11.1 *Lump-sum grants versus changing the median voter's income*

the disposable income of the median voter. The rest of the analysis is the same as for Figure 9.2.

Ignore *GCP* for now. As for Figure 9.2, a *general lump-sum grant* of *CD* is received by the local government. This shifts the budget line from *AC* (pre-grant) to *BD* (post-grant), the equilibrium shifting from e_1 to e_2. The median voter can now afford more of both *X* and *Y*. An equivalent increase in the disposable income, equal to *AB*, of the median voter would have exactly the same result as a lump-sum general grant of the same amount since it would also produce the budget line *BD* with equilibrium again at e_2. This is the *equivalence theorem*, which states that payment of a lump-sum grant to a local government stimulates the same increase in its spending as does an equivalent increase in the personal incomes of individuals who comprise that local community. In both cases, the shift is along the income consumption path (*ICP*) or curve from e_1 to e_2.

Note that, as was the case for Figure 9.2, local government expenditure increases by less than the amount of grant (x_1x_2 being less than *CD*) because some of the grant is used to finance increased consumption of *Y* (of amount y_1y_2) via reduced local taxes. Similarly, not all of the increase *AB* in disposable income is spent on non-local government outputs (y_1y_2 being less than *AB*) because some of the income is used to finance increased consumption of local government outputs (again of amount $x_1 x_2$). Again, these outcomes will be the case as long as the goods are normal goods.

Therefore, assuming that the grant received by the community is a *general lump-sum grant*, it can be shown to have the same effects, in terms of stimulating local government grantee spending, as an equivalent increase in the disposable incomes of the individuals in the community. In other words, where the money 'hits' (that is, the pockets of local citizens or in the budget of their local government) is *irrelevant* in determining the final impact on expenditures. The intergovernmental grant is simply 'a veil' for a tax cut for local voters.

This conclusion is reached in all of the traditional theories of grants-in-aid, irrespective of whether community or median voter indifference mapping is used (for example, Bradford and Oates 1971a; Romer and Rosenthal 1980; Wilde 1971). Although the preference maps represented may vary between theories, the neoclassical assumptions underlying all of the traditional models are the same, and result in the conclusions derived from them being very similar. However, Courant *et al.* (1979) note that the conclusion, shown graphically in Figure 11.1, has not been empirically verified. The empirical evidence (relating to the USA) has instead shown there to be a significant difference between the stimulatory effects of an unconditional general lump-sum grant and an equivalent increase in individuals' incomes.

Gramlich (1977b) concluded that the stimulatory effect of lump-sum grants on local government expenditures was more than four times that of equivalent increases in the incomes of private individuals. For example, Gramlich and Galper's 1973 study of US time-series data concluded that for every extra \$1 increase in intergovernmental grants-in-aid, \$0.43 is spent by the grantee, the remainder being returned to individuals via reductions in local taxes. In comparison, a \$1 increase in an individual's income would result in an increase in grantee spending of only \$0.05 to \$0.10. Hence, the stimulatory effect of lump-sum grants is more than four times greater than the effect of increased income.

This result is demonstrated in Figure 11.1. *ICP* shows the locus of consumption choices arising from the increase in median voter *income*. However, *GCP* (the grant consumption path) represents the empirical result where receipt of a lump-sum grant has a greater stimulatory effect on local government spending than an equivalent increase in median voter income, x_3 being greater than x_2. A flypaper effect occurs as long as *GCP* lies below *ICP*.

The assumption underpinning the flypaper effect is that an increase in lump-sum grants represents an increase in community income. However, as noted in Chapter 9, Brennan and Pincus (1996) argue that grants from higher to lower levels of government are matched by a reverse flow of tax payments. Hence, they assume that tax and lump-sum grant payments are exactly matched for each recipient jurisdiction. However, this exact matching seems unlikely in practice, even within a federal system.

The flypaper effect has three implications. First, as noted above, it dis-proves the traditional neoclassical theory of intergovernmental grants. Altern-atively, it demonstrates that the traditional theory of grants-in-aid is not fully developed enough to explain these seemingly contradictory results and must therefore be modified. Finally, the empirical results may themselves be flawed because statistical and/or specification errors lead to an overestima-tion of the flypaper effect. If so, then the flypaper effect is a 'mirage' and so does not disprove the traditional theory.

The first possibility was examined in detail in Chapter 10, which distin-guished between the validity of the median voter model as a model of *demand* aggregation, and its use to explain the *supply* of local government service out-puts and, hence, expenditures. The conclusion was that even if the median voter model is a valid means by which to aggregate voters' demands, it requires a supply-side component in order to be able to model local government expenditures. This chapter examines in more detail possible modifications of the model on both the demand-side and the supply-side, before examining the argument that the flypaper effect is simply a mirage.

MODIFYING THE TRADITIONAL MODEL

Three models attempt to modify the traditional utility maximization model in Figure 11.1 in order to explain the flypaper effect.

1. Hamilton's Deadweight Loss Model

Hamilton (1986) argues that the deadweight loss of welfare created by local government taxation (for example, because of disincentive-to-work effects) creates added costs for locally-raised tax revenues. In comparison, grants received from central government are free from these additional costs and therefore it is not as costly in terms of economic potential for the community to spend grant money as it is to spend taxation revenues raised locally. This of course ignores the deadweight loss created by central government taxes at national level. Moreover 'the marginal deadweight losses from taxation are typically far too small to reconcile the large differences between propensities to spend out of changes in grants and changes in private incomes' (Hines and Thaler 1995, p. 221).

2. Quigley and Smolensky's Transactions Costs Model

Quigley and Smolensky (1992) analyze the impact of transactions costs in terms of the costliness of changes in tax rates, that is the costs of reoptimizing budgets. Local government tax rates may be determined only once each year (when budgets are set) such that a mid-year unexpected change in either the disposable income of the median voter or in grants would require the full-scale redetermination of the budget if tax rates were to be altered. This would be very costly in terms of both democratic decision-making and administration. Under certain scenarios of modest adjustment costs the median voter is absolutely better off by not reoptimizing in response to receipt of a block grant (that is, returning a proportion to the voters in the form of a tax cut) but, instead, increasing local government expenditure by the full amount of the grant. Alternatively, local authorities could simply hold the extra grant as balances and return it to voters the following financial year. However, such balances may still be treated as expenditure (rather than as savings) while they are held, a case of an inappropriate variable in econometric models (see below). Reoptimization will not be necessary if grant values are announced in advance of local budgeting such that Quigley and Smolensky's model would become inapplicable.

3. King's Low-Income Constraint Model

The modification King makes to the traditional median voter model is that the median voter's utility is maximized subject to the constraint that 'the tax rate set must not leave the authority's poorest citizens with a net income below some level specified by the median voter' (King 1984, p. 114). Higher levels of output of local government services require higher local tax rates, assuming intergovernmental grants are fixed. At some point, increasing the tax rates set by the local authority would result in the poorest citizens having disposable incomes below the level specified by the median voter, assuming that all income groups are liable to pay the local tax. It is then possible to demonstrate the flypaper effect in diagrammatic terms (ibid., pp. 115–17). The validity of the low-income constraint ultimately depends upon three assumptions:

1. *Whether or not the median voter (or collectivity of voters) does seek to protect the net incomes of low-income groups* In fact, they may regard that as a central government function (see also Chapter 1).
2. *Whether local governments act in accordance with those wishes* In practice, local governments may be able to do little to protect low-income groups because of the multiplicity of factors which affect the latter's incomes (for example, recession or central government taxes) and the fact that the income-maintenance role of local government is usually limited. Local government policy-making may be heavily influenced by national policies and by other interest groups such that, in practice, there is little scope for them specifically to protect the poor.

3. *That all income groups are liable to pay local taxes*   This is invalid: by definition, the poor do not pay local income tax. The impact of a local sales tax
on the net incomes of the poorest groups depends upon which goods and
services are taxed and whether the consumption patterns of rich and poor
groups vary. The poor would be less adversely affected if food and energy
were not taxed. There may be income-related rebates for the local property
tax (as in the UK). In such cases the median voter's concerns for the welfare
of the poorest citizens will be largely unfounded.

While these three models provide examples of how the traditional median
voter model can be used to explain the flypaper effect, none has been applied
to a real-life set of data to establish the authenticity and accuracy of their theoretical predictions. They would all appear to be special cases, applicable more
to the exception than the rule. To that extent, they do not fully explain the flypaper effect and so other explanations have to be sought, which do not rely
on reformulation within the bounds of the traditional theory of grants-in-aid.

PUBLIC CHOICE THEORIES

Public choice theories attempt to explain the flypaper effect by assuming a
conflict of interests between voters and politicians/bureaucrats. The traditional model's assumption is one of a *harmony* of interests between voters
and politicians or bureaucrats. As noted in Chapter 10, this assumes either a
fiscal exchange or a fiscal transfer model of local government, whereby local
authorities act in response to citizens' preferences for services in exchange
for local taxes or seek certain degrees of redistribution of final (as distinct
from disposable) income respectively. However, Gramlich (1977b) explicitly
pointed towards *disharmony* of interests as the primary reason for the flypaper
effect and emphasized the need for revision of political theories that feature
a harmony of interests. Both Wilde (1968) and Bradford and Oates (1971a)
had previously noted that their models would be affected by the existence of
any disharmony of interests.

Disharmony of interests is not the only cause of government failure, however. It can arise in three ways, each of which could lead to a flypaper effect:

1. *Failure by institutional structure* contradicts the assumption that the political
process is highly responsive to the preferences of individuals, either
because of the restrictions placed upon the lower level of government by
higher authority, or by the rules of the local government itself. It can be
failure by neglect rather than by design.
2. *Failure by learning or habit* occurs when citizens do not know, and cannot
correctly imagine, the consequences of some proposed collective action.
If those preferences are confused, then government failure occurs.

3. *Disharmony of interests* in the form of power-hungry, self-interested politicians and bureaucrats who act in their own interests rather than those of local citizens (see Chapters 3, 5 and 10): this is the public choice model of government. The benign form of fiscal illusion (arising because of failure by learning or habit) contrasts sharply with deliberate actions of the politicians to misinform or mislead voters through the provision of false information, or information insufficient for the voters to make a well-informed decision.

These three distinct and separate causes of government failure call into question the improved allocative efficiency purportedly arising from decentralized governments, in accordance with Oates' decentralization theorem (see Chapter 2). There are a number of public choice models which fall into two groups: behavioural models and fiscal illusion models.

1. Behavioural Public Choice Models

(a) Niskanen's Model of Bureaucracy

Niskanen's model of bureaucracy was used in Chapter 5 as a microeconomic rationale for central control of local expenditure because the model predicts that bureaucrats will seek to produce excessive outputs of the services for which they are responsible. This is demonstrated graphically in Figure 11.2.

The bureau produces a single service (X) whose quantity (per period of time) is measured along the horizontal axis. The sum of the citizen's (*not* the bureaucrat's) marginal valuations of the bureau's services is represented by MV, with AV representing the sum of the average valuations. The minimum average cost for each level of output is represented by AC, with MC showing the related marginal costs for AC (pre-grant) only. The optimum level of output is $0Q_0$ (where $MC = MV$) *before* the grant is paid. Output $0Q_0$ would result in a perfectly competitive market system where local citizens themselves determine the levels of X which they wish to purchase, and where market price determines the equilibrium level of output.

Output will be $0Q_1$ if X is provided by a public sector bureau which can conceal the true marginal costs and marginal benefits of X to voters themselves. At $Q_1 AC$ equals AV, both being equal to $0B$, so total costs equal total benefits. The bureau's budget is maximized, an output in excess of $0Q_1$ being in breach of the condition that the bureau cannot exceed its budget (see Chapter 5). This is the extreme case where output doubles – that is, $0Q_1 = 2 (0Q_0)$ – but in all cases the Pareto optimal level of output is exceeded. Hence, allocative inefficiency occurs even though the bureau is X-efficient, producing output level $0Q_1$ at the minimum possible average cost $0B$. X-inefficiency would result in the cost schedules being shifted vertically upwards.

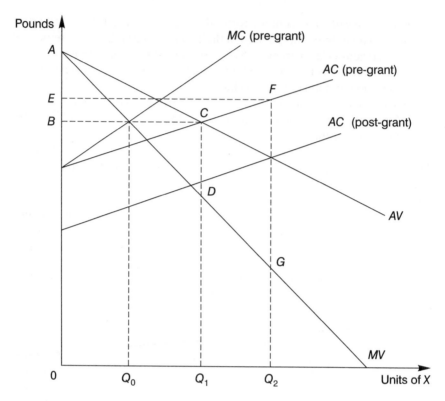

Figure 11.2   *The Niskanen model of the effect of a lump-sum grant*

Assume now that central government pays a lump-sum grant to local authorities. This shifts the average cost curve from AC to AC', and thus the budget-maximizing output (where AC equals AV) rises from $0Q_1$ to $0Q_2$. The grant is measured by $AC–AC'$ multiplied by the quantity of X produced ($0Q_2$). The budget increases from $0BCQ_1$ to $0EFQ_2$, the latter amount being the product of the now higher output multiplied by its pre-grant average cost. The grant only reduces the cost to local taxpayers: it does not reduce the actual cost of providing the output. Indeed, the average cost of the post-grant output is greater than that of the pre-grant output because marginal costs exceed average costs. *Total* benefits, measured by the area under the MV schedule, rise from $0ADQ_1$ to $0AGQ_2$, the rise being equal to Q_1DGQ_2. This increase in benefits allows the bureau to increase its budget by this same amount, thus keeping total benefits equal to total costs.

To demonstrate the existence of the flypaper effect in Niskanen's model, it has to be demonstrated that an equivalent rise in the incomes of voters would have increased the budget of the bureau by a lesser amount. If the income elasticity of demand for the local government services produced by the bureau is zero, voters would wish for no increase in those outputs. This result is demonstrated in Figure 9.3. Hence, a flypaper effect occurs. For normal goods (that is, with positive income elasticity of demand) the MV and AV schedules shift to the right, but the resultant increase in the bureau's budget will not necessarily equal the value of the grant.

Figure 11.2 demonstrates the conclusion reached in Chapter 5 that bureaucrats will use as much as possible of any increase in grants to maximize their budgets (and therefore their own welfares) rather than see any returned to voters via reduced local taxes. This will be the case even if, at the now higher level of output, voter's marginal valuation of X is less than its marginal cost. Hence, the flypaper effect occurs.

While bureaucrats' monopoly power is limited both by politicians' power and by the existence of competing bureaux, Schneider and Ji (1987) find that competition does not consistently limit the flypaper effect. They find a negative relationship between the degree of competition and the size of the flypaper effect, consistent with Niskanen's model of bureaucratic behaviour.

Competition arises through the Tiebout voting-with-one's-feet model of the local market for municipal outputs (see Chapter 4). Although Tiebout did not consider bureaucratic behaviour, the greater the degree of competition for residents among local authorities, the more constrained are bureaucrats' attempts to maximize their own welfares by maximizing their budgets. The degree of competition can be expected to be a positive function of the number of municipalities in a given metropolitan region, the migration rate between municipalities, the degree of variation in expenditures between municipalities and, similarly, the degree of variation in local tax levels. Schneider and Ji's research finds that variations in local tax levels and the number of metropolitan municipalities are positively associated with competitive pressures, the association being greater for the former than for the latter.

However, competition in municipal markets differs from that in private markets in being limited, (1) by the costs of mobility; (2) because municipalities as sellers are heavily regulated by the upper tiers of government; and (3) because the entry and exit of new producers is so heavily restricted that market contestability is limited. The local market for municipal outputs is a quasi-market, not a pure market. Consequently, competition does not consistently limit or offset fully the flypaper effect, and so the results provide qualified and limited support for the Niskanen model.

Schneider and Ji also find that wider variations in expenditures and higher levels of migration are associated with increased municipal expenditures. They explain these results by surmizing that local governments try to attract higher income families by offering better quality services to match their preferences, rather than those of current residents. In this case, a flypaper effect occurs due to politicians' (rather than bureaucrats') actions as they seek new residents in order to reduce the average costs of their services.

(b)   McGuire's 'Greedy Politicians Model'
In his 'greedy politicians model', McGuire (1975) suggests that politicians may spend all the money they can get their hands on, as long as individuals are not made any worse off, in order to maximize their chances of political survival and hence their own welfares. This is similar, in essence, to Niskanen's model. That both politicians and bureaucrats may not act in the best interests of the individuals they represent is a more comprehensive potential explanation of the flypaper effect.

(c)   Romer and Rosenthal's 'Setter Model'
Romer and Rosenthal (1979a, 1980) assume:

1. the use of referendum voting to decide upon the level of expenditure on the single public output the community is assumed to produce;
2. only the local government produces this output;
3. the expenditure level (or tax rate) voted on is proposed by a legally-designated agent which knows the preferences of the voters it represents;
4. if the proposed level of expenditure is defeated in the referendum, the level of public provision is established by an exogenous, legally-designated reversion level; and
5. the agent who sets both the proposed and reversion levels of output ('the setter') seeks to maximize the budget.

The indifference curves mapped by Figure 11.3 are those of the median voter, not the setter. Voters are faced with a choice of too much or too little spending and approve a level greater than that preferred by the median voter. The agent proposes an expenditure level where the median voter is indifferent between the proposed level and the reversion level, or is marginally better off under the proposed level, thus ensuring maximization of expenditure.
   If the reversion level were $0R_1$, the budget-maximizing setter would propose the level $0Q_1$, knowing that the median voter is indifferent between these alternatives (on the same indifference curve, I_1), or a level just below $0Q_1$ since this would put the median voter on a higher indifference curve and therefore ensure a vote in favour of the setter's desired outcome. If the reversion level were $0R_2$, the setter would propose a level of $0Q_2$, or just below it, thereby again maximizing the expenditure level, and obtaining a majority in the referendum. However, if the reversion level were $0S$, the setter would accept this level, as any higher level offered in a referendum would be rejected by the voters. Therefore, as noted by Romer and Rosenthal, 'unless the reversion level is exactly $0S$, the setter model leads to higher expenditures than the median voter model' (1980, p. 454).
   The model can now be used to analyze the effects of a lump-sum grant on the community, and thus to explain the flypaper effect. Figure 11.4, which starts from a position where the median voter's preferred level of output is

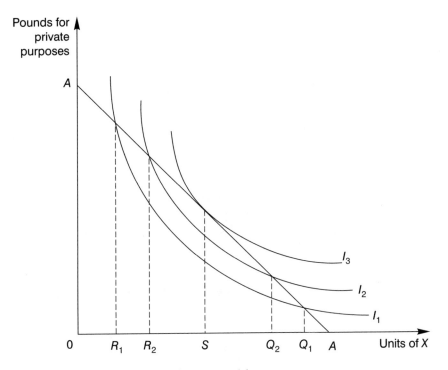

Figure 11.3   *Romer and Rosenthal's setter model*

below the initial reversion level $0R$, shows the result of a lump-sum grant and an equivalent rise in incomes on the community.

It can be seen that the rise in incomes would, in contrast to the traditional model, have no effect on the expenditure level, so long as the rise does not result in the point of tangency between the indifference curve and the new budget line rising beyond the reversion level $0R$. This is shown in Figure 11.4 when, with the reversion level remaining at $0R$, an increase in incomes occurs, resulting in a shift in the budget line from AA' to BB'. The median voter equilibrium stays to the left of RR'. Hence there is no increase in the level of expenditure; it remains at $0R$.

It is assumed that the lump-sum grant has to be spent in addition to the reversion level, thereby altering both the budget constraint and the reversion level. The budget constraint shifts from AA' to BB' while the reversion level rises from R to S (that is, by the full amount of the grant). This results in a rise in the level of expenditure to G, where the new reversion level SS' meets the new budget line BB'. Therefore the lump-sum grant causes an increase in local government output equal to the full amount of the grant, from E (where AA' intersects RR') to G (where BB' intersects SS'), the intersections at E and G being on the same horizontal line. Hence the flypaper effect occurs.

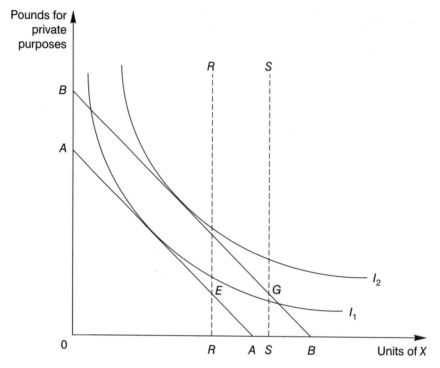

Figure 11.4 *Effect of a lump-sum grant on the setter model*

However, the Romer and Rosenthal model's results are affected by different reversion levels and the type of good (that is, normal or inferior), such that the effects of a grant can be less than an equivalent increase in income. Moreover, the assumptions of the setter model can be criticized as unrepresentative of the way local government operates, usually *without* referenda. Romer and Rosenthal developed their model to analyze US school boards and, while their model can be generalized (King 1984), their assumptions cannot.

Hence, the model would seem to be of limited applicability: another example of a special case. Though it shares budget maximization with the previous two models, it is not clear why local voters would agree to a suboptimal level of output, for example any level of output other than $0S$ in Figure 11.3. Unless there is fiscal illusion (see below), voters can be expected to agitate (express voice) in favour of maximization of their own welfares and not passively accept budget maximization. While they may be indifferent between R_1 and Q_1 and between R_2 and Q_2 in Figure 11.3, they prefer S, which can be attained by the budget represented by AA'. They could be forced to acquiesce to a suboptimal level of output if the legally-designated authority (agent, setter) has powers to override local voters' preferences. This may be the case for

US school boards, but it would certainly abrogate the underlying democratic rationale of local government.

Nor is it clear why (except in the case of US school boards with their narrow remit) all the grant has to be spent *in addition to* the reversion level. In practice, local governments provide more than one type of service output and have powers to vary from year to year their own revenues from local taxation. The setter model shares with the other models the comparative static (rather than dynamic) approach.

2. Fiscal Illusion Public Choice Models

Like the behavioural models, the fiscal illusion models are based on the assumption that the representatives of the community are self-motivated and attempt to maximize their own utility rather than that of the individuals in the community. However, they also focus upon the breakdown of another of the assumptions of the neoclassical model, that of perfect information. The difficulties of gathering information may be one of the reasons why local governments do not satisfactorily reflect the preferences of their citizens. This problem can be exacerbated by deliberate action on the part of the government to withhold information from, or to give inaccurate information to, voters.

Fiscal illusion models have been developed by Oates (1979), Courant *et al.* (1979) and Logan (1986). The first two models were developed at the same time, and the authors acknowledge their similarities. Only the Oates model will be reviewed here.

(a) Oates' Fiscal Illusion Model

As already noted in Chapter 9, the main reason for the greater stimulatory effect of open-ended matching grants compared to general lump-sum grants in the traditional model is that while the matching grants have both an income effect and a substitution effect, lump-sum grants have only income effects. However, Oates (1979) produced a model in which lump-sum grants also have substitution effects, arising because of fiscal illusion on the part of voters. Put simply, voters think that the lump-sum grant causes the tax price of the local government output to fall in much the same way as matching grants. This is clearly a mistaken belief.

The model portrays local officials as output-maximizers constrained by the preferences of the voters they represent. The *marginal* tax price to the local electorate is unaffected by the lump-sum grant. However, the local government uses the grant to deceive local voters into thinking that the cost is less, the *average* tax price. Since the average tax price is less than the marginal cost *to the electorate*, the level of output is excessive.

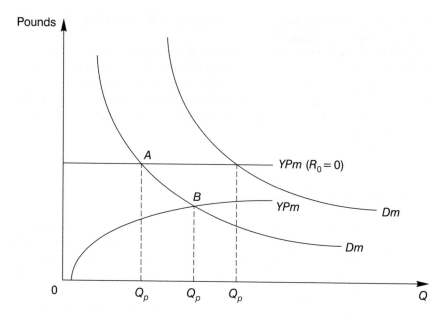

Figure 11.5   *Oates' model of fiscal illusion*

As in the traditional model, a rise in the voter-consumer's income *shifts* the demand curve to the right. However, the effect of a lump-sum grant is now depicted as a *movement along* the demand curve due to an apparent reduction in the price of the local government output. These effects are illustrated in Figure 11.5.

Dm represents the initial demand curve for the median voter, and *YPm* ($R_0 = 0$) represents the initial tax price to the median voter, where the level of intergovernmental grants (R) is nil. The initial output level is at $0Q_p$ where the fixed tax price crosses the initial demand curve. From this position, an increase in income shifts the demand curve from *Dm* to *Dm'*. This would also be the outcome if the local authority were to pass on the lump-sum grant to its voters. However, since it is assumed to maximize the level of output, the authority will retain the grant and offer the goods to the voters at a reduced tax price, represented by *YPm'*. *YPm'* is curved since the reduction in tax price as a result of the grant will reduce as quantity increases. The reduction can be measured by R/Q, where Q is quantity of output. Therefore, an increase in income causes a *shift* in the demand curve, from *Dm* to *Dm'*, while receipt of a lump-sum intergovernmental grant of the same amount will cause a *movement along* the original demand curve from A to B, with the quantity increasing from $0Qp$ to $0Qp'$.

At this point it is unclear which alternative will result in a higher level of local government output. This will depend upon both the price elasticity of demand for the local government output, and the income elasticity of demand caused by the increase in incomes. In an attempt to calculate the effects of each of the alternatives, Oates measures the rate of change of output both with respect to the level of private income, and with respect to the amount of intergovernmental grant received. For the impact of lump-sum grants to be greater than that of income, 'the ratio of absolute value of the price elasticity of demand to the income elasticity of demand [must] exceed total taxes as a fraction of private income' (Oates 1979, p. 28). By applying typical values he obtained the following results, where B is the total budget, R is the intergovernmental grant and Y is private income.

$$\delta B/\delta R = 0.4, \quad \text{and} \quad \delta B/\delta Y = 0.1$$

From these results it can be seen that the rate of change of the budget is influenced more by a change in grant than in income (by a factor of 4). While Oates acknowledged the simplicity of his model, nevertheless its results are very close to the accepted measures of the flypaper effect noted above. This suggests that his model explains the flypaper effect in showing that the stimulatory effects of a lump-sum grant are not equivalent to an increase in individuals' incomes, 'because although they may generate the same true budget constraint, they do not result in the same *perceived* budget constraint' (Oates 1979, p. 29).

Dollery and Worthington (1995) find some support for the fiscal illusion explanation in Australia, and Heyndels and Smolders (1994) find important illusionary effects in Flemish municipalities. English evidence also seems to support both the existence of the flypaper effect and fiscal illusion (Barnett *et al.* 1991; Mangan and Ledward 1997). Borge (1995) demonstrates that fiscal illusion unambiguously predicts a flypaper effect. However, Oates' theory and the public choice theories of Filimon *et al.* (1982) were rejected by Wyckoff (1991) because they were rejected statistically by his study. Moreover, both the Oates and Courant *et al.* models admit that while voters using average- instead of marginal prices can create an illusion that may lead to a flypaper effect, this may only explain part of that effect.

OTHER THEORIES

The following theories are those that do not belong to the traditional or public choice schools reviewed above.

1. The Effect of Risk and Uncertainty on Grantee Spending

Turnbull (1992) develops a model in which the lack of information available to the median voter is modelled as uncertainty rather than imperfect information. Uncertainty exists both in the form of the median voter being uncertain about factors surrounding the local output and uncertainty about the level of intergovernmental aid that will be received. Fossett (1990) also develops a model incorporating uncertainty and instability of grant revenue, but, in addition, incorporates risk-averse behaviour of local officials.

Fossett believes that the uncertainty about grants-in-aid, both in terms of the level of aid and the type of aid, results in local officials being cautious about any future support from the federal level of (US) government. There would be both political and financial risks in passing on to local voters a tax reduction made possible through the receipt of a grant this year which may not occur in future years, since local tax levels would fluctuate markedly, leading to voter discontent. Prudent local officials may therefore decide it is in the best interests of the community to spend the grant on local government outputs.

The resultant empirically-observable flypaper effect is the result of caution on the part of local officials, not of greed on the part of output-maximizing bureaucrats. Fossett therefore suggests that an inherent wish on the part of local officials to maintain certainty and stability in local finances as a general rule may provide a partial explanation of the flypaper effect. He believes that this model is more realistic in its political assumptions than the agenda-type models, and the fiscal illusion models. Certainly, there is UK evidence that local governments increased their financial balances during periods of grant instability (Audit Commission 1984a). This fiscally prudent behaviour is perhaps more likely, the higher the gearing between grants and local taxes (see Chapters 8 and 9).

2. The Effect of Pressure Groups on Public Expenditures

Dougan and Kenyon (1988) develop a model in which interest groups, rather than voters, are the key actors in budget determination. The political power of pressure groups inevitably varies from programme to programme and so the size of the flypaper effect varies according to the expenditure category. This could explain why measures of the flypaper effect vary from 0.25 to 1.00 in Table 11.1 below. However, Dougan and Kenyon's model is not tested on actual observation. Hence, its explanatory powers, like those of many of the other theories of the flypaper effect, have yet to be verified.

Additionally, use of a categorical grant rather than a general grant in their analysis may cause a bias in their model even though both types of grant may be lump-sum (see Figure 9.1). Pressure groups can be expected to be more easily mobilized is respect of categorical grants (paid in respect of specific services) rather than general grants (distributed over the generality of services). This is because any use of the categorical grant to reduce local taxation will benefit the totality of local taxpayers at the expense of the fraction of voters benefiting from the service which would otherwise experience net additional spending as a result of that grant. Put simply, the pressure group loses more than it gains from grant displacement into lower tax levels (see Chapter 5).

3. Tax Capitalization

Turnbull and Niho (1986) argue that the flypaper effect is due to tax capitalization arising from the payment of grants-in-aid (see Chapter 8). The resultant increase in the local property tax base leads to greater local tax receipts (for a given tax rate) and thus higher expenditures. However, it could be expected that, in subsequent years, voters would seek lower tax rates. Alternatively, migration may occur (Oates 1969). These potential effects emphasize the need for a dynamic model (see below).

THE MIRAGE SCHOOL

The 'mirage school' focuses upon the empirical methods used to measure the flypaper effect, and how the existence of some sort of error would invalidate the results. Empirical studies of the flypaper effect, have generally used regression analysis, the stimulatory effect of grants-in-aid on grantee spending being measured by regressing the level of expenditure on the level of grants. Some of the resulting evidence is shown in Table 11.1 where $\delta E/\delta G$ denotes the rate of change of expenditure relative to the rate of change of intergovernmental grant.

The ratio $\delta E/\delta G$ is usually summarized as the amount of a $1 increase in grants that will be used for public expenditure. Gramlich and Galper's $\delta E/\delta G$ measure of 0.43 was referred to above. Increases in individuals' incomes yield the measure $\delta E/\delta I$ (where I represents income) which lies between 0.05 and 0.10. Hence, $\delta E/\delta G$ is more than four times greater than $\delta E/\delta I$, the flypaper effect. However, Table 11.1 also makes clear the wide disparity in the measures of $\delta E/\delta G$, varying between 0.25 and 1.00. The greater the value of $\delta E/\delta G$; that is, the closer it is towards unity (1.00), the greater the flypaper effect.

That empirical studies over such a wide range of areas, using different data sets and different statistical methods, all find evidence of the effect creates difficulties for claims that the flypaper effect does not exist. Nevertheless, the extent to which the results of the empirical studies in Table 11.1 show such a wide variation suggests that a number of the studies overestimate the size of the flypaper effect. The types of errors that could occur include misspecification of the type of grant, use of an inappropriate functional form, and use of inappropriate variables in, or omitting appropriate variables from, the model.

Table 11.1   *Studies of the effects of general lump-sum grants*

Author	Year	Sample	$\delta E/\delta G$
Gramlich and Galper	1973	Time-series data of federal grants to local and state governments	0.43
Gramlich and Galper	1973	Cross-section data of federal and state aid to 10 large urban governments	0.25
Feldstein	1975	State block grants to Massachusetts towns	0.60
Bowman	1974	West Virginia untied aid to independent school districts	0.50
Weicher	1972	State school aid to fiscally independent school districts	0.59
Inman	1971	Panel study of 41 city budgets	1.00
Weicher	1972	Untied aid to 106 municipal governments	0.90[a]
Nathan *et al.*	1975	'Monitoring' of revenue sharing in 63 state or local governments	0.70[b]
Olmstead, Denzan and Roberts	1993	Missouri state aid to local school districts	0.58
Case, Hines and Rosen	1993	Federal grants to 48 states 1970–85	0.65

Source: Gramlich (1977b), Hines and Thaler (1995), Becker (1996).
Notes:
a: Gramlich states that Weicher (1972) measures $\delta E/\delta G$ at almost unity, while Hines and Thaler (1992) record the measurement as 0.90.
b: Nathan *et al.* calculate that 26 per cent of the grant led to new spending, 15 per cent to avoid cuts in programmes, 30 per cent to tax cuts, and the remainder to avoid borrowing. The flypaper effect here is the amount of the grant not used for tax cuts, as the remainder, in whatever form is grantee spending.
c: Dollery and Worthington (1996) provides a summary of the major studies of the flypaper effect undertaken during the 1980s and 1990s. Although no estimates of $\delta E/\delta G$ are given, there is overwhelming evidence in support of the flypaper effect.
d: Becker (1996) provides results for logarithmic and linear estimates.
e: Islam and Choudhury (1989) find evidence of a flypaper effect in Ontario, Canada, and Barnett *et al.* (1991) likewise for England.

1. Misspecification of the Type of Grant

King (1984) points out that one of the downfalls of a number of the flypaper studies is the lack of importance they place upon the type of grant. This deficiency is demonstrated in Figure 9.4 which shows the greater effect of a matching grant on local government spending, than an equivalent lump-sum grant. It is therefore *invalid* to use the results of an open-ended matching grant to demonstrate the flypaper effect. It will necessarily be more stimulative of local government expenditure than an equivalent increase in the median voter's disposable income and will therefore overestimate the size of any fly-paper effect. In other words, a flypaper effect may be derived if:

1. a matching grant is mistaken for a general lump-sum grant; or
2. a general lump-sum grant has some inherent matching qualities hidden within the grant programme.

An occurrence of either of these two forms of mistaken identity would result in:

(a) a flypaper effect being empirically verified when one did not exist; or
(b) the flypaper effect being overestimated.

Barnett (1993a) notes that joint use of lump-sum and matching grants within a programme of grants-in-aid is not uncommon and characterized the system of intergovernmental grants in England and Wales prior to 1990 (see Chapter 9). Such confusion of the type of grant is a *static* misspecification. A *dynamic* misspecification of grant was highlighted by Chernick (1979), who showed that the actions of the administrators responsible for allocating non-matching grants can play a significant part in the impact of the grant on local expenditure levels. Chernick observed that grant administrators, aiming to achieve the best use of the grant as possible, will enter into negotiations with potential recipients, the primary aim of which is to obtain an agreement about the level of spending by the recipient on the project. This ultimately has the effect of changing a previously non-matching grant into an *implicit* matching grant, particularly if the administrators award the grants to the recipient who is willing to commit a substantial amount of their own funds to the project. This is effectively how the UK's National Lottery grants-in-aid are distributed (see Chapter 9).

Chernick tested his model on HUD Basic Water and Sewer Facilities grants in the USA between 1966 and 1972. He found there to be 'a positive and significant relationship between the cost contribution of the recipient and the size of the grant awarded, *ceteris paribus*' (Fisher 1982, p. 338). While there has been criticism of Chernick's model for its inapplicability to general revenue-sharing grants which are truly unconditional (Hines and Thaler 1995), the model (which is based upon project grants) does highlight a problem for empirical studies. If this process of negotiation occurs for other grant programmes, then the flow of causation assumed in many of the models is questionable. The assumed flow from the amount of the grant to its stimulatory effect on the level of expenditure, can occur in the opposite direction, with the amount of the grant awarded dependent upon the grantee's agreed level of expenditure on the project. This mutual dependency destroys the distinction between the dependent and independent variables and therefore invalidates attempts to model the flypaper effect. (A similar problem was identified in

Chapter 8 in respect of econometric tests of the impact of local business taxes.)

Other types of grant misspecification include Moffitt's (1984) focus upon the AFDC (aid for dependant children) programme in the USA. Moffitt proved that treating the grants differently in econometric terms would result in a more accurate estimation of the flypaper effect. In a similar manner to Chernick, he points out that due to the structure of the programme, the expenditure level of the local government and the matching rate they received, and thus the marginal price, were determined simultaneously. To avoid creating any upward bias in the estimates, Moffitt recommends using simultaneous equations. His study shows that when the AFDC grants are treated in this way, any flypaper effect disappears. His findings are qualified through his focus upon the AFDC programme, which is a closed-ended specific matching grant programme (see Figure 9.1), and not a general lump-sum grant programme, making methodologically difficult the analysis of the flypaper effect.

A study by Wyckoff (1991), in which he applied the same set of data to four of the main explanations of the flypaper effect, showed, however, that Moffitt's model, and a similar model by Megdal (1987), do not explain the flypaper effect. Megdal shows through the use of 'Monte Carlo' evidence (that is, by running a number of tests on the model using random number generators) that, due to the upward biases of ordinary least squares (OLS) models, maximum likelihood estimates are preferable. Wyckoff compared an OLS model with one in which the bias is eliminated through the freeing of the correlation between price, income and the error term. He found that there was no significant difference between the two estimates provided by the model, and concluded that 'there is no doubt that Moffitt and Megdal have pointed out the theoretically correct way to estimate demand functions in the face of closed-ended matching grants, but their correction does not explain the flypaper effect' (1991, p. 316).

Another source of *dynamic* grant misspecification is that the distinction between effort-related grants and lump-sum grants may only apply to the year in question, rather than over a period of years. As public expenditure plans are reformulated each year, central government may feel obliged to increase the total level of grant support in line with the increased spending of local government in general and of individual local authorities in particular. Local authorities may realize that, year on year, there is a positive and significant relationship between their spending and grants, arising indirectly through the public expenditure planning process rather than directly through a matching grant mechanism. They may therefore decide to increase spending in any one year above the level that would be expected based on the median voter's income elasticity of demand, in anticipation of consequently higher lump-sum grants in the following year. In that case, lump-sum grants are not truly exogenous.

Such a behavioural response by local governments is sometimes referred to as 'grantsmanship' (that is, actions which are designed specifically to attract more grant). In effect, a lump-sum grant becomes *perceived* as a delayed matching grant and so local government expenditure is stimulated by more than would be expected on the basis of the median voter's income elasticity of demand. An intertemporal dynamic approach would therefore seem more valid.

2. Use of an Inappropriate Functional Form

Most studies use a *linear*, rather than *logarithmic*, functional form because of its ease of use. Becker (1996) shows that studies using a logarithmic form have found a smaller flypaper effect than those using a linear form. Hence, she concludes that this convenience 'may come at the cost of accurate parameter estimates' (p. 87).

According to Becker, a comparison of the studies of McGuire (1978) and Zampelli (1986) are particularly revealing. With the exception of the functional form, the studies are similar and, yet, while McGuire's linear-form study shows a significant flypaper effect, Zampelli's logarithmic-form study finds no significant flypaper effect. McGuire himself conceded that theoretically either a logarithmic form or an exponential form with constant elasticities may be more appropriate, but stated that he utilized a linear form because of its simplicity and because it allows use of linear estimation techniques.

Becker (1996, p. 97) finds that '*linear* equation produces estimates of the spending responses to grants that are inflated by a factor of nearly six', while the use of a *logarithmic* form with identical data and explanatory variables provides no evidence of the flypaper effect. In a similar vein she finds that not taking into account the biases created by endogeneity can result in the flypaper effect being inflated by a factor of almost ten. In effect, this is a measure of the impact of the interdependency between the amount of grant awarded and the recipient's expenditure promises to grant administrators identified by Chernick. Becker's paper therefore highlights not only the problem of using the correct functional form, but also the potential for the amount of the supposedly lump-sum grant, and perhaps the marginal price, to be decided endogenously rather than exogenously.

3. Inappropriate or Missing Variables

(a) Socioeconomic Status
Developing an idea of Bradford, Malt and Oates (1969), which was further developed by Oates (1977, 1981), Hamilton (1983, p. 347) hypothesizes that

'the quality of the residents of a jurisdiction is an important input in the pro-vision of local public services'. The suggestion is that a given level of service can be achieved using less resources for some types of populations than for others. For example, according to educational research, children from com-munities of higher income and higher socioeconomic status require less public expenditure to attain a particular standard than do those on lower incomes, and therefore with lower socioeconomic status. Similarly, those higher-income communities have a lower level of street crime, and therefore require less policing, again reducing the level of public expenditure required.

Hamilton is in effect claiming that other models have omitted relevant vari-ables (socioeconomic status) and are therefore incomplete. While this may be true of the economist's median voter model, use of socioeconomic vari-ables is the 'traditional approach' in some other disciplines (see Chapters 9 and 10). In its use as a proxy for socioeconomic characteristics, Hamilton uses an 'income as an input' hypothesis in the production of education to explain a significant part of the flypaper effect. He finds that, based upon obtaining reasonable parameters for the relevant variables, technology for producing local government goods, and price elasticity of demand, a significant portion (but not all) of the flypaper effect can be explained in this way.

However, Wyckoff (1991) contradicts Hamilton. His model included many socioeconomic variables mentioned by Hamilton, and some more besides. While he admits that he may have omitted some variables, he included the crucial variable of the educational level of the community. Using a non-linear model in the form suggested by Moffitt and Megdal, he compared a model with the extra variables to one without. He discovered that while the extra socioeconomic variables helped to explain expenditure *levels*, they do *not* help to explain the flypaper effect in terms of *increases* in expenditure sub-sequent to receiving lump-sum grants. This seems a reasonable conclusion since, though socioeconomic status is positively related to educational achievement, it is by no means clear whether higher or lower status would have a greater stimulatory effect on expenditure. Wyckoff concludes that 'the flypaper effect is unlikely to fade away with the inclusion of these omitted variables' (1991, p. 320)

(b)   The Local Government's Savings Ratio

The marginal propensities to save of the median voter and his or her local government are ignored in the traditional model. Flypaper models either ignore municipalities' financial balances or classify them as expenditure rather than as savings. This is clearly invalid because balances are used to finance future, not current expenditures. Econometric studies take account of median voter savings by default since they consider median voter expenditures. How-ever, to the extent that they use local government budgets inclusive of financial balances they overestimate municipal expenditures. If account were taken of municipal balances, and if savings ratios were the same for the median voter and his or her local government, the flypaper effect would disappear. Even if it is not the same as the median voter, any positive marginal propensity to save on the part of local government would mean that such econometric studies overestimate the flypaper effect.

(c) Expenditure on Private Sector Alternatives

Local government expenditure figures necessarily exclude voter expenditures on private sector alternatives (for example, for school education and leisure and recreation). Substantial alternative private sector provision could lead to median voter preferences for lower levels of public sector provision by the local public sector, preferences to which local governments may be reluctant or slow to respond, in the latter case because of delays inherent in adjusting service capacity to rapidly fluctuating (rising or falling) demand (see Chapter 6).

OVERVIEW OF STUDIES

It is clear that, as yet, there is no single explanation of the flypaper effect that has been verified both theoretically and empirically. While many of the theories reviewed here can explain some part of the flypaper effect, their authors have usually conceded that they are not full explanations. The need to distinguish between lump-sum and matching grants has been emphasized, the flypaper effect relating only to the former because of the absence of a substitution effect. Evidence based on open-ended matching grants overestimate any flypaper effect since, in addition to the stimulatory impact of the income effect, there is an additional stimulatory impact due to the reduction in the relative price of the local government output as a result of the substitution effect.

The traditional theory of grants-in-aid, based on the fiscal exchange model of government, would appear to be defective as it cannot predict the flypaper effect, accepting that the effect has been confirmed by empirical studies. Modified traditional theories relax some of those assumptions by taking account of transactions costs (incurred when reoptimizing consumption patterns) and of local deadweight losses arising from local taxation (but not from centrally financed growth), or by arbitrarily imposing a minimum disposable income constraint upon median voter preferences.

The excess burden or transactions costs must be so substantial that they create a significant divergence between gross and net stimulatory effects. Doubt has been cast on the magnitude of the excess burden, and transactions costs have been shown to depend upon the disjuncture (if any) between the chronological schedules for local budgeting and for announcement of grant allocations. The minimum disposable income constraint is at best a special case.

The traditional model, whether modified or not, implicitly assumes that local governments act in accordance with the wishes of the median voter and the constraints of grant-assisted budgets (the *fiscal exchange model* of government). In fact *despotic, benevolent* local governments may provide higher levels of output than voted for because of the public good, merit good and positive externality characteristics of their services. They may also be statutorily required to do so by national governments. In this case local government is not simply a vote-counting mechanism but, instead, pursues the public interest extending beyond the self-interest of the median voter.

Public choice theories explicitly recognize the principal–agent problem by considering the welfare functions of bureaucrats and politicians, demonstrating how their behaviour may frustrate the maximization of the median voter's welfare. Micro-level survey results from Finland suggest that the existence and size of the flypaper effect depends upon the distribution of power between the various grades of local officials and between local politicians with different committee responsibilities (Oulasvirta 1996). These results also suggest that the distribution of power can change as a result of changing grant regimes, in the Finnish case from specific to general grants.

However, even if there is a disharmony of interests, the public choice models are still deficient in failing to demonstrate how self-serving bureaucrats, politicians or the budget-setting agent (setter) acquire sufficient power to be able to override the wishes of voters (the *leviathan model* of government).

Any empirical evidence of excess expenditures may be the result of institutional failure by neglect rather than by design if, for example, there is no decision-making mechanism by which to consider lowering taxes subsequent to receiving grant. Local governments are more attuned to deciding how to spend money rather than how not to spend it (that is, return it to local taxpayers). Such outcomes could still be consistent with the despotic benevolent or fiscal exchange models of government. Alternatively they may be due to fiscal illusion on the part of voters themselves, their voted-for preferences for service levels being based on average rather than marginal tax costs. The average tax price of services leads to higher levels of output than the marginal tax price.

Of course, budget-maximizing bureaucrats may seek to engender such fiscal illusion. However, uncertainty created by any instability of intergovernmental grants from year to year may cause bureaucrats and local politicians to soak up grants in terms of services and financial balances rather than risk unpopularity by causing large annual swings in local tax levels to offset opposite fluctuations in grants. A high level of gearing between grants and local taxes (that is, where the latter are small relative to the former) would encourage such caution on the part of bureaucrats and local politicians. Local politicians may also be susceptible to pressure from, or otherwise seek to benefit, particular interest groups who stand to benefit from expansion of specific services much more than they would benefit from a reduction in local tax levels, the benefits of which are spread over the community as a whole. This would be consistent with the *fiscal transfer model* of local government.

These competing theories raise many empirical questions – for example, the size of any transactions costs and deadweight losses and whether or not voters really do experience fiscal illusion. Their importance will be exaggerated to the extent that the empirical measures of the flypaper effect are overestimated as a result of mistaken identity of open-ended matching grants for lump-sum grants and use of inappropriate functional forms by which to analyse the data. The data itself may be based on compromised definitions of income and expenditures, the resulting measures of elasticity being subject to significant margins of error.

Studies emphasizing statistical and specification errors are important in recognising the problems inherent in empirical analysis. However, the fact that so many studies, using different methods and analysing different data sets, have shown the existence of the flypaper effect makes claims that the effect does not exist at all seem rather implausible.

POSSIBILITIES FOR FURTHER DEVELOPMENT

The preceding analysis made clear that there are a number of possibilities for further development, some restricted within the confines of the median voter model, some attempting to develop further other (alternative or complementary) neoclassical economic models, some attempting to develop multi-disciplinary models, and some testing hypotheses other than the median voter hypothesis. Based on the analysis in this chapter and on that in Chapter 10, the most obvious possibilities for further development are as follows:

1. *Seek to develop further the median voter demand model* so that its predictions accord more with reality, namely by relaxing some of its most restrictive assumptions: the flypaper effect is a contradiction of the median voter hypothesis rather than of the model itself.
2. *Compare the median income with other fractiles* of income in order to confirm or deny its supposed better explanatory value, remembering to take account of any autocorrelation between fractiles.
3. *Seek to identify the median voter*, rather than simply make heroic assumptions that voter coincides with the person earning the median income in the local government's jurisdiction.
4. *Seek to determine whether the identity of the median voter changes* as a result of the receipt of an intergovernmental lump-sum grant, rather than make the heroic assumption that the median voter's identity is stable. In fact, the identity of the median voter is likely to change as a result of receipt of grant because grants have to be financed by central government taxes and the levying of such taxes will change disposable incomes, and so may change the identity of the individual with median post-tax income. Mistaken identity will also occur if not everyone votes.

5. *Develop further the supply-side models* of local government expenditure so as to model more accurately the behaviour of politicians and bureaucrats within specific 'market power' contexts (by varying the degree of monopoly power accruing to bureaux).

6. *Integrate demand-side and supply-side determinants* of local government expenditures in order to develop a more comprehensive economic model.

7. *Incorporate the economic analysis of exit and voice* into the economic models. The median voter model implies that there will always be some consumer-voters who would prefer local tax/expenditure mixes different from those offered by their current local authority. They could use voice as well as votes to reconfigure the tax/expenditure package. If unsuccessful they might migrate (exit) to another authority providing the desired mix. If different (socioeconomic) groups of voters vary in their ability or propensity to exercise voice and/or exit, and if local governments actively compete to retain and attract mobile residents, then it is unrealistic to assume that local governments slavishly obey the wishes of the current median voter. Receipt of grant may also induce migration and so change the identity of the median voter.

8. *Incorporate dynamic elements* into the exclusively static approach, for example by taking account of time lags in adjusting the supply of local government services to the current demand conditions and of time lags inherent in expressing voice or exercising exit. Allowing for grantsmanship would also add a dynamic element.

9. *Undertake more robust empirical tests* by recognizing the importance of appropriate empirical techniques and of appropriate and accurate data. Lack of such data in sufficient quantities creates substantial problems for the integrity of econometric testing.

10. *Develop a more comprehensive multidisciplinary model* by also taking account of institutional, legal, constitutional and other factors which influence the behaviour of local governments. In particular, the above analysis has made frequent references to the many groups with an interest in the provision of local government services (that is, stakeholders). These groups include service users, local citizen-voters, local government bureaucrats and agents (setters), local and national politicians, and other pressure groups. This emphasizes the need to consider the distribution of power relationships in a formal model of local government decision making and service provision. While the need to take account of the political process by which a group or community makes collective decisions has long been recognized (for example, Bradford and Oates 1971b). Such a formal model has not yet been developed. However, the importance of this issue is demonstrated in Chapters 13 and 14, which consider service quality.

CONCLUSIONS

The flypaper effect literature dates back to the early 1970s. It is overwhelmingly neoclassical in approach, attempting to improve the median voter demand model and/or temper it with public choice supply-side perspectives. While this approach provided valuable early substantial analytical insights, more recent papers seem to have contributed only marginally to an understanding of the flypaper effect, if indeed it exists at all.

Although fifty or so publications in journals and textbooks have attempted to find theoretical and/or empirical explanations of the flypaper effect, the search for a comprehensive and definitive explanation still proceeds apace. Many different avenues of research have been followed but the end result is always frustrating in that, at best, only partial explanations have been found and doubt remains about the size, and even existence, of this effect. The earlier theoretical and empirical research was almost completely restricted within the confines of neoclassical economics, the attempt being to improve the median voter demand model and/or temper it with public choice perspectives and to develop more robust empirical estimations of that model. Considering the substantial analytical and empirical insights provided by some of the earlier research, it seems that more recent research has provided rapidly diminishing marginal returns to intellectual and empirical effort.

Much of the more recent research has lacked strategic direction, has too readily accepted the validity of the median voter demand model in testing the median voter hypothesis, and has often simply tried yet another variant of earlier econometric tests. Such apparently promising avenues of research have all too often ended prematurely in culs-de-sac.

Though none of the theories offered as yet have clearly explained the anomaly of the flypaper effect, they do suggest areas where the traditional theories may fail, particularly concerning institutional structure and the behaviour of local officials. The effect of these two factors may not be as strong as the public choice models suggest, however, and it is important to note that their effect will differ between the USA, where many of these theories originated, and countries such as the UK. The power of local bureaucrats in the UK may be much less than in the USA and local politicians in the UK may more vigorously pursue output-maximizing behaviour than do bureaucrats. In addition, the institutional structure of the two economies is not the same.

If it is accepted that institutional factors play a large part in the stimulatory effect of grants, then it may be necessary to create a separate model for intergovernmental grants for each country. There is clearly a need to go beyond econometric testing of aggregate income, grant and expenditure data and to look at what actually happens inside local government administrative and decision-making structures.

More fundamentally, although a theory is validated by its predictions rather than by its descriptive reality, the major deficiency of the traditional model is that it is not an appropriate theoretical framework for the study of intergovernmental grants. These grants are paid to groups of people forming communities, rather than to individuals. The traditional model is formulated around individualized median voter, rather than collective, decision-making criteria and so cannot take account of the processes by which communities make collective decisions.

A comprehensive theory has to take account of the political and bureaucratic processes underpinning collective decision-making. This was considered in a restricted way by Romer and Rosenthal's agenda setter model and by Oulasvirta's micro-level study. However, a comprehensive model would also have to take account of political and institutional power within local government, which also affects how (and whether) voters are informed and mobilized into pressure groups.

To sum up, the economist's understanding of community preference patterns and their relationship with the preferences of individual citizen's remains primitive. It is assumed that the median voter's preferences are accurately revealed to local government decision makers through efficient voting systems, that the latter faithfully reflect those preferences in their decisions, and that those decisions are faithfully implemented by service providers. These are clearly heroic assumptions and the median voter hypothesis/model may simply be invalid. In that case, the flypaper effect is more a chimera than a mirage.

12 Public Choice Theory and Local Government Reform

INTRODUCTION

This chapter analyzes within a public choice framework the current and on-going reforms of local government described in the preceding chapters. The analysis pulls together, within a more general analytical framework, many of the theoretical propositions developed in earlier chapters relating to the behaviour of service users and providers and the financing mechanisms for local government services. It will become apparent that, in combination, those propositions create a strong theoretical base upon which to analyse the recent and ongoing reforms of local government in many countries. Note that, while many of the general reforms being introduced in different countries can be legitimized in theoretical terms, this does not mean that reforms were introduced as a direct result of public choice theory.

Nor is public choice theory the only means by which to explain the behaviour of those involved in the workings of the public sector. In contrast with the in-hospitality thesis of public choice theory, some academics believe deeply both in the need for government and in the integrity of those who work within it. They argue that the *system* of government creates inefficiencies:

> We believe that industrial-era governments, with their large, centralised bureaucracies and standardised, 'one size fits all' services, are not up to the challenges of a rapidly changing information society and knowledge-based economy. (Osborne and Gaebler 1992, p. xviii)

Hence, they are not concerned with what government should do but rather how it operates, at all levels. 'The central failure of government today is one of means, not ends' (Ibid., p. xxi). They therefore believe that government needs to be 'reinvented'.

Osborne and Gaebler argue that a preoccupation with fiduciary duty led to stifling bureaucratic controls over service inputs and processes, service outputs and outcomes being ignored as a consequence. They argue that the bureaucratic model may have been appropriate in a past slowly-changing age of hierarchy and mass markets but it is no longer appropriate in the fast moving global market place and information society. It is argued that in the post-industrial era institutions need to be more flexible and more responsive to consumer demands, leading by persuasion and incentives rather than by command, empowering citizens rather than simply serving them. This is the distinction between the traditional command council and the fiscal exchange model of local government set down in Chapter 1.

While recognizing that the applicability of public choice theory can be challenged, this chapter adopts that analytical framework to provide a theoretical base for local government reform. Recent British reforms are used to illustrate the wide applicability of those theoretical propositions to apparently *ad hoc* piecemeal reforms.

GLOBAL TRENDS

The local public sector is becoming increasingly complex in many countries. Market mechanisms are being progressively introduced in the management of public services in Western Europe, Australasia, North America, Central and Eastern Europe and in developing countries. These changes have been analysed through a number of analytical perspectives, including a post-welfare agenda (Bennett 1990; Bailey 1998b), a post-bureaucratic form (Hoggett 1996), post-fordism (Burrows and Loader 1994), hollowing-out the state (Rhodes 1994), and as a shift from government to governance (Bailey 1993).

Such categorizations are not necessarily mutually exclusive. They all emphasize a shift away from monolithic, hierarchical, highly-standardized, bureaucratic production technologies to microcorporatist networked organizations dominated by meeting the needs of consumption rather than of production. This increasingly consumerist orientation for public sector services has been occuring since the early 1980s throughout the 24 or so member states of the Organization for Economic Co-operation and Development (OECD 1987a; Batley and Stoker 1991; Bennett 1990; Bird *et al.* 1995).

The reasons for reform are many and diverse and are driven as much by cultural and philosophical considerations regarding the role of the state in society as by changing technological parameters or theoretical prescriptions. For example, some academics argue that the reforms, such as the decentralization measures detailed in Chapter 2, are a response to fundamental social and economic changes which have highlighted the inadequacies of the traditional forms of representative democracy which, in turn, have resulted in a general decline in traditional respect for professional expertize and political authority (for example, Stoker 1987). Such attitudinal changes are, of course, consistent with an increasing recognition of the validity of the behavioural (that is, self-serving) assumptions of public choice theory.

GENERAL PRINCIPLES

While cultural, practical and ideological issues influence the particular characteristics of reform in any one country, the general principles are much more widely applicable. Chapter 1 noted that the democratic argument for local government is predicated on the assumption that it secures the public interest in facilitating representative democracy. However, this assumption has been increasingly brought into question by the development of public choice theory which suggests that the self-serving behaviour of politicians, officers and bureaucrats will frustrate promotion of the public interest. Bureaucrats may maximize their own utilities rather than that of those they serve, leading to allocative inefficiency through excessive output and/or excessive unit costs (see Chapters 5 and 11).

Similarly, traditional local government may do little to stimulate participative democracy and there is no reason why participation should be restricted to formal political voting mechanisms. Chapters 3 and 4 noted that opportunities for expression of voice are limited, despite recent decentralization initiatives, and that voice may be both a costly and relatively ineffective means of expressing preferences. Therefore, economists prefer to increase the scope for exit whenever possible, utilizing voice only in cases of severe market failure. However, Chapter 4 also noted the doubts about the effectiveness of intermunicipal competition because people and households find 'voting with their feet' a costly exercise in both financial and personal terms. Hence, other means must be found by which to introduce competition into local government. These reforms do not reject the rationale for local government; instead they seek to improve its functioning.

FUNCTIONAL VERSUS POLITICAL DECENTRALIZATION

Whether the result of the system or of the people working within it, the OECD argues that, where administratively feasible, there should be a general presumption in favour of both political decentralization and administrative (or functional) decentralization to managers (OECD 1987b, 1994). The former better reflects local needs, whereas the latter improves accountability for responsibilities. Such changes in the ways local governments undertake their given functions have involved adoption of new models of public service delivery (OECD 1987b; Walsh 1995). There has been an almost universal tendency to reform administrative boundaries and functional responsibilities, and a growing tendency to create special bodies for the delivery of local public services (Martins 1995; Oates 1990).

Political decentralization is based on the principle of subsidiarity, devolving decision-making to the lowest possible level of government. Chapter 2 made clear that this is categorically distinct from the functional decentralization of service provision which, in itself, does not require decentralization of decision-making. Political decentralization requires a commitment to increase the effectiveness of voice through formal democratic processes but, in itself, does nothing to increase the scope for exit. Functional decentralization will not necessarily increase the scope for exit and will not, in itself, increase the scope for expression of voice. While other European countries have tended to concentrate on political decentralization, the UK has tended to concentrate on functional decentralization.

Functional decentralization involves a shift from a vertically-integrated corporate institutional form of direct service provision by local government to one of an enabling function within a horizontally-coordinated network of multi-agency service provision. It occurs where centrally-financed agencies operate within market and pseudo-market systems in providing local government services. It involves a fundamental reappraisal of the form of democracy and the way in which it can be secured, a questioning of the behavioural characteristics of local government in relation to the public interest, a reinstatement of the rights and responsibilities of the individual and of the family, a reduction of local government's role in providing the welfare state, and a preference for multiple solutions provided by agencies in place of monolithic provision by local government monopolies.

Although it is possible to have one without the other, political and functional decentralization are not necessarily mutually exclusive. Indeed, ideally, both would take place simultaneously and satisfy Oates' decentralization theorem while allowing economies of scale to be captured by single-service (rather than multifunctional) agencies providing services in accordance with decentralized political decisions. Such reforms have the potential to match service supply with benefit areas on a service-by-service basis (see Chapter 8). Whether they do so in practice is an empirical, rather than conceptual, question that can only be determined by research subsequent to the introduction of those reforms.

THE CHANGING SERVICE ROLE OF BRITISH LOCAL GOVERNMENT

As already noted, local government politicians in Britain are elected on a 'first-past-the-post' system of electoral representation where only one politician is elected per constituency (the candidate gaining the most votes). This tends to polarize central–local politics, socialist-dominated urban local governments often operating alongside Conservative central governments. Not surprisingly, as already noted in Chapters 5 and 9, Conservative central governments became distrustful of local government during the 1980s as central and local expenditure policies diverged and it sought to constrain local political power.

While central–local relations have become less adversarial since the election of a Labour (socialist) government in 1997, and while there are considerable differences between the main British political parties about the acceptability of individual measures, there is a general cross-party acceptance of the need for reform in order to make local councils more responsive to the needs of citizens in their localities. This perceived need for increased responsiveness reflects long-term developments in both society and in the economy, for example changing demographic and ethnic structures, expectations of increased choice and availability of service, technological changes and economic re-structuring. These issues are arguably more important than the political complexion of the party in power at any one point in time.

British local government lost responsibility for the supply of electricity and gas early in the twentieth century, followed by health in the late 1940s and water supply and sanitation between the mid-1970s and later 1990s (Bailey 1995, chs 13 and 14). All but health care (and water and sewerage services in Scotland) were sold to the private sector during the 1980s and early 1990s. Privatization was intended to constrain public choice inefficiencies by intro-ducing market forces. Services remaining the responsibility of British local government by the later 1990s include school education, police, fire, personal social services, public transport (but not railways), roads (but not motor-ways), refuse collection and disposal, libraries, museums and galleries, envir-onmental services, leisure and recreation, spatial planning and rental housing.

The rapid postwar growth in service expenditures went hand-in-hand with the growth of the welfare state and was consolidated by the mid-1970s reforms which created relatively large and powerful local governments through-out Britain (see Chapter 2). However, the general consensus about the desir-ability of continued expenditure growth began to break down with the onset of a recessionary economic climate and as central government sought to control (reduce) public expenditure in general and local government spend-ing in particular (Bailey 1982c).

The result was a sharp deterioration in central–local relations during the later 1970s, 1980s and early 1990s. Conflict replaced consensus and central government took an increasingly interventionist stance in local financial affairs. This led to successive reforms of the intergovernmental grant system, culminating in 1990 in the replacement of the local domestic property tax by a local poll tax, and the nationalization of the property tax on business pre-mises (see Chapters 8 and 9). By the early 1990s, central government directly controlled about two-thirds of local government income and also had powers to cap local tax rates as well as having a significant influence on other revenue sources such as rents for municipal houses (see Chapter 7).

The increasing financial constraints of the 1980s and early 1990s are not merely a reflection of economic necessities. They also reflect a fundamental questioning of the role of the public sector, of the relative responsibilities of the state and of the individual, of the balance between the market and non-market sectors and of the very meaning of democracy itself. While it is not possible to define democracy in terms of institutional form or in terms of par-ticular public sector services, it is clear that local government is strengthened by having responsibility for a wide range of services which are influential in people's everyday lives (see Chapter 2).

Reduction in financial autonomy and loss of service responsibilities have inevitably been interpreted as a centralizing attack on local government (Burgess and Travers 1980; Jones and Stewart 1985; Newton and Karran 1985). In fact the real agenda is not so simple. A major transformation in the way in which functions are provided by British local government has become evident. There are two distinct elements to this transformation:

1. There has been a move away from the tradition of direct provision by corporatist local governments towards an enabling role whereby they increasingly secure the desired levels and standards of services by contracting provision from the private sector.
2. There is no longer a presumption in favour of the institutional framework of local government as a promoter of democratic accountability. The very idea of local democracy is changing from one of simply political representation (indirect democracy) to one which also includes universal individual participation in decision-making (direct democracy).

REDEFINING DEMOCRACY

Direct forms of democracy include referenda on specific issues and pseudo-market mechanisms which allow for increased individual choice. These forms of *functional* democracy and *market* democracy are beginning to replace or supplement *representative* democracy. One could question whether the meaning of democracy is being redefined to suit ideological imperatives. However, there is no absolute definition of democracy that is durable for all time and all conditions. The real question is one of balance between the various forms and meanings of democracy. It could be argued that there has been too great a dependence in many countries on the representative form of democracy in the past and that this led to increasing centralization of both political and bureaucratic power within the state at both central and local levels.

Put simply, the idea of one politician representing all individual citizens in his or her constituency irrespective of political persuasion is questionable (Meadowcroft 1991). Ideals of uniformity and integration are giving way to an acceptance (and even a welcoming) of diversity and differentiation consistent with individual preferences and effort. Simple forms of representative government are becoming increasingly inadequate in representing an increasingly diverse multicultural society with divergent socioeconomic conditions and in ensuring public choice and accountability. Democratic choices can be facilitated by participation as well as by representation, especially at local level (Jones and Ranson 1989) and by the deliberative role of government in the tradition of J. S. Mill (Reich 1987).

Representative democracy is made necessary because voting systems are mechanically incapable of consistently aggregating a multitude of individual wishes into a single set of collective wants – the 'Arrow problem' (see Chapter 10). This problem is overcome by electing politicians who can be trusted to make the right decisions on behalf of citizens. However, as already noted in Chapters 3, 5 and 11, public choice theory suggests that the various parties to the public expenditure process may in fact pursue their own self-interest at the expense of the public interest. Public choice theory has an inhospitality thesis, arguing that it is idealistically naïve to regard governments as protectors and promoters of the 'public interest', if such a paternalistic concept could be defined.

Voting systems do not gauge the intensity of preferences: voters are known to be poorly informed about alternative policies on offer, and it is quite rational for the voter not to bother to be well informed when voting or, given the insignificant impact of his or her vote on personal well-being, even to vote at all (Downs 1957; Tullock 1967). Furthermore, the voter's knowledge may be heavily biased in favour of his or her special interests, the imbalance between benefits and costs arguably leading to excessive public spending on voted-for services (see Chapter 5 and Buchanan and Tulloch 1962).

This supposed asymmetry in voter behaviour was said to be compounded in Britain by the lack of a direct relationship between those who vote for, those who pay for and those who use local government services (see Chapter 8). The British central government argued that there was a general belief that someone else would pay. The 'someone else' were national taxpayers financing intergovernmental grants, local businesses paying local non-domestic property taxes while having no vote and the minority of voters who paid local domestic property taxes as heads of household. Hence, the British government believed there was an in-built tendency for voters to vote for excessive local government spending.

Deficiencies in demand articulation and lack of competition may allow both local politicians and bureaucrats to act opportunistically. Politicians may seek to increase their chances of re-election and political survival rather than promote the public interest. Bureaucracies tend to become larger (empire-building) and, since bureaucrats themselves have votes and are perhaps more likely to use them than other groups, they can acquire sufficient political power to guarantee self-preservation and self-interest. Furthermore, they may themselves be local politicians.

While taking care not to exaggerate, there is considerable confusion among voters in Britain regarding the political control of their local authority (London being a notable exception), about which particular public sector services are provided by local government, their relative importance in expenditure terms, how they are financed and the relative proportions of income sources from intergovernmental grants, local taxes and so on (DOE 1992). The same source reveals that three-quarters of those eligible to vote have little or no interest in local politics, less than 10 per cent having attended a council or committee meeting or a public meeting on a local issue within the previous year. Less than a fifth of voters appear willing to vote against their council if it proposed something of which they strongly disapproved. Nonetheless, irrespective of low levels of knowledge of and participation in local government affairs, three-quarters of voters appear satisfied with their council's activities.

Such disinterest in local politics (often reflected in low rates of voter turnout at elections) creates organizational slack and suggests that there is scope for discretionary behaviour by bureaucrats, by local politicians and by distributional coalitions seeking to obtain the largest possible share of output for their members (see Chapter 5). Distributional coalitions introduce an additional potential public choice inefficiency through the combination of heterogenous preferences, the asymmetry of effective political power, the inflexibility of tax payments for financing services and the largely discretionary nature of service takeup.

Chapter 5 noted that the major part of redistribution at the local government level is through service usage and that there is an incentive to seek to vary the level of output and/or to change its distribution within a given tax cost. Indeed, there is evidence of 'middle-class capture' of subsidy through service usage (Bramley *et al.* 1989; Le Grand and Winter 1987; Pampel and Williamson 1989) and these socioeconomic groups (owner-occupiers, better qualified and educated) are more likely both to vote and to participate in local groups and meetings (DOE 1992).

The ability of local government to adapt to changing socioeconomic conditions is therefore severely constrained precisely because services tend to be targeted at particular groups or localities and because any reduction of services would see a reduction in the benefits accruing to them but no change in tax liability. Hence, local government services are difficult to cut back and this characteristic serves to reinforce self-serving behaviour by local bureaucrats and politicians.

Possible solutions are on both the demand side and the supply side. *Supply side measures* are designed to constrain the pursuit of self-interest by bureaucrats. They include value for money audits, performance review, efficiency studies and the opening up of in-house provision to competitive forces. *Demand side reforms* could make voters better informed, for example through larger electoral assemblies and annual elections to single-tier local governments (to strengthen the connection between voters and their political representatives) or by single-issue voting (referenda). However, it is simply too expensive (in terms of time and effort) for voters to become knowledgeable on all issues and they may simply prefer to trust politicians to make the right decisions. Central government's distrust of local politicians has resulted in limits having been set on the ability of higher-tier British local government officers to hold local political office in order to limit the potential self-indulgent feedback between bureaucracies and politicians. In addition, various legislative measures have been taken to limit local authorities' use of 'political propaganda'.

Proportional representation could replace the 'first-past-the-post' system as a way of protecting the interests of people who are in a minority. However, successive British central governments remained committed to the existing system of electoral representation at both national and local levels. Introduction of proportional representation at the local level while maintaining 'first-past-the-post' at national level will not necessary depolarize political representation everywhere.

None of these demand side and supply side approaches are categorically different from the *status quo*, since the concepts of both democracy and service remain the same. Moreover, there is little scope to increase municipal competition in the form envisaged by Tiebout, whereby local governments modify their service and tax packages to attract affluent residents (see Chapter 4). Institutionalized democracy is therefore thought to be seriously deficient and dissatisfaction with monolithic public sector solutions has become increasingly evident since the late 1970s. Central governments attempted to reduce local political power and increase the power of the individual citizen as (non-political) consumer of local services, operating within a private market or pseudo-market framework to allow increased scope for exit.

The need for increased flexibility in service provision was recognized by local authorities themselves in their attempts to stimulate participation and multiple solutions through tenant management schemes, community involvement in spatial planning and architecture, increased school council activities, outreach programmes for public library services and so on (see Chapter 4). However, there are practical limits to the ability of local authorities in this respect and there is no obvious reason why the replacement of monolithic by multiple solutions should be contained within the existing institutional framework of local government itself, nor even within the public sector.

The lack of clear answers to socioeconomic problems is increasingly seen as requiring more variety of response and multiple solutions. It may be regarded as unreasonable that individuals should have to uproot themselves and move between individual local governments to secure preferred service packages (voting with one's feet). They should perhaps be in a position to shop around alternative providers of local public services within their present locality. Monolithic public sector solutions were increasingly being seen as both inappropriate and inimical to promoting choice through expression of voice and so increased attention was given to increasing the scope for exit.

The increasing fragmentation of UK public sector decision-making during the 1980s through specially appointed central government agencies with explicit remits and special boundaries (especially for local economic development initiatives) was in direct and uneasy contrast with the consolidating, over-arching corporatist approach of local government. Multiple solutions implied not just fragmentation of public sector decision-making but also a reduction of politico–bureaucratic control and responsibility and a restatement of the rights and responsibilities of the individual, family and community.

The perceived solution was to promote consumerism (rather than producerism) and this raised the question as to the legitimate stategic role of local government within a governmental system which appeared to be steadily fragmenting. The conventional argument about the need to enshrine and protect the role and very existence of British local government within a written constitution gave way to a more fundamental questioning of the meaning of citizenship, its rights and responsibilities. This, in turn, led to a reappraisal of the respective roles of governments and markets.

THE ENABLING ROLE

The UK Conservative government's 1991 White Paper 'Competing for Quality' stated that

> the Government's model for local government in the 1990s and into the 21st century is that of the enabling authority ... This implies a move away from the traditional model of local authorities providing virtually all services directly and a greater separation of the functions of service delivery from strategic responsibilities. (Cm 1730, p. 22)

The former Conservative government expected a plurality of provision to encourage competition and so stimulate cost-effectiveness, innovation and choice. Even where British local government retains full responsibility for services, direct provision is giving way to an enabling role, consistent with facilitating increased choice for individual consumers. The term 'enabling' can have a number of different interpretations or emphases:

1. *The private market* can be enabled to participate more fully in service provision.
2. *The individual* can be enabled to receive services most suited to his or her own specific needs and requirements.
3. *Community development* can be enabled.

These three different conceptions of enabling are neither necessarily mutually exclusive nor mutually reinforcing. Educational reforms may enable both the individual and the community to maximize their potential, but may not stimulate private provision of the service. Improvements in public transport may achieve all three forms of enablement. The enabling local authority is clearly a multifaceted concept and there is some evidence that local authorities have a different perception of the enabling role, emphasizing personal and community development rather than market development (Wistow *et al.* 1992).

The most significant feature of enabling is the separation of the specification and delivery of services. If these reforms are as significant as the former UK Conservative government intended, the ultimate effect will be to replace multi-purpose local governments by a network (co-ordinated or not) of service specification and multi-agency provision.

It is in this context that current use of the term *'government'* implies a standardized form of polity, a highly organized and coordinated form of civil government. The term *'governance'* refers to the act, manner or function of governing and does not have the modern connotation of uniformity, comprehensiveness or standardization of 'government'. 'Governance' suggests a multiplicity of ways in which representation is achieved and in which services are delivered. It implies fragmentation at the local level, a return to the British system of the late nineteenth century which the reforms of the twentieth century had done so much to consolidate and corporatize. This is because the needs of local residents allegedly became subservient to the needs of the organization.

FROM GOVERNMENT TO GOVERNANCE

A shift from government to governance has profound implications for the way in which services are delivered, the way in which local political processes operate, the respective roles of local politicians, administrators, service providers and service users, the management function, budgeting, the contribution of voluntary action and 'voluntarism', the interface between the public and private sectors and the emphasis on consumerism as distinct from producerism. The development of local public service networks requires a shift away from the relatively simple vertically-integrated collegial hierarchy within local government to a form of contractual relationships between individual departments operating as competitive internal consultancies charging for professional services.

External relationships already exist between local authorities and the private and voluntary sectors but they are becoming more comprehensive and encompass the new agencies providing education, training and other services, part of a complex disaggregated, horizontally-linked system of explicit or implicit service-level agreements. Local democratic public accountability remains as part of the enabling function but local government is increasingly defined by new forms of accountability relating to the fulfilment of contractual and quasi-commercial arrangements with contractors, residents, partners in the voluntary and commercial sectors and even with central government (Parkinson 1987; Stewart and Stoker 1989; Alexander 1991; Cochrane 1991; Hollis *et al.* 1992; Walsh *et al.* 1997).

This wider form of accountability permeates not just the local authority–contractor–client relationship but also the relationships between and within

Funding

		Public	Private
Production	Public	1	2
	Private	3	4

Figure 12.1   *Modelling the shift from government to governance*

departments within local authorities. Political power and authority is increasingly giving way to negotiation and persuasion. This implies a number of other changes if the enabling role is to be fulfilled. Local councillors' internal committee responsibilities have to be supplemented by increased representation on the boards of external agencies. Increased emphasis on negotiation and persuasion requires behavioural changes on the part of officers and councillors alike. Power relationships are being transformed as functional representation of different interest groups increasingly takes place through a variety of elected and non-elected organizations of which local government is only one (even if the main) constitutional form.

The policy implications of public choice theory can be summarized in Figure 12.1, adapted from Klein (1984). Cell 1 is the case where the state directly produces as well as finances public sector services which are free at the point of use. Privatization in the form of sale of assets is denoted by cell 4. Services which cannot be privatized (or are thought unsuitable for privatization) could be charged for at the point of use. Introduction of full-cost user-charges for publicly-provided services causes a shift to cell 2. Where user-charges are levied at less than full cost (so that publicly-financed, partial subsidies continue), the result is a cross-over between cells 1 and 2 (where public production continues). If voluntarily-incurred user-charges can fully finance production costs, there is not necessarily any reason why production of the service should remain within the public sector: it could be privatized. A shift from cell 2 to cell 4 (representing privatization) would then occur. However, as noted in Chapter 7, charges will only improve allocative efficiency if there is full consumer sovereignty and no aspects of market failure.

A move to cell 3 occurs where the state wishes to maintain control of service provision but contracts provision to a private sector producer. It requires a formal division between the purchaser (public sector) and the provider (the private sector producer). Cell 1 can include both a formal split between purchaser and (public sector) provider or no such split. Figure 12.2 is therefore required to clarify the distinction between contracting and non-contracting arrangements for public service providers. It is used specifically to refer to local government.

Purchaser?

		No	Yes
Provider?	Yes	1	2
	No	3	4

Figure 12.2   A model of the purchaser–provider split

In cell 1 of Figure 12.2 the local government directly provides the service with no division or split between purchaser and provider. Cell 3 represents transfer of responsibility for service provision outwith local government. It includes provision of services by quangos (see Chapter 4) and schools opting-out of local authority control (see below). In Cell 2 service provision is *contracted-in*, local government employees winning service contracts in competition with private companies. In cell 4 provision of the service is *contracted-out* to a private producer (ideally by competitive bidding) and so purchased by the local government. Both Cells 2 and 4 depict *the purchaser–provider split*.

The purchaser–provider split separates the functions of service delivery from strategic responsibilities. It creates contestability for providers but not for purchasers. In effect, market features are combined with a modified hierarchy of control to created managed markets. Increased centralization (of strategy) and decentralization (of self-managed functional units) are achieved simultaneously.

It is held that the public sector will not only benefit from exposure to market forces but also from the concomitant adoption of commercial management models. In particular, the principle is that those with responsibilities for administering the competition process should have no direct interest in its resulting outcome. Hence the purchaser supposedly becomes the advocate of the consumer, there no longer being a conflict of interest with the defender of the provider (its employees).

This a priori expectation is developed more fully in Chapter 13 and is empirically tested in Chapter 14. Hence it is sufficient for now to note that doubts have been expressed about the arguments for the purchaser–provider split:

> The purchaser–provider split is at the core of the development of the new public management, and is accepted surprisingly widely both on the Right and the Left, with little questioning either of its theoretical basis or examination of the empirical evidence on its effects. . . . It can be argued that the role of the purchaser is to operate at a strategic level. The danger is that the concept of strategy can be so broad and vague as to mean little. The

divorce between strategy and practice may make strategic decision difficult, because of lack of adequate knowledge of service. There is a danger
that the introduction of market mechanisms for the management of the
public service will make it difficult to adjust to changed circumstances and
make policy changes. (Walsh 1995, pp. 255–6)

THE MAIN BRITISH REFORMS

The main reforms fall into two categories. The first attempts to give service
users increased scope for voice and exit (see Chapters 3 and 4), particularly
for education and housing. The second attempts to create increased competition for the supply of services in order to reduce X-inefficiency (see Chapters
5 and 13).

1. Increasing the Scope for Voice and Exit in Education and Housing

(a)   School Education
Prior to the introduction of these reforms, local education authorities
(LEAs) planned the distribution of pupils and resources between schools in
their own jurisdictions. The reforms gave parents statutory rights regarding
choice of school for their children, even the right to cross LEA boundaries
(that is, increased scope for exit from an individual school or LEA). Parents
also have the right to information and to attend annual meetings reporting
on school performance (that is, increased scope for voice). The composition
of school governing bodies was revised and their powers increased, the inten-
tion being to make them less political, so increasing the voice of the individual citizen as service user (as consumer rather than as citizen).

Some reforms have been intended to reduce X-inefficiency by giving service
units greater responsibility for managing their own affairs. First, LEAs were
required to delegate budgets to individual schools in order that they manage
their own finances. Second, individual schools could apply to central government to 'opt-out' of local government control altogether, becoming directly
funded by central government (refered to as 'grant-maintained schools'). Central government effectively purchases school places from opted-out schools
and requires them to provide minimum educational standards.

The Conservative government (with hindsight, over-optimistically) expected
numbers of schools opting-out to expand significantly, with most secondary
schools (ages 11–18) opting-out by 1997. In fact by early 1997 only 658 of
England's 3594 state secondary schools (18 per cent) had opted-out of local
control to become grant-maintained by central government, this despite large
financial inducements to opt-out. Similarly, only 504 of the 18480 English
primary schools had opted-out, less than 3 per cent. Proportions were even

lower in Scotland and Wales. In 1997, the newly elected Labour government announced that no more schools would be allowed to opt-out of LEA control.

A number of changes have been intended to encourage diversity in provision directly, rather than await the outcomes of increased scope for voice and exit, perhaps in recognition of both the limited influence of parental choice regarding what is taught and the limited resources (time and knowledge) which they can apply to educational matters. A national curriculum was imposed upon primary and secondary schools, replacing LEA discretion regarding the range of subjects taught. However, central government allowed secondary schools to specialize in one or more subjects. Specialisms can relate to the teaching of modern European languages, modern applications of science and technology, music, creative arts, business and management studies and so on. Additional central government finance for selected comprehensive schools was provided in order to improve provision and encourage excellence in technology subjects. This was complemented by the provision of new form of institution for secondary school education: City Technology Colleges. They were established outside the control of LEAs, being directly financed by central government with some finance pledged by private business. These (ultimately very limited) measures served to differentiate schools and so facilitate choice through increased scope for exit within local authorities within which they are situated.

(b) Education Beyond School Age
Local authorities lost control of the former polytechnics and colleges providing higher education (HE). They were absorbed into the traditional university system in the early 1990s (most in 1992). LEAs also lost control of further (vocational) education (FE) in their areas in 1993. FE colleges now control their own budgets, central government either paying grant directly to them or indirectly through training agencies. FE colleges have an increased incentive to expand provision of vocational courses in order to attract students for whom fees are paid. As for school education, these changes were also intended to give colleges freedom from political influence, promote competition, and therefore increase the scope for exit within the FE and HE sectors. This would encourage them to cater more effectively for the needs of their areas. The Conservative government believed that independence allows colleges to become more innovative and entrepreneurial in providing courses and so provide more effective choices to local people. College principals shared the same view (*THES* 1992).

The rationale for these reforms was that the government wished to depoliticize education at the local level, it being a value judgement that education should be depoliticized (and perhaps an unrealistic aspiration that it could be). The government believed that LEAs were not the best judges of educational requirements. Instead, parents, pupils and students (now increasingly referred to as 'clients') were believed to know where their strengths and interests lie, not school teachers or lecturers, not educational theorists, not local bureaucrats, not local politicians, not the LEA. Although the subsequent Labour government expressed a more conciliatory attitude towards schools and colleges, it retained all the reforms except for opting-out. Put simply, the approach being increasingly adopted is that of informed choice on the part of service users.

(c) Housing

Whereas the former Conservative government continued to favour owner-occupation, it believed that the private rented housing sector had been subject to excessive control in favour of local governments which, in the past, were expected to provide the bulk of rental housing. It believed that this led to a lack of tenant choice and monolithic council estates often with inadequate standards of housing services. Reforms were intended to stimulate consumer choice (exit) by encouraging both owner-occupation and a greater diversity of landlords. The subsequent Labour government has been of much the same view, although perhaps recognizing the need to facilitate expression of voice further.

Owner-occupation has been facilitated by giving council tenants a legal 'right to buy' the properties they rent from their local authorities. Central government encouraged the decision to purchase, rather than rent, by heavily discounting the selling prices of those properties and by forcing up rents for municipal housing. The discount was made proportional to the length of the tenancy: the longer the tenant had rented the house, the greater the proportion by which the selling price was discounted.

Central government increasingly forced rents up to market levels by reducing the specific grant it paid to local governments in respect of municipal housing. Rents increasingly related to current rather than to historic costs, the former being greater than the latter if only because of inflation. This provides financial incentives for those who can afford to do so to buy rather than rent their houses. Council tenants can also choose individually (for houses) or collectively (for flats and maisonettes) to transfer their existing homes to another landlord. These are both forms of privatization (see Figure 4.2, Chapter 4).

A greater rental sector diversity has been encouraged by subjecting local government provision to increasing competition. Deregulation of the private rental sector leaves landlords free to negotiate improved services and higher rents. The social rented sector has been diversified by expanding the housing association sector. Despite the fact that they are unelected quangos (see Chapter 4), individual housing associations are, nevertheless, thought to be flexible and able to respond sensitively to differing housing needs. Local governments can also voluntarily transfer some or all of their housing stock to housing associations or other landlords if holding onto isolated housing stock becomes increasingly untenable. Competition in housing management was expected to lead to improvements in management practice, and was to be encouraged by competitive contracting (see below).

If the reforms had had the effects intended by the previous Conservative government, local political manipulation of local rent policies would have ceased and local regulatory and enabling responsibilities would have superceded local government manipulation of subsidy through low-rent policies and transfers from general revenue accounts to housing revenue accounts. Tenants would therefore supposedly have been given clearer signals about the performance of their council's housing management and would have been able to decide whether to exercise their right of exit (buy or opt for another landlord). Decentralization of management to the individual estate level would break up monolithic provision and more closely relate supply to benefit areas (estates and neighbourhoods).

In practice, however, these reforms have had much more limited impact than the former Conservative government intended. First, the 'right-to-buy' has not been widely exercised in many local authorities, especially those with relatively high unemployment, those with poorer quality municipal housing, and those with high proportions of flats and apartments within their rental stock. Second, many local authorities 'went out of subsidy' as increasing rents and rental income reduced their eligibility for central government's specific housing grant. The result was that central government's influence on rent levels was drastically reduced in those local authorities. Third, the private rental and housing association sectors did not expand fast enough and relatively few local authorities and tenants were keen to transfer their housing to them. Tenants generally feared even higher rents if they transfered and most local authorities wished to retain responsibility for the service, it being a crucial part of the local welfare state.

2. Increasing Competition for the Supply of Services

This was achieved through the purchaser–provider split which required the contractual specification of a number of services. Those contracts then became subject to compulsory competitive tendering (CCT) so that the most efficient provider would be able to provide the service. This constitutes decentralization to markets within, rather than outwith, local government (see Figure 4.2, Chapter 4). In its extreme form (Ridley 1988; ASI 1989), the enabling role replaces the universal provider role.

CCT was introduced in 1980 for local government's construction-related activities, including new building and renewal, building repairs and maintenance, and highways construction and maintenance. CCT was extended in the late 1980s for the internal cleaning of buildings, refuse collection, street cleaning, school and welfare catering, other catering (for example, for municipal office workers), vehicle maintenance, grounds maintenance (such as parks), and management of sports and leisure services. During the later 1990s CCT was extended to housing management and to other professional services. In 1997 the newly elected Labour government announced that the CCT regime would be replaced by a more comprehensive system designed to achieve 'best value' even in areas where competition for service contracts was limited or non-existent. Nonetheless, there is still an expectation that competitive tendering is usually the most effective means of achieving best value (see Chapters 13 and 14).

EVALUATION

The reforms outlined above are clearly intended, *inter alia*, to increase *individual choice and participation* whether through choice of service outlet (such as a particular school) or through choice within a pseudo-market system (such as type of landlord). But will service provision and choice necessarily improve as a result of the new arrangements? The answer depends upon a simultaneity of affirmatives, namely that councillors will be provided with more effective mechanisms to enable them to fulfil a representative (rather than service committee) role; that agencies are better providers than local governments; that co-ordination and articulation is effective; that local or central government can regulate agencies effectively; that disjointed funding mechanisms, central–local conflict, increasing centralization, continuing change and uncertainty are not obstructive; and that outcomes are monitored and results assessed by independent research rather than by ideological stance (Brooke 1992).

Irrespective of political persuasion, opinion polls in Britain found an overwhelming satisfaction with the existing system of local government among the general population (John and Block 1991). Hence, there must be a presumption in favour of local government which has the major advantage of democratic legitimacy compared with non-elected agencies. Reference to public choice theory and corroborative evidence is not sufficient to justify change. Rationally at least, alternative modes of provision must be demonstrably superior to existing provision for change to be justified.

In practice, it is difficult to specify precise contracts for services such as residential care of the elderly and sports centre facilities. This makes it difficult to monitor the extent to which a move towards enabling, agency and market provision achieves the benefits claimed by a priori analysis. Asset specificity and bounded rationality were already the case under local authority control but they will now be combined with the opportunism of profit-seeking market agents, leading to potentially high transaction costs (see Chapter 3). Hence, it is not self-evident that these reforms necessarily achieve the benefits expected of them. The manifestation of the public choice problem will have changed, not the problem itself. There are four main issues for evaluation.

1. Individual Choice

This has not been increased by the competitive tendering of contracts for refuse collection and disposal because service delivery characteristics largely remain a collective decision because of the area-based nature of refuse collection rounds. The same seems to apply to the personal social services where need for service (such as residential care for an elderly person) is assessed by a multidisciplinary network of professionals (health, housing, social work and so on). Individual choice regarding education has inevitably been constrained by the finite capacities of popular schools. It has been claimed that popular schools became increasingly selective, selection being determined by socio-economic or other criteria, including previous examination performance. This was ameliorated within further and higher education by a subsequent expansion of student places but partially counteracted by increased financial restraints facing students as subsistence grants were cut in real terms. The outcomes for housing, sports and public transport depend on the behaviour of private suppliers acting within or outwith local government regulatory constraints.

2. Cost-Effectiveness

Higher costs may have resulted from the increased fragmentation of services. However, at the input and process stages the main economies of scale are related to sizes of individual schools, of housing management areas, of transport operations and so on (see Chapter 2). There may in fact be significant managerial diseconomies which increase with system size and which may be reduced by functional decentralization. At the output and outcome stage higher costs relate to the inspection and monitoring of outputs of a multiplicity of agencies and to ensure their compliance with contractual specifications and any subsequent enforcement costs. A 'before and after' comparison is invalid here if it is accepted that increased attention should have been paid to outputs and outcomes of services previously provided directly by local government. Evaluation of cost-effectiveness was also complicated because opting-out did not reach appreciable proportions. However, evidence for Community Care suggests that long-term contracts (for residential care of the elderly and so on) written to detailed specifications lose a degree of flexibility and, while *unit* costs may be reduced, organizational structures may be made less responsive by the contract culture and become less cost-effective *in aggregate* (Common and Flynn 1992). This outcome would appear to reduce, rather than increase, individual choice.

3. Equity

To claim that increased choice increases equity assumes equal capacity for choices among all socioeconomic groups. In fact poorer groups may accept lower standards of service because they have less information about alternative service levels and lower expectations than affluent goups. This may be reinforced by the behaviour of service providers serving to restrict choices available to lower-income groups. This may arise within education from increased selectivity by opted-out schools. It may arise within housing if local authorities become residuary welfare housing authorities providing low-standard accommodation to those who cannot afford to buy their council houses or afford the higher rents (which one hopes reflect improved housing services) of opted- out estates. Provision of personal social services will still depend on (say) elderly people applying for community care services. However, poorer groups tend to have relatively low takeup rates for welfare services. Similar considerations apply to other services such as sports and leisure facilities and public transport where, as noted above, the evidence suggests higher participation rates by more affluent groups and middle-class capture of subsidy.

4. Expenditure Control

It is not necessarily any easier for central government to control spending when dealing with a greater number of agencies than of local governments. The same pressures will exist (such as demographic change and increased expectations of service provision) as will the same problems of public choice generally. There is now an even greater disparity between those who vote for, pay for and use local services than existed under local government. For example, there is no longer any local tax contribution to opted-out schools or further education colleges.

CONCLUSIONS

The public choice perspective questions the behavioural characteristics of local government in promoting the public interest and implies a preference for multiple solutions provided by competitive or pseudo-market agencies in place of monolithic provision by local government monopolies. It also implies a fundamental change of organizational form, namely the separation of the specification and delivery of services. Functional plurality and consumerism complements (if not completely replaces) political pluralism and producerism. Devolution of responsibilities to individual service production units and allowing both these units and service users to opt-out of local government control represents functional decentralization. This is in marked contrast to increasing political decentralization in other European countries. It is intended to increase individual citizens' choices regarding the package of service consumption as distinct from local collective choices.

There is a danger of giving a misleading impression of radicalism. Certainly there is much innovation, but the main differences are the perception of the role of the state and the culture of its management. Many countries are seeking more diverse approaches to long-standing problems and issues because they are less sure of their capacity to know how best to achieve social and economic objectives. The role of the state is increasingly seen in terms of its core functions of strategic policy-making, thereafter encouraging the private and voluntary sectors to make greater contributions in the delivery of welfare services.

The shift from the highly standardized and co-ordinated polity of government to the fragmentation and agency functionalism of governance is perhaps a more subtle and accurate description of events than the proclaimed demise of British local government. The vertically integrated corporate institutional form of direct service provision by British local authorities is increasingly becoming one of an enabling function within a horizontally coordinated network of multi-agency service provision. This transition is based on a fundamental reappraisal of the form of local democracy and the way in which it can be secured. Rather than adopt a new system of electoral representation (such as proportional representation) which may be expected to bring more of a convergence between central and local political priorities, central government sought to constrain local political and bureaucratic power. The rights and responsibilities of the individual and family are reaffirmed and local government's role in providing the welfare state is reduced.

These reforms were intended to reduce the dominance of public paternalism. It is no longer assumed that the state knows better than the individual in all aspects of welfare planning and provision. This is not to deny a crucial role for local government but it does not necessarily require the traditional institutional form making direct provision of services to levels and standards determined through a framework of collective choice. Instead, the role of the state is to facilitate individual choice, *enabling* service provision by means of a plurality of agencies to provide local service networks. Hence, the framework of provision becomes more diverse, explicitly adaptive and evolutionary: less monolithic and standardized.

While such divisions of responsibilities allow for the possibility of multiple solutions, they also create a danger of fragmented and uncoordinated approaches to strategic policy planning and service provision serving to restrict choice. This assumes that co-ordination and planning was successful previously, a particularly contentious assumption. Besides, it is arguable that the need for detailed planning is reduced by the introduction of competitive forces within market, pseudo-market and internal market systems. Nonetheless, successful implementation of this strategic policy and the associated reforms of services proved to be highly problematic, emphasizing the need for monitoring and for evaluation of outcomes. This is the subject of Chapters 13 and 14.

13   Competition and Quality

INTRODUCTION

Competition in public sector procurement is increasingly common in many countries, having developed beyond the purchase of supplies and materials to the allocation of contracts for service delivery. Competition has become increasingly popular because it is seen as a fair way of securing best value for money spent. This view is based on the premise that the provision of services by government is wasteful and unnecessarily bureaucratic. However, competition within local government extends far beyond the purchase of supplies and services.

Earlier chapters have highlighted the three main forms of competition within local government, namely political competition (Chapter 10), competition between local governments (Chapter 4) and competition within a single jurisdiction (Chapter 12). This chapter examines the meaning and degree of competition in more detail to provide the context within which to examine the theory and practice of the purchaser–provider split and assess its impact upon both the cost and quality of local government services.

It compares the a priori theoretical results with empirical research findings relating to UK local government services subject to the purchase–provider split and considers whether that split is both a necessary and sufficient condition for the improvement of quality of service. First, however, a formal theoretical exposition of competition within local government is necessary to highlight both the potential efficiency gains and losses. This chapter assesses the possible cost and quality outcomes for the generality of UK local government services subject to the purchaser–provider split, while Chapter 14 does likewise for two case-studies: the management of sports and leisure services and provision of school meals. Those two case-studies will be used to illustrate the need for a broad multidisciplinary approach in studying the effect of competition on the quality of service.

THE MEANING AND DEGREE OF COMPETITION IN LOCAL GOVERNMENT

1. Political Competition

Political competition within any one local authority occurs as different political parties compete for power. This is implied by Oates' decentralization theorem (see Chapter 2). However, Chapters 10 and 11 noted that elections create only periodic contestability and cast doubt on the proposition that parties tend to adopt the preferences of the median voter. Empirical research finds little correlation between median voter preferences and tax and expenditure levels across local authorities. Politics may, in fact, have little to do with local tax and expenditure levels, these perhaps being determined by socioeconomic factors, past commitments and national (rather than local) party ideology and control. Hence, the effectiveness of political competition may be severely limited in practice. Moreover, neither political competition nor performance review necessarily ensure X-efficiency since local voters may have little knowledge of the cost conditions of local government services (see Chapter 5). There is therefore a general principle in favour of increasing competition in the supply of local government services wherever possible.

2. Competition between Local Governments

Competition between local governments occurs as they offer alternative tax/ expenditure packages in order to attract mobile (voting-with-their-feet) citizens (see Chapter 4). In effect, local governments are viewed as an industry in which local politicians and bureaucrats act as sellers of local services to their buyers: citizens, households and local businesses. The buyers choose where to locate, paying for local services through local tax-prices. The level of competition between local governments is a function of three factors: local government structure, local autonomy and the extent of central funding (Boyne 1996b).

(a) Local Government Structure

Local government structure can facilitate both *horizontal* competition (between authorities on the same tier of local government) and *vertical* competition (between different tiers of local and regional government). Horizontal competition is positively related to the number of local governments serving a given area or population. The *decentralization hypothesis*, developed by Brennan and Buchanan (1980), posits that the greater the decentralization of tax-raising powers and public expenditures, the smaller the share of national income accounted for by government. The hypothesis (sometimes also referred to as the *Leviathan hypothesis*) holds that the greater the degree of decentralization the greater the constraints upon both budget-maximizing bureaucracy and special interest groups' self-serving behaviour. This is because citizens' power of exit from any one local government increases the greater the number of local governments in which one can choose to reside. In effect, the greater the size of local governments the more *institutional factors* predominate over the preferences of the median voter.

The decentralization hypothesis is analogous to the market structure perspective of monopoly and competition in the private sector, namely that large monopoly governments exploit their citizens. In the extreme case, local government is controlled by a rent-seeking monopolist who maximizes government 'profit' or economic rent by exceeding the spending levels desired by the median voter (Epple and Zelenitz 1981). Many smaller governments have to compete for citizens such that such exploitation is held in check (Courant *et al.* 1979; Oates 1985; Bender and Fixler 1989; Forbes and Zampelli 1989).

On the other hand, smaller jurisdictions may forgo economies of scale, the resultant rise in the unit costs of service provision leading to higher total expenditures because many local government services are price inelastic (Deacon 1978; Borcherding 1985). In addition, it has been claimed that more local governments provide more points of access for distributional coalitions to lobby for higher spending on local government services (Grodzins 1960). The opposite case is argued by Tullock (1959), however, namely that a centralized public sector provides interest groups with more opportunities for undemocratic agreements between politicians involving mutual favours and vote trading (referred to as 'logrolling' in the USA).

Given these conflicting arguments, the actual relationship between local government structure and its spending levels can only be determined by empirical research. While the international evidence is rather mixed, on balance successive studies tend to support the decentralization hypothesis (Oates 1989; Raimondo 1989; Joulfaian and Marlow 1990; Nelson 1992; Miller 1993). Conflicting research results may be due to failure to take adequate account of the diverse nature of decentralization, which cannot simply be measured by the number of local authorities serving a given region or population (see Chapter 4). They may also be explained by the public choice caveats of Chapter 4, namely that decentralization does not necessarily reduce the power of groups operating within and alongside local government institutions. It may simply redistribute that power. Moreover, for any given local government structure, competition between local governments is enhanced by high levels of local autonomy and of self-financing of expenditures.

(b) Local Autonomy
Local autonomy stimulates competition in terms of both the quantity and quality of services because service provision is not heavily constrained by central government controls.

(c) The Extent of Central Funding
The extent of central funding is important for local competition since too high a level of central funding serves to disguise the real cost of local authority services (fiscal illusion), including any excessive costs, and so blunts the operation of the tax-price mechanism and, likewise, reduces the incentive to migrate.

For competition between local governments to be stimulated, all of these conditions must be satisfied simultaneously, namely a fragmented structure of highly autonomous local governments with low levels of central government funding which do no more than equalize for differing per capita needs and resources. Previous chapters (in particular, 2, 8 and 9) showed that none of these three factors is the case for the UK. The UK has relatively large local governments, tax and budget capping, nationalization of the former local business property tax, and grants far in excess of those needed for equalization purposes. These serve to destroy competition within the local government market. Moreover, vertical competition in the UK's two-tier system of local government was criticized as wasteful and duplicative, the upper tier being abolished in some areas during the 1980s and 1990s.

3. Competition within a Single Jurisdiction

Competition within a single jurisdiction can occur between different departments and/or between a local authority and other organizations for contracts to provide services within its own area (that is, competitive contracting). Ideally, the introduction of competition involves creating *external* markets whereby organizations outwith local government (such as private sector firms and voluntary organizations) are invited to bid for service contracts, usually in competition with the local government's own internal (in-house) production units. Where this is not possible, for example because of inadequate private sector capacity, or not allowed by law, it may still be possible to create *internal* markets between different parts of the local government. Chapter 12 noted that creation of internal and external markets implies a radical reform of the structure of local government.

Consistent with the concept of competing distributional coalitions (see Chapter 5) departments may compete with each other in order to win a greater share of the local authority's budget. They would have an incentive to demonstrate that their service provides better value for money than those provided by other competing departments. In effect, this internal market for cash flow allocations is comparable with that of the multidivisional (M-form) structure of the modern corporation which, if it operates properly, separates strategic and operating issues and assigns cash flows to high-yield uses (Williamson 1986). This can be expected to involve internal control through monitoring the efficiency of each division or department and providing appropriate incentives. However, in the UK case at least, there is little evidence that local politicians actively scrutinize departmental budgets (Elcock and Jordan 1987). Even where they do, bureaucrats may provide information biased in favour of their own interests (Tullock 1965), especially given the difficulties in measuring output (Jackson 1995).

Hence, internal competition between departments would seem to be of limited effectiveness in stimulating greater efficiency. This perhaps explains the UK's emphasis on 'league table' comparisons of single functions and services across local authorities, comparisons of departmental efficiency being more effective across (rather than within) local government boundaries (see Chapter 5).

External competition within a single local authority's jurisdiction includes opting-out provisions for schools and for municipal housing and so on. In effect, users of local government services could switch services between alternative suppliers of, for example, rental housing. This destroys local municipal monopolies by removing barriers to entry in the market for local government services. However, Chapter 12 noted that these competitive measures have not developed as fully as was intended within the UK and, in the schools case, have been limited by capacity constraints at popular schools. The result has been that competitive pressures within a given jurisdiction are severely constrained. Hence, the main form of external competition has been requiring local governments to put specified services out to competitive tender, part of the purchaser–provider split.

THE PURCHASER–PROVIDER SPLIT: ECONOMIC THEORY

Conventional economic theory regarding the degree of competitiveness in any industrial or service sector is based on the static 'structure, conduct, performance' typology, namely that the greater the market share of the dominant firm the greater the degree of monopoly power and the greater the risk of exploitation of the consumer through high prices (see Chapter 5). As already noted, the traditional local authority service model in the UK is one of direct provision of services by the local government itself (see Chapters 4 and 12).

While allowing local authorities to retain strategic responsibility for services as *purchasers*, both efficiency and quality of service could be maximized if alternative potential *providers* are required to compete for the right to deliver the service (competitive contracting). In theory, this purchaser–provider split separates the demand for and supply of services, in sharp contrast with direct delivery by the local authority itself. Purchasers supposedly act on behalf of service users, concentrating on identifying need for service. The purchaser specifies the service to be delivered by the provider within a fixed budget.

While it implies a formal contracting regime, the purchaser–provider split does not necessarily introduce or require contestability for contracts to provide services. Non-competitive contracting regimes may be used where there are fears that the organization winning the contract might face such severe financial pressures that they reduce quality and/or levels of service in order to cut costs. Such fears explain the use of non-competitive contracting in the UK in respect of residential care services for elderly people.

In general, however, these aspects of value for money will not be achieved where competition for service contracts is not in place (non-competitive contracting) because, in theory, monopoly provision removes incentives to minimize the costs of a given level and quality of service.

Quasi-Markets

Competitive tendering for public sector service contracts typifies a quasi-market in that service users do not pay for the service at the point of consumption. Moreover, their preferences are mediated through the purchaser, who ultimately retains control of the total service budget and who may, in turn, be subject to central government control. The market may also operate under a non-profit rule. These characteristics mean that the market is a managed, rather than a free, market (Le Grand 1990; Le Grand and Bartlett 1993). Nevertheless, such managed competition will, in theory, yield cost savings and/or improved quality of service because there is competition for the right to provide the service.

Contestability

If competitive conditions prevail, it does not matter who provides the service, whether a public or private sector supplier. In theory, it is competition rather than ownership of the enterprise that promotes efficiency (Bishop and Kay 1988). Moreover, competition does not necessarily require a large number of providers of a given service or of potential providers bidding for service contracts. Instead, it is the *threat* of competition, rather than the number of bids, which is crucial in creating the incentives for increased efficiency (Baumol *et al.* 1982; Shepherd 1984).

In theory, the greater the threat of market entry by potential competitors, the greater the efficiency of incumbent firms, irrespective of their actual number or of the proportion of the market for which they account. As long as there are no restrictions on the ability of organizations to tender for service contracts, the number of competing bids for those contracts will be fewer the more efficient the incumbent service provider. This is because potential providers who cannot undercut the incumbent provider's costs realise that their bids will be unsuccessful. Hence, competitive conditions may not correspond to those of the economist's classic model of perfect competition (created by many providers), but instead be determined by the *threat* of competition.

A competitive market therefore is one into which new providers or enterprises are able to enter, but of which only one or a few may ultimately attempt so to do (Sorensen 1993). The reduction or removal of statutory barriers to entry into a public sector service market will therefore increase the level of contestability and so force the incumbent service provider to improve its efficiency by reducing X-inefficiency in order not to lose the service contract at the next round of tendering. In theory, the greater the degree of contestability, the greater are the cost savings and improvement in service quality (Ellwood 1996). There is some evidence in support of these theoretical propositions (Almquist 1999).

The lower the sunk costs of market entry and the lower the irrecoverable costs of market exit by service providers, the greater the contestability of an individual market, and so the greater the pressures on incumbent firms to achieve maximum economy, efficiency and effectiveness. Hence, public policy should attempt to maximize wherever possible the scope for contestability, rather than necessarily attempt to increase the number of companies or organizations producing a particular good or service. There are, however, few industries or service sectors where sunk costs can be made so low that markets are perfectly contestable in the sense of 'hit-and-run' entry into the market.

Competition for Markets or Users?

This market theory is qualified in its application to the purchaser–provider split in that the provider competes for the service contract: that is, for the market, *not* for the service user. Hence, while the theory demonstrates that the efficiency of the service provider will be improved (X-efficiency), the total output or quality of the service may remain suboptimal (allocative inefficiency) if the purchaser does not fully reflect users' wishes in the service contract and if the service user has no ability to vary his or her takeup of the service. In other words, there may still be exploitation of the service user by the purchaser, even if any exploitation of service users by the service provider is eliminated as a result of competitive contracting. The needs of the service user may be met more fully because the purchaser–provider split supposedly weakens the influence of the provider in terms of the specification of services.

Exit and Voice

It is more likely that service specifications reflect the service users' (rather than the provider's) needs under either or both of the following conditions:

1. if there is competition in supply so that service users have effective choices between alternative suppliers;
2. if purchasers fully reflect the needs and wants of service users.

In the first case exit from the service provider is facilitated. In the second case, there may need to be some improvement in the administrative arrangements for expression of voice by the service user. In theory, voice is more effective than exit the greater the degree of market failure (see Chapter 3).

Either or both of increased scope for voice and/or exit will facilitate the move from a service-led to a needs-led approach to service delivery. However, such a transition will be constrained if the purchaser pursues its own self-interest rather than those of the service user, for example under the leviathan (self-serving) model of government. The transition to a needs-led service assumes a fiscal exchange model of government. The despotic benevolent model of government also takes account of wider social benefits and costs. Hence, the extent to which users' needs are more fully reflected in service specifications under the purchaser–provider split depends crucially on the model of government (see Chapter 1 and Dunleavy 1991).

Possible Adverse Outcomes of Competition

It is possible that attempts to increase contestability may lead to suboptimal outcomes.

(a)   The Winner's Curse
Competitive pressures may lead potential entrant companies to submit unrealistically low tender prices for public sector service contracts in order to win contracts, the true costs of service provision being unintentionally underestimated. This is quite distinct from bidding for a contract as part of a 'loss leader' strategy to enter the market. The winner's curse may subsequently lead to default by the contractor with consequent disruption of service.

(b)   Transaction Costs
Local governments may be inexperienced in dealing with large private sector companies and may easily be 'exploited' by such contractors. In particular, assuming profit maximization, cost reduction subsequent to award of contract can be achieved by specifically seeking to reduce quality of service, even though contracts may specify that quality should be maintained at the levels existing prior to the award of the service contract (PSPRU 1992; Abbot 1993). This outcome is more likely where it is difficult to specify precise measures of quality in contracts with the result that judgements regarding the effect of competitive tendering on quality are largely subjective (Propper 1992a, 1992b), a point returned to below.

Ideally, explicit guidelines and social objectives are clearly set out in the contracts awarded by local governments and actual outcomes rigorously monitored. However, community-wide social objectives for such activities as sports and leisure are broad and vague and performance measurement against objectives is often haphazard. This creates the possibility of high transaction

Table 13.1 *Transaction costs for services subject to CCT*

Service	Bounded rationality	Opportunism	Asset specificity
Refuse collection	Low	Medium	Medium
Street cleaning	Low	Medium	Low
Building cleaning	Low	Medium	Low
Catering	Medium	High	Medium
Vehicle maintenance	Medium	High	Medium
Grounds maintenance	Low	Medium	Low
Leisure services	High	Medium	High

costs; that is, the costs of using contracts to secure the intended levels and qualities of services (see Chapter 3).

A typology of transaction costs surmised by Stewart and Stoker (1989) in respect of UK local government services subject to competitive contracting during the 1980s and 1990s is reproduced in Table 13.1. While the rating of bounded rationality, opportunism and asset specificity is open to debate, the level of transaction costs seems greatest for the management of leisure services (see Case-Study 1 in Chapter 14). First, it is difficult to specify precisely what its objectives are (for example, improved physical and mental health, less crime and vandalism) and to determine whether they are being satisfied (bounded rationality). Second, assets such as sports and leisure centres are highly specific to those uses and cannot easily be redeployed. Third, the management of those facilities could pursue opportunistic revenue-raising strategies by increasing the provision of chargeable activities and programmes and by increasing the levels of charges already levied. Such revenue-raising strategies may be contrary to access objectives for low-income groups. In contrast, objectives are easily specified for building cleaning (such as offices), assets (that is, unskilled labour) are not highly specific and scope for opportunism is limited since work can easily be checked.

Note, however, that such an outcome depends on the *simultaneous* occurence of opportunism, bounded rationality and asset specificity and that the conditions for transaction costs will occur whether the service is contracted-in to the local government's own employees or contracted-out to private companies or other external organizations. Contracting would only cause a shift from expense preference (assuming a Niskanen model of bureaucracy) to profit preference (assuming the normal profit maximizing objective of firms).

To suggest, *a priori*, that such a shift would occur implicitly assumes that power and discretion resides with the contractor; this is not necessarily the case. In particular, it ignores the existence of a range of interest groups (stakeholders) who may seek to influence contract specifications and monitoring arrangements. In other words, the extent of transaction costs is sensitive to governance structures and changes in those structures (Dietrich 1994). It also assumes that any profits or income accrue to the contractor whereas payments may be on a 'management fee only' basis.

(c)   Demotivation of Employees

Contracting service provision to replace direct-provider arrangements results in a change of governance and in the conventions regarding service delivery. It may make employees feel less a part of the local authority, even when still employed by the contracting service provider. Hence, it would be too simplistic to interpret sunk costs only in terms of technology. In practice human capital and employee motivation may be more important than the up-front costs of physical capital. Demotivation may occur where contracts are highly prescriptive, especially where the client local authority retains developmental functions and the contractor is simply an administrator. An example could be a sports and leisure management contract where the performance yardstick is income generated per square metre of floorspace.

The associated increase in monitoring activity may also reduce trust between client (the principal) and contractor (the agent), with the result that employees shift from commensurate to perfunctory performance as disaffected workers reduce effort in non-monitored tasks (see Chapter 5 and Williamson 1993). The import of this hypothesized effect depends on the nature of the service, presumably less the more routine the tasks involved and greater the more discretionary the developmental aspects of the task. Hence, demotivation effects may be of greater importance for white-collar and professional activities (usually requiring considerable training and experience) than for blue-collar tasks (usually low-skilled). Depending on its precise form and nature, monitoring may improve motivation, especially if undertaken in a non-punitive, positive way as part of an ongoing process of service improvement.

(d)   Knowledge/Skill Embeddedness

Quality may be critically dependent on the expertise of the current set of particularly long-serving employees and may lack transferability, so reducing the scope for governance by the market (Williamson 1985). This embeddedness is a form of asset specificity (see Chapter 3). It would seem to be less of a constraint for low-skill blue-collar services than for white-collar services requiring considerable training and experience. However, not all white-collar activities involve embeddedness, for example many clerical and administrative functions, and some which do are still provided by the market (for example, legal and architectural services).

(e)   Discouragement of Investment in Capital Facilities

Transient contractors will have little incentive to incur the costs of acquiring dedicated capital facilities, where assets are specific to the service activity.

This is less likely to be a problem for generic services such as cleaning and vehicle maintenance where the required capital assets and equipment are not peculiar to local government contracts. It is more likely to be a problem for sports and leisure management contracts where, as noted above, sports centres and other physical facilities are highly specific assets imposing high entry costs for new providers. In the UK, however, in making such facilities available to potential contractors (LGMB 1994), local authorities have reduced the costs of entry into the market for sports and leisure contracts and so minimized the potentially adverse impacts on quality of service caused by under-investment in high-cost dedicated capital assets.

Summary of Possible Adverse Outcomes

The degree of transaction costs, demotivation of employees, knowledge/skill embeddedness and lack of investment may be in inverse proportion to the length of contracts. This will be the case if longer contractual periods reduce the motivation to make quick returns, increase the identity of contractor employees with the client authority and facilitate accumulation of skills and experience and task-specific assets. On the other hand, excessively long contract periods may confer right of incumbency upon current contractors, so limiting competition through contestability and facilitating opportunistic behaviour.

THE PURCHASER–PROVIDER SPLIT: ORGANIZATIONAL THEORY

The purchaser (client) deals with client-side functions, namely planning the service, defining the work to be undertaken by the contractor, contract preparation, tendering processes, tender evaluation and letting and managing the contract. The provider's (contractor's) role is to fulfil contractual requirements. The contractor may previously have been part of the department having direct responsibility for the service (that is, contracting in) or alternatively, an external private sector company (that is, contracting out), see Figure 4.2. Local politicians supposedly become more concerned with service strategy as part of the enabling role, rather than being involved in day-to-day operations.

Previously, when local governments were the direct providers of the services now subject to the purchaser–provider split, they were concerned with all stages of service production: inputs, processes, outputs and outcomes:

1. *Inputs* are the resources used to provide the service. Personnel are the principal inputs for most services, other inputs including consumable materials, equipment and other facilities.

2. *Processes* are the procedures, methods and approaches by means of which services are provided. They may be codified as standard operating procedures in conformance with any statutory requirements (for example, for health and safety in sports facilities or race relations in housing allocation), professional codes of conduct (for example, for chartered surveyors, accountants or solicitors), professional management standards (for example, use of the BS 5750 [ISO 9000] Quality Management System by architects, solicitors and housing managers), good practice guidelines and so on.
3. *Outputs* are the services or products delivered by the contractor. Products include meals, reports, data, records, instructions to counsel and so on. Services include cleaning, servicing vehicles, satisfactory resolution of housing applications and enquiries, training, vacant properties or posts filled and so on. Standards (that is, quality of service) relate to such aspects as the comprehensiveness, reliability, availability, accuracy, relevance and timeliness of such outputs. Some standards are more easily specified than others, for example timeliness versus palatability of meals.
4. *Outcomes* are the results, effects or benefits derived from the service outputs. Outcomes will be of most concern to users of services. Contractors should generally be able to control (and clients to monitor) outputs. However, there is not necessarily a direct link between outputs and outcomes since the relationship between them will be influenced by other factors. For example, the outcome of housing management services will be affected by the characteristics of particular potential or actual users.

Subsequent to the purchaser–provider split, local governments are no longer formally responsible for *inputs and processes*, these being the responsibility of the private companies or public sector organizations holding service contracts. Instead, local governments are supposedly concerned only with controlling *outputs and outcomes*. The purchaser buys the service output in order to secure an outcome consistent with its policy strategy. It is the purchaser's responsibility to ensure that the output achieves the desired outcome at the lowest cost. In theory, this should result in a transformation from a *production-orientated public organization* to a *consumption-orientated regulatory body*. Hence, auditing and 'value for money' studies (in respect of inputs) and management initiatives such as efficiency studies and performance review (in respect of processes) are now supposedly the concern of the providers of services. Audits of outputs and of outcome effectiveness or quality are supposedly now the main concern of purchasers.

COMPETITION AND QUALITY OF SERVICE

It is arguable that competition for service contracts necessarily improves service quality. There is a well-developed academic rationale for this belief, namely public choice theory, although it is not without its critics (Mueller 1993; Self 1993; Udehn 1996). Put briefly, competition serves both to promote cost reductions (including elimination of wasteful bureaucracy) as firms compete through lower prices and improve quality to increase the competitive edge of the good or service. The argument is that quality improves because competitive firms are more responsive to consumer wants. This argument adopts a consumerist definition of quality which may not be appropriate in the case of the purchaser–provider split because the purchaser may not act solely on behalf of service users but, in addition, also act on behalf of the local electorate (not all of which may use the service directly).

Service quality may also be a part of the bureaucratic utility function which service managers and professionals are assumed to attempt to maximize (see Chapter 5). In this case, rather than increasing the welfare of service users, the benefits of improved quality are appropriated by employees, whether located in the client local authority or contractor side of the contract. Competitive forces can perhaps be assumed to limit the potential for contractor-side employees to capture the benefits of service quality, especially where there is a clear and categorical purchaser–provider (client–contractor) split. Such a split is most common for blue-collar activities. In comparison, client-side officers may seek to increase service quality (perhaps only according to their particular definitions) by emphasizing the need for further developmental activity (in which they participate) so as to maximize the budgets over which they exercise control. That part going to users will be greater the more choice they have in using the service and the greater the proportion of finance coming from user charges rather than from compulsory local and national taxes. That part going to users and to contractors will presumably be less, the greater the political power within the organization held by client-side officers. It, therefore, becomes difficult to justify further developmental activity in which service users are not fully represented.

Choice relates to scope for exit. However, exit is necessarily limited since, as already noted, CCT creates contestability for markets rather than for consumers. CCT does not create choices for local residents, for example regarding which firm will empty their bins or manage their local sports centres. Despite these caveats, in its 1991 White Paper 'Competing for Quality' the UK government stated that 'competition is the best guarantee of quality and value for money' (Cm 1730, p. 1).

However, as already noted in Chapter 11, a public choice framework for analysing quality demonstrates that an appreciation of any particular approach to (or definition of) quality can only be understood in terms of the institutional model, the policy and objectives of a particular institution and the dominance of particular stakeholders, defined as 'all those individuals or bodies inside or outside an organisation who are directly affected by what the organisation does' (Allen 1988, p. 8). If there is no user representation in the provision of services then those responsible for providing services may be constrained by their own political agendas, by the conflicting needs of individuals and groups and by limited resources (Younis 1995).

Case-studies covering the UK public sector suggest that it has been managers who have been empowered rather than consumers, there having been

> little or no real effort to democratise and open producer interests to new external considerations.... A narrow emphasis on 'value for money' and conformance ... has not sat well with the more ambitious talk about extending the involvement of users in the design, delivery and assessment of public services. (Kirkpatrick and Martinez Lucio 1995, p. 273)

This fits the *technocratic model* of power relationships within local authorities (see Chapter 1).

Other UK research results (reported in Chapter 14) support KML's analysis in finding high rates of no prior consultation with service users, especially in respect of external (as distinct from internal) end users, low rates of use of citizen/customer charters and a distinct lack of commitment to the future development of such charters. Hence, the scope for expression of voice by service users still seems to be limited.

These research findings are consistent with the claim that quality assurance mechanisms, customer care, performance measurement and decentralization are 'technologies' of control (Miller and Rose 1990). 'Public organisations, like any other, are "negotiated orders" in which there exists ample scope for human agents to interpret top-down initiatives, transform them and use them for alternative purposes' (Kirkpatrick and Martinez Lucio 1995, pp. 9–10). Indeed, Chapter 5 noted that bureaucrats will have an incentive to frustrate shirking control devices by advocating definitions and measures of performance which protect their positions.

Pollitt (1990, p. 439) notes the argument that 'far from being neutral representatives of the general will, managers have their own territorial interest'. Whether deliberately or by default of negligence, asymmetries of information restrict effective user participation in the design of services. This marginalization of users may be outweighed by the securing of other objectives relating to expenditure control and reduction, increasing control over professional groups and reducing trade union influence. In such cases, 'getting closer to the customer' is simply rhetoric because no substantive attempt has been made to actively involve users.

A FORMAL MODEL OF COST-EFFECTIVENESS

The claim that competition secures cost-effectiveness was noted above. For value for money to be achieved, competition must secure economy in the purchase of inputs and efficiency in the use of inputs to produce outputs. For quality of service to be achieved outputs must achieve the required outcomes in accordance with service objectives.

Costs (C) are the financial value of resources used in provision of the service, either derived directly from markets for inputs or imputed. Benefits (B) are measured in financial terms although, as already noted, in practice it may be difficult to derive accurate financial values of benefits. The financial benefit of service provision divided by its financial cost provides a measure of the relative value of the service $\frac{B}{C}$.

Both cost and benefit are direct functions (possibly non-linear) of output (O). These relationships are summarized in Identity 1.

$$\frac{B}{C} = \left(\frac{O}{C}\right)\left(\frac{B}{O}\right) \qquad \text{Identity 1}$$

Identity 1 can be disaggregated to demonstrate the compositional relationships between inputs (I) and effectiveness (E), both measured in nonfinancial terms. These are derived in Identity 2.

$$\frac{B}{C} = \left(\frac{I}{C}\right)\left(\frac{O}{I}\right)\left(\frac{E}{O}\right)\left(\frac{B}{E}\right) \qquad \text{Identity 2}$$

Identity 2 can be rearranged to derive a measure of *cost-effectiveness*. This is demonstrated in Identity 3.

$$\frac{E}{C} = \left(\frac{I}{C}\right)\left(\frac{O}{I}\right)\left(\frac{E}{O}\right) \qquad \text{Identity 3}$$

These identities can be used for the evaluation of performance, labelled in terms which directly relate to the purchaser–provider split.

E/C denotes *cost-effectiveness*;
I/C denotes *economy* in the purchase of inputs;
O/I denotes *efficiency* in the translation of inputs into outputs;
E/O denotes *outcome effectiveness* or *quality*.

The competition facilitated by the purchaser–provider split is assumed to improve cost-effectiveness. However, this depends on improvements in *either* the production function $\left(\frac{I}{C} \times \frac{O}{I}\right)$ *or* the outcome effectiveness (quality) function $\left(\frac{E}{O}\right)$ in Identity 3. Hence, Identity 3 clearly illustrates the possibility of a trade-off between efficiency gains and deterioration of quality. This would occur if competitive pressures to minimize the costs of inputs resulted in the purchase of lower quality inputs which were unable to produce the required quality of service, for example inadequately skilled or trained labour. If, however, there was substantial inefficiency in service provision prior to competitive contracting, it may be possible to reduce costs while simultaneously maintaining or improving quality of service.

There has been a substantial amount of research on the $\left(\frac{I}{C} \times \frac{O}{I}\right)$ component (see Chapter 14). In contrast with the extensive research regarding the impact of competitive tendering on service costs, there has been only very limited systematic empirical research of the effects of competitive tendering on quality of service, that is, on the $\left(\frac{E}{O}\right)$ component. This may be because of the difficulties of devising suitable measures of the quality of outcomes. It may also be because improvements in economy and efficiency can be secured much more quickly than improvements in quality.

A FORMAL ECONOMIC MODEL OF SERVICE QUALITY

Economists concerned with the accuracy of price indices (used to measure changes in the cost of living) have long recognized the need to take account of changes in the quality of goods and services in order to make standardized and accurate comparisons of the purchasing power of money at different points in time. The quality of commodities often changes over time, reflecting technological progress and innovation. Thus many consumer durables (such as television sets or cars) are of much better quality now than twenty or thirty years ago, both in terms of reliability and the features they incorporate. Much the same can be said of services provided by banks, telecommunications companies and so on. A comparison of the cost of a given product at two different points in time would therefore have to subtract the value of any increased quality in order to derive a methodologically valid measure of changes in the cost of living over time.

An improvement in the quality of a given product or service can be measured by assessing consumers' maximum willingness to pay for that improved quality or by the amount of money which they would have to give up in order to maintain their utility constant. Likewise, any deterioration in quality can be measured in terms of the amount of money that would have to be paid to consumers in order to compensate them fully for the reduction in their utility.

The valuation of changes in the quality of public services is still at the developmental stage, making use of *compensating variation* (Barnett 1993b; Cave *et al.* 1993; Payson 1994). Compensating variation is the amount of money that an individual is willing to accept (WTA) after an undesirable economic change in order to leave the individual with the same level of utility as before the change. Alternatively, compensating variation is the amount that the individual would be willing to pay (WTP) in order to secure a beneficial change. This can be illustrated in Figure 13.1 for an improvement in quality.

Figure 13.1 measures a change in the quality of a particular food item (such as a school meal – see Case-study 2 in Chapter 14). Quality can relate to taste, texture, appearance, nutritional value and so on. The last aspect of quality is used in the example because it can be measured objectively – unlike, say, flavour.

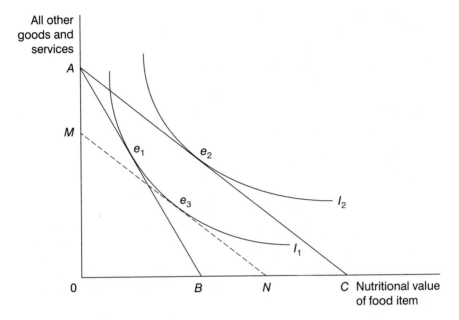

Figure 13.1 Economic measures of changes in quality

If Figure 13.1 related to a reduction in price of the food item, then the budget line pivots on point A from AB to AC, the equilibrium shifting from e_1 to e_2 as the individual moves to the higher level of utility represented by indifference curve I_2. The compensating variation would be measured by the value of AM, since that would be the reduction in total income that would be necessary in order to return the consumer to his or her original indifference curve I_1. The line MN is parallel to AC because it retains the same price relativities, with the result that the compensating variation equilibrium is e_3 – compared with e_1 before the price reduction.

However, rather than measuring the effect of a change in price, Figure 13.1 represents an improvement in quality. It assumes that the nutritional value of the food item can be measured on a linear scale. Any change in nutritional value is therefore a change in quality of the product. Assume that an improvement in nutritional value causes the same shift from AB to AC in Figure 13.1. The change in quality is therefore measured by AM, the compensating variation.

The economist's approach to measuring the quality of marketed outputs via *WTA* or *WTP* is therefore *positive* in attempting to determine the forces that cause changes in quality, and in objectively measuring those changes in monetary terms. Many other disciplines adopt a *normative* approach saying that it is desirable that quality *should* improve. Social policy commentators often argue that the quality of public sector services should be continually improved and can be improved by targeting them on low-income, deprived, or needy prioritized groups. Economic theory can objectively measure such subjective stances by measuring the median voter's *WTA* or *WTP* in terms of local tax costs. In this case, voter sovereignty for non-marketed outputs replaces consumer sovereignty for marketed commodities.

However, measures of *WTA* and *WTP* rely upon answers to hypothetical questions and are therefore subject to 'hypothetical bias' in that responses to questions about *WTA* and *WTP* are not in respect of real transactions. Responses may also display 'strategic bias' where respondents believe that they can profit by not revealing their true preferences (for example, understating *WTP* and overstating *WTA*). Such problems often result in implausible results and measures of *WTA* exceeding those of *WTP*, for example, comparing the amount of compensation required in respect of a deterioration in quality with willingness to pay for an improvement of the same amount. In addition, there may also be problems created by information asymmetries between producer and consumer and by a normative belief that services should be free, rather than paid for directly, at the point of use. Figure 13.1 also assumes that the individual's utility is independent of that of others and that the only constraint is income. Other problems relate to who should define and assess quality and the weighting of measures of *WTA* and *WTP* (necessary because averaging gives more weight to the views of those with high incomes than to those with low incomes). These issues are examined in more detail in Chapter 14.

OTHER APPROACHES TO QUALITY OF SERVICE

The economic analysis of quality of output is highly formalised, making use of compensating variation and *WTP* or *WTA*. Other academic disciplines analyse quality of service in much more eclectic and pragmatic ways, especially in considering the quality of inputs, processes, outputs and outcomes. The quality literature has an almost incomprehensible number of approaches to, and definitions of, quality (Davidson and Bailey 1995). Table 13.2 is therefore necessarily a reductionist and simplified summary of approaches to quality across a range of academic disciplines:

1. *The traditional approach* to assessment of quality is often described in terms such as expensive, superior or surpassing excellence. It implies exclusivity, whereas public services may seek inclusivity.
2. *The output-based approach* assumes that quality is a precise and measurable variable in which differences in quality are actually differences in features specific to the product, such as durability and reliability. The focus is on the finished product and how well it performs its function(s). Quality

Table 13.2 *A taxonomy of approaches to quality*

Approach	Characteristics and features		
Traditional	superior	exclusive	transcendant
Output-based	reliability	features	product
Process-based	production	manufacturing	managerial
Professional	absolutist	expert	scientific
User-based	individual	consumerist	
Value-based	democratic	social	

control in manufacturing is about reducing variations in production while quality in the service sector may require increased variations to take account of the differing needs of individuals.

3. *The process-based approach* assumes that it is possible to design managerial systems which ensure quality in the transformation of inputs into outputs, without necessarily having to precisely define and measure the quality of output itself. Although the end result (the output) is obviously important, the emphasis is on the *process* of production rather than on the *product*.

4. *The professional approach* is about meeting need but the emphasis is on how the supplier – as the acknowledged expert – defines that need in absolutist and scientific terms and how it can best be met.

5. *The user-based approach* is based on the premise that quality 'lies in the eye of the beholder' and that high-quality products are those that best meet the needs of the individual end-user. The consumerist approach underpins the UK's Citizen's Charter (Pollitt 1994) and the economist's approach to quality assessment based on willingness to pay.

6. *The value-based approach* is perhaps the one most appropriate to the public sector because it seeks to achieve a balance between different interests, in the interests of the community as a whole. It defines quality as fitness for purpose, responsive *and* empowering, the last characteristic relating to the active involvement of both users and citizens in the planning and delivery of services (i.e. voice). Thus, although this has elements of the consumerist approach, it is mainly based on collective and social issues expressed through democratic (rather than market) mechanisms. One such mechanism is decentralization (see Chapter 4).

Each of these various approaches to quality has a number of dimensions, Table 13.3 provides summary examples.

The tripartite categorization of Table 13.3 recognizes that both provider and user will have their own perspective of what constitutes quality of service. Process quality could be flawed since the professional view and the customer's view of service requirements need not coincide. As for customer

Table 13.3   *Dimensions of quality*

Customer quality	Professional quality	Process quality
service surroundings	core service	communication
amenity	technical	delivery
provider–user relationship	specification	people and systems
interpersonal relationship	performance	responsiveness
security	durability	competence
aesthetics	features	credibility
perceptions	reliability	
access	serviceability	
courtesy	conformance	
understanding		

quality, the interaction between user and provider may be a major influence on how the user judges quality. The importance of user–provider interaction depends on the particular service and the degree of interaction (for example, social worker and client), the important point being that the interpersonal relationship can influence the success of the service and even determine its nature (for example, the type of treatment).

CONCLUSIONS

This chapter has considered the meaning of competition within local government and outlined the conceptual and theoretical analysis of competition and quality. It demonstrated how both competition and quality can be promoted through the purchaser–provider split but also noted some possible adverse consequences of that split.

In so doing, it generated a number of testable hypotheses: for example, first, that the reduction in service costs and improvement in service quality are more substantial the greater the degree of competition for service contracts; and, second, that local authorities become transformed from production-orientated to consumption-orientated regulatory bodies.

Such hypotheses can only be tested by means of case-studies of particular services in countries which have introduced the purchaser–provider split. Hence, the next chapter examines the results of case-studies in the UK. It then provides a more informed and fuller conclusion in respect of the theoretical and a priori results of this chapter.

14 The Impact of the Purchaser–Provider Split in the UK

INTRODUCTION

Chapter 13 provided an exposition of the meaning and degree of competition in local government and considered how it can be enhanced via the purchaser–provider split. Reference was made to both economic theory and organization theory and a formal model of cost-effectiveness was developed. That model distinguished in conceptual terms the hypothesized impacts on both service costs and service quality. While retaining an economic perspective on service quality, it was recognized that the conceptualization of service quality requires a much broader approach than that conventionally adopted by economists.

This chapter tests some of the theoretical predictions of the impact of competition and of the purchaser–provider split on service costs and quality. It focuses on the UK experience, particularly in respect of quality of service. The management of sports and leisure services and provision of school meals are analysed as two case-studies in order to illustrate the need for a broad multidisciplinary approach in studying the effect of competition on the quality of service.

UK EVIDENCE

The purchaser–provider split underpinned the UK's compulsory competitive tendering (CCT) regime described in Chapters 12 and 13. During the 1980s and early 1990s the CCT regime was applied to the services listed in Table 13.1 plus local government construction-related activities. While the situation varies between UK local governments of differing political complexions, there is some evidence that the purchaser–provider split is having some of the expected effects.

The Role of Local Politicians

There appears to be a shift of local politicians' involvement away from concern with direct provision (and the necessity to win contracts to safeguard the jobs of local government employees) and towards a concern for service in general and a focus on the customer in particular (Walsh and Davis 1993). An unpublished Local Government Management Board (LGMB) survey of organizational change in 285 authorities, reported in Rao and Young (1995), found that in 43 per cent of authorities local politicians were 'closely involved' in developing policy and in 47 per cent they were 'closely involved' in setting standards. In contrast, only 15 per cent were 'closely involved' in specifying contracts and only 14 per cent likewise for monitoring them.

This progressive shift may reflect the development of the client side as a counterbalance to the contractor side of the purchaser–provider split. Generally, however, local politicians' involvement tends to be very limited, if only because of substantial delegation from local government service committees to both the client and contractor side. In the latter case, this is because local government committee cycles are not suited to the need for rapid decision making by the local authorities' in-house production units, known as Direct Labour Organizations (DLOs) for construction-related activities or Direct Service Organizations (DSOs) for the other services subject to CCT.

Hence, local politicians' involvement on the contractor side tends to be more sporadic, in response to particular issues. Their involvement on the client side is often through their position with external bodies, particularly school governing bodies. The end result is inadequate reporting of contract performance to, and monitoring by, local government committees. This structural deficit seems to have been reinforced by a cultural disjuncture, in that 'the division of client and contractor did not fit easily into the members' [that is, local politicians'] understanding of their roles' (Walsh and Davis 1993, p. 23).

Management Structures

Competition may lead directly to improved efficiency on the contractor side (see below) but will not necessarily have any impact (whether direct or indirect) on the client-side governance structures. The client-side management structure may be highly centralized (in the form of a single specialist client unit in the chief executive, treasurer or personnel departments), highly decentralized (individual service departments responsible for their own contracts), or the partially decentralized case of the 'lead client' department (for example, an education department taking on the client role for all building, cleaning, education and welfare catering or grounds maintenance work).

Notwithstanding the rationale for the purchaser–provider split, the regulations introduced by the 1992 Local Government Act do not specify the precise nature of that split. The result is that, rather than a distinct client–contractor split being all-pervasive, with DSOs and contracting units in separate departments (a 'hard split' – usually the case for refuse collection), some authorities have adopted 'twin-hatted' arrangements with client and contractor (DSO) roles being managed within the same service department (a 'soft split'). In the latter case, while formally separated, the client and contractor units (DSO) report to the same management structure, this being common for sports and leisure management (LGMB 1992). The most common approach is a multi-functional DSO where stand-alone DSOs operate multiple contracts (Walsh 1991).

Does Competitive Contracting Reduce Service Costs?

While results are necessarily qualified by methodological problems (Marsh 1991; Cope 1995), the evidence (some of which relates to countries other than the UK) is that competitive contracting yields significant cost savings in the supply of local authorities' services (for example, Audit Commission 1984b, 1987, 1988; Carnaghan and Bracewell 1993; Chaundy and Uttley 1993; Cubbin *et al.* 1987; Domberger *et al.* 1986, 1988; Ganley and Grahl 1988; IPF 1986; Kerley and Wynn 1991; Parker and Hartley 1990; Szymanski and Wilkins 1993; Uttley and Harper 1993; Vining and Boardman 1992; Voytek 1991; Walker 1993; Walsh 1991; Walsh and Davis 1993). Cost savings have arisen mainly from improved technical efficiency, changes in the capital–labour mix, better asset management and reductions in overheads – rather than through wage cuts and forced redundancies.

There may, of course, be cases where costs increase. This will especially be the case where markets are not truly contestable such that production function cost savings (if any) are insufficient to offset the administrative costs of contracting. Moreover, the figures for cost savings vary widely depending on the nature of the service, the country to which the data relate, and whether data are net of the costs of contracting and monitoring. However, gross savings of about 20 per cent are thought to be fairly representative (Bailey 1995; Cabinet Office 1996; Domberger and Jensen 1997).

These cost savings may be visualized in terms of a shift onto the agent's production possibility frontier (PPF). In addition, competitive contracting may result in the agent offering that combination of outputs on the PPF which maximizes the principal's welfare (see Figure 5.2). In that case, the reported cost savings underestimate the total economic gain to the principal.

Does Competitive Contracting Improve Quality of Service?

A 1995 survey of all local governments in Britain found that they were still closely concerned with the inputs and processes (defined in Chapter 13) used to produce services subject to CCT, perhaps even more so as a result of the rigours of contracting between the now split purchaser and provider (Bailey and Davidson 1996, 1997, 1999; Davidson and Bailey 1996). On balance, the purchasers' concern with quality is predominantly in respect of *processes* rather than *inputs* (both supposedly the responsibility of the provider) or *outputs* and *outcomes* (both supposedly the responsibility of the purchaser).

The emphasis on process – as evidenced by a reliance on mechanisms such as service delivery, error rectification and response times – suggests a heavily managerial process-driven approach to quality which is not necessarily balanced by any mechanisms related to effective outcomes. This predominantly managerial approach has not necessarily resulted in the purchaser becoming the advocate of the consumer. There is still a belief that it is the management of the process which will ensure a quality outcome. There may therefore still be a conflict of interest between client and contractor on the one hand and the user on the other.

The interpretation of these results is open to question, however, because Bailey and Davidson's finding that client-side officers devote the bulk of their time to inputs and processes does not necessarily prove a lesser interest in outputs and outcomes. Indeed, other UK research found that improvements in quality of outcomes had resulted from CCT because local authorities were forced to review services and improve monitoring of standards, now explicitly specified in contracts (Walsh and Davis 1993). That evidence is qualified, however.

First, it was based on evidence gained from a panel of only 40 English authorities, to the exclusion of those in Scotland and Wales. Second, the data was necessarily based on the subjective impressions of respondents (officers and politicians) during interviews (Walsh 1991). The research therefore adopted the definitions of quality implicit in the minds of those respondents. This was inconsistent with the admission that 'the user must be involved in the assessment' (Stewart and Walsh 1991, p. 24).

The strong possibility of bias on the part of the respondent should not be ignored. While it would be unrealistic to expect officers and managers to 'get it right first time' they would naturally have been reluctant to concede that quality of service had not been broadly maintained, since to admit that it had deteriorated would probably indicate failure to meet strategic service objectives. Failure to secure quality standards could relate to the mechanics of quality assurance systems (pre-tender questionnaires, contractual specifications, monitoring and arrangements for remedial action) or to broader corporate approaches to, and conceptions of, quality.

Objective evidence is harder to come by. While there were standards before CCT was introduced, quality simply was not actively monitored (Walsh and Davis 1993). Standards were tacit rather than written. Subsequent to introduction of CCT, the highly detailed nature of preparing, letting and monitoring contracts meant that this was largely officer-led. Local politicians usually set only very general guidelines, having little involvement and normally accepting recommendations to the service client committees on which they sat (Walsh 1991).

Specific objective standards cannot be written into contracts. Even if quality could have been effectively operationalised in early contracts, it is not necessarily the case that quality will have been secured since there were cases where standards were not being achieved. Effective monitoring and prompt remedial action is critical in such cases but will not have been helped by the finding that client-side information was commonly seen as poor and that the client side often lacked the necessary expertize in management skills.

Third, the Walsh and Davis evidence relates only to the first few years of the CCT regime (prior to 1993) whereas financial incentives to cut costs by reducing quality could persist beyond that date. According to Gaster (1995b, p. 132) 'one thing is certain. A quality programme takes a long time, three to five years at the minimum.'

Hence, it would seem that the Walsh and Davis research results regarding the maintenance of quality were, at best, highly provisional. This same caveat applies to an even more limited survey of nine local governments and twelve health authorities for 1989 and 1990 (the former usually involving the authority's treasurer or deputy) which concluded that 'for the majority of contracts (113 out of 199) quality was broadly maintained' (McMaster 1995, p. 421).

Sentiments regarding the need to involve service users over protracted periods of time are shared by the Audit Commission. In 1992/93, the Commission undertook detailed fieldwork in 13 English authorities, as well as shorter visits to an unspecified number of other authorities, and sampled another 40 authorities by means of a questionnaire on client-side aspects. It also consulted relevant professional bodies. While concluding that many local authorities continued to provide good quality services, elsewhere

> failings stem from one single cause – failure adequately to involve the consumers of the service in the contract process. In a well-managed authority the general public, the headteacher on behalf of the school, its students and their parents, the housing tenant and other consumers of the services delivered by the contractor play an important part in the specification and monitoring of a contract. (Audit Commission 1993, p. 1)

Expression of voice is clearly important in ensuring quality of service (see Chapters 3 and 4).

While Domberger and Hensher (1993) also found that, if anything, quality had improved, such improvements were not restricted to services subject to CCT. A government-sponsored survey of public opinion found that a majority of respondents thought that the standards of 28 public services had been improved or maintained during the previous year (ICM Research 1993). Such improvements seem to have been the result of local initiatives and influences more general than CCT, and not only of the Citizen's Charter (Pollitt 1994). Indeed, with the benefit of hindsight, Walsh (1995, p. 239) notes 'quality of service has become the overarching concept for the discussion of change in public service management'.

Rao and Young (1995) argue that managers are now looking at services from the perspective of the user and community rather than purely from their own perspective as providers. However, this research was also very limited in being based on face-to-face interviews with officers and councillors in only ten councils in England, Wales and Scotland. The authors describe their results as 'qualitative impressions' (Ibid., p. 1). In fact, specifically in respect of CCT, Davies and Hinton (1993) found that interest in quality was mainly the outcome of officer-led (rather than councillor-led) initiatives. This was a small-scale pilot study limited to north-west England and north Wales, such that its results must also be treated with caution.

The Bailey and Davidson research results also show that, notwithstanding the involvement of elected members, the approach to quality is, to a very great extent, determined by client officers and departments. Service users had little involvement in determining and monitoring contract standards in the first rounds of CCT. In particular, it was found that *technical* standards (such as error rectification, complaints procedures, response times and health and safety issues) are more commonly specified than *non-technical* standards (such as service output and expected outcomes). Standards which are of a non-technical nature are less amenable to precise specification and even less amenable to monitoring (LGMB 1995). As noted above, this emphasis on *process* is not balanced by any mechanisms related to effective *outcomes*. The role of service users is mainly that of complainant, a highly restricted negative and reactive role consistent with their limited role in determining standards. The clear implication is that purchasers are monitoring what is monitorable rather than what should be monitored (see Chapter 5). This raises the question as to how the client officers and other officials identified in this and earlier research can be so sure that service standards have remained constant or improved.

A REAPPRAISAL OF THE PURCHASER–PROVIDER SPLIT

Perhaps it is not surprising that British local governments continued to focus on inputs and, particularly, on processes. First, the quality of outputs ultimately depends on the quality of inputs and the ways in which they are used in order to deliver services. Second, the quality of outputs and outcomes is difficult to measure, especially so for white-collar and professional services. The specification of standards for outputs and outcomes may be partial or incomplete and it may be easier to define standards for inputs and processes. In such cases, recourse has to be made to assessing the quality of inputs and processes in order to gain a more comprehensive assessment of quality. Third, local authorities may wish to reduce the risk of occurence of inferior quality of outputs or outcomes because of the social, financial and political consequences. Hence they will wish to secure quality inputs and processes in order to reduce that risk.

Local governments as purchasers are naturally wary of allowing providers too much leeway in deciding how best to satisfy the authority's service requirements, both in terms of cost reductions and innovative practice. Hence, it is more often a question of the appropriate balance of quality specifications for inputs, processes, outputs and outcomes. This rationale for an emphasis on inputs and processes serves to qualify the UK government's guidance that quality specifications should relate to outputs wherever possible.

Indeed, the LGMB recommended that local authorities examine the competences and qualifications of staff employed by potential contractors. These characteristics can be assessed by requiring companies wishing to bid for a contract to complete a pretender questionnaire. Unnecessarily detailed questionnaires with an overemphasis on specifications for inputs and processes may be deemed anticompetitive. This is especially the case for those with irrelevant questions in respect of non-commercial matters such as employment conditions of own staff or political affiliation. Otherwise, staff qualifications, details of registration with professional bodies, bankruptcy, criminal offences, professional indemnity insurance, experience with similar contracts, quality management systems such as TQM (see Figure 3.4) and ISO 9000 (see Case-study 1 below), and other matters essential to the delivery and quality of service are of legitimate concern.

More generally, the optimal approach to securing the required quality and quantity of services will be likely to vary between local governments with different circumstances (for example, size and scope of contracts and service objectives) and within local governments for different services. However, it is unlikely that local governments will set standards for inputs, processes, outputs and outcomes without reference to the capabilities of potential contractors.

DOES THE PURCHASER–PROVIDER SPLIT SECURE BEST VALUE?

It is questionable whether the purchaser–provider split is necessary in order to obtain best value for money and whether competition is the best means by which the split can be operationalized. It has been argued that the purchaser–provider split has led to duplication, divisiveness and adversarial relationships within local government (between departments, between purchaser and provider, between senior managers and front-line workers) and that it is not clear that reorganization along market lines is more effective than hierarchies in delivering public services (Lewis *et al.* 1996).

This last point has been explicitly recognised by the UK central government in its report 'Competing for Quality' (Cabinet Office 1996). Although the report reviewed central government services subject to competitive contracting, its general conclusions are also applicable to local government because many of the same kinds of services were involved. In finding that the main source of cost savings were new working practices, irrespective of whether services were supplied by private sector organizations or in-house teams, it concluded that 'this casts doubt on the widely held presumption that the private sector is able to bring about efficiencies in ways the public sector cannot' (ibid., p. 8, para. 3.18).

The report therefore recommended greater selectivity in the use of competition to secure cost savings. 'If the only scope [for cost savings] arises from better management to make staff work harder, the answer is probably to improve management not contract out' (ibid., p. 17, para. 3.53). Other cost savings arise from securing economies of scale, re-engineering service processes, giving greater flexibility for in-house teams to suggest more cost-effective approaches to service delivery, avoiding unnecessarily small service contracts and, of course, ensuring adequate competition. Nonetheless, 'competition should be judged against other mechanisms for achieving improvements in value for money in the light of the nature of the activity, the capabilities of the market, and the best approach determined on a case by case basis' (ibid., p. 17, para. 3.49).

Within local government specifically, adversarial relationships, divisiveness and demotivation of employees may be avoided by twin-hatted arrangements facilitating common purpose and collaboration between purchaser and provider. Nonetheless, interdepartmental rivalry created by a more clear split may inhibit the development of co-operation and partnership (Rao and Young 1995). Hence, contrary to the efficiency arguments for interdepartmental rivalry noted above, the ultimate impact on policy and strategy may be rather more complicated (see Shaw *et al.* 1993).

Collaboration, participation and co-operation may be more effective than market forces, for example where workers feel that they 'own' internal rather than external processes. Moreover, in many cases, being in the non-profit sector, providers are not motivated by profits and service users have little scope for choice. Both of these characteristics are at odds with private markets upon which much of the theory is based. Collaboration may also be less costly than competitive contracting, especially in terms of the costs of implementing the formal tendering, contracting and monitoring regimes. The regimes used for public procurement of physical items may not be as easily adapted for the supply of personal social services as for the collection of household waste. Put more formally, transaction costs are perhaps much greater for professional than for manual services (see Table 13.1).

These and other considerations led the UK government to announce that it intends to replace the CCT regime with a more comprehensive 'Best Value' regime (DOE 1997). The Best Value regime will be concerned not just with economy and efficiency but also with effectiveness and the quality of local government services. The new regime will therefore address cost-effectiveness (defined in Chapter 13) and will cover all local government services, not just those previously subject to CCT.

There will continue to be a clear presumption in favour of open competition where there are other potential providers in the market. Local authorities will have to demonstrate why competition is inappropriate in particular circumstances. Hence, while competition will continue to be an important part of the new regime, it will no longer be the only means of securing value for money.

In effect, CCT is to be replaced by voluntary competitive tendering (VCT) within a permissive framework which emphasizes local choices and local accountability (that is, voice) rather than central prescription. It is being extended to other local government activities, including the management of municipal housing, construction-related professional services (architecture, engineering and property management services), computing, legal services, financial services, personnel, and corporate and administrative services.

Although the Best Value regime was still evolving at the time of writing (early 1998), it is likely that the purchaser–provider split will be maintained for many aspects of local government service provision. Best Value highlights the need for local authorities to produce meaningful and robust information in order that those who pay for and benefit from their services can judge performance. As will be demonstrated by the case-studies below, the CCT regime has largely failed to involve service users in the specification and monitoring of service standards. If it has the effects expected of it, the Best Value regime will shift the focus more towards outputs and outcomes and so address the undue focus on inputs and processes under the CCT regime.

QUALITY OF SERVICE CASE-STUDIES

Many of the above general points and analysis, in both this chapter and Chapter 13, can be illustrated by studying the impact of competitive contracting on the quality of two services: sports and leisure management and catering. Without such case-studies it is very difficult to appreciate fully the many aspects of the purchaser–provider split, competitive tendering and quality of service.

Case-Study 1: Sports and Leisure Management

Sports and leisure management is a particularly interesting case-study since, compared with the other services subject to CCT, it has greater variety and requires greater flexibility. This makes evaluation of tenders for contracts more problematic and requires a greater element of negotiation between client and contractor regarding service characteristics, including any requirement to upgrade capital facilities either before or during the course of contracts. Hence, contractors would appear to have more leeway as regards day-to-day operations and so there is more potential for high transaction costs (see Chapter 13).

A general discussion of the types of sports and leisure facilities provided by local authorities is available elsewhere (Bailey *et al.* 1993). The most relevant characteristic is that sports and leisure management competes for customers since they have the option of using (and usually paying for) the service – unlike, say, for collection of domestic refuse.

The CCT legislation defines this service as the management of sports centres, golf courses, swimming pools and so on. LGMB data show that 56 per cent of sport and leisure management contracts up to 1995 were awarded without competition and that, as for catering (education and welfare), the average number of bids per contract was less than two. However, as already noted, the number of bidders is not an accurate measure of the degree of contestability. There may have been many potential bidders, of which only a few actually bid – perhaps because they already knew that the DSO was operating efficiently. On the other hand, it may take time for the private sector to develop sufficiently to be able to contest contracts. Nonetheless, it is the *threat* of competition, rather than the number of bidders, which is the measure of contestability and which drives incumbent DSOs to improve their operating efficiency.

LGMB figures also show that over four-fifths of (non-franchise) work for this service remained in-house (91 per cent by value and 85 per cent of contracts by 1995). In other words, contracting-in was the norm (see Figure 4.2). The limited extent of contracting-out for this and other services subject to CCT suggests that the realization of economies of scale by one contractor holding many small contracts will have been significant in only a relatively few local authorities (see Chapter 2).

Average contract value was just under £0.5 million per annum in 1995, usually on a 'management fee only' basis. The Audit Commission (1993) estimated that client-side cost averaged 1.5 per cent of total annual expenditure, the second lowest average client-side cost after catering (education and welfare), presumably for the same reasons and with the same caveat about the need for effective involvement of users (see Case-study 2 below).

Daily or weekly supervision of contractors is common (two-thirds of local authorities) and both the incidence of routine (as opposed to responsive) meetings with contractors (again two-thirds) and use of quality management systems (a fifth) to facilitate monitoring is highest for this service. Some 59 per cent of authorities have customer complaints procedures in place, this the second highest after refuse collection. However, while sports and leisure management has the most developed and diverse monitoring systems, only 7 per cent use customer sampling techniques. Only a fifth of authorities have a contractual requirement that contractors achieve certification under BS EN ISO 9000.

Walsh and Davis (1993) found that, among their panel of 40 English authorities, there was a tendency towards two-part contract specifications: the first stating the authority's general philosophical position and strategy (for example, people-based recreation for all, rather than elite sports and sporting excellence), the second providing detailed specifications for programmes, equipment, staffing and so on. Hence, being a complex service and recognizing the expertise and detailed knowledge of contractors, there was more of a tendency in leisure management than in other services to ask the contractor to interpret contract conditions in cases where precise definitions were not possible. In addition, the major responsibility for marketing of programmes and facilities, as well as for service development, rested with the contractor.

All of the Walsh and Davis panel authorities adopted deficit guarantee contracts, usually with income sharing or profit sharing (see Bailey 1995, ch. 15 for a full discussion of the different types of contract). This means that client authorities cover debt charges and costs of building maintenance and pay a management fee to the contractor. As already noted in Chapter 13, this increases contestability by reducing high entry costs and the high sunk costs of exit. The contractor meets all other costs and retains any income from user-charges in accordance with any agreement regarding sharing income or profits with the client. This arrangement minimizes risk for the client and provides incentives for the contractor to increase usage rates. It does, however, require fairly intensive financial monitoring (although this is aided by computerised till systems).

Walsh and Davis (1993) found that the proportion of work inspected more than doubled from 15 per cent before CCT to 40 per cent after (compared with an increase for all services from 24 to 42 per cent). Because of the nature of the service, monitoring was seen as requiring a mixture of generalist and specialist activity.

Sports and leisure management makes relatively extensive use of statistical sampling, reflecting the use of computers to monitor financial aspects of contracts in particular. Their use also for systematic monitoring of the views of users meant that there was most involvement of the public for monitoring in the case of sports and leisure management. This illustrates how political decentralization via consultation can complement decentralization to markets (see Figure 4.2). Walsh and Davis found that 78 per cent of their panel of authorities used public surveys, 35 per cent made use of user complaints, 19 per cent employed user panels, and 11 per cent had established user-consultative committees for this service. However, Wheeler and Richards (1993) argue that the widespread absence of non-financial measures of performance makes it very difficult, if not impossible, to monitor the effectiveness of sports development policies.

The service has to be firmly based within the leisure strategy of local authorities. Sports and leisure management contracts therefore presumably encompass the authority's political stance applied to leisure policy. That political stance may relate to considerations of equity in the distribution of service outputs between high and low income groups. It may also relate to considerations of efficiency in that sport is not a pure private good but, instead, exhibits positive externalities (and merit good characteristics) in terms of improved health and well-being.

However, there was some concern that the client–contractor split would lead to fragmentation of the service, and also that the decline in stand-alone specialist leisure departments would mean a loss of skilled and experienced personnel. In that case authorities would be less likely to develop sports and recreation strategies. This illustrates *knowledge/skill embeddedness* (see Chapter 13).

Research in the early 1990s by the Sports Council found that less than half of local authorities had a general leisure strategy and only a third had a specific sport and recreation strategy. Sports development policy was rarely accompanied by specific measurable throughput targets. Hence, even where contractors were given policy parameters within which to work, in most cases the client local authority was unable to monitor outputs and so unable to determine whether policies were actually being implemented and objectives met. This illustrates *bounded rationality* (see Chapter 13).

Initially, contracts were usually prepared by small groups of professional leisure officers (on both the client and contractor sides), sometimes assisted by consultants and following advice from the local authority associations and such bodies as the Institute of Leisure and Amenity Management (Walsh and Davis 1993). Dependence on use of professionals occured if only because of the absence of explicit written policies and inadequate management information systems (including data bases). Indeed, lack of a strategic review of the objectives of the service during contract preparation seems to have been the rule rather than the exception (Nicholls 1995a). This posed particular difficulties for client officers and others when drafting contract specifications, for example how programmes and prices promoted achievement of service objectives.

Drawing on his rather small sample of 12 local authority leisure departments, Nicholls goes as far as to suggest that, in creating the new role of client officer, CCT has introduced another powerful stakeholder (defined in Chapter 13) to the policy context of the leisure and recreation service. Such new officers 'could have a very significant impact on determining the direction of the service through the contract specification. They could also influence future decision making through the dissipation of new information collected in the course of their monitoring function' (Nicholls 1995a, p. 52). This is especially so because, according to Nicholls' research, councillors' intervention was limited since they lacked technical expertize, there was insufficient time at the first round of tendering for them to become fully conversant with contract specifications, and they were more concerned with who won the contract (prefering the DSO to win rather than the private contractor) than with what precisely was in it.

While it was more difficult for non-specialists to be involved at the initial stage, many contracts made provision for market research and for increased user involvement through, say, annual open public meetings and/or user surveys, as well as in formal monitoring systems. Such actions are supposedly made necessary by the fact that users often pay for services and alternatives exist elsewhere. In this sense, users have *exit* as well as *voice* (see Chapters 3 and 4). Hence the service has to be customer responsive. Of particular concern is the need during the contract period to ensure service development in response to changing tastes and demands, always provided appropriate to public needs. Static contract specifications could inhibit evolution of a customer-responsive service.

However, Nicholls (1995a) argues that client officers could selectively feed councillors information in order to influence their decisions on particular issues (as distinct from high-level decision-making). Such influence is constrained because the client officer acts as part of a corporate centre along with the chief leisure officer and possibly the chairperson of the leisure committee. Nevertheless, the increased frequencies with which councillors meet in committee and the increased volume of information means that client officers can exert more influence on the development of service strategies. This is consistent with Niskanen's model of bureaucracy and the public choice analytical framework (see Chapters 5, 11 and 13).

In addition to possible client officer distortions of service objectives through selective use of information, Nicholls (1995b) argues that it is difficult to design a contract that ensures that contractors' behaviour achieves those objectives. Contract specifications that are flexible enough to allow the service to adapt to changing public demand (for example, for step aerobic classes or provision for the unemployed) require a high degree of trust. There is therefore a high degree of *bounded rationality* with respect to future service requirements, together with a considerable scope for *opportunism* on the part of the contractor because of the diverse nature of the services specified in contracts. Hence, there is a tradeoff between the need for flexibility of contract specifications and the need to limit the scope for opportunistic behaviour by contractors.

Opportunistic behaviour could occur at the tendering stage pre-contract if tenderers submitted unrealistically low bids (that is, for payment to manage the service). If successful, *adverse selection* occurs (that is, the winner's curse – see Chapter 13). Such contractors could exploit flexible contract specifications in order to reduce management costs, for example employing poorly-qualified staff. However, such short-term incentives are balanced by longer-term incentives relating to contract renewal, the contractor having to be seen to provide a good quality of service consistent with the spirit, as distinct from the letter, of the contract. This is especially the case if contractors have invested in capital facilities which they do not own.

The policy implication is that local authorities should seek capital investments by contractors (to create *asset specificity* on the contractor side, balancing that on the client side) and limit contract length (to increase the threat of imminent competition). Shorter contract periods also facilitate faster responses to both clients' learning by experience and market development. Contractors will presumably favour longer contracts with limited investment, DSOs (unlike private sector companies) not having access to investment finance.

These qualifications do not, of course, obviate the need to tighten up the letter of contract specifications so as to reduce the scope for opportunistic behaviour by contractors. Nicholls (1995b) argues that small local authorities will face particular difficulties in this respect because they have fewer specialist officers available to work on contract specifications. Such authorities may perhaps have more to gain from use of consultants for such purposes.

The key relationship in this context is between the client officer and the contractor (for example, the DSO manager), one which Nicholls describes as a long-term tactical investment in a contractual relationship (if not altruism), both parties deriving economic value from preserving the contract. Ultimately, they must have a good working relationship with each other if a quality service is to be provided in accordance with the spirit of the contract and so that the chances of contract renewal are increased. Such a working relationship is likely to have been improved where contracts have been prepared by small groups of professional leisure officers on both the client and contractor sides.

Provision of a quality service can lead to an accumulation of 'political capital' which can also improve chances of success in bidding for extra resources for the service and for contracts to be renegotiated by mutual consent. Such incentives are substantially reduced if either the contractor does not expect or want contract renewal or if DSO managers are convinced that there is no need to guard against future competition, either because it does not exist or because the local authority is ideologically opposed to external contractors. The scope for opportunism is increased in such cases. Given that it is generally accepted that management processes have been improved, any transaction costs post-CCT should be compared with any organizational slack (X-inefficiency) that existed prior to CCT (see Chapter 5).

Conclusions on Competition for Sports and Leisure Management

In summary, this sports and leisure management case-study illustrates the need to take account of institutional form and the nature of the contract (including any sharing of income or profits) when considering the validity of the neoclassical economist's argument that competition necessarily improves cost effectiveness (that is, increased quality and/or cost reductions). It is clear that sports and leisure management contracts have to reach a satisfactory balance between a number of potentially conflicting criteria: the authority's social objectives, the financial objectives of contractors, the changing demands of users, and the need to maintain the semblance of effective competition alongside stability of service. It cannot simply be assumed that increased competition through increased contestability will necessarily improve service quality. The governance structure is the crucial factor.

Case-Study 2: School Meals Catering

The school meals service had already undergone substantial changes during the 1980s, prior to the introduction of CCT (Audit Commission 1993; Walsh and Davis 1993). The average annual contract value for this service was £1.7 million in 1994, just under half of current contracts having been won without competition from private sector catering companies (LGMB 1994). The average number of bids per contract was less than two, local authorities' own Direct Service Organizations (DSOs) winning 75 per cent of contracts, 85 per cent by value.

Despite this general lack of competition for contracts, there is – as in sports and leisure management – competition for customers (in this case with food outlets outside schools). Again like sports and leisure management, contractors have incentives to attract customers and increase sales because of the positive effect on revenues. Hence, it is increasingly important to take account of consumers' views, both because schools have increasing autonomy in managing their own budgets (see Chapter 12) and because paying pupils can go elsewhere. Those views could be expected to relate to contract specifications and monitoring, aided by effective provision of information and effective use of complaints systems and suggestions.

The UK 1980 Education Act gave local education authorities (LEAs) control over both charges and nutritional standards for meals served in their schools. It therefore changed the balance of power between the various stakeholder groups. School pupils are only one of a number of stakeholders, others including nutritionists (who use expert criteria to assess the quality of meals), social policy commentators (who argue that free school meals are an instrument of social policy in favour of low-income families), the UK Treasury (which is concerned with the public expenditure costs of meals), trades unions (which have favoured labour-intensive, cooked, meals to protect jobs), parents of pupils (who may regard school meals as a useful means of keeping children at school all day) and pupils (who can be expected to judge meals in terms of individual rather than collective choice, particularly as regards taste and fashion).

Ultimately, the institutional framework determines the number and range of stakeholders (see Chapter 13) whose views are taken into account when defining and monitoring quality. Any such definition is necessarily influenced by the relative power of different groups of stakeholders, whether in terms of purchasing power or of political power.

Even if nutritionists regard pupils and their parents as not competent to judge what food is good for them (that is, school meals are regarded as a merit good), pupils (more so than parents) have the choice whether to pay for and eat the food, to pay for it yet discard it, or not to buy the meal at all. Both lack of customers and 'plate waste' may be proxy measures of quality of service as judged by the ultimate service user.

The 1980 Act reduced the influence of nutritionalists by doing away with the statutory requirement for LEAs to provide the traditional cooked meal of meat, two types of vegetable and a dessert. This type of meal has become increasingly inappropriate in multi-ethnic schools and in terms of the internationalization of food tastes (such as pizzas, pasta and beefburgers). Prior to 1967, the Treasury paid LEAs a specific subsidy for each school meal served. However, that subsidy was subsumed into the general block grant (see Chapter 9) paid to local governments so that schools face a much greater incentive to adopt a cafeteria-style service with snacks (rather than labour-intensive cooked meals) in order to reduce their costs. Moreover, in 1975, the then Department of Education and Science noted that closely prescribed nutritional standards were incompatible with allowing pupils to choose from a menu what they wish to eat (Rose and Falconer 1992). Hence, the 1980 Act allowed LEAs to provide snacks as part of a cafeteria service. School children can choose to buy snacks such as biscuits and drinks in order to supplement any food from home which is eaten in the cafeteria. Hence, pupils have a much greater degree of choice than a decade or so ago.

More than 4 million school meals are served daily in the UK, over 1 million children receiving free meals in 1995/96 because their parents qualified for Income Support (a state welfare payment). The numbers of children eligible for free school meals rose sharply during the early 1990s. These figures qualify the perception that the customer pays because the proportion of pupils actually paying for their meals has been falling, particularly sharply in some economically-depressed LEAs. This emphasizes the increasingly important welfare implications of school meals for low-income groups.

Whereas low-paid employment is supplemented by Family Credit, a state benefit which includes provision for school meals costs, nonetheless the children of such families may also be heavily dependent upon school meals in providing a substantial proportion of their daily nutritional requirements at comparatively low cost. A school meal, the average cost of which in 1995 was £1.09, provides between 30 and 43 per cent of a child's average daily energy intake (Doughty 1995). However, between 1979 and 1991, the numbers of children in England taking school meals dropped by a third from 64 to 42 per cent. Moreover, the lower takeup rates of free school meals for secondary pupils (aged between 11 and 18 years) than for primary pupils (aged 5–11) in London suggests a more discriminating clientele (Brindle 1994).

The supposed causes of these trends are that children increasingly prefer to take packed lunches in order to reduce time queuing (and so allow time for lunch-hour clubs and other activities), to allow them to sit with whom they choose, to reduce costs, and to allow more individualized choice as regards food. Parents also have more control of their children's diet, including its complementarity with evening meals. CCT for the school meals service has increased the pressure (on both private contractors and DSOs, the latter having to achieve a 5 per cent rate of return on capital) to sell meals and snacks that children want, rather than what might be deemed good for them.

However, there have long been concerns about the health aspects of the average diet (that is, the negative externalities arising from a poor or nutritionally-unbalanced diet). These concerns have been highlighted since the abolition of statutory dietary requirements in 1980. The National Heart Forum (NHF), which represents 35 health and nutrition organizations in the UK, argues that, as a consequence, the nutritional quality of meals varies considerably between different parts of the country and children's diets have deteriorated despite greater choice (Weale 1995). The NHF and the School Meals Campaign argue that many school meals contain too much fat and that too few LEAs regularly check that the content of their school meals is healthy. The NHF note that British schoolchildren eat too much fat, sugar and salt and not enough fruit and vegetables. Such a diet is thought to cause heart disease and cancer later in life, as well as tooth decay and obesity during childhood. More recently, the 'BSE in beef' ('mad cow disease') scare highlighted the other health aspects of quality, namely how food is produced. Some LEAs themselves decided to remove beef products and/or pure beef from menus in all schools, some only in primary schools (on the grounds that secondary school pupils are capable of making their own decisions) and some only decided to alter menus after consulting either headteachers and/or parents.

This pattern of decision-making illustrates a number of points. First, the complexity of perceptions about who constitutes the customer and the extent to which individual consumers of different age groups can be left to make their own consumption decisions based on conflicting views of the health-related aspects of the foods they eat. Second, whether LEAs have a protective paternalistic role separate from that of both the UK Department of Health and the Ministry of Agriculture Fisheries and Food (and even from that of the European Union). Third, it emphasizes the role of professional pressure groups outwith (as well as within) local and central government. Fourth, the income-protection aspects of free school meals emphasize the social welfare characteristics of the service.

It is evident that there are various aspects of the quality of school meals including nutritional value, public confidence in the safety of prepared foods, and pupil choice. However, quality criteria suitable for inclusion in contracts need to be much more specific. Illustrative examples of a school catering contract are provided by the Audit Commission (1993). *Inter alia*, such a contract can be expected to state that school meals be nutritious (possibly utilizing central government's voluntary nutritional guidelines) and tasty, based on a rotating four-week cycle menu, kitchens being regularly inspected for conformance with health and safety regulations, and with a 'hot line' for complaints. It may also require a cafeteria service (to allow pupils flexibility regarding timing and lunch partners) and that food intended to be hot is just that. Some of these criteria are technical and hence easy to monitor (such as temperature). But who should determine what is in the menu, what constitutes 'tasty' and how effectively are complaints dealt with?

It is the responsibility of management to provide the leadership, commitment and support necessary to develop quality assurance. It is therefore vital that management (whether at individual school level or local education authority level) has a clear understanding of quality assurance in respect of school meals. Besides the quality of *inputs* (ingredients for school meals and so on), education and training (maintenance of food hygiene and so on) are necessary components of the production *process* in order to enhance the abilities of the workforce and to foster their participation in quality improvements.

The *outcome* or effectiveness of the final *output* depends upon both technical and behavioural aspects of quality. The behavioural aspect relates to how (or even if) the output is used and the extent to which it satisfies the needs or wants of the final user. The behaviour of pupils in respect of their school meals choices is a case in point, choosing whether or not to eat them in the first place and, if so, which particular food items.

It is questionable whether such contractual quality criteria result in greater levels of satisfaction among service users. The Audit Commission found that *prior to CCT*, consumers were often dissatisfied with the service provided. Any specifications were usually set by the service departments rather than by headteachers at the point of service delivery. What is more, those specifications were not always followed and it was difficult for consumers to obtain redress. The Commission says that all this *should* have changed as a result of introduction of CCT.

In fact, 'a survey of 150 schools carried out by the Commission's auditors in a sample of authorities revealed significant dissatisfaction with the provision of catering services. In answer to the question: "how well do you feel the present contract meets your needs?", nearly a third of respondents answered "badly" or "not very well"' (Audit Commission 1993). Although based on a very small percentage sample, these results are supported by another survey on the impact of the Local Management of Schools (LMS) initiative with over a quarter of respondents judging services to be 'poor' or 'very poor' (LGMB 1992).

The explanation of these continuing levels of dissatisfaction may be that the first round of contracts tended to codify existing inputs or processes. This possible explanation is supported by the fact that, of the services subject to CCT, catering had been found to be the service where there was *least* failure to perform against contract, highly dispersed services such as building cleaning and grounds maintenance having experienced the highest failure rates (Walsh and Davis 1993). Nonetheless, Walsh and Davis found evidence of reduced choice, 'menu fatigue' and switching from fresh to frozen foods, perhaps explained by the limited scope for further cost savings noted above.

Currently, with the exception of some very small single-institution contracts, most contracts are for all schools in an authority. All-schools contracts necessarily constrain the extent to which schools' preferences can be catered for, this perhaps being particularly significant where schools differ markedly in the proportions of ethnic and/or religious minorities with differing dietary cultures.

The research results described and analysed elsewhere (Bailey 1998b) suggest that the ultimate users of the school meals service (that is, the pupils themselves) are relatively underrepresented in quality assurance procedures. This is perhaps the inevitable result of the institutional and policy context within which the school meals service operates. Nonetheless, those who ultimately eat the food (or who choose not to) are not significantly involved in the determination of quality criteria. Their role tends to be residualized to that of complaints, after the event of unsatisfactory service. Their voice in the determination of quality standards has therefore not been significantly increased. While users do have the power of exit to private sector caterers outwith school premises, this is limited by the high levels of dependence on free school meals in certain LEAs. Provision of free meals becomes part of the social policy of local authorities with multiply-deprived neighbourhoods within their administrative areas. Nevertheless, the fact that high proportions of meals are provided free should not of itself qualify the extent to which pupils have a say in the determination of quality.

In practice, however, the representation of users' views is operationalized through school headteachers and/or through parents' representation on school governing bodies. School pupils themselves seem restricted to limited choices through cafeteria services. Plate waste and/or eating elsewhere are the ultimate pupil sanctions.

Bailey (1998b) found that the approach to quality (for example, value-based or user-based – see Chapter 13) was overwhelmingly determined by elected members and service managers. Elected members could be acting on behalf of service users and/or incorporating their own set of values into quality of service. If, in fact, members simply approve (rather than initiate) the policy recommended by service managers, then a managerial approach is dominant. Managers' recommendations could already incorporate the value set of local politicians, such that there is no need for the latter to initiate the contractual specification of service policy. However, it would be more difficult for local politicians actively to represent users (schools and their pupils) in such a case. The quality standards required were almost invariably determined by the purchasing local authority, current users only featuring in half of cases and potential/future users in only a quarter. Complaints procedures had not been prioritized as an aspect of quality management. Instead, there had been a much broader approach to setting and monitoring standards.

Conclusions on School Meals and Competition
CCT and LMS have given school pupils and their parents more of both political and market power, perhaps qualified by the high levels of free school meals in some authorities. In this sense, school meals quality is both a politicized concept and one which is increasingly subject to market forces. The definition of quality requires a pluralistic approach which must be underpinned by effective communication between all stakeholders so as to allow the achievement of quality within a framework that is economically efficient, dynamic and responsive.

This case-study has made clear the multifaceted nature of service quality in respect of school meals catering. To believe that competition would necessarily lead to an improvement in service quality as perceived by the ultimate service user is clearly oversimplistic. The impact on service quality ultimately depends on the ways in which competition changes management practice, changes the relationships between managers and local politicians and changes the financial leverage of schools (in terms of awarding their own contracts) and their pupils (in choosing whether or not to buy meals).

CONCLUSIONS

Chapter 13 made clear that there is considerable scope for competition to be introduced within the local government sector. Of the many ways within which competition can be introduced, the purchaser–provider split is the most radical in terms of its implications for local governance structures and in terms of its focus on the cost-effectiveness of services. However, despite the a priori deductive logic of the purchaser–provider split, the UK evidence is that local governments continue to be concerned with inputs and, particularly, processes rather than just with outputs and outcomes. Indeed, the purchaser–provider split seems to have resulted in British local governments paying more attention to inputs and processes because of the formalities of contracting. This concern permeates every stage of the CCT regime, from pre-selection (shortlisting) procedures, through tender evaluation and acceptance, to monitoring performance of the contractor.

In this sense the theoretical development of the purchaser–provider model is too simplistic in hypothesizing that client local authorities will only be concerned with outputs and outcomes and so be able to concentrate on strategic policy issues. To hypothesize that they will entrust to contractors concern about inputs and processes is clearly wrong. This argument is based on a simplified market scenario where purchasers and providers are anonymous parties to transactions. While this may be an accurate depiction of most retail markets, such anonymity seems rare elsewhere.

Purchaser and provider are often in a highly interdependent relationship, the latter providing components or services to the former and both being equally concerned with the quality of the intermediate product. Even where there is a clear purchaser–provider split, a close working relationship between contractors and contracting units may develop in order to resolve operational difficulties. Providers may also be concerned with service development, especially if it is likely to increase their chances of contract renewal. There is little firm evidence from the UK's CCT regime that can substantiate claims of improved services to users, as distinct from improved managerial processes.

Given the human, social and political consequences of failure to provide local government services in the desired quantities and qualities, it is likely that local governments will increasingly have a highly structured and comprehensive approach to ensuring delivery of quality services by the contractors upon whom they depend. Such a focus is clearly not solely due to difficulties in measuring and assessing the quality of outputs and subsequent outcomes.

The above analysis of research results effectively questions whether competition is both a necessary and sufficient condition for an improvement in the quality of local government services. A public choice analysis of the operations and outcomes of quasi-markets casts doubt on claims that quality is necessarily improved for service users, as distinct from other stakeholder groups. Hence, there is still a long way to go before it is certain that the purchaser–provider split has brought about the shift of emphasis to service strategy in respect of outputs and outcomes. Clearly, the transformation of local governments from production-orientated to consumption-orientated organizations is much more complex than implied by the a priori deductive logic of the purchaser–provider split.

Voice is undoubtedly of much greater importance than exit for the services typically subject to competitive tendering. Quality of service is crucially dependent upon the ways in which consumers, users and citizens can express their needs and influence the ways in which they are met. At present, however, UK research finds that user involvement is limited and is more reactive than proactive. This suggests that user voice remains weak. The exceptions tend to be in those services where users can be clearly identified – such as tenants' associations.

Though quality of service can be improved by taking account of the wishes of users, there is still a need for a strategic vision of how each service should develop in the future. Without such a vision, stakeholders (including customers) have no precise focus for discussion of their expectations of the service. In other words, increased use of customer satisfaction surveys is not necessarily a proper substitute for collective representation and public discussion about the nature of public services. All stakeholders should be able to influence plans for services directly, be involved in their monitoring and evaluation and be able to suggest ways of improving them. A true partnership between producers and consumers should be achieved, one which involves all stakeholders. Determination of quality should not be predominantly one-sided. The author is clearly taking a normative stance in this respect.

To claim that the UK's CCT regime has maintained or improved service quality remains an unproven assertion derived from a particularly narrow stakeholder perspective which is predominantly managerial and professional in content. The evidence is clear that CCT has improved technical efficiency by economizing on the use of inputs and reducing organizational slack on the contractor side. It is still open to doubt, however, that CCT has improved either allocative efficiency or quality or is even necessary for the latter's improvement.

In addition, CCT may have caused adverse equity outcomes to the extent that it reduced real wages and led to a deterioration in other conditions of employment. There may also have been knock-on implications in terms of greater social security payments as a result of lower rates of pay and higher unemployment. However, cuts in wages and forced redundancies have generally not been the main source of cost savings. Instead, the main cost savings seem to have arisen from improved technical efficiency, changes in the capital–labour mix, better asset management and reductions in overheads.

More generally, the emphasis on customer, as distinct from citizen, requires radical changes in the traditional forms of public sector organization and control. The traditional emphasis on legality, statutory duties, value for money and equality of treatment based on need is increasingly complemented by direct accountability to service users as one group within a changing spectrum of stakeholders. Put simply, the conception of quality is increasingly less a collectivist, paternalistic and inward-looking, institution-based, concept and increasingly more an outward-looking responsive relationship with individual customers.

Even if increased attention is given to the preferences of service users, the conceptualization and implementation of the quality of public sector services is necessarily much broader than the market-based approach adopted by economic theory. This broader approach offers much more scope for the immediate implementation of measures to improve quality. Moreover, it explicitly recognises the public policy context within which the quality of public sector services is determined. The dimensions, characteristics and features of service quality can only be determined through public debate and democratic deliberation. Consumer sovereignty is not the sole determinant of the quality of local government services.

15 Conclusions

INTRODUCTION

The previous chapters demonstrated the increasingly wide scope of the economics of local government. It shares with public sector economics many broad theoretical and policy issues relating to allocative and X-efficiency, public expenditure, taxation, borrowing, public sector pricing, and so on. Nevertheless, local government economics is a distinctive area of economics worthy of study in its own right. Like other areas of applied economics, such as housing, transport and labour economics, local government economics has to fit within a broad multidisciplinary framework if it is to contribute fully to the study of local government.

Having examined the many economic theories, models and research findings relating to local government, the reader may ask what precisely economics has to say which is of direct relevance for local government. Indeed, the introduction to Chapter 1 noted that the ultimate objective of this book is to develop a set of economic principles justifying the existence of local government and providing guidance in respect of its functions, size, structure, financing, method of operation, and freedom from central control of its expenditures.

The answer is that in some areas economics has developed a clear set of principles with which to guide policy-makers and practitioners, but that in other areas much further theoretical and empirical development is required before economic theory can fully contribute to local government studies. In other words, in its current state, economic theory provides a useful (if not perfect) analytical framework with which to judge current practice in any one country and suggest appropriate measures for its improvement.

After listing these economic principles in the next section, subsequent sections consider why they do not necessarily require, or result in, commonality of practice and why economic models of local government expenditures need further development. The multidisciplinary framework is then re-emphasized and international developments of relevance to local government economics briefly noted. The chapter closes with a final comment on the need for inclusion of local government economics in local government studies.

ECONOMIC PRINCIPLES FOR LOCAL GOVERNMENT

The rationale for the economic principles listed below can be found in earlier chapters, no attempt being made to explain them here. That rationale cannot be fully understood without reading the full text. Nevertheless, the numbers of the most relevant chapters are noted for each set of principles. Each set could be used for class discussions and for assessing one's own understanding of earlier chapters.

Economic Principles for the Functions of Local Government (mainly Chapter 1)

1. The majority of public sector services should be provided by local government because their benefits are localized.
2. Central government should only provide national pure public goods such as defence and foreign policy.
3. Local government should restrict its provision of services to those cases where local market failure is high and the risk of government failure is low.
4. This implies that local governments should restrict their service provision to core functions, irrespective of any powers of general competence conferred upon them by central government.

Economic Principles for Local Government Size and Structure (mainly Chapter 2)

1. Local government should be as small as possible without forgoing the potential efficiency gains of economies of scale.
2. The jurisdictional areas of local governments should, as far as practically possible, be conterminous with the areas benefiting from their provision of services.
3. These benefit areas should also match financing areas so as to prevent tax exporting.
4. Matching of financing and benefit areas may require regional (rather than local) government for the provision of some services.
5. Benefit areas will have to be periodically reconfigured as service technologies and transport infrastructures change over time.

Economic Principles for the Financing of Local Governments (mainly Chapters 7, 8 and 9)

1. Charges should be the primary means of financing local government services because most are not pure public goods.
2. Where other forms of market failure occur, such as positive externalities, services should also be part-financed by local taxes.

3. The size of the locally-financed subsidy should not exceed the monetary value of positive externalities or merit good characteristics.
4. Subsidies should be targeted on users rather than on facilities.
5. Local governments should tax bases that have low mobility, are not heavily redistributive, are evenly distributed across the country, and whose revenues rise in line with service costs without having to raise the tax rate.
6. Intergovernmental grants-in-aid should generally be restricted to services where unavoidable spillover effects are so great that significant allocative inefficiency would occur.
7. Equalization grants intended to achieve horizontal equity are best financed by local governments themselves on the 'Robin Hood' principle.
8. Otherwise, any centrally-financed equalization grants should be no greater than those levels required to secure the required degree of equalization.

Economic Principles for the Operations of Local Government (mainly Chapters 3, 4, 10, 12, 13 and 14)

1. The systems of voting and of political representation should maximize the scope for political competition.
2. Irrespective of the systems of voting and of political representation, scope for exit should be maximized wherever possible.
3. Scope for exit should be facilitated by maximizing the scope for inter-municipal competition for residents and by the decentralization of service provision to alternative providers within a single local government jurisdiction.
4. Contestability of service contracts should be maximized as far as practically possible at reasonable relative cost in order to gain best value for money.
5. Competition is best facilitated by liberalization initiatives which allow the possibility of private sector provision of local government services.
6. Internal markets should be created where it is not possible to create external markets or where to do so would compromise service objectives.
7. Service vouchers are an effective way of facilitating internal and external markets and exit in that the money follows the service user.
8. Where exit is restricted by natural local monopolies, voice should be strengthened as far as possible by political decentralization within local government.
9. Irrespective of the use of internal or external markets, shirking-control devices should be employed to reduce organizational slack.
10. Efficiency studies should be undertaken periodically.

Economic Principles for the Control of Local Government Spending (mainly Chapters 5, 6 and 11)

1. If the above principles are put into practice, the need for central government control of local government spending is significantly reduced.
2. Otherwise local government expenditures have to be centrally controlled for both macroeconomic and microeconomic purposes.
3. Central government control should be limited to centrally-provided finances as long as locally-determined financing mechanisms accurately relate voting decisions to willingness and liability to pay local taxes and user-charges.
4. In that case, local governments should have considerable discretion to set their own levels of local taxes and user-charges.

THE DIVERSITY OF ARRANGEMENTS FOR LOCAL GOVERNMENT

While now well developed, these economic principles do not necessarily require that all countries adopt the exactly the same local government structures, functions, financing arrangements, operational procedures and control mechanisms. This is because economic, technological, social, cultural, democratic and other relevant factors vary from country to country – and even among regions within any one country. These factors affect the scope for both the articulation of demand for and the organization of supply of individual local government services. In particular, the scope for exit and voice differ in reflection of differing constitutional, cultural and other contexts among and within countries (see Chapters 3, 4 and 12). Likewise, the diversity of potential supply arrangements reflect the capacities of both the public and private sectors within particular countries (or regions within any one country) and so restrict or facilitate the securing of economies of scale (see Chapters 2, 13 and 14).

For similar reasons, although the standard sources of finance are intergovernmental grants, local taxation and user-charges, there is a great diversity of models for financing local governments in different European countries. This diversity has been made apparent by the discussions in Chapters 7, 8 and 9. It persists despite a general trend to greater fiscal pressures on European local governments during the 1980s and 1990s, and despite ongoing and cumulative moves towards greater fiscal harmonization within the European Union.

Perhaps this diversity should not be surprising because case-studies of individual countries throughout Europe and Scandinavia show that most countries have developed in isolation their own systems of financing local government. They have typically paid little attention to financing models used in other countries. Moreover, fiscal harmonization has also made relatively little progress in respect of tax regimes at the central (as well as local) government level within the member states of the European Union.

It has proved particularly difficult to develop economic theories explaining the diversity of models for financing local governments. This is because it has also proved difficult to develop economic theories explaining the diversity of local government structures and functions among European countries. This problem is not peculiar to economics, however. It is also experienced by other academic disciplines. Political, economic, constitutional, and other theories are not fully developed enough to explain differences throughout Europe in the structures, functions, financing and operational procedures of local government. A comprehensive model would have to be multidisciplinary in approach. There is, therefore, a large variation between countries which remains to be explained by historical, economic, geographical, political, institutional and other such variables.

Nonetheless, this text has made clear the well-developed economic principles to guide central and local governments in their use of intergovernmental grants and of local taxes and charges. However, rather than increasingly adopting these generally applicable economic principles, there is instead some evidence of an increasing diversity of financing arrangements. This increasing diversity may be exacerbated by the arbitrary and unsystematic adoption of user-charges.

Put perhaps rather too simply, the degree of market failure and of (the complementary concept of) non-market failure varies from country to country, from area to area, and over time with the result that the arrangements for local government will also vary and, in many cases, will not be optimally organised at any point in time (Young 1976).

A RE-EVALUATION OF THE ROLE OF USER-CHARGES

Fully democratic processes are a necessary but not sufficient condition for allocative efficiency because they do not necessarily satisfy the other economic principles listed above. In particular, rather than charges being the residual method of financing local government services (after income from local taxes and intergovernmental grants have been determined), the benefit model of local government finance makes charges the primary means of finance. In that case, local taxes and grants become subsidiary methods of financing local government's provision of services. This reverses the common conception of the means of financing local government and contrasts sharply with the traditional situation in the UK and some other countries, where intergovernmental grants are the main means of financing local government, followed by local taxes then charges.

User-charges may have much greater potential in promoting equity than is acknowledged by conventional wisdom. Their introduction requires a more accurate identification of both service costs and service users. Hence, in tandem with means-tested and categoric subsidies, they could facilitate a more accurate targeting of service benefits on prioritized groups and secure a more equitable financing arrangement. However, it is insufficient to argue that a policy change should go ahead simply because there is an excess of benefits over costs or because there are more gainers than losers. Service providers and users are as concerned to avoid sharp reductions in service provision as they are to secure even modest improvements. This explains the incrementalist approach to changes in service delivery and denies the voluntary introduction of radical financial reforms on the part of local governments.

On the same grounds, a sudden leap into the idyll of maximum efficiency is not possible and will most likely be at the cost of severe disruption to the achievement of both service objectives and equity. Local governments are not solely regulatory arrangements for the promotion of efficiency and any proposal for a new charging regime has to accept that constraint.

Taking these caveats and preconditions on board, there is considerable potential for the increased use of user-charges for local government services, allowing individual service users greater discretion over their takeup of services and relating charges to it. There is a need for a coherent philosophy for user-charges, certainly not just an attempt to restrain service takeup or generate additional revenue. The implications for management practice would be quite profound. They could be used to promote municipal services actively (levels, quality and accessibility), a positive tool of social policy rather than a negative one of public expenditure restraint and a consequence of tax limitation schemes.

The UK and USA case-studies of user-charges revealed that user-charges are both widespread and numerous, with the highest cost-recovery rates in property-related services (see Chapter 7). User-charges for property-related services are probably easier to assess and enforce, have the least visible deterrence of service use and the benefits are both more clearly attributable and restricted to individuals or to particular groups of service users. Charges for people-based services tend to have lower cost-recovery rates and are often accompanied by means-tested or categoric state-financed welfare payments.

ECONOMIC MODELS OF LOCAL GOVERNMENT EXPENDITURE

The above lists of principles make clear that there are well-developed and clearly articulated economic models of local government functions, structure, financing, and operations. In contrast, Chapters 10 and 11 demonstrated that economic models of local government expenditures are neither well developed not clearly articulated. Despite being first articulated in the 1920s and more extensively developed in both theoretical and empirical terms in subsequent decades, the theoretical and empirical validity of the median voter model remains seriously in doubt. Moreover, being a demand-side model, its exclusion of supply-side factors makes it inadequate as a model of local government expenditures.

The median voter hypothesis is simply a by-product of the median voter model. While the model provides substantial analytical insights into a pure theory of voting, it is incomplete as a model of public sector supply. When the model is combined with the median voter hypothesis, in its crudest form it has only one independent variable which determines local government expenditures, namely the income of the median voter. Even though more recent versions of the model have included more independent variables, they can only improve the modelling of voting outcomes, not of public sector supply. The supply-side models of production by public sector bureaux developed by Niskanen and others are neither fully developed enough in themselves nor integrated with demand-side models.

The substantial data and econometric difficulties faced when trying to test the median voter model/hypothesis do not invalidate either the model or the hypothesis. These difficulties are common to many economic models (for example, the Tiebout model of intermunicipal competition) and are inherent feature of the theory of knowledge (i.e. that models can never be proven, only disproven – and even to disprove them is extremely difficult). Nevertheless, the paucity of variables employed by economic models of public sector supply, contrasts sharply with the more eclectic models of political science and other disciplines. The discussion in Chapter 9 of expenditure needs assessment as part of the equalization procedures employed in the distribution of intergovernmental grants, demonstrated how some countries use a multiplicity of factors in attempting to explain the expenditure patterns of their local governments. Given the poorly articulated and inadequately developed economic models of public sector supply, it is therefore not surprising that local government spending seems to be greater than that implied by median voter incomes.

LOCAL GOVERNMENT ECONOMICS IN A MULTIDISCIPLINARY CONTEXT

It is important to note that, despite their claims to be neutral (that is, making positive rather than normative statements), economists are in fact partisan advocates of efficiency. Their principles are intended to improve both allocative and X-efficiency. These efficiency principles will necessarily be tempered by social policy, constitutional, political and other considerations. Note, however, that the 're-evaluation of charges' section (above) emphasized that the supposed tradeoff between efficiency and equity may not be as severe as generally thought. Indeed, where user-charges are used to target subsidy, there may be no tradeoff at all – instead a complementarity between efficiency and equity. Note also that these economic principles do *not* conflict with the proper operation of democratic processes. Indeed, allocative efficiency requires fully democratic processes, economic theory analysing those processes through models of voting.

This demonstrates the multidisciplinary context within which economics does and must fit. An attempt has been made in this book to set economic theory within that context. Frequent reference has been made throughout this text to academics from other disciplines. For example, the discussion of exit and voice, and especially initiatives in respect of the latter, drew on the work of academics from political science, public sector management, social policy, and so on. The discussion of fiscal stress made reference to the work of those disciplines as well as others, most notably economic geography. Much the same can be said of the discussion of the median voter model and the shift from government to governance. This emphasizes that economics has to fit within a multidisciplinary framework of academic studies if it is to contribute its full potential to the study of local government.

Local government economists must therefore study the work of political scientists, economic geographers, sociologists, public management experts and others in order that they may see how their own efficiency principles can be (and are being) applied in the local government sector. Local government economists must not restrict themselves to the narrow boundaries of neoclassical economics.

An understanding of the factors influencing local government expenditures requires economists to go beyond aggregate macro-level econometric approaches and to undertake disaggregated micro-level studies of the decision-making processes and power structures within local governments in different countries. Fiscal federalists have recently attempted to develop theories incorporating a range of non-economic factors and which focus more on political processes. The development of institutional economics also holds much promise in this respect.

The increased use of micro-level studies is inevitable as the relative balance of attention shifts from fiscal federalism and tax issues to the study of supply-side initiatives such as internal markets, output-control devices, shirking-control devices and performance reviews. Given that X-inefficiency is thought to be of greater magnitude than allocative inefficiency, the local government economist has much to contribute through micro-level studies of local government service inputs, processes, outputs and outcomes – including service quality. Nonetheless, macro-level studies are still relevant because some areas of empirical research require large data-sets and because local government expenditures and taxation are crucially important for macroeconomic policy.

INTERNATIONAL DEVELOPMENTS AND LOCAL GOVERNMENT ECONOMICS

Almost all of the member states of the Council of Europe have signed the 1985 European Charter of Local Self-Government and the European Union has adopted the decentralization principle under the name of 'subsidiarity', namely that government powers should be exercised at the lowest level of government possible (Council of Europe 1994). Together with the increasing accumulation of powers within EU institutions, the supposed decline of nation states and growth of a 'Europe of the Regions' implies considerable and fundamental reforms to the systems of local and regional government throughout the EU.

Outside Western Europe, decentralization measures have often been aided by international development agencies and bilateral assistance programmes. These include the World Bank's Fiscal Decentralization Initiative, the European Union's PHARE programme (which provides finance in support of economic and democratic reform in central and eastern Europe), the United Nations' Centre for Human Settlements (UNCHS) and the Council of Europe's LODE (an acronym for LOcal DEmocracy) Programme.

Put simply, the adoption and implementation of subsidiarity and of other decentralization measures substantially increases the scope for applied economics at the local government level.

CONCLUSIONS

The foregoing chapters have made clear the pervasiveness of allocative efficiency and of X-efficiency considerations within local government. Allocative efficiency in local government brings together voting mechanisms, Oates' decentralization theorem, Tiebout's voting-with-one's-feet and other exit mechanisms, voice mechanisms, the Niskanen model of bureaucratic supply, the flypaper effect, and user-charges, taxes and grants. X-inefficiency brings together performance review, competitive contracting, internal markets, service vouchers, and other measures to reduce organizational slack.

Analysis of local government functions, size, structure, financing and operations in terms of allocative efficiency and X-efficiency has been used to derive a clear set of economic principles. These principles could be used to guide the constitutional arrangements for local government. Indeed, they underpin Articles 3, 4, and 9 of the European Charter of Local Self-Government to a remarkable degree. However, the foregoing chapters make clear that many European countries still have a long way to go before these principles and Articles are fully adopted, as distinct from being ratified by a signature.

Those who believe that economics has little to offer the study of local government fail to recognize the all-pervasiveness and importance of efficiency considerations within its structure, functions, financing and operational procedures. Local government economics is therefore a crucial component of local government studies and its exclusion from such study programmes is a serious omission.

Bibliography

Abbot, B. (1993) *Patterns of Privatisation and Market Trends in Local Government Services*, Kingston Business School Working Paper Series (London: Kingston University).

Accounts Commission (1998) *The Challenge of Charging: A Managed Response* (Edinburgh: Accounts Commission).

Ahmad, E. (ed.) (1997) *Financing Decentralised Expenditures: An International Comparison of Grants* (Cheltenham: Edward Elgar).

Alaszewski, A. and J. Manthorpe (1988) 'Literature Review: Decentralising Welfare Services', *British Journal of Social Work*, **18**(1): 63–74.

Alcaly, R. E. and R. Mermelstein (1977) *The Fiscal Crisis of American Cities* (New York: Vintage).

Alexander, A. (1991) *Managing Fragmentation: Democracy, Accountability and the Future of Local Government*, Inaugural Professorial Lecture Scottish Local Authorities Management Centre (Glasgow: University of Strathclyde).

Allen, M. (1988) *The Goals of Universities* (Milton Keynes: Open University Press).

Almquist, R. (1999) 'Measuring the Threat of Competition: Elderly Services in the City of Stockholm', *Local Government Studies*, **25**(2).

AMA (1994) *Changing the Face of Quangos: Proposals for the Reform of Appointed Bodies in England and Wales* (London: Association of Metropolitan Authorities).

Aronsson, T. and M. Wikstrom (1996) 'Local Public Expenditure in Sweden: A Model where the Median Voter is not Necessarily Decisive', *European Economic Review*, **40**(9): 1705–16.

Arrow, K. J. (1959) 'Rational Choice Functions and Orderings', *Economica*, **26**: 121–7.

Arrow, K. J. (1963) *Social Choice and Individual Values* (2nd edn) (New Haven and London: Yale University Press).

ASI (1989) 'Wiser Counsels', *The Reform of Local Government* (London: Adam Smith Institute).

Atkins, D., T. Champion, M. Coombes, D. Dorling and R. Woodward (1996) *Urban Trends in England: Latest Evidence from the 1991 Census* (London: HMSO).

Audit Commission (1984a) *The Impact on Local Authorities' Economy, Efficiency and Effectiveness of the Block Grant Distribution System* (London: HMSO).

Audit Commission (1984b) *Further Improvements in Refuse Collection: A Review by the Audit Commission* (London: HMSO).

Audit Commission (1987) *Competitiveness and Contracting Out of Local Authorities' Services* (London: HMSO).

Audit Commission (1988) *Competitive Management of Parks and Green Spaces* (London: HMSO).

Audit Commission (1993) *Realising the Benefits of Competition: The Client Role for Contracted Services* (London: HMSO).

Bahl, R. (1978) *The Fiscal Outlook for Cities* (New York: Syracuse University Press).

Bailey, S. J. (1982a) 'Central City Decline and the Provision of Education Services', *Urban Studies*, **19**(3): 263–79.

Bailey, S. J. (1982b) 'Do Fewer Pupils Mean Falling Expenditure?', in R. Rose and E. Page (eds), *Fiscal Stress in Cities* (Cambridge University Press).

Bailey, S. J. (1982c) 'The Political Economy of Local Government Finance', *The Fraser of Allander Institute Quarterly Economic Commentary*, **8**(2): 49–64.

Bailey, S. J. (1984) 'The Costs of Sixth Form Rationalisation', *Policy and Politics*, **12**(1): 53–69.

Bailey, S. J. (1987) 'A Poll Tax for Scotland?' *Critical Social Policy*, 20 (Autumn): 57–65.

Bailey, S. J. (1988a) 'Local Government Finance in Britain', in R. Paddison and S. J. Bailey (eds), *Local Government Finance: International Perspectives* (London: Routledge).

Bailey, S. J. (1988b) 'Information Requirements of the Community Charge', *BURISA Newsletter*, 83 (British Urban and Regional Information Systems Association).

Bailey, S. J. (1989a) 'Charging for Public Library Services', *Policy and Politics*, **17**(1): 59–74.

Bailey, S. J. (1989b) 'The Revenue Support Grant: A Better Grants System?', *Public Policy and Administration*, **4**(2): 22–34.

Bailey, S. J. (1990a) 'Implementing Public Choice: The Community Charge', in T. Younis (ed.), *Implementation in Public Policy* (Aldershot: Dartmouth).

Bailey, S. J. (1990b) 'Charges for Local Infrastructure', *Town Planning Review*, **61**(4): 427–53.

Bailey, S. J. (1990c) 'The Poll Tax in Scotland: The First Year', *Local Government Studies*, **16**(5): 57–80.

Bailey, S. J. (1991) 'Fiscal Stress: The New System of Local Government Finance in England', *Urban Studies* **28**(6): 889–907.

Bailey, S. J. (1993) 'Public Choice Theory and the Reform of Local Government in Britain: from Government to Governance', *Public Policy and Administration* **8**(2): 7–24.

Bailey, S. J. (1994) 'Charging for Local Government Services: A Coherent Philosophy', *Public Administration*, **72**(3): 365–84.

Bailey, S. J. (1995) *Public Sector Economics: Theory, Policy and Practice* (Basingstoke: Macmillan).

Bailey, S. J. (1998a) 'Cities and Services: A Post Welfarist Analysis', in R. Paddison and W. F. Lever (eds), *Handbook of Urban Studies* (London: Sage).

Bailey, S. J. (1998b) 'Assuring the Quality of UK Local Government Services: A Case Study of School Meals Catering', *Public Policy and Administration*, **13**(1): 95–106.

Bailey, S. J. and S. Connolly (1997) 'The National Lottery: A Preliminary Assessment of Net Additionality', *Scottish Journal of Political Economy*, **44**(1): 100–12.

Bailey, S. J. and C. Davidson (1996) *Assuring Quality of Local Government Services Subject to Compulsory Competitive Tendering: Results of a Two-Year Research Project* (Glasgow: Glasgow Caledonian University).

Bailey, S. J. and C. Davidson (1997) *Did Quality Really Increase Under Local Government CCT?*, in L. Montanheiro *et al.* (eds), *Public and Private Sector Partnerships: Learning for Growth* (Sheffield: SHU Press).

Bailey, S. J. and C. Davidson (1999) 'The Purchaser–Provider Split: Theory and UK Evidence', *Government and Policy* **17**(1).

Bailey, S. J., P. Falconer, M. Foley, M. Graham and G. McPherson (1998) *To Charge or Not to Charge: A Study of Museum Admission Policies* (London: Museum and Galleries Commission).

Bailey, S. J., P. K. Falconer and S. McChlery (1993) *Local Government Charges: Policy and Practice* (Harlow: Longmans).

Bailey, S. J. and R. Paddison (eds) (1988) *The Reform of Local Government Finance in Britain* (London: Routledge).

Barnett, R. R. (1993a) 'The (Non) Equivalence Theorem When There are Matching Grants as Well as Lump-Sum Grants', *Public Choice*, **75**(4): 363–9.

Barnett, R. R. (1993b) 'Preference Revelation and Public Goods', in P. M. Jackson (ed.), *Current Issues in Public Sector Economics* (Basingstoke: Macmillan).

Barnett, R. R., R. Levaggi and P. Smith (1991) 'Does the Flypaper Model Stick? A Test of the Relative Performance of the Flypaper and Conventional Models of Local Government Budgetary Behaviour', *Public Choice*, **69**: 1–18.

Barr, J. and O. A. Davis (1966) 'An Elementary Political and Economic Theory of Expenditures of Local Governments', *Southern Economic Journal*, **33**: 149–65.

Batley, R. and G. Stoker (eds) (1991) *Local Government in Europe: Trends and Developments* (Basingstoke: Macmillan).

Baumol, W. J. (1967) 'Macroeconomics of Unbalanced Growth: The Anatomy of Urban Crisis', *American Economic Review*, **57**(1): 415–26.

Baumol, W. J. and D. F. Bradford (1970) 'Optimal Departures from Marginal Cost Pricing', *American Economic Review*, **60**(2): 265–83.

Baumol, W. J., R. Panzer and R. D. Willig (1982) *Contestable Markets and the Theory of Industry Structures* (New York: Harcourt Brace Jovanovich).

Beale, V., P. Coen and L. Homer (1994) 'Community Government in Hertfordshire – Devolution and Delegation', *Local Government Policy Making*, **20**(4): 37–44.

Becker, E. (1996) 'The Illusion of fiscal illusion: Unsticking the flypaper effect', *Public Choice*, **86**(1–2): 85–102.

Bender, B. and D. Fixler (1989) 'The Median Voter, Voting and Local Government Employment', *Journal of Regional Science*, **29**: 29–46.

Bennett, R. J. (1980) *The Geography of Public Finance* (London: Methuen).

Bennett, R. J. (1982) *Central Grants to Local Governments* (Cambridge University Press).

Bennett, R. J. (1987) 'Local Business Taxes in Theory and Practice', *Oxford Review of Economic Policy*, **3**(2): 60–80.

Bennett, R. J. (ed.) (1990) *Decentralization, Local Governments and Markets: Towards a Post Welfare Agenda* (Oxford: Clarendon).

Bennett, R. J. and Fearnehough, M. (1987) 'The Burdens of Non-Domestic Rates on Business', *Local Government Studies*, **16**(3): 23–6.

Bergstrom, T. C. and R. P. Goodman (1973) 'Private Demands for Public Goods', *American Economic Review*, **63**: 280–96.

Bird R. M. (1976) *Charging for Public Services: A New Look at an Old Idea* (Toronto: Canadian Tax Foundation).

Bird, R. M., R. D. Ebel and C. I. Wallich (1995) *Decentralization and the Socialist State: Intergovernmental Finance in Transition Economies* (Washington: IBRD/ World Bank).

Bishop, M. and J. Kay (1988) *Does Privatisation Work? Lessons from the UK* (London Business School).

Black, D. (1948) 'On the Rationale of Group Decision-Making', *Journal of Political Economy* **56**: 23–34. Reprinted in C. K. Rowley (ed.), *Social Choice Theory: Volume 1* (Aldershot: Edward Elgar) pp. 50–61.

Black, D. (1958) *The Theory of Committees and Elections* (Cambridge University Press).

Blair, P. (1993) 'Financial Equalisation Between Local and Regional Authorities in European Countries', in J. Gibson and R. Batley (eds), *Financing European Local Governments* (London: Frank Cass) pp. 7–27.

Blake, B., P. Bolan and D. Burns (1991) *Local Budgeting in Practice: Learning from Two Case Studies* (Bristol: School for Advanced Urban Studies).

Boadway, R. W. (1979) *Public Sector Economics* (Cambridge, Mass.: Winthrop).

Bond, S., K. Denny, J. Hall and W. McCluskey (1996) 'Who Pays Business Rates?' *Fiscal Studies*, **17**(1): 19–35.

Borcherding, T. E. (1985) 'The Causes of Government Expenditure Growth: A Survey of the US Evidence', *Journal of Public Economics*, **28**: 359–82.

Borcherding, T. E. and R. T. Deacon (1972) 'The Demand for the Services of Non-federal Governments', *American Economic Review*, **62**: 891–901.

Borge, L. E. (1995) 'Lump-Sum Intergovernmental Grants Have Price Effects: A Note', *Public Finance Quarterly*, **23**(2): 271–4.

Bowen, H. R. (1943) 'The Interpretation of Voting in the Allocation of Economic Resources', *Quarterly Journal of Economics*, **58**(1): 27–48. Reprinted in C. K. Rowley (ed.), *Social Choice Theory: Volume 1* (Aldershot: Edward Elgar) pp. 28–49.

Boyne, G. A. (1988) 'The Extent and Impact of Local Fiscal Stress', *Public Policy and Administration*, **3**(2): 15–26.

Boyne, G. A. (1995) 'Population Size and Economies of Scale in Local Government', *Policy and Politics*, **23**(3): 213–22.

Boyne, G. A. (1996a) 'Assessing Party Effects on Local Policies: a Quarter Century of Progress or Eternal Recurrence?', *Political Studies*, **44**: 232–52.

Boyne, G. A. (1996b) 'Competition and Local Government: A Public Choice Perspective', *Urban Studies*, **33**(4–5): 703–21.

Boyne, G. A. (1996c) 'Constraints, Choices and Public Policies', *Research in Urban Policy*, **6** (London: JAI Press Ltd).

Bradbury, K. L., A. Downs and K. A. Small (1982) *Urban Decline and the Future of American Cities* (Washington DC: The Brookings Institution).

Bradford, D., R. Malt and W. E. Oates (1969) 'The Rising Cost of Local Public Services: Some Evidence and Reflections', *National Tax Journal*, **22**: 185–202.

Bradford, D. F. and W. E. Oates (1971a) 'The Analysis of Revenue Sharing in a New Approach to Collective Fiscal Decisions', *Quarterly Journal of Economics*, **85**(3): 416–39.

Bradford, D. F. and W. E. Oates (1971b) 'Towards a Predictive Theory of Intergovernmental Grants', *American Economic Review*, **61**(2): 440–8.

Bradford, D. F. and W. E. Oates (1974) 'Suburban Exploitation of Central Cities and Governmental Structure', in H. M. Hochman and G. E. Peterson (eds), *Redistribution Through Public Choice* (New York: Columbia University Press) pp. 43–90.

Bramley, G., A. Evans, P. Leather and C. Lambert (1983) *Grant Related Expenditure: A Review of the System* (SAUS WP 29) (Bristol: School for Advanced Urban Studies).

Bramley, G., J. Le Grand and W. Low (1989) 'How Far is the Poll Tax a Community Charge? The Implications of Service Usage Evidence', *Policy and Politics*, **17**(3): 187–205.

Brennan, G. and J. M. Buchanan (1980) *The Power to Tax: Analytical Foundations of a Fiscal Constitution* (Cambridge University Press).

Brennan, G. and J. J. Pincus (1996) 'A Minimalist Model of Federal Grants and Flypaper Effects', *Journal of Public Economics*, **61**(2): 229–46.

Brindle, D. (1994) 'Poverty Highlighted by School Meals Survey', *Guardian*, 31 Jan.

Brooke, R. (1992) 'Local Government in the 1990s: 15 Key Questions for Research', *Local Government and Policy Making*, **18**(5): 33–40.

Broom, D. and D. Wild (1996) 'Manhattan Transfer', *Public Finance*, 23 August: 10–13.

Brown, C. (1984) *Black and White Britain* (London: Heinemann Policy Studies Institute).

Brown, C. V. and P. M. Jackson (1990) *Public Sector Economics* (Oxford: Basil Blackwell).

Brueckner, J. K. (1997) 'Infrastructure Financing and Urban Development: The Economics of Impact Fees', *Journal of Public Economics*, **66**: 383–407.

Buchanan, J. M. and G. Tulloch (1962) *The Calculus of Consent: Logical Foundations of Constitutional Democracy* (Ann Arbor: University of Michigan Press).

Burgess, T. and T. Travers (1980) *Ten Billion Pounds: Whitehall's Takeover of the Town Halls* (London: Grant McIntyre).

Burns, D., R. Hambleton and P. Hoggett (1994) *The Politics of Decentralisation: Revitalising Local Democracy* (Basingstoke: Macmillan).

Burrows, R. and B. Loader (eds) (1994) *Towards a Post Fordist Welfare State* (London: Routledge).

Cabinet Office (1996) *Competing for Quality Policy Review: An Efficiency Unit Scrutiny* (Efficiency Unit, Cabinet Office) (London: HMSO).

Cameron, G. C. and S. J. Bailey (1987) 'The Fiscal Costs of City Decline: A Case Study of Education', in L. Berg, L. S. Burns and L. H. Klaassen (eds), *Spatial Cycles* (Aldershot: Gower).

Carnaghan F. and B. Bracewell (1993) *Testing the Market: Competitive Tendering for Government Services in Britain and Abroad* (London: Institute of Economic Affairs).

Castles, F. G. (ed.) (1982) *The Impact of Parties: Politics and Policies in Democratic Capitalist States* (London: Sage).

Cave, M. *et al.* (1993) *The Valuation of Changes in Quality in the Public Services: Report Prepared for HM Treasury by Brunel University* (London: HMSO).

Champion, T., D. Atkins, M. Coombes and S. Fotheringham (1998) *Urban Exodus: A Report for CPRE* (London: Council for the Protection of Rural England).

Chandler, J. A. (1996) *Local Government Today* (2nd edn) (Manchester: Manchester University Press).

Chandler, J. A., M. Gregory, M. Hunt and R. Turner (1995) *Decentralisation and Devolution in England and Wales* (Luton: Local Government Management Board).

Charters, S. (1994) 'Participation and the Role of Councillors in a Decentralised Authority: The Case of Tower Hamlets', *Local Government Policy Making*, **20**(4): 24–30.

Chaundy, D. and M. Uttley (1993) 'The Economics of Compulsory Competitive Tendering: Issues, Evidence and the Case of Municipal Refuse Collection', *Public Policy and Administration*, **8**(2): 25–41.

Chernick, H. A. (1979) 'An Economic Model of the Distribution of Project Grants', in P. Mieszkowski and W. H. Oakland (1979) *Fiscal Federalism and Grants-in-Aid* (Washington: The Urban Institute).

Chicoine, D. L., N. Walzer and S. C. Deller (1989) 'Representative versus Direct Democracy and Government Spending in a Median Voter Model', *Public Finance*, **44**(2): 225–36.

Cm 324 (1988) *Financing Our Public Library Service; Four Subjects For Debate* (London: HMSO).

Cm 1730 (1991) *Competing for Quality: Buying Better Public Services* (London: HMSO; Office of Public Service and Science).

Cm 2970 (1995) *The Citizen's Charter: The Facts and Figures. A report to mark four years of the Charter programme* (London: HMSO; Office of Public Service and Science).

Cm 3658 (1997) *Scotland's Parliament* (London: HMSO).

Cm 3718 (1997) *A Voice for Wales: The Government's Proposals for a Welsh Assembly* (London: HMSO).

CML (1983) *Municipal Services and User Charges in Colorado* (Denver: Colorado Municipal League).

Cmnd 6453 (1976) *Local Government Finance: Report of the Committee of Enquiry (The Layfield Report)* (London: HMSO).

Cmnd 7643 (1979) *Central Controls over Local Authorities* (London: HMSO).

Cmnd 8449 (1981) *Alternatives to Domestic Rates* (London: HMSO).

Cmnd 9714 (1986) *Paying for Local Government* (London: HMSO).

Cmnd 9797 (1986) *The Conduct of Local Authority Business* (Chairman D. Widdicombe QC) (London: HMSO).

Cochrane, A. (1991) 'The Changing State of Local Government: Restructuring for the 1990s', *Public Administration*, **69**: 281–301.

Cole, M. and G. Boyne (1995) 'So You Think You Know What Local Government Is?', *Local Government Studies*, **21**(2): 191–202.

Commission for Local Democracy (1995a) *Taking Charge: The Rebirth of Local Democracy* (London: Municipal Journal Books).

Commission for Local Democracy (1995b) *The Quango State: An Alternative Approach*, CLD research report no. 10 (Commission for Local Democracy).

Common, R. and N. Flynn (1992) *Contracting for Care* (York: Joseph Rowntree Foundation).

Cope, S. (1995) 'Contracting Out in Local Government: Cutting by Privatising', *Public Policy and Administration*, **10**(3): 29–44.

Council of Europe (1986) *The Response of Local Authorities to Central Government Incitement to Reduce Expenditure*, Study Series Local and Regional Authorities in Europe no. 37 (Strasbourg).

Council of Europe (1992) *Decentralisation and the Strengthening of Local Self-Government*, Local and Regional Authorities in Europe no. 48 (Strasbourg: Council of Europe).

Council of Europe (1994) *Definition and Limits of the Principle of Subsidiarity*, Local and Regional Authorities in Europe no. 55 (Strasbourg: Council of Europe).

Council of Europe (1995a) *The Size of Municipalities, Efficiency and Citizen Participation*, Local and Regional Authorities in Europe no. 56 (Strasbourg: Council of Europe).

Council of Europe (1995b) *Economic Intervention by Local and Regional Authorities*, Local and Regional Authorities in Europe no. 57 (Strasbourg: Council of Europe).

Council of Europe (1997) *Local Finance in Europe*, Local and Regional Authorities in Europe, no. 61 (Strasbourg: Council of Europe).

Courant, P. N., E. M. Gramlich and D. L. Rubinfield (1979) 'The Stimulative Effects of Intergovernmental Grants or Why Money Sticks Where it Hits', in P. Mieszkowski and W. H. Oakland (eds), (1979) *Fiscal Federalism and Grants-in-Aid* (Washington: The Urban Institute).

Crawford, P., S. Fothergill and S. Monk (1985) *The Effect of Business Rates on the Location of Employment* (University of Cambridge Department of Land Economy).

Criz, M (1982) 'The Role of User Charges and Fees in City Finance', *Urban Data Service Reports*, **14**(6) (Washington DC: International City Management Association).

Cubbin, J., S. Domberger and S. Meadowcroft (1987) 'Competitive Tendering and Refuse Collection: Identifying the Sources of Efficiency Gains', *Fiscal Studies*, **8**(3): 49–58.

Cullis, J. and P. Jones (1998) *Public Finance and Public Choice* (2nd edn) (Berkshire: McGraw-Hill).

Cyert, R. M. and J. G. March (1963) *A Behavioral Theory of the Firm* (New Jersey: Prentice-Hall).

Damania, D. (1986) 'The Impact of Non-Domestic Property Taxes on Employment: A Comment', *Urban Studies*, **23**: 413–18.

Davidson, C. and S. J. Bailey, (1995) *Quality: A Literature Review and Analytical Framework*, Department of Economics Discussion Paper no. 26 (Glasgow: Glasgow Caledonian University).

Davidson, C. and S. J. Bailey (1996) 'What Caused Improved Quality of Local Government Services Subject to Compulsory Competitive Tendering? Two Case Studies', in L. Montanheiro *et al.* (eds), *Public and Private Sector Partnerships: Working for Change* (Sheffield: PAVIC Publications).

Davies, K. and P. Hinton (1993) 'Managing Quality in Local Government and the Health Service', *Public Money and Management*, **13**(1): 51–4.

Davis, O. A., M. A. H. Dempster, and A. Wildavsky (1966) 'A Theory of the Budgetary Process', *American Political Science Review*, **60**: 529–48.

Deacon, R. T. (1978) 'A Demand Model for the Local Public Sector', *Review of Economics and Statistics*, **60**: 184–92.

Derrick, P. (1988) 'Local Fiscal Crisis: Diagnosis and Remedies', *Regional Studies*, **22**(3): 238–41.

Dietrich, M. (1994) *Transaction Cost Economics and Beyond* (London: Routledge).

Dilger, R. J. (1993) 'Residential Community Associations: Their Impact on Local Government Finance and Politics', *Government Finance Review*, **9**: 7–10.

DOE (1981) *Local Government Financial Statistics: England and Wales 1979/80* (Department of the Environment London: HMSO).

DOE (1991) *Local Government Financial Statistics: England No 2. 1990* (London: Department of the Environment).

DOE (1992) *Public Perceptions of Local Government: Its Finance and Services* (Department of the Environment London: HMSO).

DOE (1997) *Compulsory Competitive Tendering: Changes to Regulations and Guidance*, Department of the Environment Transport and the Regions/Welsh Office Consultation Paper, 25 July (London: Department of the Environment).

Dollery, B. E. and A. C. Worthington (1995) 'Federal Expenditure and Fiscal Illusion: A Test of the Flypaper Hypothesis in Australia', *Journal of Federalism*, **25**(1): 23–34.

Dollery, B. E. and A. C. Worthington (1996) 'The Empirical Analysis of Fiscal Illusion', *Journal of Economic Surveys*, **10**(3): 261–97.

Domberger, S. and D. Hensher (1993) 'On the Performance of Competitively Tendered Public Sector Cleaning Contracts', *Public Administration*, **71**(3): 441–54.

Domberger, S. and P. Jensen (1997) 'Contracting Out by the Public Sector: Theory, Evidence, Prospects', *Oxford Review of Economic Policy*, **13**(4): 67–78.

Domberger, S., S. Meadowcroft and D. Thompson (1986) 'Competitive Tendering and Efficiency: The Case of Refuse Collection', *Fiscal Studies*, **7**(4): 69–87.

Domberger, S., S. Meadowcroft and D. Thompson (1988) 'Competition and Efficiency in Refuse Collection: A Reply', *Fiscal Studies*, **9**(1): 86–90.

Dougan, W. R. and D. A. Kenyon (1988) 'Pressure Groups and Public Expenditures: The Flypaper Effect Reconsidered', *Economic Inquiry*, **26**(1): 159–170.

Doughty, R. (1995) 'Chips with Everything?', *Guardian*, 14 November, Education Guardian Section p. 16.

Dowding, K., P. John and S. Biggs (1994) 'Tiebout: A Survey of the Empirical Literature', *Urban Studies*, **31**(4/5) 767–97.

Downs, A. (1957) *An Economic Theory of Democracy* (New York: Harper & Row).

DTp (1993) *London Congestion Charging: A Review of Technology for Road Use Pricing in London* (London: Department of Transport).

Dunleavy, P. (1991) *Democracy, Bureaucracy and Public Choice: Economic Explanations in Political Science* (Brighton: Harvester Wheatsheaf).

Elcock, H. and G. Jordan (1987) *Learning from Local Authority Budgeting* (Aldershot: Gower).

Elcock, H., G. Jordan and A. Midwinter (1989) *Budgeting in Local Government: Managing the Margins* (Harlow: Longman).

Ellwood, S. (1996) *Cost-based Pricing in the NHS Internal Market* (London: Chartered Institute of Management Accountants).

Epple, D. and A. Zelenitz (1981) 'The Implications of Competition Among Jurisdictions: Does Tiebout Need Politics?' *Journal of Political Economy*, **89**: 1197–1217.

Evans, A. W. (1985) *Urban Economics: An Introduction* (Oxford: Basil Blackwell).

Evans, A. (1988) *No Room! No Room! The Cost of the British Town and Country Planning System* (London: Institute of Economic Affairs).

Eversley, D. E. C. (1972) 'Rising Costs and Static Incomes: some economic consequences of Regional Planning in London' *Urban Studies*, **9**: 347–68.

Feldstein, M. S. (1972) 'Pricing and Efficiency in Public Sector Pricing: The Optimal Two Part Tariff', *Quarterly Journal of Economics*, **86**(2): 175–87.

Filimon, R., T. Romer and H. Rosenthal (1982) 'Asymmetric Information and Agenda Control', *Journal of Public Economics*, **17**: 51–70.

Fisher, R. C. (1982) 'Income and Grant Effects on Local Expenditure: The Flypaper Effect and Other Difficulties', *Journal of Urban Economics* **12**(3): 324–45.

Flynn, C. L. *et al.* (1981) *Using User Fees: A Guide for Massachusetts Cities and Towns SP-129*, Local Government Series Community Resource Development Program (Massachusetts: University of Massachusetts and Massachusetts Municipal Association).

Forbes, K. F. and E. M. Zampelli (1989) 'Is Leviathan a Mythical Beast?', *American Economic Review*, **79**: 568–77.

Foster, C. D., R. A. Jackman and M. Perlman (1980) *Local Government Finance in a Unitary State* (London: Allen & Unwin).

Fossett, J. W. (1990) 'On Confusing Caution and Greed, A Political Explanation of the Flypaper Effect', *Urban Affairs Quarterly*, **26**(1): 95–117.

Fothergill, S. and G. Gudgin (1982) *Unequal Growth: Urban and Regional Employment Change in the UK* (London: Heinemann).

Frenckner, P. (1989) 'Costs of Using Capital and Determination of Net Income in Capital Intensive Firms', in Bo Fridman and L. Ostman (eds), *Accounting Development: Some Perspectives* (Stockholm: Ekonomiska Forskningsinstitutet) pp. 133–49.

Ganley, J. and J. Grahl (1988) 'Competition and Efficiency in Refuse Collection: A Critical Comment', *Fiscal Studies*, **9**(1): 80–5.

Gaster, L. (1993) *Organisational Change and Political Will – Decentralisation and Democratisation in Harlow* (Bristol: School for Advance Urban Studies).

Gaster, L. (1994) 'Quality, Choice and Efficiency: The Case of Harlow's Neighbourhood Offices', *Local Government Policy Making*, **20**(4): 18–23.

Gaster, L. (1995a) 'Quality in Service Contracts at the Local Level: the Case of Environmental Services in Harlow District Council', in G. Bouckaert and C. Pollitt (eds) *Quality Improvement in European Public Services* (London: Sage).

Gaster, L. (1995b) *Quality in Public Services: Managers' Choices* (Buckingham: Open University Press).

Gaster, L. and P. Hoggett (1993) 'Neighbourhood Decentralisation and Local Management', in N. Thomas, N. Deakin and J. Doling (eds), *Learning from Innovation: Housing and Social Care in the 1990s* (Birmingham: Birmingham Academic Press).

Gaster, L. and M. O'Toole (1995) *Local Government Decentralisation: An Idea Whose Time Has Come?*, Working Paper 125 (Bristol: School for Advanced Urban Studies).

Gaster, L. and M. Taylor (1993) *Learning from Consumers and Citizens* (Luton: Local Government Management Board).

George, H. (1966) *Progress and Poverty* (London: Hogarth).

Gibb, K. (1992) 'The Council Tax: The Distributional Implications of Returning to a Tax on Property', *Scottish Journal of Political Economy*, **39**(3): 302–17.

Gibson, J. G. and R. Batley (eds) (1993) *Financing European Local Governments* (London: Frank Cass).

Gibson, J. G., P. Smith and P. A. Watt (1987) 'Measuring the Fiscal Pressure on English Local Authorities under the block grant system', *Environment and Planning C: Government and Policy*, **5**: 157–70.

Glasby, J. (1981) 'Principles of Charging in Local Government', *Public Finance and Accountancy*, February: 13–14.

Glassberg, A. (1981) 'The Urban Fiscal Crisis Becomes Routine', *Public Administration Review*, **41**: 165–72.

Gould, F. and F. Zarkesh (1986) 'Local Government Expenditures and Revenues in Western Democracies: 1960–1982', *Local Government Studies*, **12**(1): 33–42.

Gramlich, E. M. (1976) 'The New York Fiscal Crisis: What Happened and What is to be Done', *American Economic Review*, **66**(2): 415–29.

Gramlich, E. M. (1997a) *Financing Federal Systems: The Selected Essays of Edward M. Gramlich* (Cheltenham: Edward Elgar).

Gramlich, E. M. (1977b) 'A Review of the Theory of Intergovernmental Grants', in W. E. Oates (ed.) (1977) *The Political Economy of Fiscal Federalism* (Lexington, Mass.: Lexington Books).

Gramlich, E. M. and H. Galper (1973) *State and Local Fiscal Behaviour and Federal Grant Policy* (Brookings Papers on Economic Activity 1).

Gramlich, E. M. and D. L. Rubinfield (1989) 'Micro-estimation of the Demand for Schooling. Evidence from Michigan and Massachusetts', *Regional Science and Urban Economics*, **19**: 381–98.

Grayson, L. and H. Davis (1995) 'Quangos', *Inlogov Informs*, **5**(1) (whole issue).

Grodzins, M. (1960) 'American Political Parties and the American System', *Western Political Quarterly*, **13**: 974–98.

Gudgin, G. (1995) 'Regional Problems and Policy in the UK', *Oxford Review of Economic Policy*, **11**(2): 18–63.

Gyford, J. (1987) 'Decentralisation within Authorities', in M Parkinson (ed.), *Reshaping Local Government* (Oxford: Transaction Books).

Haine G. and A. Keen (1994) 'Improving Quality Services – Decentralisation in Birmingham', *Local Government Policy Making*, **20**(4): 13–17.

Hambleton, R. (1988) 'Consumerism, Decentralisation and Local Democracy', *Public Administration*, **66**(2): 125–47.

Hambleton, R. (1992) 'Decentralisation and Democracy in UK Local Government', *Public Money and Management*, **12**(3): 9–20.

Hambleton, R., P. Hoggett and D. Burns (1994) 'A Framework for Understanding Area-based Decentralisation', *Local Government Policy Making*, **20**(4): 5–12.

Hamilton, B. W. (1983) 'The Flypaper Effect and other Anomalies', *Journal of Public Economics*, **22**: 347–61.

Hamilton, J. H. (1986) 'The Flypaper Effect and the Deadweight Loss from Taxation', *Journal of Urban Economics*, **19**(2): 148–55.

Hansson, I. and C. Stuart (1984) 'Voting Competitions with Interested Politicians: Platforms do not Converge to the Preferences of the Median Voter', *Public Choice*, **44**(3): 431–41.

Harris, R. and A. Seldon (1976) *Pricing or Taxing*, IEA Hobart Paper 71 (London: Institute of Economic Affairs).

Heald, D. (1983) *Public Expenditure: Its Defence and Reform* (Oxford: Martin Robertson).

Heald, D. (1990) 'Charging by British Government: Evidence from the Public Expenditure Survey', *Financial Accountability and Management*, **6**(4): 229–61.

Heyndels B. and C. Smolders (1994) 'Fiscal Illusion at the local level: Empirical evidence for the Flemish municipalities', *Public Choice*, **80**(3–4): 325–38.

Hill, R. C. (1977) 'State Capitalism and the Urban Fiscal Crisis in the United States', *International Journal of Urban and Regional Research*, **1**(1): 76–100.

Hines, J. R. and R. H. Thaler (1995) 'Anomalies: The Flypaper Effect', *Journal of Economic Perspectives*, **9**(4): 217–26.

Hirschman, A. O. (1970) *Exit, Voice and Loyalty: Responses to Decline in Firms, Organisations and States* (Cambridge, Mass.: Harvard University Press).

Hirschman, A. O. (1974) 'Exit, Voice and Loyalty: Further Reflections and a Survey of Recent Contributions', *Social Science Informs*, **13**(1): 7–26.

Hirschman, A. O. (1976) 'Political Economy: Some Uses of the Exit–Voice Approach: Discussion', *American Economic Review*, **66**(2): 386–89.

Hoggart, K. (1991) 'Adjusting to Fiscal Stress: City Expenditure in the San Francisco-Oakland Metropolitan Area', *Local Government Studies*, **17**: 57–75.

Hoggett, P. (1996) 'New Modes of Control in the Public Service', *Public Administration*, **74** (Spring): 9–32.

Holcombe, R. G. (1989) 'The Median Voter Model in Public Choice Theory', *Public Choice*, **61**: 115–25.

Hollis, G., G. Ham and M. Ambler (1992) *The Future Role and Structure of Local Government* (Harlow: Longman).

Hotelling, H. (1929) 'Stability in Competition', *Economic Journal*, **39**: 41–57.

Houston, L. O. (1996) 'Business Improvement Districts', *Development Commentary*, **20**(1): 4–9.

ICM Research (1993) *Citizen's Charter Customer Survey: Research Report* (London: ICM Research).

Inman, R. P. (1979) 'The Fiscal Performance of Local Governments: An Interpretative Review', in P. Mieszkowski and M. Staszheim (eds), *Current Issues in Urban Economics* (Baltimore: Johns Hopkins University Press).

IPF (1986) *Competitive Tendering and Efficiency: The Case of Refuse Collection* (London: Institute of Public Finance).

Islam, M. and S. A. Choudhury (1989) 'The Flypaper Effect and the Revenue Impact of Grants-In-Aid', *Economics Letters*, **30**(4): 351–6.

Jackman, R. (1982) 'Does Central Government Need to Control the Total of Local Government Spending?', *Local Government Studies*, **8**(3): 75–90.

Jackman, R. (1988) 'Local Government Finance and Macroeconomic Policy', in S. J. Bailey and R. Paddison (eds) *The Reform of Local Government Finance in Britain* (London: Routledge), pp. 172–89.

Jackson, P. M. (ed.) (1993) *Current Issues in Public Sector Economics* (Basingstoke: Macmillan).

Jackson, P. M. (1995) *Measures for Success in the Public Sector* (London: CIPFA).

Jackson, P. M., W. J. Meadows and A. P. Taylor (1982) 'Urban Fiscal Decay in UK Cities, *Local Government Studies*, **8**(5): 23–43.

John, P. and A. Block (1991) *Attitudes to Local Government: A Survey of Electors* (York: Joseph Rowntree Foundation).

John, P., K. Dowding and S. Biggs (1995) 'Residential Mobility in London: A Micro-level Test of the Behavioural Assumptions of the Tiebout Model', *British Journal of Political Science*, **25**: 379–97.

Johnson, D. N. (1980) 'The Use of Service Charges and Fees to Finance Local Government in Oregon: An Overview', *Finance Bulletin No 10 Bureau of Governmental Research and Service School of Community Service and Public Affairs* (University of Oregon).

Johnstone, L. (1992) *The Rebirth of Private Policing* (London: Routledge).

Jones, G. W. and S. Ranson (1989) 'Is There a Need for Participative Democracy? An Exchange', *Local Government Studies*, **15**(3): 1–10.

Jones, G. W. and J. Stewart (1985) *The Case for Local Government* (2nd edition) (London: Allen & Unwin).

Jones, G. W., J. Stewart and T. Travers (1986) 'A Rejoinder to Jackman', *Local Government Studies*, **12**(4) 59–63.

Joulfaian, D. and M. Marlow (1990) 'Government Size and Decentralisation: Evidence from Disaggregated Data', *Southern Economic Journal*, **56**(4): 1094–1102.

Karran, T. (1988) 'Local Taxing and Local Spending: International Comparisons', in R. Paddison and S. J. Bailey (eds), *Local Government Finance: International Perspectives* (London: Routledge).

Kennett, S. (1980a) *Local Government Fiscal Problems: A Context for Inner Areas*, Inner Cities Working Party (London: Social Science Research Council).

Kennett, S. (1980b) *The Inner City in the Context of the Urban System*, Inner Cities Working Party (London: Social Science Research Council).

Kerley, R. and D. Wynn (1991) 'Competitive Tendering: The Transition to Contracting in Scottish Local Authorities', *Local Government Studies* (September/October): 35–41.

King, D. (1984) *Fiscal Tiers: The Economics of Multi-Level Government* (London: George Allen & Unwin).

King, D. (1988) 'The Future Role of Grants in Local Government Finance', in S. J. Bailey and R. Paddison (eds), *The Reform of Local Government Finance in Britain* (London: Routledge).

King, D. (ed.) (1992) *Local Government Economics in Theory and Practice* (London: Routledge).

King, D. (1993) 'Issues in Multi-Level Government', in P. M. Jackson (ed.), *Current Issues in Public Sector Economics* (Basingstoke: Macmillan) pp. 156–82.

King, D. (1996) 'A Model of Optimum Local Authority Size', in G. Pola, G. France and R. Levaggi (eds) (1996) *Developments in Local Government Finance: Theory and Policy* (Cheltenham: Edward Elgar) pp. 55–76.

Kirkpatrick, I. and Lucio M. Martinez (eds) (1995) *The Politics of Quality in the Public Sector: the Management of Change* (London: Routledge).

Kirwan, R. M. (1980) 'The Fiscal Context', in G. C. Cameron (ed.) *The Future of the British Conurbations* (London: Longman).

Klein, R. (1984) 'Privatisation and the Welfare State', *Lloyds Bank Review*, no. 151 (January): 12–29.

Lamb, C. (1995) Quangos and Sub-national Executive Agencies: Problems of Unconstrained Power and Some Remedies', *Local Government Policy Making*, **21**(4): 61–8.

Laramie, A. J. and D. Mair (1993) 'The Incidence of Business Rates: A Post-Keynesian Approach', *Review of Political Economy*, **5**(1): 55–72.

Laramie, A. J. and D. Mair (1996) 'The Short-Period Macroeconomic Incidence and Effects of State and Local Taxes', in G. Pola, G. France and R. Levaggi (eds), *Developments in Local Government Finance: Theory and Policy* (Cheltenham: Edward Elgar).

Lavery, K. (1995) 'Privatisation by the Back Door: The Rise of Private Government in the USA', *Public Money and Management*, **15**(4): 49–53.

Le Grand, J. (1990) 'Quasi-markets and Social Policy', *Studies in Decentralisation and Quasi-Markets*, no. 1 (Bristol: School for Advanced Urban Studies).

Le Grand, J. and W. Bartlett (1993) 'The Theory of Quasi-markets' in J. Le Grand and W. Bartlett (eds), *Quasi-markets and Social Policy* (London: Macmillan).

Le Grand, J. and D. Winter (1987) 'The Middle Classes and the Defence of the British Welfare State', in R. Goodin, J. Le Grand *et al.*, *Not Only The Poor: The Middle Classes and the Welfare State* (London: Allen & Unwin).

Leach, S., J. Stewart and K. Walsh (1994) *The Changing Organisation and Management of Local Government* (Basingstoke: Macmillan).

Leibenstein, H. (1966) 'Allocative Efficiency versus X-Efficiency', *American Economic Review*, **56** (June): 392–415.

Levaggi, R. (1991) *Fiscal Federalism and Grants in Aid: The Problem of Asymmetrical Information* (Aldershot: Avebury).

Levitt, S. D. (1996) 'How Do Senators Vote? Disentangling the Role of Voter Preferences, Party Affiliation and Senator Ideology', *American Economic Review*, **86**(3): 425–41.

Lewis, J., P. Bernstock, V. Bovell and F. Wookey (1996) 'The Purchaser–Provider Split in Social Care: Is It Working?', *Social Policy and Administration*, **30**(1): 1–19.

Lewis-Beck, M. S. (1977) 'The Relative Importance of Socioeconomic and Political Variables for Public Policy', *American Political Science Review*, **71**: 559–66.

LGIU (1988) *LGIU Guide to the Poll Tax* (London: Local Government Information Unit).

LGIU (1994) 'Quangos Under Examination', *LGIU Briefing*, no. 7 (London: Local Government Information Unit).

LGMB (1992) *CCT Information Service: Client/Contractor Relationships Report 1992* (London: Local Government Management Board).

LGMB (1994) *CCT Information Service Survey Report*, no. 10 (London: Local Government Management Board).

LGMB (1995) *Quality in the Balance: Safeguarding Quality in CCT for White Collar and Professional Services* (London: Local Government Management Board).

Logalbo, A. T. (1982) 'Responding to Tax Limitation: Finding Alternative Revenues', *Governmental Finance*, **11**(1): 13–19.

Logan, R. R. (1986) 'Fiscal Illusion and the Grantor Government', *Journal of Political Economy*, **94**: 1304–18.

Losch, A. (1954) *The Economics of Location* (New Haven: Yale University Press).

Lowndes, V. (1994) 'Decentralisation: The Continuing Debate', *Local Government Policy Making*, **20**(4): 1–4.

Lowndes, V. and G. Stoker (1992a) 'An Evaluation of Neighbourhood Decentralisation Part 1: Customer and Citizen Perspectives', *Policy and Politics*, **20**(1): 47–61.

Lowndes, V. and G. Stoker (1992b) 'An Evaluation of Neighbourhood Decentralisation Part 2: Staff and Councillor Perspectives', *Policy and Politics*, **20**(2): 143–52.

Luksetich, W. A. and M. D. Partridge (1997) 'Demand Functions for Museum Services', *Applied Economics*, **29**: 1553–59.

MacLennan, D. (1982) *Housing Economics: An Applied Approach* (London: Longman).

Mair, D. (1984) 'Towards a Kaleckian Theory of the Short-Period Incidence of the Property Tax', *Environment and Planning C: Government and Policy*, **2**: 117–34.

Mair, D. (1987) 'The Incidence of Business Rates: Preliminary Estimates', *Environment and Planning C: Government and Policy*, **5**: 99–103.

Mair, D. and A. J. Laramie (1992) 'The Incidence of Business Rates on Manufacturing', *Scottish Journal of Political Economy*, **39**(1): 76–94.

Mangan, J. and R. Ledward (1997) *Local Authority Grants and the Flypaper Effect in England*, Staffordshire University Business School Division of Economics Working Paper no. 97.7 (Stoke-on-Trent: Staffordshire University).

Marlow, M. L. (1992) 'Intergovernmental Competition, Voice and Exit Options and the Design of Fiscal Structure', *Constitutional Political Economy*, **3**(1): 73–88.

Marsh, D. (1991) 'Privatisation under Mrs Thatcher: A Review of the Literature', *Public Administration*, **69**(4): 459–80.

Martins, M. (1995) 'Size of Municipalities, Efficiency, and Citizen Participation: A Cross-European Perspective', *Environment and Planning C: Government and Policy*, **13**: 441–58.

Martlew, C. and S. J. Bailey (1988) 'A Poll Tax for Britain?', in S. J. Bailey and R. Paddison (eds), *The Reform of Local Government Finance in Britain* (London: Routledge).

Mathis, E. J. and C. E. Zech (1986) 'An Examination into the Relevance of the Median Voter Model: Empirical Evidence Offers Support for the Model and Certain Uses', *American Journal of Economics and Sociology*, **45**(4): 403–12.

Matland, R. E. (1995) 'Exit, Voice, Loyalty, and Neglect in an Urban School System', *Social Science Quarterly*, **76**(3): 506–12.

McCarthy, K. *et al.* (1984) *Exploring Benefit Based Finance for Local Government Services: Must User Charges Harm the Disadvantaged?* (Washington DC: US Department of Health and Human Services).

McGuire, M. C. (1975) 'An Econometric Model of Federal Grants and Local Fiscal Response', in W. E. Oates (ed.), *Financing the New Federalism* (Baltimore: Johns Hopkins University Press).

McGuire, M. C. (1978) 'A Method for Estimating the Effect of a Subsidy on the Receiver's Resource Constraint: With an Application to US Local Governments, 1964–71', *Journal of Public Economics*, **10**: 25–44.

McKay, D. H. (1985) 'A Reappraisal of Public Choice Theory of Intergovernmental Relations', *Government and Policy*, **3**: 163–74.

McKelvy, R. D. (1976) 'Intransitivities in Multi-dimensional Voting Models and Some Implications for Agenda Control', *Journal of Economic Theory* **12**(3): 472–82.

McKelvy, R. D. (1979) 'General Conditions for Global Intransitivities in Formal Voting Models', *Econometrica*, **47**(5): 1085–1112.

McMaster, R. (1995) 'Competitive Tendering in UK Health and Local Authorities: What Happens to the Quality of Services?', *Scottish Journal of Political Economy*, **42**(4): 409–27.

Meadowcroft, M. (1991) *The Politics of Electoral Reform* (London: Electoral Reform Society).

Megdal, S. B. (1987) 'The Flypaper Effect Revisited: An Econometric Explanation', *Review of Economics and Statistics*, **69**: 347–51.

Mercer, L. T. *et al.* (1985) *California City and Country User Charges: Change and Efficiency Since Proposition 13* (Berkeley: Institute of Governmental Studies University of California).

Midwinter, A. and C. Mair (1987) *Rates Reform: Issues, Arguments and Evidence*, (Edinburgh: Mainstream Publishing).

Midwinter, A. and C. Monaghan (1991) 'Reversing the Revaluation Effect – The Spatial Impact of the Poll Tax', *Local Government Studies*, **17**(2): 47–55.

Mieszkowski P. and W. H. Oakland (1979) *Fiscal Federalism and Grants-in-Aid* (Washington: The Urban Institute).

Miller, G. H. (1993) 'Are There Too Many Governments in the Tenth District?', *Economic Review Federal Reserve Bank of Kansas City*, **78**(2): 67–77.

Miller, P. and N. Rose (1990) 'Governing Economic Life', *Economy and Society*, **19**(1): 1–31.

Moffitt, R. A. (1984) 'The Effects of Grants-in-Aid on State and Local Expenditures', *Journal of Public Economics*, **23**: 279–305.

Morgan, W. D. and L. T. Mercer (1981) *City and County User Charges in California: Options, Performance and Criteria*, California Policy Seminar no. 12 (Berkeley: Institute of Governmental Studies University of California).

Morgan C. and S. Murgatroyd (1994) *Total Quality Management in the Public Sector* (Buckingham: Open University Press).

Morgan, D. R. and W. J. Pammer (1988) 'Coping With Fiscal Stress', *Urban Affairs Quarterly*, **24**(1): 69–86.

Mouritzen, P. E. (ed.) (1991) *Managing Cities in Austerity: Urban Fiscal Stress in Ten Western Countries* (London: Sage).

Mueller, D. C. (1972) 'Hirschman's Exit, Voice, and Loyality: A Review Article', *Public Policy*, **20**(3): 473–7.

Mueller, D. C. (1993) *Public Choice II: A Revised Edition of Public Choice* (Cambridge University Press).

Mulgan, G. (1994) 'Democratic Dismissal, Competition, and Contestability among the Quangos', *Oxford Review of Economic Policy*, **10**(3): 51–60.

Musgrave, R. A. and P. B. Musgrave (1989) *Public Finance in Theory and Practice* (New York: McGraw-Hill).

Mushkin, S. J. and C. L. Vehorn (1977) 'User Fees and Charges', *Governmental Finance*, **6**(4): 42–8.

NAO (National Audit Office) (1985) *Department of the Environment: Operation of the Rate Support Grant System* (London: HMSO).

Nathan, R. P. and C. Adams (1976) 'Understanding Central City Hardship', *Political Science Quarterly* **91**: 47–62.

Nelson M. A. (1992) 'Municipal Amalgamation and the Growth of the Public Sector in Sweden', *Journal of Regional Science*, **32**(1): 39–53.

Nelson, R. H. (1987) 'The Economics Profession and the Making of Public Policy', *Journal of Economic Literature*, **25**: 49–91.

Nelson, R. R. (1976) 'Political Economy: Some Uses of the Exit-Voice Approach: Discussion', *American Economic Review*, **66**(2): 389–91.

Netzer, D. (1983) *Local Alternatives to the Property Tax: User Charges and Non Property Taxes*, Working Paper no. 4, Tax Analysis Series (Washington DC: Academy for State and Local Government).

Newton, K. (1980a) 'Central Government Grants, Territorial Justice and Local Democracy in Post War Britain', in D. E. Ashford (ed.), *Financing Urban Government in the Welfare State* (London: Croom Helm).

Newton, K. (1980b) *Balancing the Books: Financial Problems of Local Government in West Europe* (London: Sage).

Newton, K. (1981) 'The Local Financial Crisis in Britain: A Non Crisis Which is neither Local nor Financial', in L. J. Sharpe (ed.), *The Local Fiscal Crisis in Western Europe* (London: Sage).

Newton, K. (1988) 'The Death of the City and the Urban Fiscal Crisis', in J. M. Stein (ed.), *Public Infrastructure Planning and Management* (London: Sage).

Newton, K. and T. Karran (1985) *The Politics of Local Expenditure* (London: Macmillan).

Nicholls, G. (1995a) 'The Role of the Client Officer in Leisure Services', *Local Government Policy Making*, **22**(3): 52–60.

Nicholls, G. (1995b) 'Contract Specification in Leisure Management', *Local Government Studies*, **21**(2): 248–62.

Niskanen, W. (1968) 'Nonmarket Decision Making: The Peculiar Economics of Bureaucracy', *Applied Economic Review* (Supplement), **58**: 293–305.

Niskanen, W. (1971) *Bureaucracy and Representative Government* (Chicago: Aldine-Atherton).

Niskanen, W. (1975) 'Bureaucrats and Politicians', *Journal of Law and Economics*, **18**: 617–43.

Nolan, Lord (1995) *Standards in Public Life: First Report of the Committee on Standards in Public Life Volume 1* (Chairman Lord Nolan), Cm 2850-I (London: HMSO).

Oates, W. E. (1969) 'The Effects of Property Taxes and Local Public Spending on Property Values: An Empirical Study of Tax Capitalisation and the Tiebout Hypothesis', *Journal of Political Economy*, **77**: 957–71.

Oates, W. E. (1972) *Fiscal Federalism* (New York: Harcourt Brace Jovanovich).

Oates, W. E. (ed.) (1977) *The Political Economy of Fiscal Federalism* (Lexington, Mass.: Lexington Books).

Oates, W. E. (1979) 'Lump-Sum Grants have Price Effects', in P. Mieszkowski and W. H. Oakland (1979) *Fiscal Federalism and Grants-in-Aid* (Washington: The Urban Institute).

Oates, W. E. (1981) 'On local finance and the Tiebout Model', *American Economic Review*, **71**: 93–8.

Oates, W. E. (1985) 'Searching for Leviathan: An Empirical Study', *American Economic Review*, **75**: 748–57.

Oates, W. E. (1989) 'Searching for Leviathan: A Reply and Some Further Reflections', *American Economic Review*, **79**: 578–83.

Oates, W. E. (1990) 'Decentralization of the Public Sector: An Overview', in R. J. Bennett (ed.), *Decentralization, Local Governments and Markets: Towards a Post Welfare Agenda* (Oxford: Clarendon).

Oates, W. E. (1991) *Studies in Fiscal Federalism* (Aldershot: Edward Elgar).

Oates, W. E. (ed.) (1998) *The Economics of Fiscal Federalism and Local Finance* (Cheltenham: Edward Elgar).

O'Connor, J. (1973) *The Fiscal Crisis of the State* (New York: St Martin's Press).

OECD (1987a) *Managing and Financing Urban Services* (Paris: Organization for Economic Co-operation and Development).

OECD (1987b) *Administration as Service. The Public as Client* (Paris: Organization for Economic Co-operation and Development).

OECD (1992) *Revenue Statistics of OECD Member Countries, 1965–1991* (Paris: Organization for Economic Co-operation and Development).

OECD (1994) 'Performance Measurement in Government: Issues and Illustrations', *Public Management Occasional Papers*, no. 5 (Paris: Organization for Economic Co-operation and Development).

OECD (1997) *OECD Revenue Statistics 1965–1996* (1997 edn) (Paris: Organization for Economic Co-operation and Development).

O'Hare, M. (1993) 'The Council Tax', *Economic Review*, **10**(4): 11–13.

Olson, M. (1965) *The Logic of Collective Action: Public Goods and the Theory of Groups* (Cambridge, Mass.: Harvard University Press).

Olson, M. (1982) *The Rise and Decline of Nations: Economic Growth, Stagflation and Social Rigidities* (New Haven: Yale University Press).

Olson, M. (1986) 'A Theory of the Incentives Facing Political Organisations: Neo Corporatism and the Hegemonic State', *International Political Science Review*, **7**(2): 165–89.

Osborne, D. and T. Gaebler (1992) *Reinventing Government: How the Entrepreneurial Spirit is Transforming the Public Sector* Mass.: Addison-Wesley).

Oulasvirta, L. (1992) 'Municipal Public Finance in the Nordic Countries', *Local Government Studies*, **18**(4): 106–35. Also published in J. G. Gibson and R. Batley (eds), *Financing European Local Governments* (London: Frank Cass) pp. 106–35.

Oulasvirta, L. (1996) 'Real and Perceived Effects of Changing the Grant System from Specific to General Grants', *Public Choice*, **91**: 397–416.

Owens, J. and G. Panella (eds) (1991) *Local Government: An International Perspective* (Amsterdam: North-Holland).

Paddison, R. and S. J. Bailey (eds) (1988) *Local Government Finance: International Perspectives* (London: Routledge).

Page, E. C. and M. J. Goldsmith (eds) (1987) *Central and Local Government Relations: A Comparative Analysis of West European Unitary States* (London: Sage).

Palmer, A. J. (1992) *Practical Consequencies of the Theory of Public Choice: The Role of the Audit Commission as a Control Device*, Working Papers in Economics no. 2 (Bristol: University of the West of England).

Pampel, F. C. and J. B. Williamson (1989) *Age, Class, Politics and the Welfare State* (Cambridge: Cambridge University Press).

Parker, D. and K. Hartley (1990) 'Competitive Tendering: Issues and Evidence', *Public Money and Management*, **10**(3): 9–16.

Parkinson, M. (1987) *Reshaping Local Government* (Hermitage: Policy Journals).

Paul, S. (1992) 'Accountability in Public Services: Exit, Voice and Control', *World Development*, **20**(7): 1047–60.

Payson, S. (1994) *Quality Measurement in Economics: New Perspectives on the Evolution of Goods and Services* (Aldershot: Edward Elgar).

Peacock, A. T. (1979) *The Economic Analysis of Government and Related Themes* (Oxford: Martin Robertson).

Peacock, A. T. (1983) 'Public X-inefficiency: Informational and Institutional Constraints', in H. Hanusch (ed.), *Anatomy of Government Deficiencies* (Berlin: Springer-Verlag).

Peacock, A. T. and J. Wiseman (1964) *Education for Democrats*, Hobart Paper no. 25 (London: Institute of Economic Affairs).

Pola, G., G. France and R. Levaggi (eds) (1996) *Developments in Local Government Finance: Theory and Policy* (Cheltenham: Edward Elgar).

Pollitt, C. (1990) 'Doing Business in the Temple? Managers and Quality Assurance in the Public Services', *Public Administration*, **68**: 432–52.

Pollitt, C. (1994) 'The Citizen's Charter: A Preliminary Analysis', *Public Money and Management*, **14**(2): 9–14.

Pommerehne, W. (1978) 'Institutional Approaches to Public Expenditure: Empirical Evidence from Swiss Municipalities', *Journal of Public Economics*, **9**: 255–80.

Poole, K. T. and H. Rosenthal (1984) 'The Polarisation of American Politics', *Journal of Politics*, **46**(4): 1061–79.

Poole K. T. and H. Rosenthal (1996) 'Are Legislators Ideologues or the Agents of Constituents?', *European Economic Review*, **40**: 707–17.

Prest, A. R. (1982) 'On Charging for Local Government Services', *Three Banks Review*, (133): 3–23.

Propper, C. (1992a) *Quasi-markets, Contracts and Quality* (Bristol: School for Advanced Urban Studies).

Propper, C. (1992b) *Is Further Regulation of Quasi-markets in Welfare Necessary?* (Bristol: School for Advanced Urban Studies).

PSPRU (1992) *Privatisation Disaster for Quality* (London: Public Services Privatisation Research Unit).

Quigley J. M. and E. Smolensky (1992) 'Conflicts Among Levels of Government in a Federal System', *Public Finance*, **47** (Supplement): 202–15.

Quirk, B. (1986) 'Paying for Local Government: Beyond the Financial Issue', *Local Government Studies*, **12**(5): 3–11.

Raimondo, H. J. (1989) 'Leviathan and Federalism in the United States', *Public Finance Quarterly*, **17**(2): 204–15.

Rao, N. and K. Young (1995) *Competition, Contracts and Change: The Local Authority Experience of CCT* (York: Joseph Rowntree Foundation).

Reich, R. B. (1987) *The Power of Public Ideas* (New York: Harper Business).

Rhodes, R. A. W. (1994) 'The Hollowing Out of the State: The Changing Nature of the Public Services in Britain', *Public Administration*, **65** (2): 138–51.

Rhodes, T. and S. J. Bailey (1979) 'Equity, Statistics and the Distribution of the Rate Support Grant', *Policy and Politics*, **7**(1): 83–97.

Rice, T. W. (1985) 'An Examination of the Median Voter Hypothesis', *Western Political Quarterly*, **38** (2): 211–23.

Ridley, N. (1988) *The Local Right: Enabling not Providing*, Policy Study no. 92 (London: Centre for Policy Studies).

Ritchie, P. (1989) 'The Relationship between Needs Assessment and Local Taxes', *Public Policy and Administration*, **4**(2): 48–56.

Romer, T. and H. Rosenthal (1979a) 'Bureaucrats versus Voters: On the Political Economy of Resource Allocation by Direct Democracy', *Quarterly Journal of Economics*, **93**: 563–88.

Romer, T. and H. Rosenthal (1979b) 'The Elusive Median Voter', *Journal of Public Economics*, **12**: 143–70.

Romer, T. and H. Rosenthal (1980) 'An Institutional Theory of the Effect of Intergovernmental Grants', *National Tax Journal*, **33**(4): 451–8.

Rose, R. (1984) *Do Parties Make a Difference?* (London: Macmillan).

Rose, R. (1990a) 'Charging for Public Services', *Public Administration*, **68**: 297–313.

Rose, R. (1990b) 'Inheritance before Choice in Public Policy', *Journal of Theoretical Politics*, **2**(3): 263–91.

Rose, R. and P. Falconer (1992) 'Individual Taste or Collective Decision: Public Policy on School Meals', *Journal of Social Policy*, **21**(3): 349–73.

Rose R. and E. Page (1982) 'Chronic Instability in Fiscal Systems', in R. Rose and E. Page (eds), *Fiscal Stress in Cities* (Cambridge University Press).

Rowley, C. K. (1993) *Social Choice Theory: Volume 1* (Aldershot: Edward Elgar).

Rubin, I. S. (1985) 'Structural Theories and Urban Fiscal Stress', *Urban Affairs Quarterly*, **20**(4): 469–86.

Sachs, S. and R. K. Andrew (1975) 'User Charges and Special Districts', in J. R. Aronson and E. Schwartz (eds), *Management Policies in Local Government Finance* (Washington: International City Management Association) pp. 166–83.

Santerre, R. (1986) 'Representative versus Direct Democracy: A Tiebout Test of Relative Performance', *Public Choice*, **48**(1): 55–63.

Schneider, M. and B. M. Ji (1987) 'The flypaper effect and competition in the local market for public goods', *Public Choice*, **54**(1): 27–39.

Schott, K. (1982) 'The Economic Behaviour of Local Authorities', *Fiscal Studies*, **3**(1): 39–45.

Scott, A. D. (1952) 'The Evaluation of Federal Grants', *Economica,* **19**: 377–94.

Self, P. (1993) *Government by the Market? The Politics of Public Choice* (Basingstoke: Macmillan).

Sharp, E. B. (1984) 'Exit, Voice, and Loyalty in the Context of Local Government Problems', *Western Political Quarterly*, **37**(1): 67–83.

Sharp E. B. and D. Elkins (1987) 'The Impact of Fiscal Limitation: A Tale of Seven Cities', *Public Administration Review*, **47**(5): 385–92.

Sharpe, I. J. and K. Newton (1984) *Does Politics Matter? The Determinants of Public Policy* (Oxford University Press).

Shaw, K., J. Fenwick and A. Foreman (1993) 'Client and Contractor Roles in Local Government: Some Observations on Managing the Split, *Local Government Policy Making*, **20**(2): 22–7.

Shepherd, C. (1994) 'Community Councils and the Citizen in Middlesbrough', *Local Government Policy Making*, **20**(4): 31–6.

Shepherd, W. G. (1984) '"Contestability" vs. Competition', *American Economic Review*, **74**(4): 572–87.

Simon H. A. (1952) 'A Behavioural Model of Rational Choice', *Quarterly Journal of Economics*, **69**: 98–118.

Simon H. A. (1959) 'Theories of Decisionmaking in Economics and Behavioural Science', *American Economic Review*, **49** (June): 253–83.

Smith, B. (1986) *Cost Savings in Ontario Municipalities* (London: Chartered Institute of Public Finance and Accountancy).

Smith, B. C. (1985) *Decentralization: The Territorial Dimension of the State* (London: George Allen & Unwin).

Smith, P. (1988) 'The Potential Gains from Creative Accounting in English Local Government', *Environment and Planning C: Government and Policy* **6**: 173–85.

Smith, S. and D. C. Squire (1986) 'The Local Government Green Paper', *Fiscal Studies*, **7**(2): 63–71.

Smith, T. (1989) 'Literature Review: Decentralisation and Community', *British Journal of Social Work*, **19** (April): 137–48.

Sorensen, R. J. (1993) *The Efficiency of Public Service Provision* (London: Sage).

Sorensen R. J. (1995) 'The Demand for Local Government Goods: The Impact of Parties, Committees, and Public Sector Politicians', *European Journal of Political Research*, **27**(1): 119–41.

Stewart, J. D. and G. Stoker (eds) (1989) *The Future of Local Government* (Basingstoke: Macmillan).

Stewart, J. and K. Walsh (1991) *The Search for Quality* (Luton: Local Government Management Board).

Stoker, G. (1987) 'Decentralisation and the Restructuring of Local Government in Britain', *Local Government Policy Making* **14**(2): 3–11.

Stoker, G., S. Baine, S. Carlyle, S. Charters and T. Du Sautoy (1991) 'Reflections on Neighbourhood Decentralisation in Tower Hamlets', *Public Administration*, **69**: 373–84.

Stoker, G. and V. Lowndes (1991) *Tower Hamlets and Decentralisation: The Experience of Globe Town Neighbourhood* (Luton: Local Government Management Board).

Stone, P. A. (1978) 'The Implications for the Conurbations of Population Changes (with particular reference to London)', *Regional Studies*, **12**: 95–123.

Szymanski, S. and S. Wilkins (1993) 'Cheap Rubbish? Competitive Tendering and Contracting Out in Refuse Collection 1981–88', *Fiscal Studies*, **13**(3): 109–30.

TACIR (1981) *Municipal Current Charges and Alternative Revenue Sources* (Austin: Texas Advisory Commission on Intergovernmental Relations).

Ter-Minassian, T. (1997) *Fiscal Federalism in Theory and Practice* (Washington: International Monetary Fund).

Teske, P. and M. Schneider (1994) 'The Role of Entrepreneurs in the Local Market for Public Goods', *Research in Community Sociology*, **4**: 135–51.

THES (1992) *The Times Higher Education Supplement*, 31 January, pp. 1 and 4–5.

Tiebout, C. M. (1956) 'A Pure Theory of Local Expenditures', *Journal of Political Economy*, **64**: 416–24.

Todo-Rovira, A. (1991) 'Empirical Analysis of the Provision of Local Public Goods: An Alternative to the Median Voter Model', *Public Finance* **46**(3): 490–511.

Toft, G. S. and B. J. Warnecke (1980) *Local Revenue Diversification with User Fees in Indiana*, Research Report 80–3, Centre for Public Policy and Public Administration (Indiana: Purdue University).

Travers, T. and J. Weimar (1996) *Business Improvement Districts: New York and London* (London School of Economics and Political Science).

Trotter, S. D. (1985) 'The Price Discriminating Public Enterprise, With Special Reference to British Rail', *Journal of Transport Economics and Policy*, **19**: 41–55.

Tullock, G. (1959) 'Problems of Majority Voting', *Journal of Political Economy*, **67**: 571–9.

Tullock, G. (1965) *The Politics of Bureaucracy* (Washington: Public Affairs Press).

Tullock, G. (1967) *Towards a Mathematics of Politics* (Ann Arbor: University of Michigan Press).

Turnbull, G. K. (1992) 'Fiscal Illusion, Uncertainty, and the Flypaper Effect', *Journal of Public Economics*, **48**: 207–23.

Turnbull, G. K. and S. S. Djoundourian (1994) 'The Median Voter Hypothesis: Evidence from General Purpose Local Governments', *Public Choice*, **81**(3–4): 223–40.

Turnbull, G. K. and P. M. Mitias (1995) 'Which Median Voter?', *Southern Economic Journal*, **62**(1): 183–91.

Turnbull, G. K. and Y. Niho (1986) 'The Optimal Property Tax with Mobile Nonresidential Capital', *Journal of Public Economics*, **29**: 223–39.

Udehn, L. (1996) *The Limits of Public Choice: A Sociological Critique of the Economic Theory of Politics* (London: Routledge).

Uttley, M. and N. Harper (1993) 'The Political Economy of Competitive Tendering', in T. Clarke and C. Pitelis (eds), *The Political Economy of Privatisation* (London: Routledge).

Vining, A. and A. Boardman (1992) 'Ownership versus Competition: Efficiency in Public Enterprise', *Public Choice*, **73**: 205–93.

Voytek, P. (1991) 'Privatising Government Service Delivery: Theory, Evidence and Implications', *Government and Policy*, **9**: 155–71.

Wagner, R. E. (1991) *Charging for Government: User Charges and Earmarked Taxes in Principle and Practice* (London: Routledge).

Walker, B. (1993) *Competing for Building Maintenance: Direct Labour Organisations and Compulsory Competitive Tendering* (London: HMSO).

Walsh, K. (1988) 'Fiscal Crisis and Stress: Origins and Implications', in R. Paddison and S. J. Bailey (eds), *Local Government Finance: International Perspectives* (London: Routledge).

Walsh, K. (1991) *Competitive Tendering for Local Authority Services: Initial Experiences* (London: HMSO).

Walsh, K. (1995) *Public Services and Market Mechanisms: Competition, Contracting and the New Public Management* (Basingstoke: Macmillan).

Walsh, K. and Davis, H. (1993) *Competition and Service: The Impact of the Local Government Act 1988* (London: HMSO).

Walsh, K., N. Deakin, P. Smith, P. Spurgeon and N. Thomas (1997) *Contracting for Change: Contracts in Health, Social Care, and Other Local Government Services* (Oxford: Oxford University Press).

Weale, S. (1995) 'Heart Disease Alert over Children's Eating Habits', *Guardian*, 3 November, p. 8.

Wheeler, M. and R. Richards, (1993) 'Weighing Up the Competition', *Leisure Management,* December: 24–6.

Whynes, D. K. (1993) 'Can Performance Monitoring Solve the Public Services' Principal–Agent Problem?', *Scottish Journal of Political Economy*, **40**(4): 434–46.

Wildasin, D. (1986) *Urban Public Finance* (London: Harwood Academic Publishers).

Wilde, J. (1968) 'The Expenditure Effects of Grants-in-Aid Programs', *National Tax Journal*, **21**(3): 340–8.

Wilde, J. (1971) 'Grants-in-Aid: The Analytics of Design and Response', *National Tax Journal*, **24**(2): 143–55.

Williamson, O. E. (1963) 'Management Discretion and Business Behaviour', *American Economic Review*, **53** (December): 1032–57.

Williamson, O. E. (1974) *The Economics of Discretionary Behaviour: Managerial Objectives in a Theory of the Firm* (London: Kershaw).

Williamson, O. E. (1976) 'The Economics of Internal Organisation: Exit and Voice in Relation to Markets and Hierarchies', *American Economic Review*, **66**(2): 369–77.

Williamson, O. E. (1985) *The Economic Institutions of Capitalism: Firms, Markets, Relational Contracting* (London: Macmillan).

Williamson, O. E. (1986) *Economic Organisation: Firms, Markets and Policy Controls* (Brighton: Wheatsheaf).

Williamson, O. E. (1993) 'Transaction Cost Economics and Organisation Theory', *Industrial and Corporate Change*, **2**(2): 107–56.

Wilson, D., C. Game, S. Leach and G. Stoker (1994) *Local Government in the United Kingdom* (Basingstoke: Macmillan).

Wilson, D. and C. Game (1998) *Local Government in the United Kingdom* (2nd edn) (Basingstoke: Macmillan).

Wistow, G., M. Knapp, B. Hardy and C. Allen (1992) 'From Providing to Enabling: Local Authorities and the Mixed Economy of Social Care', *Public Administration*, **70**: 25–45.

Wolman, H. (1982) 'The Fiscal Problems of US Cities', *Local Government Studies*, **8**(2): 67–88.

Wyckoff, P. G. (1991) 'The Elusive Flypaper Effect', *Journal of Urban Economics*, **30**(3): 310–28.

Young, D. R. (1976) 'Consolidation or Diversity: Choices in the Structure of Urban Government', *American Economic Review*, **66**(2): 378–85.

Young, K. (1988) 'Local Government in Britain: Rationale, Structure and Finance', in S. J. Bailey and R. Paddison (eds), *The Reform of Local Government Finance in Britain* (London: Routledge).

Youngman, J. M. and J. H. Malme (1994) *An International Survey of Taxes on Land and Buildings* (The Netherlands: Kluwer Law and Taxation Publishers).

Younis T. A. (1995) Quality Service: Consumer Responsiveness in the Public Sector', in L. Montanheiro *et al.* (eds), *Public and Private Sector Partnerships in the Global Context* (Sheffield Hallam University).

Younis, T. A., S. J. Bailey and C. Davidson (1996) 'The Application of Total Quality Management to the Public Sector', *International Review of Administrative Studies*, **62**(3): 369–82.

Zampelli, E. M. (1986) 'Resource Fungibility, the Flypaper Effect, and the Expenditure Impact of Grants-In-Aid', *Review of Economics and Statistics*, **68**: 33–40.

Index